Mirages of International Justice

This book is dedicated to my daughter Mia Bernadette, who was born while the first draft was still underway. To bring human life into the world is a sobering responsibility, all the more so when one views human nature, and humankind's political institutions, through a pessimistic prism of insatiable egotism. The book is testament to some of the grand follies and political hallucinations of politicians who have sought to stamp a moral writ upon the world of international relations. In seeking to warp the globe into an unnatural mould shaped by their ideals, they are guilty of a fatal conceit. That my daughter might track her own moral direction in life, valuing kindness and sympathy in the face of irrepressible human self-interest, must be the wish of any father. That she and others find inspiration from a source other than the hypocrisy of idealism, is my abiding hope.

Mirages of International Justice

The Elusive Pursuit of a Transnational Legal Order

Matthew Parish

Visiting Fellow, British Institute of International and Comparative Law; Of Counsel, Akin Gump Strauss Hauer & Feld LLP, Geneva, Switzerland

Edward Elgar

Cheltenham, UK • Northampton, MA, USA

Published by
Edward Elgar Publishing Limited
The Lypiatts
15 Lansdown Road
Cheltenham
Glos GL50 2JA
UK

Edward Elgar Publishing, Inc.
William Pratt House
9 Dewey Court
Northampton
Massachusetts 01060
USA

A catalogue record for this book
is available from the British Library

Library of Congress Control Number: 2010939212

MIX
Paper from responsible sources
FSC www.fsc.org FSC® C018575

ISBN 978 1 84980 408 0 (cased)

Typeset by Servis Filmsetting Ltd, Stockport, Cheshire
Printed and bound by MPG Books Group, UK

Contents

Preface

Does international law really achieve the goals we want it to? This book suggests not. We hold high hopes for international law, from banning landmines and cluster munitions, to upholding human rights in the face of domestic repression, to fostering coordination of international solutions to climate change, to prosecuting war criminals and holding senior politicians accountable for genocides, to mediating conflicts and preventing wars. Almost uniquely amongst areas of law, international law is vested with moral significance by its advocates; it is said that many of the world's international and even domestic problems can be resolved by upholding international law. Yet therein lie its dangers. I suggest these aspirations are bound to be disappointed.

I am not the first to express such pessimism; several scholars have expressed the view that in an anarchic world of self-interested states harbouring their own military force to defend and conquer, there is no good reason to expect the high aspirations of international law to be observed. But I do not think international law is irrelevant. I am of the view that it makes a real difference to international relations and even domestic politics. It makes the world of international relations vastly more complex, by adding to the anarchy of states a series of autonomous international institutions, each with their own interests, goals and powers. International courts exist, purporting to mete out international justice. Yet this image, so carefully cultivated, is a charade. International courts exist not to resolve disputes impartially, but to cement their ever tenuous positions and pursue the growth of yet more international law. International courts are necessarily weak, because no strong and rational state would agree to create a genuinely strong and independent institution, lest it subsequently turn against it. Forever fearful of irrelevance, the international courts that exist seize power for themselves where they can, and otherwise make decisions in accordance with the wishes of the strong. They also promote the intellectual and bureaucratic growth of the discipline of international law which sustains them. Their overriding goal is self-perpetuation. This book examines several such international courts, and finds them wanting in these ways.

I first became interested in international law, and by extension the international organisations that propagate it, when I worked for two such institutions. One was the World Bank (until 2005); the other was the Office of the High Representative of Bosnia and Herzegovina (until 2007). I must express gratitude for my employment by both of them. The former, because it gave me the opportunity to live in Washington, DC, a wonderfully metropolitan city with an exceptionally high quality of life; the latter, because I met my wife while working there, I wrote my first book as a result and I spent over two years enjoying the most fascinating professional experience of my career. Yet both organisations, in related ways, were the most abysmal employers one could imagine. In the World Bank, I was initially astonished by its gross over-staffing. It employed far too many people, each of whom in consequence had not nearly enough to do. This was a surprising observation to make in respect of one of the world's most prestigious financial institutions: the greater majority of the staff spent the greater part of their time spinning wheels. I was therefore led to the question: how could it be, that such a renowned institution could employ so many people to do so little of relevance? The next surprise in store for me was the frequently perplexing bureaucracy: as a pretext to justify their existences, these surplus employees had created interminable internal procedures and rules to sustain their otherwise superfluous roles.

Moreover, the World Bank was exceptionally poor in terms of the service it offered its clients. The procedures it followed were so cumbersome that its sovereign borrowers increasingly preferred to turn to regular commercial lenders for financing. Whereas the World Bank would take upwards of two years from project inception to signing a loan agreement, and then perhaps another six months for the initial disbursement of funds, a commercial bank could lend money within six weeks. The World Bank would also tie its borrowers up in the bureaucracy of its procurement procedures – sometimes requiring changes in domestic legislation – and endless paperwork required to comply with World Bank project management and reporting requirements. Lost in a sea of its own procedures, the organisation seemed incapable of competing within the real world. Perhaps the most challenging question that faced me was why its members – that is to say, almost every country of the world – did not simply shut it down and save themselves a lot of time and money.

Yet the organisation also showed great tenacity in perpetually reinventing itself. It went from a bank lending money principally to middle income sovereigns for infrastructure projects, to a 'knowledge bank', opening its own research institute and presenting itself as a pioneer in the latest fashions in development thinking. It also started lending to low income countries, a difficult decision to justify in policy terms given such nations lacked sufficiently robust institutions to manage and spend the money in accordance with coherent projects or policies. It started lending to the private sector. It even developed itself as an international arbitration centre. The World Bank became a pioneer in self-preservation, through endless reincarnations. That way, perhaps nobody would spot just how poor it was at its core function – lending money. Thus it remains in existence today, going from strength to strength, arguably sturdier than ever.

The Office of the High Representative of Bosnia and Herzegovina (OHR), the international governor of the country created by the peace agreement ending the 1992–95 war, was also dysfunctional, but in quite different ways. Whereas the World Bank was grossly overstaffed, OHR was absurdly undermanned. I was expected to run a complex legal and judicial reform project with just a handful of people. The task was impossible. At the same time, I worked for an international civil servant with the most extraordinary and draconian powers of imposition over Bosnia's domestic elected leaders, without any form of due process or review. We were dictators, at times even tyrants. The ways we used, and misused, our powers, were the subject of my earlier book and a number of articles.[1] This led me to the question why the states who staffed and funded the organisation, including the British government, allowed the institution to get away with conduct so reprehensible in its disregard for basic principles of constitutionalism and rule of law that it would never have been tolerated in those countries' home jurisdictions. I then sought to draw broader lessons from my twin experiences. As an international lawyer, I started to wonder whether the deficiencies I had observed in the way international law is practised by international organisations were attributable to my misfortune in choosing infelicitous working environments, or reflected a more structural malaise in the field as a whole.

In time, I came to realise that absence of legal or any other kind of accountability was a recurrent feature of international organisations, a theme I developed in an earlier extended essay.[2] Despite these institutions being responsible for the propagation and implementation of the greater weight of international law and treaties, they operate beyond the scope of that law or of any law. They are also, I came to discover, remarkably autonomous from the interests of the states that have ostensibly come together to create them, that fund them and imagine they direct their activities. The lack of legal accountability within these organisations also had one remarkable common consequence: they are unpleasant places to work. Unaccountable to anyone, their managers setting their own direction without reference to national or international law or the wishes or interests of their donors, staff become freed from the common decencies expected in civilised workplaces. Being heaving bureaucracies in which process is valued over results, they are seldom meritocratic. There is no rational division of labour between staff, no system for ensuring successful people are promoted, and managers (of which there are far too many) have no incentive to ensure their departments work effectively. Sexual and other sorts of harassment are known to be rife, as are corruption and nepotism. International organisations have no independent mechanisms for resolving complaints by or against staff. Their work is not open to the public eye, because they are typically exempt from freedom of information legislation in the countries in which they operate. Indeed they are almost invariably exempt from all domestic laws, through a doctrine of 'legal immunity' which provides that international organisations are impossible to sue in any court. Nor, as a rule, can they be sued in international courts. They operate in a legal vacuum.

Despite these unsettling features, international organisations play an enormously important role in the development of international law. First, they draft it. International organisations are involved in the preparation of most, if not all, international treaties. The World Bank's loan agreements had the status of international treaties; OHR would issue executive decrees which purported to have effect in international law. Second, they monitor and even administer international law. Third, they purport to enforce it. The various international courts and tribunals which this book describes are themselves international organisations, with all the attendant unusual features and internal problems that I found in the organisations for which I worked. If organisations so dysfunctional are responsible for propagating, adjudicating, monitoring and developing international law, what is that likely to say about international law itself? These were the questions that led me to write this book. I wanted to understand what it is about the international system that renders it so pathological.

I appreciate that coming to this preface for the first time, the reader may not yet be persuaded that the dysfunction I experienced is as pervasive as I suggest. One of the purposes of this book, therefore, is to provide evidence of widespread peculiarities within international law, as propagated by international organisations. Most importantly, I wish to demonstrate that international law has none of the features we consider characteristic of effective domestic law. It stands in a class of its own, and not one towards which other legal systems should aspire. Moreover, there is no reason to believe that international law will develop the characteristics we have come to expect of effective legal systems. The other purpose of this work is to develop a general theory that explains why international law, while so prevalent, is so ineffective – in other words, why it exists at all in its unsatisfactory contemporary condition. Most theories of international relations and international organisations so far developed in the literature do not achieve that. I therefore develop a somewhat different theory of international relations, which takes its lead from a so far modest literature on dysfunction in international organisations, and I try to expand it into an account of the political economy of international law.

This book commences with a discussion about the two principal theories of international relations, realism and liberalism. My own theory of international relations emerges from a discussion of the strengths and weaknesses of each of these two fundamentally opposed positions. I am often surprised by the inability of scholars in each camp to understand the perspectives of the other; for both positions clearly have merit, and yet the possibility of compromise between the two schools is apparently impossible, reflecting cemented ideological divisions. I attempt to break these divisions down, and sketch out the principles of my own theory which (I hope) incorporates the wisdom of both sides of the debate, through developing a more sophisticated account of the determinants of states' behaviour than prior theories have hitherto considered. The book then proceeds to a chapter which considers the growth, since the end of World War II, of international organisations and international law. The purpose of this study is to trace the relationship between international law and international organisations, and to suggest that the proliferation of the two is intimately related.

There follows a series of chapters considering specific international courts and tribunals that purport to apply and enforce international law. I consider in each case whether these tribunals operate in accordance with the standards we expect of domestic legal systems. With one intriguing partial exception, I conclude that every international tribunal under consideration is grossly lacking in one or more fundamental ways. I ask in each case why this is, and I seek to explain such structural deficiencies in the international structures states have set up. My closing chapter asks whether things might get better – whether the current unsatisfactory state of international law is a mere passing phase, a staging post on the road to Damascus. I conclude this is most unlikely, because the political and economic dynamics that motivated development of effective and independent court systems in western countries are lacking in the international system. International law is an aberration, developed by mischievous and flawed analogy with domestic legal systems. International law will never transform itself into the sort of robust transnational legal system we would hope for.

Writing this book has involved not just copious quantities of empirical and academic research, but also many intensive and critical discussions with friends and colleagues to ensure my thesis stands respectably robust in the face of a wealth of scholarly literature already written on the subject. Gratitude for help and inspiration in bringing this work to completion is due to Phil Bocking, Stephen Browne, David Chandler, Victoria

Curzon-Price, Ed Flaherty, Veijo Heiskanen, Sarah Hunt, Matthew Kanna, Suzie Kurdi, Nick Miles, Katie Oliver, Howard Parish, Margaret Parish, David Potterbaum, Natasha Proietto, Jean-Marc Rickli, Joseph Rieras, Nicole Schwab, Alexandre Vautravers, Greg Wilson, Rebecca Wise and anonymous reviewers. I must extend particular thanks to Eric Posner, whose enthusiastic support for my occasionally eccentric theories of international relations was crucial inspiration, and without which this book would never have been written. Also due a gargantuan tranche of love and appreciation is my wife Mirjana, who supported me and kept me sane during the six months in which I laboured over the greater body of the text, while she was pregnant, and then after she gave birth to our beautiful daughter. Significant gratitude is also due to Robert McCorquodale and all the staff of the British Institute of International and Comparative Law, with whom I was a visiting fellow during 2009 and 2010 and whose support for this work is hugely appreciated. Last but by no means least, I would like to thank my commissioning editor Ben Booth, whose patience, good humour and exceptionally high standards of professionalism immeasurably assisted my bringing this text to fruition. Notwithstanding all the valuable counsel and assistance I have received, responsibility for all errors and omissions remains mine alone. Finally, I should express debts of gratitude to my second home, the city of Geneva, whose peaceful and civilised air contributed to a sense of calm so essential to complete this manuscript; and to the Athenaeum, a haven of tranquillity in central London where much of the research was undertaken.

NOTES

1. See in particular Parish, Matthew (2009), *A Free City in the Balkans: Reconstructing a Divided Society in Bosnia* (London: I.B.Tauris); Parish, Matthew (2009), 'The demise of the Dayton protectorate', *Journal of Intervention and Statebuilding*, Special Supplement December; Parish, Matthew (2009), 'International officials', *Austrian Review of International and European Law*, **13**, 79; also available on the Social Science Research Network at http://ssrn.com/abstract=1651519 (last accessed 2 November 2010).
2. Parish, Matthew (2010), 'An essay on the accountability of international organizations', *International Organizations Law Review*, **7**(2), 277. A number of the themes of this work are foreshadowed in that paper.

Acronyms

AB	Appellate Body
BiH	Bosnia and Herzegovina
BIT	Bilateral Investment Treaty
CEARD	Convention on Elimination of All Forms of Racial Discrimination
CEDWA	Convention on Elimination of All Forms of Discrimination Against Women
CPRMW	Convention on Protection of the Rights of Migrant Workers and their Families
DRC	Democratic Republic of Congo
DSB	Dispute Settlement Body
DSU	Dispute Settlement Understanding
ECHR	European Court of Human Rights
ECJ	European Court of Justice
ECSC	European Coal and Steel Community
EEC	European Economic Community
EFTA	European Free Trade Association
FDI	Foreign Direct Investment
GATT	General Agreement of Trade Tariffs
ICC	International Criminal Court
ICCPR	International Covenant on Civil and Political Rights
ICESR	International Covenant on Economic, Social and Cultural Rights
ICISS	International Commission on Intervention and State Sovereignty

ICJ	International Court of Justice
ICSID	International Centre for the Settlement of Investment Disputes
ICTR	International Criminal Tribunal for Rwanda
ICTY	International Criminal Tribunal for the former Yugoslavia
ILC	International Law Commission
ILO	International Labour Organisation (formerly International Labour Office)
ITO	International Trade Organisation
KFOR	Kosovo Force
MEP	Member of the European Parliament
MFN	Most Favoured Nation
OAS	Organisation of American States
OHR	Office of the High Representative (Bosnia and Herzegovina)
PCA	Permanent Court of Arbitration
PCIJ	Permanent Court of International Justice
QMV	Qualified Majority Voting
RPF	Rwandan Patriotic Front
RPT	Reasonable Period of Time
TEU	Treaty on European Union
TFEU	Treaty on the function of the European Union
UNCTAD	United Nations Conference on Trade and Development
UNHCR	United Nations High Commission for Refugees
WTO	World Trade Organisation

1. Mirages

> If one party resolves to demand what the other resolves to refuse, the dispute can be determined only by arbitration; and between powers who have no common superior, there is no other arbitrator than the sword.
>
> Samuel Johnson
> *Thoughts on the late transactions respecting the Falkland's Islands*, 1771[1]

International law is an industry. It is driven not by a demand for justice, but by the pursuit of its own self-propagation. The determinants of its growth are not principally exogenous but endogenous. It achieves remarkably few of the goals it purports to advance. It is not a legal system at all in the conventional sense. At best it is a bogus and impotent bureaucracy; at worst a rhetorical cloud that obscures naked exercise of political power. Yet it is here to stay, it is liable to grow and prospects for its reform are bleak. Those are the themes of this book. In arguing for my stark conclusions, I shall explore how international law is made, how it is discussed, and how it is enforced. In fact, I shall conclude, it is not enforced at all. This book focuses upon the international courts and tribunals that purport to apply international law, and I should warn the reader that my intention is to make those bodies appear effete and futile. I shall also spend some time considering the institutions that create international law. For the most part states, while signatories to international treaties, are not the prime movers behind international law. Instead, those prime movers are international organisations. International law is an industry, and international organisations are the industrialists. They work with unceasing effort to propagate this branch of law, because in doing so they propagate themselves. Fascinatingly, they are gifted at avoiding the application of international law to themselves. They thus preserve the appearance of being impartial dispensers of a superior regime of international law governing all states and all persons worldwide, and yet through the most expert of intrigues they themselves evade its withering clutches. This is one of the most profound mysteries in international law, and it is not immediately clear why the community of states allows this pretence to continue. This book tentatively suggests how this astonishing state of affairs can have come about, and what it means for international relations in the modern world.

In describing international law as an industry, this book seeks to pursue a hitherto under-explored theory within international relations, and to develop it in a new direction. The theory with which I have sympathy has gone by the name of 'constructivism',[2] although this label has arguably never been adequately defined. We shall persevere with the term constructivism, but for no other reason than the lack of a better alternative. However, this chapter will aim to describe a distinct version of the doctrine, and to differentiate it from the two principal themes in international relations that have dominated twentieth-century discussion of the subject. This is not primarily a theoretical work; but it begins with some theory, to entice the reader to consider how it might be possible to make rational order of the seemingly senseless cacophony of events that constitute the way states interact with one another.

The hope is that the patient reader will find the various subsequent chapters to be at least roughly coherent pieces in a jigsaw that this book will help him or her construct. Alas, the jigsaw shall never be complete: one can never present conclusive proof that any theoretical perspective is canonical. International relations is too empirically complex for that. Moreover, the subject has an infinity of hidden facets which represent not empirical findings, but are rather indices of the observer's philosophical predispositions. International relations theory is not a science in the way of physics; it is more like one's favourite pair of old reading glasses. One knows the lens is replete with imperfections, and the view as a whole may even be distorted. But the image offers comfort to the reader, and helps him or her bring a modicum of comprehension to an otherwise baffling world. These glasses fit better than any other. When one is eased into the perspective they bestow, they become comfortably a part of a person's ideology.[3] Given the obligation to respect the copious volumes written by historians in particular descriptions of the multiplicity of events over which international relations theory seeks to generalise, that is the bravest statement one may properly make about any wide-ranging theory of international relations.

THE DARK PESSIMISM OF REALISM

The two theories to which this book will contrast constructivism conventionally go by the labels 'realism' and 'liberalism'. These are both theories which, like economics, try to understand the behaviour of their subjects by reference to generalisations about the incentives and decision-making capacities of their subjects. Whereas in economics that subject is the individual within society, or the firm, in international relations theory the subject is the state amongst other states. Realism considers the principal motivating factor in states' decisions to be rational self-interest.[4] Suspended in the balance of power, states pursue their own self-preservation and their own self-aggrandisement. They acquire territory and wealth from trade, manufacture and plunder, and colonise and subjugate where they see it as in their interests to do so. This self-interest periodically motivates formation of alliances. States will enter into international treaties where the states in question share common interests. But alliances will shift perpetually, as states' interests (or their perception of those interests) evolve. For the realist, international law is nothing more than a series of agreements that facilitate cooperation between states whose interests are temporarily aligned. But there is no permanence, and no legitimacy, to international law of this kind. International law has no morally mandatory quality; that is not its purpose. States will withdraw from international treaties at any time when they perceive it as within their interests to do so.

Of course states do not often speak as though realism is correct. Taking political discourse in international relations at face value, the evidence goes against the veracity of realism. Statesmen do not typically talk in terms of national interest in characterising the rationales for their foreign policy decisions – or, not exclusively so. Typically governments frame foreign policy decisions in terms of principles, whether they be self defence, resistance against aggression, protection of human rights, humanitarian considerations or other altruistic motives. The rationale given for the Second Gulf War was to disarm a dangerous regime, not to gain influence over the country's oil reserves. The reason given for supporting the independence of Kosovo was the right to self-determination, not the concern that handing back Kosovo to Serbia would precipitate indefinite international military involvement to constrain an Albanian insurgency. Notwithstanding the lofty ideals captured in the language typical of international diplomacy, the realist asserts that the true rationale for foreign policy decisions is, as a rule, naked self-interest. For the realist, the world of international relations is a bleak place, untinged by mercy or decency. Behind the language of principle and respect for others, there exists an unconstrained battle for power between states. In the words of the realist scholar Hans Morgenthau, '[t]he statesman must think in terms of the national interest, conceived as power among other powers. The popular mind, unaware of the fine distinctions of the statesman's thinking, reasons more often than not in the simple moralistic and legalistic terms of absolute good and absolute evil.'[5]

Modern realist thinkers have characterised the principal driving force in international relations as a 'security dilemma'.[6] Having no central authority, the international system is characterised by anarchy, in which the danger of attack by a foreign power always exists, no matter what alliances or treaties one may have entered into. States are thus bound to develop offensive military capabilities to ward off the risk of attack. Moreover, they will sometimes engage in aggressive military behaviour even without having been attacked first, as the most effective way of preserving their interests and mitigating the risk of future successful attacks against them. States' overriding motivations are to preserve a relative gap in power between them and their adversaries, to deter enemies from attacking; this may require wars of aggression to increase one's relative position. States must be concerned with relative gains, not absolute ones: the gap in offensive capability between a state and its adversaries must be kept as large as possible.

In anarchy, perpetuation of war is inevitable as the most effective response to a prisoners' dilemma in which international cooperation cannot be relied upon. In the absence of a central enforcement authority, an international treaty which seeks to set out limits on the permissibility of inter-state aggression, such as the UN Treaty (which prescribes that war is permissible only in self defence or pursuant to a resolution of the UN Security Council),[7] is of little value. If a country elects to ignore such a treaty, the UN has no army. Unlike the circumstances in which a contract is breached, there is no independent court to adjudicate the issue; and there is no bailiff to enforce the court's judgment once made. The contract analogy as a paradigm for the circumstances in which international cooperation may or may not work is worth considering carefully, and will be returned to throughout this book. The realist maintains that like a contract without a legal system, treaties are legally insecure, and can have no permanence or constancy because there is no sanction for their observance beyond the self-interest of the parties involved. When men lived in caves, there could be no law, and there could be no contracts. Might ruled; men guarded their caves and others attacked them. Fellow cave dwellers might have joint understandings for mutual protection of their territory; but such understandings were inevitably a temporary convenience, to be cast aside in favour of the spilling of blood as soon as one party chose to form an alliance with the next village instead. So it is with states. International organisations, lacking the independent enforcement capacity necessary to keep the barbarian states in line, cannot effectively temper the prevailing anarchy. In the words of John Mearsheimer, a contemporary realist scholar, 'institutions cannot get states to stop behaving as short-term power maximizers'.[8]

One of the most persuasive realist historians in recent times is the controversial former US Secretary of State Henry Kissinger. In his book

Diplomacy, Kissinger provides a compelling account of how security dilemmas drove European history from Richelieu to Hitler.[9] Essential for preserving peace in Europe, in Kissinger's view, was sustenance of a 'balance of power' between the various nations of the continent. Where no one state dominated Europe, wars could be kept under control, as minor or peripheral affairs, the larger states bringing pressure to bear to end those confrontations. Europe's most destructive wars occurred where one of the European powers became so strong as to disrupt a sense of mutually assured destruction. Thus Richelieu's skill in keeping the Germanic states of central Europe small and weak in the seventeenth century ultimately led to the Napoleonic wars, as France eclipsed its neighbours. Bismarck's success in unifying those same states and making Germany the most powerful continental power at the end of the nineteenth century ultimately led to World War I and II. After the end of the World War II, the balance of power dynamic was adopted by the USA and the USSR. The relative military power of each again provided credence to the fear of mutually assured destruction, which kept the peace, save on the peripheries, for some 45 years. That balance of power was disrupted with the collapse of the USSR in the 1990s, which led to another round of wars and bloodshed. The realist thesis draws on insights of this kind to illustrate the underlying *realpolitik* that motivates statesmen. In conditions of anarchy, the only thing that restrains states is the power of other states and the fear this may create.

There is clearly a sense in which this dark picture of international relations is inconsistent with much of the contemporary dialogue about international law. Human rights law assumes common standards of treatment of citizens to which all nations are bound. International criminal law criminalises wars of aggression. The World Trade Organisation sets out common legal standards by which states agree to the import of one another's goods. The World Health Organisation stipulates international legal standards of health care and medical treatment. The United Nations High Commissioner for Refugees propagates legal standards for treatment of refugees, and coordinates international relief efforts. The list goes on. It has been estimated that there are over 1,800 international organisations worldwide,[10] or more than nine for every country in the world.

If the international system is an anarchy, two principal puzzles emerge. One is to ask why treaties creating such extensive international cooperation exist at all. Realism should predict far less international cooperation, and of a far more precarious kind, than actually occurs. Second, it is not clear that international law, or the international organisations that propagate it, can make any difference. If by reason of the lack of independent enforcement capacity, states are minded only to act in their own interests, and thus only to comply with treaty obligations when it suits them, then international law is in some sense irrelevant. International law supervenes on the acts of states: that is to say, it is undoubtedly a creation of them, but the causal relationship is one-way. States create international law and international organisations, but those organisations, and that law, do not determine what states do. The sole (or principal) determinant of states' behaviour is the balance of power; international organisations have no power; therefore they are causally irrelevant.

Faced with the existence of apparent significant levels of international cooperation which seemingly belie the realist thesis, one might reject realism as false. Even if there is a sense in which the global system is an anarchy, in that there is no 'universal policeman' to enforce the dictates of international law, nonetheless states have incentives beyond pure self-interest and reacting to security dilemmas.[11] Another approach is to explain why, consistent with the realist thesis, states might create such an extensive network of international organisations and international law that can have no realistic effect upon their decisions or upon the decisions of other states. The version of constructivism advanced in this book adopts both these courses. Although there is a significant kernel of truth in realism, it is too simple in its analysis of states' motivations, albeit its errors are not those its critics have hitherto supposed.

Realists may hope to explain the existence of international cooperation notwithstanding their pessimistic view of the dynamic of interstate relationships in the following way. Game theory is sometimes used to analyse compliance with contracts: observance of one's contractual obligations is a 'game' in which both parties to the contract may choose compliant or non-compliant strategies. If A meets B in the street and the two individuals enter into a contract, but anticipate never contracting or interacting again, then the value of any agreement they reach depends entirely upon the prospects of external enforcement. The parties will not trust one another to comply with any obligations that are not to be satisfied there and then, because the dominant incentive will be to cheat one another. However, if A and B anticipate a further relationship, whether commercial, or through family or friends, then they may have a reason not to cheat. Cheating may invite retaliation, may carry reputation costs and may make it impossible for those two individuals to do business again in the future. Thus contractual obligations may be observed notwithstanding the absence of an independent enforcement authority, if a perception of dishonesty in failing to comply with contractual commitments creates negative reputational and retaliatory consequences. In the language of game theory, one solution to a prisoners' dilemma is an indefinite repeat play game. If a party wants (or is obliged) to play the contract game more than once, then breaching the contract will invite a tit-for-tat counter response in future games.

This analysis may explain why, in countries with weak legal institutions and poor enforcement of court judgments, people will do business only with family and close friends; whereas in countries in which contractual enforcement using the law is easier, people will do business with those they do not know.[12]

Applying this logic by analogy to states rather than private individuals, treaties may set forth rules which, if observed, will create a cooperative surplus and benefit both parties. If for example two states agree to delimit their borders, their observance of that agreement can reduce conflicts detrimental to both. Such treaties are observed, because the number of states in the world is relatively small, and repeat play games are inevitable. If one state double crosses another on one treaty commitment, the aggrieved state may do the same thing for another treaty commitment. Third states, knowing of the breach of the treaty obligation, may come to regard the state breaking the law as unreliable or treacherous. Thus they may decline to enter into treaties with that nation, or become less concerned about observing their own international obligations. In this manner, observance of treaty obligations, and the effectiveness of international law in general, become matters of upholding one's international reputation.

Alas, this logic is only superficially compelling. The reality is that states breach their treaty commitments all the time. They seem to care not a jot for their reputations when more fundamental interests are at stake. Thus the United States invades countries without a UN Security Council resolution authorising it to do so.[13] Nuclear missiles proliferate in Iran and North Korea, contrary to those countries' commitments under the Nuclear Non-Proliferation Treaty. The EU and the US perpetuate unlawful subsidies and trade barriers, contrary to WTO commitments. Countries the world over torture prisoners and condemn them to cruel punishments after unfair and politicised trials, contrary to their commitments under human rights treaties, in particular the International Covenant on Civil and Political Rights. Many countries formally discriminate against women, contrary to obligations under the same treaty. Louis Henkin, an American scholar of international relations theory, once ventured the proposition 'Almost all nations observe almost all principles of international law and almost all of their obligations all the time'.[14] This maxim seems astonishing because it is so demonstrably false. A better aphorism would be that almost all nations are in violation of at least some of their obligations under international law almost all the time. If reputational risks are supposed to motivate treaty compliance, the incentives thereby created are manifestly hopelessly weak.

It is worth pausing briefly to enquire why this is. Part of the answer lies in the possibility of autarchy. Whereas autarchy is not a realistic option for individuals, it is, to some degree, a plausible option for states. Faced with international condemnation of its conduct, a country can simply withdraw from the international community, as have Iran, Myanmar (Burma) and North Korea in recent times and to varying degrees. Diplomatic isolation will rarely be matched by economic sanctions of any effectiveness. Where the impugned country has significant international trade and investment relations with the outside world, business interests will coalesce to lobby hard against sanctions that would damage their participation in the country. UN sanctions in practice require the agreement of all five permanent members of the UN Security Council, a frustratingly difficult consensus to achieve given those nations' competing interests. Where external economic links are fewer, sanctions may be easier to agree upon, but are unlikely, *ex hypothesi*, to be an effective form of pressure. Where there is little trade to start with, trade sanctions will be of proportionately nominal effect. Reputation costs turn out to be remarkably easy to bear. Second, even if reputational damage has a real cost for states, that cost may be suffered by the country's citizenry and not by its leaders, as was seen with sanctions upon Iraq between the first and second Gulf Wars (1991–2003). In countries in which the lines of political accountability between rulers and governed is tenuous (as is typical in undemocratic states), the retaliatory actions of foreign states, short of invasion and overthrow, may have minimal effect upon the decision-makers.

The other way in which the prisoners' dilemma of cooperation failures between states can be overcome is for the states in question to agree upon an impartial adjudication and enforcement mechanism for the international obligations it undertakes. One of the prevailing themes of this book is that this virtually never happens in practice. The vast majority of the dispute resolution mechanisms that have been created in international law are not impartial. Still fewer are effective, in the sense that the decisions they issue can be enforced. Those that once might have been effective are being systematically undermined. Arguably the most ambitious international legal instrument ever created, the Treaty of San Francisco creating the United Nations, was conspicuous both in its failure to create an international military force to carry out the organisation's edicts, and in placing the Security Council, an essentially political, rather than impartial legal, institution, at the heart of its decision-making. Likewise, the International Criminal Court has no independent police force; it depends upon the member states who created the court to apprehend its indictees. These are just a few hints of the themes that will be explored in future chapters. Suffice it to say for now that genuine delegation to a third party of judicial capacity to adjudicate states' non-compliance with treaty obligations, still less to enforce those obligations, is exceptionally rare.

IMPORTING LIBERAL ASSUMPTIONS

The conventional realist explanations of how international law comes to exist at all – as solutions to prisoners' dilemmas in cooperation problems which rely upon the reputation costs of non-compliance – therefore appears wanting. Nonetheless, the paradox facing the realist is that there is an overwhelming level of international cooperation between states, existing in virtually every sphere of activity. There is barely a field of human activity where there is not some treaty or other, and some international organisation created thereby with a mandate to oversee international coordination in the pertinent field. The realist has trouble, using his conventional starting point of states' self-interested incentives, in explaining how all this international law came about and why it persists. One reaction to this paradox is to reject realism as painting too narrow, and too negative, an account of states' motivations in their interactions in the international sphere. That is the starting point of realism's chief ideological opponent in international relations: liberalism. Liberalism is commonly associated with its principal twentieth-century proponent, US President Woodrow Wilson, who was the architect of the first global organisation to promote international cooperation, the United Nations' predecessor the League of Nations, in the aftermath of World War I. We will explore the birth of the League of Nations in Chapter 2, but it is worth noting for now that Wilson's thought would radically influence the course of international relations, and in all likelihood permanently. His theory of liberalism marked a sea change in the way international relations is practised. Without his work, this book would have had no subject matter.

The logical starting point of liberalism is that in one sense, realism is obviously wrong. The incentives affecting states are hugely complex, and to boil all the causal influences upon any nation's foreign policy and international actions into a hypothesis of unadulterated self-interest is a gross over-simplification. Most importantly, one of the errors of realism is to assume that the principal determinants of a state's external behaviour are themselves external to that state – i.e. the relative powers and threats of other states, and the fear of their actions that creates security dilemmas. The theory fails to acknowledge that purely domestic political considerations may have a profound influence upon a nation's foreign policy. This is the principal insight of liberalism, which divides the world, very broadly, into two types of state.

For dictatorial states, oppressive of their citizens' rights and without democratic representation in government of the popular will, realism may be an accurate model of international behaviour. Such states may order their foreign policy upon the same principles as they order their internal affairs: with a view to the ruling elite maximising its own welfare, constantly fearful of violent overthrow, whether from within or without; acting without regard to the interests of their populations, or to the interests of the global polity as a whole. The tools by which such governments stay in power means that their conduct is necessarily amoral, and this lends credence to the realist theory of what motivates states in their international relations. However, a democratic and liberal state need not be motivated in this way – or not exclusively so. To the extent that the domestic polity within a state has respect for ethical ideals in the conduct of international relations, those values may find themselves reflected in the way a nation practises its foreign policy. It may have domestic imperatives to show that it is doing something to ensure respect for the human rights of foreign citizens, refraining from conducting wars of aggression and pursuing foreign policy goals, such as humanitarian intervention, that are at odds with a narrow account of its self-interest. Indeed a government may be compelled to pursue such policies, because the electorate responsible for placing the government in office, motivated by public interest groups and media outlets, demands it. They will vote their elected officials out of office if their liberal humanitarian concerns are not catered to in their government's foreign policy decisions.

Wilson anticipated a world in which liberal democracies would cooperate willingly to achieve common goals. Because they value peace and prosperity over defeat of enemies and domination, democratic countries do not, as a rule, go to war with one another, and therefore need not be concerned with forever bolstering their offensive capabilities to resist acts of external aggression. States are thus liberated to pursue absolute gains rather than relative gains, and genuine long-term cooperation may achieve outcomes from which every participating state benefits. Democratic states may have moral preferences that motivate their foreign policies, that supplant (or at least complement) the raw self-interest posited by the realist. Where states' moral preferences coincide, cooperation may be facilitated through international organisations and international law. Wilson's theory suggests a bottom-up mode of democratic political expression: where there is a free liberal society and genuine democratic political accountability, the populace will have moral preferences about the conduct of their state, which will influence the government's foreign policy through voting decisions. This in turn will drive both the creation of vehicles for cooperation and voluntary compliance with international law, through an expression of moral preferences in foreign policy, notwithstanding the absence of an enforcement mechanism to sanction non-compliance.

In its modern form liberalism in international relations was developed by an American, Woodrow Wilson, yet there are a number of notable historical paradoxes about the role of liberalism in contemporary American international relations. Liberalism might be thought close to a recent political movement, neoconservatism, which was associated with certain academics and policy-makers close to the US Presidency of George W. Bush (2001–2009).[15] Neoconservatism involved the view that US power should be used to overthrow dictatorial regimes, associated with the propagation of political instability worldwide, and replace them with liberal democratic states. The wars in Afghanistan (2001–) and Iraq (2003–) were justified on this basis. It is not hard to find the theoretical underpinnings of neoconservatism in liberal international relations theory. According to liberalism, foreign states may be dangerous precisely because they are undemocratic and thus there is no upward pressure from the country's voting population to require expression of ethical precepts in its foreign policy. Therefore an undemocratic state will remain fixated with relative gains rather than absolute ones, and thus will consider itself permanently trapped in a security dilemma. Thus it will pose a security risk to the external world. Liberalism is also used to advocate intervention in other states on humanitarian grounds that reflect the moral principles inherent in the foreign policy of a democratic state.[16] From this precept, it is a small step to advocate 'humanitarian' intervention in a foreign nation to correct its democratic deficit and render null that country's threat to international liberal peace and stability.

Notwithstanding this connection, many of the persons associated with the contemporary neoconservative movement, traditionally a bastion of recent Republican politics in the United States, might be horrified to be associated with Wilsonian liberalism, traditionally associated with left-leaning Democratic politics. Realist thinkers, in contrast to both Wilsonians and neoconservatives, are altogether more cautious in practice about the wisdom of foreign policy interventions. Their prevailing view is that foreign policy should be confined to maintaining the balance of power, acting to ensure that no country becomes too dominant in world affairs. For realists, dangers to the peace are the consequence not (principally) of dictatorships but of any one country becoming substantially more powerful than its neighbours. In consequence, realists advocate creating networks of alliances to constrain powerful states, or entering a war to balance an advantage that otherwise exists in favour of another powerful state. Realists would seldom advocate the sort of regime change neoconservatives have pushed for. It turns out that the hard right and left wings of American politics have something in common. Realism, it transpires, sits in the middle of American policy-making, a sceptical strain of diplomacy that advocates undertaking the least consistent with ensuring no one nation becomes too powerful. Statesmen should action certainly not undertake significant and risky courses of action in the name of pursuing liberal democracy.

AMERICAN EXCEPTIONALISM

The other tension in contemporary liberal thinking in the United States is its relationship with American exceptionalism. 'Exceptionalism' is the view, periodically prevalent in US thinking about foreign relations, that American constitutional democracy is inherently superior to other forms of social organisation. Perhaps this is an Anglo-Saxon disease; the British also tend to suffer from it, holding equivalent views about the superiority of our parliamentary democracy and court system. Wilson himself was an exceptionalist, believing in the inherent morality of the American constitutional system and the spirit of American society.[17] He believed that a benign international polity could be forged from export of American political values, a thought popular more recently amongst neoconservatives. Kissinger describes liberalism as a quintessentially American point of view, driven by a belief that American values are universally applicable and are capable of forming the basis of international polity motivated by principle rather than merely the balance of power. He notably chastises Stalin – a statesman for whom one might infer Kissinger otherwise has considerable respect – for underestimating the American tendency to make decisions in accordance with principle rather than national interests. Stalin's greatest foreign policy mistakes, he suggests, were to assume that every other foreign leader would act with such ruthlessly single-minded pursuit of his state's own self-interest as did Stalin himself.[18] On the Wilson-Kissinger view, therefore, exceptionalism is the source of liberalism and pits the United States against the realist pragmatism in foreign affairs characteristic of the rest of the world.

But this analysis of the United States' intellectual support for liberalism might seem quite dated to the contemporary reader. Reading Jeremy Rabkin, a conservative American scholar of international relations, one might reach a quite contrary view, namely that American exceptionalism is the source of the country's rejection of international law and the role of international organisations. This anti-cooperative position in international affairs has recently come to be perceived as characteristic of modern American foreign policy.[19] Rabkin's argument is that the exceptional characteristics of the American constitutional system are reasons why the United States should not sign up to international legal obligations, which are of an altogether less robust character than the rights accorded under the US Constitution. Respect for constitutional democracy, he suggests, precludes derogation of sovereignty to international legal obligations created through the contemporary network of international organisations and treaties. For Rabkin, the lack of any mechanisms for independent enforcement of international law makes the entire discipline 'soft' law, susceptible to a multitude of interpretations, and thus inferior to US domestic law.

Moreover to protect its constitutional prerogatives, the United States must have the right, he argues, to declare war whenever it deems fit. Every sovereign must have a mandate to protect its people; for Rabkin, it will never do that this mandate is subcontracted to a series of fuzzy international standards set out in the UN Charter. Therefore exceptionalism justifies unilateralism in the name of a realist conception of international relations. The American system is sufficiently precious that, in a dangerous world, the United States must not abrogate its sovereignty in the name of an international order that cannot achieve its stated aspirations because it cannot be impartially enforced. This robust defence of the American unilateral prerogative is contrasted, perhaps a little contemptuously, with what Rabkin calls 'Eurogovernance'.[20] The promotion of international legal norms is something he associates with the European Union, and which he conceives as a historical development of universal and imperial tendencies from the Holy Roman Empire through Napoleonic Europe to the rise of Nazism. The European Union's quest for transnational order is, he suggests, an extension of these historical movements by which European nations seek to impose their values on everyone else. Although modern Europe apparently now operates by some universal precepts set out in the EU treaties, the European mistake is to imagine that European nations' own capacity to absorb European law into their domestic legal and political systems is an experiment capable of being repeated across the remainder of the world through international treaties. On this analysis, it is Europeans who are liberals and Americans who are realists. According to Rabkin the American view is preferable, because to protect themselves in a hostile world Americans must free themselves from the universalist illusions of international law propagated by the Europeans as a result of their distinct historical experiences.

Rabkin's assertion that European nations delude themselves over the truths of realism might seem surprising given that many of the early proponents of the doctrine – Machiavelli, Richelieu, Bismarck and Pitt – were all Europeans. European countries having fought countless wars over centuries in the name of preserving the 'balance of power', one might likewise be surprised by his insinuation that understanding the capacity of nations to pursue their relative self-interest is not a feature of the psyche of European nations. Nonetheless, what a comparison of Wilson and Rabkin reveals is how the competing philosophies of realism and liberalism may find favour at different times, depending on the prevailing political winds. It may simply be that the unilateralism implied by realism is more convenient to nations at certain points within their histories. When European nations were the centre of gravity of the international system, and they spent time and resources fighting one another for control not just over Europe but over their colonial possessions, realist individualism was a convenient philosophy for them to embrace to explain their perennial battles. When international relations became more global, particularly after the end of World War II, European politics were eclipsed by a struggle between superpowers. In the modern era, one superpower has fallen, but others threaten to take its place. In the face of such tectonic movements, European cooperation may be premised upon a realisation that the only way any European nation can have an influence in the contemporary global system is to pool resources. For that to work, intensive legal cooperation is necessary. The experience of the United States, by contrast, has gone in precisely the opposite direction since the end of the Cold War. Being for a time the sole superpower, it has embraced unilateralism precisely because it has the economic, military and diplomatic force to propagate its values around the world. The justifications for it doing so have at times been realism of Rabkin's variety, a useful theory to brush off criticism of the United States for withdrawal from its treaty commitments. At other times the United States has relied upon liberalism of the neoconservative variety, useful to justify regime change in Iraq on the grounds that it contributes towards international polity in which democracy prevails.

The curious relationship between liberalism and the practice of American foreign policy notwithstanding, as a political theory liberalism suffers from its own weaknesses. First, like realism, it is over-simplistic. As the foregoing discussion shows, different (democratic) countries may display different levels of loyalty to ethical principles in foreign policy at different periods. Individual statesmen may weigh such factors in different ways. Kissinger contrasts Theodore Roosevelt and Woodrow Wilson, near-consecutive US Presidents,[21] who adopted entirely different philosophies in international relations with quite different policy outcomes. Roosevelt was a colonialist, seizing Puerto Rico, Cuba and the Philippines from Spain; Wilson established the League of Nations, the United Nations' interwar predecessor. Moreover, issues of national interest may simply outweigh ethical considerations, even in the most liberal democracies. The voters may insist upon it. The bottom-up lines of political accountability that liberalism posits may compel that a nation acts in its own self-interest. That may be precisely what the voters want. If it is a choice between spending money reforming healthcare and spending money relieving humanitarian catastrophe or sending peacekeepers to far-flung corners of the world to subdue civil wars, the voters may insist upon the former. None of these hypotheses seems innately implausible within a democratic system. Significant US public support existed for the indefinite internment of inmates in Guantánamo Bay,[22] contrary to international legal standards of treatment of prisoners in wartime and of due process for persons suspected of crimes. In such circumstances, the ethical principles said to be created by the domestic political pressures existing within liberal democracies may not emerge. Liberalism appears at best an ideal, from which states may frequently, or even mostly, depart.

The second critical problem for liberalism is to explain why when states develop international law, they do not create independent mechanisms for adjudication and enforcement of disputes that arise under it. Perhaps the principal theme of this book is that when we ordinarily talk of law, we refer to a system that, at least in western democracies, we think of as tolerably just. The features we consider characteristic of justice are not present in international law. Those features include an impartial and independent tribunal to adjudicate disputes. They require consistent application of the law, in which precedents are followed and legal rules are applied consistently from one case to the next. They entail a fair procedure, in which all affected parties have both access to the tribunal and an opportunity to be heard. A forum must be available for those adversely affected by a breach of the law, to have his complaint heard and to seek an effective remedy. Justice must be administered quickly enough that it does not suffer from what Shakespeare decried as 'the law's delay'.[23] Decisions must be made in accordance with principle only, without regard to political influence. The relative political power of the parties involved in a dispute should not be a determinant of its outcome. Finally, decisions yielded by the adjudicatory process must be respected. There must be a procedure for enforcing them, in the final resort by force.

Many of these features are lacking in many of the world's legal systems. However, we hope that one of the distinguishing features of liberal western democracies is that most or all of these principles are upheld most or all of the time. In international tribunals, those features are disregarded on an astonishingly widespread basis, as this book will seek to demonstrate from Chapter 3 onwards. The liberal must explain why this is so. If well-meaning liberal democracies were determined to cooperate to promote common ideals through binding international treaties, why would they not agree to create rigorous adjudication and enforcement mechanisms of the kinds we find in robust domestic legal institutions? As shall be seen, the international tribunals that states actually agree to form are susceptible to egregious political influence. Liberalism cannot explain why the enlightened democracies wish to perpetuate at an international level such bastardised shadows of impartial and effective justice. The proper administration of justice is a matter which those countries know so well from their domestic experiences. This intimate knowledge of impartial and effective justice is supposed, on the liberal thesis, to motivate those states' foreign policy. Yet in fact it does not.

CONSTRUCTED INCENTIVES

Both realism and liberalism turn out to be over-simplistic accounts of states' motivations. The debate between the two poles is irreconcilable because states' behaviour is influenced by a variety of factors, some in the nature of self-interested atoms suspended in the anarchic balance of power, and some in the nature of genuine altruism and a desire to propagate certain values beyond their borders. Yet we cannot hope to develop a perfect account of international relations just by combining the insights of these two perspectives. A theory that sought to blend liberalism and idealism in a linear spectrum, attributing every act of a state, and thus every international act, along a sliding scale between two extremities, would not be complete either. There is a third influence on states' behaviour, which renders a fulsome portrait of international relations at least three-dimensional. This is the propensity for international actors to behave in accordance with ideas, rules, procedures or standards, for the reason that the rules exist and that their existence legitimises courses of action purporting to be consistent with them. In economics this is sometimes known as 'path dependence', and applied to international organisations this is a central insight of constructivism. In the words of one constructivist scholar, '[i]nternational politics is shaped by persuasive ideas, collective values, culture, and social identities'.[24]

Rules, and the institutions that embody them, create legitimacy for certain ideas, and the states that create such institutions may do so because they wish to be associated with those ideas. On this analysis, international organisations are created not, as economists imagine, just to resolve cooperation problems, and to achieve common goals the states have in mind, but also to embody values with which states wish to associate themselves. International law is the same: it reflects values with which states wish to be associated. In the words of Michael Barnett and Martha Finnemore, in their groundbreaking paper on constructivism and international organisations, 'organizations may be created and supported not for what they do but for what they are – for what they represent symbolically and the values they embody'.[25] States may sign human rights treaties not because they want to enforce them (or have those treaties enforced against them), but because they wish to be associated with the values those treaties represent. This may explain why some of the world's worst human rights abusers feel comfortable signing treaties of this kind.

Persist for a moment with the example of human rights treaties. A country with a poor human rights record may be able to massage that fact by agreeing to such a document. To any criticism that it harbours poor human rights standards, it can respond that it has agreed to the same standards of human rights as the rest of the world. Moreover, it has an incentive to agree to an overarching international institutional structure to accompany the treaty – for example, a Human Rights Council, of the kind that exists under the auspices of the Office for the High Commissioner of Human Rights. A country can demonstrate its commitment to human rights, and the seriousness it accords to treaty norms, through participation in such a body. It may send delegates, comment on the agenda and even provide funding, all in demonstration of its international commitments. None of this may make any difference to its domestic practice, but there is real political value in participating in such a treaty – as long as there is no genuine and credible independent mechanism by which the treaty might be enforced within the member's territory. Why then do countries with strong constitutional traditions of upholding human rights sign human rights treaties? If they understood the motives of their less ethical counterparts, why would they go along with the charade?

The simplest answer is that they wish to be associated with precisely the same human rights values. There may be a political benefit at home to an argument that they are promoting human rights worldwide. Signing a treaty and contributing some funds to an international organisation is a far cheaper and more convenient way of saying you are playing a part in the promotion of international standards of human rights, than invading nations and overthrowing their governments to correct their human rights abuses. It is also cheaper than imposing economic sanctions on nations that abuse human rights. It signals a commitment to a value, for relatively nominal cost. Once the number of signatories to a treaty reaches a critical mass, there may be a domestic or international reputation cost to pay in refusing to sign up to an instrument most other countries in the world have agreed to, as the American government discovered when it signed, but subsequently refused to ratify, the Rome Statute establishing the International Criminal Court (ICC).[26] Its decision attracted a degree of global opprobrium. The global values associated with the ICC were so obvious that other civilised nations held it against the United States that it refused to support them.

These are constructivist reasons for states' participation in international law and international organisations. They are not reasons comprehensible to a realist. Realists must believe that states adhere to international treaties only where they have real cooperation problems to resolve. International human rights is not a real cooperation problem – the United States has no (or no strong) interest in human rights being observed in China, because Chinese citizens do not vote in US elections. Liberalism predicts the participation of liberal democracies in human rights treaties, but not dictatorships or human rights abusers. It also predicts agreement upon proper enforcement mechanisms. Therefore neither theory can provide a perfect account of why such treaties exist in the form they do. The plethora of actual human rights treaties that exist, and the institutions created to ensure their observance, will be considered in Chapter 7. However, the important point for now is that the desire to be associated with legitimacy is an important part of the picture of states' incentives that explains how such treaties have evolved into their current form. Realism and liberalism both assume that states, as rational actors, do things with a view to achieving results: selfish results for realists, altruistic results for liberals. Constructivism sees an association with legitimacy as an independent desirable goal for states, irrespective of whether the legitimate aims in fact achieve fruition.

If states can be motivated in this way, there is manifestly some danger. Values, one might think, are barely worth having within the international sphere unless they are respected. If they are honoured in the breach, they become a mere smokescreen for concealed realist wickedness. The only truth in liberalism lies in its being a dishonest charade behind which lies sinister pursuit of naked self-interest. If international law served only this function, its crime might be only to reflect in international relations the hypocrisy prevalent in other spheres of human political activity. Yet the constructivist hypothesis goes further. Both liberalism and idealism deny the autonomy of international law and its actors. They understand international institutions, and the legal rules those institutions propagate, as being proxies for amalgams of state incentives. For the realist, international law makes no difference to international relations, because states will take no notice of their international commitments unless it is in their own interests to do so. Without an enforcement authority, states have no independent incentive to comply with the international law to which they have agreed in their treaty commitments, beyond the threat of retaliation by an aggrieved state. Yet this threat would have existed even had the commitment not been entered into in the first place.[27] Interestingly, the same is also true for liberals. Where ethical states propagate international rules, those ethical states would comply with such rules anyway, precisely because they are ethical. Unethical states may not comply with those ethical obligations, and ethical states may cooperate and force them to do so. But states could cooperate to force unethical states to act in the ethical ways they require in any event, irrespective of the existence of international law or international organisations.

Indeed there are many such examples of their doing so. The NATO aerial bombardment of Serbia and subsequent occupation of Kosovo in 1999 was a good example of countries acting with humanitarian motives without the slightest regard for international law. So arguably was the 2003 invasion of Iraq, the purpose of which was apparently – perhaps incredibly – to remove a tyrant. The self-interested motives for the invasion cited at the time, which centred around pre-emptive self-defence against a state with weapons of danger to the rest of the world, have since proved to lack credibility.[28] For both realist and liberal theories, international law has causal relevance only at the margins. It is primarily an expression of state incentives to cooperate, and creates a forum to facilitate their cooperation. But ultimately, states could and would do what they are going to do anyway even if international law did not exist at all. International law is a reflection of state incentives. It does not shape them. There is no possibility within these theories that international law creates a new value or principle which does not have its origin in a combination of the values of the states that have combined to create it. Constructivism parts company with both liberalism and idealism on this point. It advances the view that international law may have a content autonomous from the incentives of the states whose joint action have created it.

This autonomy spills over into international organisations which propagate and administer that law. For the liberal proponent of international organisations, those institutions remain an amalgam of states' interests, albeit ethical or principled ones. The World Health Organisation expresses the joint desire of its members to pursue a moral goal, namely global eradication of serious disease. There could be no possibility of the institution adopting an agenda out of kilter with the preponderance of the desires of its members. The institution, and the legal rules it propagates, are a construct of its member states' preferences. Constructivism denies this model. The development of international law is, says the constructivist, only partially controlled by the state actors who come together to create it. It may develop its own trajectory, much as the mob may riot even when it was not the wish of any (or very few) of its members, considered individually, for that result to come about. For constructivism, the sum is greater than the parts that comprise it. Based upon anecdotal evidence, this must seem right: there are far more international organisations than there are states, and the number of treaties globally is almost innumerably large. International organisations, themselves the subject of treaties, even sign treaties with each other, creating new international organisations, which presumably might continue to sign more treaties creating more international organisations, creating an exponential avalanche. Both realists and liberals have difficulty capturing the insight that international relations involves something more than a simple combination of the preferences of states. These theories focus on the state whereas the locus of attention in some cases should be the international organisations themselves, the creations of international law. The slave may become the master; and constructivism suggests that this may well occur. There are a number of explanations of how this might come about.

THE POLITICAL ECONOMY OF INTERNATIONAL ORGANISATIONS

First, we might study agency problems to suggest how international law develops an autonomous quality. Assume that four people want to buy a property together. Rather than all four of them looking at properties, they hire an agent to look for them. The agent is retained to resolve the cooperation problem. It might well be more efficient for the agent to undertake the search than for all four principals to undertake the search collectively. But that does not mean that the agent will execute his principals' collective intentions impeccably. Each principal may have his own wishes. One may want a property with a certain number of rooms; one may place emphasis on the garden; and the like. The principal who is on the telephone most frequently to the agent may have his preferences better reflected in the agent's choices, notwithstanding the relative poverty of his financial contribution to the transaction. The inputs the agent receives may not be a composite linear amalgam of financial or other power.

Furthermore, the agent will have his own incentives, which may be unrelated to the principals' interests. He may be receiving his commission from the vendor; thus an extra incentive may be inserted into the decision-making process. More subtly, the agent may have interests in selling properties in a certain part of town, where (s)he is seeking to expand the business. Alternatively, there may be purely internal incentives, which have nothing to do with the business incentives of any of the parties involved. The agent may wish sales to be directed through one particular sales official on the staff, because that person is his or her cousin; and that person sells only maisonettes, or only detached houses. Thus the internal structure of the agent determines the range of choices facing the principals. Where international organisations are the agents, and the number of principals is so high (up to 192, corresponding to the 192 UN member states), these agency problems are magnified. International organisations are immensely complex bureaucratic structures, in which the principals' interests are liable to be lost in the system.

This may occur even where the principals' interests are closely aligned, if those interests are not particularly strong. In theory, principals with aligned interests can collectively tell their agent that if that agent does not execute their combined will, they will penalise the agent: in the case of an international organisation, they may do that by ceasing to fund it, or even collectively withdrawing. However, in practice they will often not take such dramatic measures. That is because the efforts required to influence an agent to depart from following the course prescribed by its internal incentives is often significant; and that effort may be more than the prospective benefit the disgruntled principals, individually or collectively, stand to gain from forcing the organisation to comply with their will. International organisations may be ingenious in their ability to divide their principals who seek to cooperate to prevent those organisations' autonomy. Although principals may agree on one issue, they may differ on a variety of other issues. The organisation may exploit those differences, and that danger may be something no principal wants to risk. Moreover, international organisations often have formidable publicity machines, in which their work is idolised as promoting the very best practice, and the most ethical conduct, in international relations. International organisations frequently promote themselves as impartial experts and arbiters in differences between states, leading any state that seeks to force its view upon the organisation liable to be branded as an international delinquent from the institutional norm.

States are frequently dissatisfied with the work of international organisations, and are exasperated by their inefficiency and their tendency to pursue their own autonomous agendas. But the trouble involved in confronting the organisations and squeezing the agency problems out of the system is typically just not worth the effort. This is all the more the case where the costs of the ultimate sanctions a state has against a recalcitrant international organisation – withdrawal or suspension of funding – yield such modest advantages. Withdrawal from international organisations is rare, and is usually a highly political act, as when France withdrew from NATO high command,[29] or Russia withdrew from the Energy Charter Treaty, a 1994 multilateral investment treaty designed to promote foreign investment in Eastern European extractive industries.[30] The detrimental consequences for international cooperation, as other countries conclude the state in question is an unreliable international partner in other areas unrelated to the organisation from which one is withdrawing, may be too high a price to pay. The only states that have sought to withdraw from the

UN Treaty have soon thereafter resumed their membership.[31] Similarly, the United States has an established history of withholding its dues from the United Nations, in an attempt to force reform.[32] Despite its being the largest single donor to the UN's budget, this pressure has not worked. Each time the UN has waited until a friendlier administration is elected in Washington, DC, then offered modest reforming concessions to revive US funding. Because the institution receives by far the greater bulk of its funding from other states, and because the UN is periodically useful to the United States (for example by providing *ex post facto* cover for the 2003 invasion of Iraq),[33] it can afford to wait.

The agency problems involved in establishing international organisations can be described in another way by observing that their lines of political accountability are exceptionally diffuse. The principal decision-makers in an international organisation are not democratically elected. Unlike a national government, the electorate cannot replace the decision-makers if they disagree either with their policies or with the means of their implementation. The leaders of international organisations are free to formulate their policies and develop the bureaucracy within which they work as they please, without regard to the price an electorate might force them to pay for unpopular decisions. The question then arises, what pressure exists to keep those organisations faithful to their proper course? One may reply that the democratic deficit is ameliorated by the fact that the participant members in an international organisation are democracies. But of course this is not wholly true – indeed for most international organisations, it is not even mostly true. The majority of members of the United Nations are not functional democracies (although many purport to be so).[34] International organisations are accountable not to a democratic polity at all, but to an unholy mélange of the world's dictatorships.

Even for those members of international organisations that are democracies, the voting population has little interest in the decisions of international organisations. The decisions they make are too far removed for voters to cast their votes based upon them. The line of causation from voter to domestic politician to official within an international organisation appointed by the domestic politician is too tenuous, for this theory of democratic accountability to be expected to act as a restraining influence upon international organisations. It is hard enough to persuade voters within the European Union to take an interest in European affairs: the average turnout across the EU in the 2009 European elections was 43 per cent, significantly lower than the average turnout in domestic elections. It will be harder still, therefore, for members of the global population to take a sufficient level of interest in the activities of the United Nations, such that they are prepared to change the way they vote in order to influence the organisation's operation. In a world in which different national members of international organisations inevitably have differing interests, corresponding to the different wishes of their populations (or of controlling elite interest groups within undemocratic or imperfectly democratic political systems), it is all too easy for the decision-makers within an international organisation to play the members off against one another. The result is that the indirect lines of democratic responsibility are inevitably fractured.

Moreover, this democratic accountability theory misrepresents the role international organisations play in the domestic polity of their members. National politicians do not take an interest in what the electorate thinks about international issues, and then cast their votes within the decision-making structures of international organisations accordingly, to ensure the organisations' managers observe the strictures required by their electorates. That account is back to front. Instead, the international organisations promote a series of standards by which national governments are held to account. If a national government is disinclined to observe the rules or principles an international organisation promotes, the organisation may publicise that fact, or the government's domestic political opponents may highlight the issue. In other words, international organisations and the standards they propagate may become weapons wielded by politicians within domestic debates. The electorate may be urged to vote down its national government by reason of its officials' failure to comply with international law, a story unfolding within the United Kingdom as this text is being written, in the course of the inquiry into the legality of the Iraq war.[35] Thus international organisations are not constrained by the domestic electorate; instead they serve to shape the electorate's preferences, through a perception that they exist in some sense as neutral arbiters of the domestic government's conduct.

INTERNATIONAL ORGANISATIONS AS STANDARD-SETTERS

This capacity of international organisations to insert themselves into the domestic political sphere as purportedly neutral actors, who set standards against which nations should be assessed, goes to the core of the constructivist thesis. The insight suggested is that the capacity to set and administer legal rules may have an effect upon parties to whom they are addressed, even without the means for the enforcement of them. This might appear a surprising thesis. I may be the village crank, pinning to the town hall notice board a series of prescriptions about what colours people walking in the street should or should not wear on given days of the week. I am not the police, and I have no means to enforce these rules. Thus I remain a crank, and everybody ignores my rules. However, as soon as I acquire the capacity to hire officers in uniform, suitably armed, to enforce my rules, I cease to be the crank, and people will start obeying my laws. When purporting to make law, everything apparently turns upon the capacity to enforce.

Superficially attractive as this reasoning is, the constructivist suggests it is wrong – or, at least, incomplete. When propagated and administered by an authority claiming to occupy a privileged ethical viewpoint, those rules may acquire some level of causal force even if there is nobody to punish directly their infraction. The constructivist thesis explains why, in Nazi-occupied Denmark for a period of six months in 1944–45 when the country had no police force, there was no appreciable increase in many types of crime.[36] In some circumstances at least, people observe rules simply because they have been promulgated by a body declaring itself to be authoritative. Constructivists in international relations suggest that states, and international organisations, may also find incentives of this kind to obey international legal rules.

This is what the German sociologist Max Weber meant when he referred to 'rational-legal authority' as the characteristic form of control exercised by the modern state.[37] Weber saw the distinguishing feature of contemporary government as a rational authority, creating rules and then impartially applying them, avoiding the appearance of discretion, preference or arbitrariness. This authority would be legitimised through division of power between several poles – executive, legislative, judicial, national, federal, local – each of which would serve to temper the powers of the others, but also through so doing would lend the others legitimacy. In earlier Hobbesian forms of government the absolute power of the sovereign could be wielded arbitrarily, and there was no other authority within government to which one could turn when one disagreed. By contrast under the modern constitutional bureaucratic form of government, the impartial and diffuse way in which power is wielded creates a legitimacy which renders subjects hesitant to disobey overtly. The moral force of rules propagated within a legitimate system of government creates a reason to act, irrespective of the imminence of the policeman's brute force in the event of infraction. To be sure, this type of incentive is not as strong as the pursuit of self-interest in the absence of enforcement. In domestic society, the coincidence of self-interest and legitimate imperative is remarkably uniform, through the knowledge that for the social deviant, the policeman is never far away. But for states, there is no policeman – or, at least, no impartial one. Thus the causal dynamic of a legitimating authority is somewhat different, and the deviant state is not effectively restrained.

Once states cooperate to create international organisations, the constructivist maintains, those organisations create rules in the form of international law that bind those same states. To some degree, states become hostages to the organisations that have created them. There are several causal pathways by which this may occur. The international organisation may shame states into not complying with them, through adverse publicity that inserts itself into the domestic politics of the nation concerned. Domestic pressure groups with an interest in the rule in question may lobby to make compliance with a given area of international law a domestic priority. Other states may highlight a nation's non-compliance with international law. Domestically, politicians, judges and others may have their own reasons to argue for compliance with international law. The domestic legal profession may have an interest in asserting that international law forms part of domestic law: it may give them more clients, more arguments, more work. Judges may wield more power if they can use international law to override domestic law. Opposition politicians may use non-compliance with international law to attack the government. There are plenty of ways in which international law has causal effects.

Indeed the foregoing account of the causal influence of international law may sound entirely positive: there are ways in which international law may be applied and enforced, notwithstanding the non-existence of a global policeman. The challenge for international law, however, is precisely that: in the absence of the policeman in whose impartiality one may have confidence, each state is entitled to develop its interpretations of international law in whatever way it wishes, within the bounds of intellectual credibility, and sometimes outside them. In the endless conversations about the content of international law, everyone has a never-ending say. There is no court that may be trusted to apply, interpret and develop the law in a neutral way and whose rulings will be final. In an essentially contested political environment of the kind that exists in international relations, with no world government, international courts and tribunals are occupying a role quite different from their domestic counterparts. One of the principal themes of this book is to examine what this role is. The suggestion that emerges is that what they are doing is not always a good thing.

Imagine a group of 192 people who come together in an anarchy to agree some set of rules about how they ought to live together, share common resources, respect one another's demarcated territory and the like. However, our 192 founding fathers do not pursue the possible progressions from the state of nature envisaged either by Hobbes or by Rousseau. The former saw a powerful sovereign forcibly taking over from the anarchy and imposing his (or her) own law. The latter saw a voluntary agreement between citizens to create a republican authority to enforce the law. Instead, our founding fathers agree to create institutions to develop the law, but do not create any authority to enforce it. They leave it to one another to enforce the law as they see fit. They may agree to create courts to adjudicate disputes; but the courts have no power to order anyone to imprison, hurt or kill someone who breaks the law. In such a legal system, how would the courts then behave in interpreting the law? If they apply the law against someone who has more guns, that person may come to the door of the court to imprison, hurt or kill them. This does not happen in a civilised society, because the court officials themselves have more guns; states have an (overwhelming) monopoly on the use of force. Civilisation requires it. Without that monopoly everything starts to break down.

Without its own power of enforcement, the court in our thought experiment will still want to uphold the law its 192 citizens have created, because its own self interest will lie in doing so: if the law lacks credibility, the court will be disregarded, and it will soon be finished. The court might therefore follow a strategy of applying the law against weak parties at the request of strong ones; but not vice versa. But this will lead to a charge of partiality, the antithesis of the rational legitimacy that gives the system authority. Thus the court will develop complex and abstruse yet flexible doctrines, which enable it to reach whatever result is most convenient to its own survival, consistent with professing of an impartial application of theory. Any public administration on which these 192 citizens have agreed will do likewise: it is the only mechanism for self-defence when it is the only actor in the society without any guns. At the same time, the administration will promote itself as a propagator of impartial values in a chaotic world and seize greater budgets, justifying ever greater areas into which the administration should peer. It will do everything it can to grow, playing its 192 members off against one another, for in truth it is answerable to none of them. The optimal self-preservation strategy of the administration is to create ever more laws to administer, always taking care that the rules it creates are never applied in such a way that one of the more powerful citizens takes exceptional umbrage. Such is the dynamic of a multi-polar world occupied for over 50 years by a dense glut of international organisations. Assessed by the standards of rule of law and administrative effectiveness by which we in the privileged west like to assess our own legal institutions, the organisations created on this hypothesis would inevitably be highly dysfunctional.

It should be clear from this picture that if it is accurate, then the institutions of international law have significant autonomy. They are not slaves of the states that create them; they are unaccountable in important ways. They make decisions which are important to the states that have created them, and yet which those states cannot fully control. They are constrained in their actions; they cannot cross their most important members' most vital interests without precipitating a potentially damaging backlash. This is all the more the case where the balance of power in the world revolves as it has since 1945, around a small number of comparatively powerful states. But by playing off rival member states one against the other, international organisations have a remarkable degree of leeway. To the extent they can tap into domestic interest groups and member states' politics, and offer an association of international rationality and legitimacy with a domestic political cause, international organisations can also grow, even if the majority of their members may prefer that they do not. They can branch out into new areas of operation, new fields of international law can be created and if necessary funded by just a small constituency of member nations.

Even if many or most powerful nations are opposed (as with the International Criminal Court), these new areas of international law can still flourish. Some nations will support them, and pay for them; having only rational-legal authority rather than authority backed by might, nobody sees their growth as sufficiently threatening. They lack political accountability, since there is no electorate complaining their growth is wasteful. Their expansion is capped only by the limits to the intellectual creativity of those who work within them, in finding a new area into which to expand; and the financial willingness of some enthusiastic group of states within the global community prepared to fund their growth. That is why we live in a world with over nine times as many international organisations as states. Once established, the institutions can carry on potentially indefinitely; due to their legitimating authority, no member state, responsible in part for an organisation's creation, wants to be seen to undermine it, implying as that would an abandonment of the principles underlying it. Thus international law and organisations only grow.

Another intriguing feature of the politics of international organisations that derives from their political autonomy is the power of middle managers. Due to the diffuse lines of accountability to each individual member, the level of representation the members can press for is limited. Ostensibly, the members must appear to be in control. Therefore the governing boards of international organisations are typically composed of representatives of those members. The World Bank has a Board of Executive Directors, whose sanction is required to approve projects. The Executive Directors are appointed by the member states, and vote in proportion to the members' shareholdings (which in turn is proportionate to their financial contributions). In the UN, the Security Council ratifies all principal decisions; its membership is composed of representatives of member states. Not all member states can sit simultaneously on the Council; therefore they rotate, albeit with five permanent members.

However, to assume that the Security Council of the UN or the Executive Directors of the World Bank are the principal loci of power within these institutions might be a mistake. Although the press is used to reporting heated debates within the Security Council between the Great Powers, threatening to exercise their vetoes over controversial resolutions relating, for instance, to the 2003 invasion of Iraq,[38] the greater bulk of Security Council business does not involve such vexed confrontations. Underneath the formal decision-making council, staffed by national civil servants posted for short-term assignments to the international organisation in question, lies a morass of professional managers who have spent their career in the international organisation and have exclusive access to the organisation's institutional knowledge and sole familiarity with its procedures. Through selective release of that knowledge to the board of principals, they can exert significant influence over the majority of decisions the organisation makes. An initiative pushed by a member state can easily be killed within the folds of the organisation's bureaucracy, if it does not please the managers' objectives. Similarly, a controversial feature of an initiative can be hidden from view by the managers in the way they present their proposals to the decision-making board.

Managers can also use their powers to filter the projects that reach the board. International organisations are staffed, for the most part, by civil servants recruited and promoted through autonomous human resources procedures into which member states have no input. Therefore the way these civil servants make their decisions remains wholly outside the influence of their members. International organisations also encourage their staff to build their entire careers around the institution in question, almost always promoting to senior management positions from within, and providing tenure to senior staff in a way increasingly incomprehensible in the western world in either public or private sectors. All staff therefore have a vested incentive in keeping the system as it is, and not 'blowing the whistle' to member states. Save where overwhelming considerations of realist political relations between member states take hold (as where one Great Power wants to invade a country over the wishes of another Great Power), the power within the organisations lies not with the representatives of the member states, but in the autonomous managers who owe no allegiance to the member states and instead have every incentive to withhold complete information about the organisation's activities from them.

It therefore turns out that some of the principal decision-makers within international organisations are not even indirectly politically accountable to member states or their electorates. They are accountable to the internal bureaucracy alone. This concern is exacerbated because the other principal form of constraining influence that exists for public organisations (at least in western societies) – namely the obligation to answer to an independent court for failure to respect the tenets of a detailed administrative law – is also absent for international organisations. As this book will explore, international organisations are almost never subject to lawsuits to test the legality of the decisions they make. Indeed the legal framework of their decision-making procedures is opaque or in some cases even non-existent. Virtually every international organisation relies upon all-pervasive doctrines of legal immunity from suit of any kind in domestic courts; yet no international courts have jurisdiction to review their decisions either.[39] This stands in stark contrast to the decisions of public bodies in western countries, which as a rule are subject to detailed and vigorous procedures of judicial review by reference to often exacting standards of due process, proportionality, *ultra vires* and legitimate purpose.

This lack of legal accountability is compounded by an absence of publicly available information about international organisations' operations. Sitting above the domestic legal systems of the countries in which they operate, international organisations are not subject to freedom of information legislation. Neither the public at large, nor the member states, can compel international organisations to produce information pursuant to a judicial process. Although they often profess openness, international organisations decide for themselves which documents they release into the public domain. Naturally, they release only those that paint themselves in a good light or advance their managers' strategic goals. Without obligations either to report to a court of law or to release their internal documents to the public, international organisations are a law unto themselves, over which it is exceptionally difficult to bring external scrutiny to bear. Subject to neither legal nor political accountability to any significant degree, it is no surprise that they exhibit such marked tendencies towards autonomy in their decision-making. If international organisations are above the law in these elementary ways, yet are responsible for creating and even implementing international law, then the law that is produced as a result may turn out to be rather strange. This book will explore that strangeness.

WHY CONSTRUCTIVISM?

This chapter should close by explaining why this book uses the label 'constructivism' to characterise my view of the operation of international law and international organisations, and how my view is differentiated from 'conventional' constructivism. Constructivism within international relations has traditionally been conceived as a somewhat more optimistic alternative to realism. Realists conclude that self-interest and fears of other states' aggressive capabilities lead independent states in an anarchic system to security dilemmas and defensive competition. By contrast, constructivist thinkers prefer not to ascribe any motives to states *a priori*. Instead, the constructivist suggests that relations between states are 'socially constructed', i.e. formed by such matters as the history of the nations' relations and the values embodied within the discourse those states have with one another.[40] Realism is not necessarily wrong in many, or even most, cases; it is just that it is not inevitable. According to these theories, the socially constructed reality that influences international relations is potentially a force for good. International organisations may reflect the values that exist in states' dialogues with one another, which may ameliorate the harsh realist world. At its most radical, one constructivist writer maintains that the values colouring international relations may change so radically that in time the very concept of the sovereign nation state may break down. The common demand by the world's citizens for equal respect and recognition will lead in time to a 'global government'.[41]

The form of constructivism advanced here is far less bold and altogether more pessimistic. Although states may, for example by reason of their historical relationships, engage with one another in ways that realism cannot explain, there is a limiting factor to effects of this kind. When states' national interests are strong, historical relationships, customs or social discourse will inevitably yield to realist considerations of self-interest. Ideology prevails only when it is in the ideologue's self-interest to perpetuate it. Where state interests are weak, some causal space is created for social constructions. These constructions are typically moral, economic, social and legal values that involve a Kantian respect for universalism. Characteristic values are the universality of freedom of expression, uniform rule of law standards across divergent legal systems or access for all persons to an unpolluted environment. Such ideals are a driving force for the creation of international law and international organisations, which routinely promote common standards across all nations.

Because they operate only where states' interests are weak, the international institutions and legal rules promoting these standards fall upon the horns of an acute dilemma. Where a state's interests remain weak, that state will have no long-term concern about what international law and international organisations are doing. It has already blessed the social values the organisation represents, by contributing to its establishment and its budget. It has no interest in engaging in the knotty politics of trying to force the organisation to do anything in particular, given all the other states' potentially contrary interests. Thus the values the institution represents give way to a dangerous autonomy, wherein the organisation can develop those values in any direction it wants. On the other hand, where a state's interest is strong, the organisation, and the socially constructed values it represents, will simply be ignored. In the words of realist scholar Hans Morgenthau, 'it is the iron law of international politics, that legal obligations must yield to the national interest'.[42] Thus the values the conventional constructivists posit are either harmful or irrelevant. There is an internal incoherence to international law, which arises from its pretensions to universality on the one hand and its being confined to a policy space where there are few strong state interests on the other. International law is an ideological construct to fill those spaces, and seeks to secure its observance by persuading states and people that the system is neutral and just. Yet it cannot be so, because it occupies so small a space that its universality is necessarily illusory.[43]

It is easy to feel ambivalent about the label 'constructivism'. Talk of social construction of values, that influence international relations, sounds scholastic and theoretical. Using language that verges upon the obscure is dangerous, because it may hide the relatively straightforward assertions about the operation of international organisations and international law that this work seeks to convey. Those assertions are that states have incentives to create and fund international law and international organisations, but far weaker incentives to ensure those organisations achieve significant results; political accountability of those organisations is exceptionally diffuse; legal accountability is non-existent; such institutions can develop an unhealthy autonomy and therefore the behaviour of institutions that purport to administer international law tends to be very strange, and sharply divergent from western conceptions of the rule of law tradition. The truth of constructivism within this picture is that, contrary to the realist thesis, ethical values have a real role to play in international relations. But unlike either liberal supporters of international institutions or more conventional constructivists, this book portrays the influence of those values as detrimental to an otherwise ruthless, but at least honest, realist polity.

With these remarks, we now conclude this opening theoretical chapter. This work aims principally to be empirical, drawing inferences from case studies of individual institutions within the global system of international law. The first of these case studies will consider the extraordinary development of international law from the end of the nineteenth century to the beginning of the twenty-first. We find ourselves today in an international legal system that nobody could have imagined a hundred years ago. We need to understand how this extraordinary transformation in the international legal system came about in a relatively short period of human history, and in just what this change truly consists. That is the task facing us in the next chapter.

NOTES

1. Johnson, S. (1777), *Thoughts on the Late Transactions Respecting the Falkland Islands*, London: T. Codell (available at http://www.samvdjdison.com/falklands.html, last accessed 6 November 2010).
2. The first scholar to coin the term 'constructivism' in connection with international relations was perhaps Nicholas Onuf (1989), *World of our Making*, Columbia, SC: University of South Carolina Press.
3. This book is not the first to use an analogy of distorting spectacles to describe international relations theory. See also Holsti Ole (2004), 'Theories of international relations', in Hogan, Michael and Thomas Patterson (eds), *Explaining the History of American Foreign Relations*, Cambridge: Cambridge University Press.
4. So-called 'neorealists', of which the first was arguably Kenneth Waltz (1979), *Theory of International Politics*, Reading, MA: Addison-Wesley, try to divorce the realist thesis from any type of statement about human or state incentives. Instead, they suggest, the realist view of international relations follows straight away from a set of premises about the anarchy of the international sphere, being the lack of any independent enforcement mechanism for obligations in international law. It seems unlikely that one can make this leap. Even in anarchy, if actors were altruistic, or motivated by honour, decency or some other sentiment to abide by their legal obligations, then international law ought to be possible even though there is no independent enforcement mechanism. Attribution of self-interested motives to states appears an essential premise for the realist thesis that international law is honoured in the breach. Moreover, if states were not self-interested, then they would agree to forego anarchy, and by cooperation would create the independent enforcement mechanisms sufficient for true world government. One theme of this book is that independent enforcement mechanisms are virtually never created.
5. Morgenthau, H. and Kenneth Thompson (1985), *Politics Among Nations*, 6th edition, New York: McGraw-Hill, p.165.
6. See e.g. Jervis, Robert (1978), 'Cooperation under the security dilemma', *World Politics*, **30**(2), 167.
7. Article 2(4) of the UN Charter contains a general obligation upon states 'to refrain in their international relations from the threat or use of force against the territorial integrity or political independence of any state'. Article 42 provides for the UN Security Council to authorise military action 'to restore international peace and security'. Article 51 provides for the 'inherent right of individual or collective self-defence if an armed attack occurs against a member of the United Nations'.
8. Mearsheimer, John (1995), 'A realist reply', *International Security*, **20**(1), 82.
9. Kissinger, Henry (1994), *Diplomacy*, New York: Simon & Schuster, Chapters 4 *et seq.*
10. Figure provided by the Union of International Associations, Brussels, based on data from the 2001 Yearbook of International Organisations.
11. For an example of so-called 'liberal institutionalists' who cite the existence of extensive international cooperation as evidence for the falsity of the realist thesis, see e.g. Keohane, Robert O. and Lisa L. Martin (1995), 'The promise of institutionalist theory', *International Security*, **20**(1), 47.
12. See North, Douglass C. (1990), *Institutions, Institutional Change and Economic Performance*, Cambridge: Cambridge University Press, Chapters 6 *et seq.*
13. Some of the more notable major US military actions against the sovereign territory of other states undertaken without UN Security Council approval since 1980 include Grenada (1983), Serbia (1999), Bosnia (1995), Iraq (2003–) and Afghanistan (2001–).
14. Henkin, Louis (1979), *How Nations Behave*, New York: Columbia University Press, p.47.
15. This point is made with some force by Mearsheimer, John (2005), *Hans Morgenthau and the Iraq War: realism versus neoconservatism*, London: openDemocracy.
16. See the report of the International Commission on Intervention and State Sovereignty (ICISS) (2001), *The Responsibility to Protect*, Ottawa, ON: International Development

Research Centre, for a liberal theory of intervention in foreign states on humanitarian grounds. The ICISS report was sponsored by the Canadian government.

17. For an exploration of Wilson's exceptionalist views, see Blum, John Morton (1956), *Woodrow Wilson and the Politics of Morality*, London: Little, Brown & Co.
18. See Kissinger, ibid., *Diplomacy*, Chapter 13.
19. See Rabkin, Jeremy (2005), *Law without Nations? Why Constitutional Government Requires Sovereign States*, Princeton: Princeton University Press.
20. Rabkin, ibid., Chapter 6.
21. Roosevelt's Presidency ended in 1909; Wilson's began in 1915. They were interceded by a single four-year term of William Howard Taft.
22. See Gallup, 'Americans approve of most Obama actions to date', 2 February 2009 (noting that only 44 per cent of Americans approved of President Obama's stated policy to close the controversial prison camp).
23. *Hamlet*, Act III Scene I.
24. Barnett, Michael (2007), 'Social constructivism', in Baylis, John, Steve Smith and Patricia Owens (eds), *The Globalization of World Politics*, 4th edition, Oxford: Oxford University Press.
25. Barnett Michael N. and Martha Finnemore (1999), 'The politics, power, and pathologies of international organizations', *International Organization*, **53**(4) (Autumn), 699.
26. President Clinton signed the Rome Treaty on behalf of the United States in 2000. He declined to submit it to the Senate for ratification, and in May 2002 his successor President George W. Bush sent a note to the UN Secretary General in which he declared he was 'suspending' the USA's signature of the Treaty. The ICC is discussed in detail in Chapter 4.
27. A marginal exception to this principle might be made for the indefinite repeat play game. Where a state has relied to its detriment upon the commitment of another state expressed in an international treaty, it might be more inclined to retaliate than had the commitment never been made. By reason of reliance, retaliation in repeat play games may produce a net worse outcome than the default non-compliance option in one-off prisoners' dilemmas.
28. It rapidly became clear in the aftermath of the war that few of those involved in the decision to go to war could genuinely have believed the Iraqi regime was a threat to anyone else. It had suffered such excruciating sanctions after the first Gulf War in 1991 that it was not in a position to fight any other nation; and it was surrounded by other powerful and hostile nations, including Iran and Israel, that could have ruined it had it tried. The Anglo-American invasion of Iraq was thus a remarkable piece of evidence for the liberal thesis, embodied in neoconservative philosophy.
29. France withdrew its Mediterranean fleet from NATO command in March 1959; in 1966, it withdrew entirely from NATO military integrated command and the United States withdrew some 200 military aircraft from ten airbases across France. France rejoined NATO command in 2009.
30. Russia withdrew from the Energy Charter Treaty on 30 July 2009. The motivation for doing so was apparently a lawsuit brought under the Charter against Russia by shareholders in the nationalised Russian oil giant Yukos. This case is discussed further in Chapter 5.
31. The UN Charter contains no formal provisions for states' withdrawal from it, but that has not prevented states from doing so. Syria withdrew from the UN in 1958 upon its joinder with Egypt to form the United Arab Republic. In 1961 it seceded from the United Arab Republic and resumed separate membership. In 1965 Indonesia withdrew in protest at its then-rival Malaysia taking a seat on the UN Security Council. After a coup later the same year, Indonesia decided to 'resume full cooperation with the UN'.
32. The saga of US refusal to pay its dues to the UN has continued at least since 1985. The level of arrears owed has varied since 1995 between US$738 million and over US$1.3 billion.
33. See e.g. UNSCR 1483 (22 May 2003), recognising the US and the UK as the occupying

powers in post-invasion Iraq; and UNSCR 1511 (16 October 2003), recognising the Coalition-imposed 'Governing Council' as the Iraqi government.

34. The 2010 Bertelsmann Stiftung Transformation Index surveys a set of 123 countries that aspire to be democracies, and concludes that 59 per cent of the countries surveyed have a 'limited democracy' ranking or lower.
35. The Chilcot Inquiry into the United Kingdom's role in the 2003 invasion of Iraq commenced public hearings in November 2009. It was part way through hearing witness evidence, including from the then British Prime Minister Gordon Brown, when the UK general election intervened in May 2010 and resulted in the government being voted from office. Particular public attention in the course of the Inquiry focused upon the evidence of the British Attorney General at the time, the Government's Chief Legal Adviser, who had apparently changed his mind on the conformity of the invasion of Iraq with international law over a short period of time.
36. In September 1944, the German army began arresting virtually all the police officers in Denmark, due to their failure to cooperate with Nazi administrators' demands. Many were subsequently deported to concentration camps. In the aftermath, crimes in many categories saw a sharp and immediate increase, in particular property offences such as theft and burglary. However, incidence of more serious crimes, including murder and rape, did not suffer an appreciable increase. For discussion see Cavadino, Michael and James Dignan (1992), *The Penal System: An Introduction*, Thousand Oaks, CA: Sage; Gardiner, Gerald (1958), 'The purposes of criminal punishment', *Modern Law Review*, **21**(2), 117.
37. The other types of domination a government could exercise were described by Weber as traditional authority (obedience commanded by social tradition) and charismatic authority (obedience commanded by the personal qualities of an individual). While all three forms of authority are found in combination, Weber characterised the development of the modern state as being associated with a rise in the relative importance of rational-legal authority. See Weber, Max (1958), 'Three types of legitimate rule', *Berkeley Publications in Society and Institutions*, **4**(1), 1.
38. A draft Security Council resolution dated 7 March 2003, proposed by Spain, the United States and the United Kingdom, would have authorised the US-led invasion of Iraq that ultimately took place in April 2003. Russia, Germany and France issued a joint declaration on 5 March 2003 opposing such a resolution and declaring that Russia and France, permanent members of the Security Council, would veto any resolution authorising use of force against Iraq. Thus the draft resolution was never put to a vote.
39. See Parish, Matthew (2010), 'An essay on the accountability of international organizations'. *International Organizations Law Review*, **7**(2), 277. International courts are most reluctant to undertake a review of the actions of international organisations, even where there might (as with the European Court of Human Rights) be a plausible jurisdictional basis for their doing so, for fear of the unfunded docket growth this would promote. See Case No. 71412/01 *Behrami and Behrami v France*; Case No. 78177/01 *Saramati v France, Germany and Norway*, Decision of 31 May 2007 (ECHR may not review acts of KFOR (Kosovo Force) peacekeeping soldiers even though all soldiers were seconded to KFOR by member states of the European Convention on Human Rights).
40. See e.g. Wendt, Alexander (1992), 'Anarchy is what states make of it: the social construction of power politics', *International Organization*, **46**, 391; Finnemore, Martha (1996), *National Interests in International Society*, Ithaca, NY: Cornell University Press.
41. Wendt, Alexander (2003), 'Why a world state is inevitable', *European Journal of International Relations*, **9**, 491.
42. Morgenthau, Hans (1951), *In Defence of the National Interest*, New York: Alfred A. Knopf.
43. This notion of international law as an ideology bears some similarity with what is known as the 'critical theory' school within international relations. See e.g. Purvis, Nigel (19991), 'Critical legal studies in international law', *Harvard International Law*

Journal, **32**, 81; Boyle, James (1985), 'Ideas and things: international legal scholarship and the prison-house of language', *Harvard International Law Journal*, **26**, 327; Koskenniemi, Martti (1989), *From Apology to Utopia: The Structure of International Legal Argument*, Cambridge: Cambridge University Press.

2. International law: the legacy of the twentieth century

If we had to choose one person as the father of modern international law, it would be not Grotius but Woodrow Wilson. These two figures are worth comparing briefly. Their goals were similar. Both sought to develop sets of legal rules which dictate the behaviour of states in their mutual confrontations. The subject matter of these rules in both cases was the circumstances in which states were entitled to go to war with one another, and the way those wars should be fought when they occur. Both advanced their ideas in the context of wars that had exacted a brutal toil on human life. Grotius wrote in the midst of the bloody Thirty Years War, in which it is estimated that between 3 and 12 million people died. Wilson advanced his ideas in the aftermath of World War I, in which between 15 and 30 million people may have died. The purpose of the international law they developed was to prevent the horrors of future warfare and massive loss of life.

Yet there was a profound difference in the sorts of international legal regime each thinker advocated. Grotius's masterpiece *De Jure Belli ac Pacis* (1625) was the first attempt to set out detailed rules for the conduct of states in their hostile relations with one another. The array of topics he addresses is exceptionally broad, including performance of treaty obligations, duties to respect foreign property, authority of agents to bind sovereigns, embassies and diplomatic immunity, prisoners of war, plunder of conquered territory, treatment of civilians, neutrality, the obligations of states in administering criminal justice and a great deal more. For the most part his authorities are the ancient Roman and Greek writers; there is very little reference in his work to contemporary events, although the horrors of the Thirty Years' War, raging in the background as he wrote, no doubt motivated his appeal to moderation. However, he clearly perceived war as to a degree inevitable, and thus something to be regulated rather than eliminated. Most revealingly, Grotius makes no attempt to explain how the principles of international law that he sets out are to be enforced. Presumably he thought that states themselves would enforce his principles against other states; but that begs the question, how they would do so in circumstances of hostility between one another that triggered the need for this area of law in the first place?

Although to the modern eye this may appear a surprising lacuna in Grotius's writings, it was perhaps less surprising to his readership. This was an era in which the study of law was not a practical matter of how to administer justice impartially between individuals; rather it was an affair of scholarship, of study of Roman law. Certainly the notion of an independent judiciary, neutrally applying the law apart from the sovereign who propagated it, was only dimly understood in the era. It would not be until events preceding the English Civil War, in the period beginning ten years after Grotius published his work, that the tradition of judicial independence from the sovereign would find expression in a series of cases in which the English courts sided with parliament, and against the crown. The notion of an independent judicial authority existing to assess the sovereign's compliance with legal obligations would have appeared to Grotius, writing before these momentous events, as bizarre or even seditious.

International law would remain a set of lofty scholarly ideals that European sovereigns in their wisdom and unquestioned authority, often asserted as being derived from the divine, might be expected to observe. It would not be enforced *per se* against a recalcitrant sovereign; there would be no need. International law at the time was seen as a kind of 'natural law',[1] an account of the way things really are, rather than a set of rules to be imposed under threats of sanction for noncompliance. This was, perhaps, a natural legal philosophy for those dependent upon the will of a near absolute sovereign for enforcement of the law. Inevitably, as soon as one relaxed the assumptions about the Monarch's beneficence and infallibility, the lack of an enforcement mechanism for Grotius's edicts would become of acute concern. But for Grotius himself, relaxing those assumptions was unthinkable. For lawyers to enter the political realm in such a way, in an era of absolute power held by sovereigns who could wield that power arbitrarily and at will, could be exceptionally dangerous. In 1618, Grotius had been arrested and sentenced to life imprisonment for authorship of an edict promoting religious tolerance (although he escaped in 1621). In the future his legal writings would remain of an entirely academic nature.

International law continued in this principally academic vein for the next 290 years. The Thirty Years' War ended with the Peace of Westphalia, a series of treaties in 1648 which demarcated the internal boundaries of the states within the Holy Roman Empire and delineated the powers between the Emperor and the states in a decentralising direction. It is said that the treaties comprising the Peace of Westphalia established the principle of sovereignty within international law: that is to say, the notion that states are free to do whatever they please within their own borders, so long as they respect the borders of others.[2] However, that inference is an academic abstraction; the principles of sovereignty are prescribed nowhere in the Westphalian treaties. Indeed those treaties say a fair amount about the internal operations of states, including a federal distribution of powers between Holy Roman Emperor and constituent nations; and guarantees of freedom of worship to Christian minorities within the territories of the Empire.

The association of Westphalia with the notion of sovereignty may derive from the fact that international territorial boundaries were recognised by other states, which promised to honour them. The notion of mutual respect by republican governments for one another's territory promised to be the foundation of what Immanuel Kant called a 'Perpetual Peace' in 1795, in his influential essay of that name. Nonetheless, the principles of international relations Kant proposed – which included abolition of standing armies, the prohibition of secret treaties planning for future wars, prohibitions on national debts and a ban on interference with the internal affairs of other states – remained aspirations only. Kant saw them as hortatory: principles which, if observed, would lead to the idealised state of peace to which he aspired. Kant's international law, like that of Grotius, was more akin to moral philosophy than law in the sense of judges, juries, police and prosecutors. Although the nineteenth century saw considerable growth in international law, in the form of a wealth of treaties between nations, again these treaties were modelled on Kant's conception of international law. Little thought was given to the question of whether the domestic authorities within a state might fail to comply with their international legal obligations, and the philosophical thinking necessary to develop international law beyond an abstract discipline did not take place.[3]

WILSONIAN INSTITUTIONS

The sea change in international law occurred at the end of the First World War when one man, the US President Woodrow Wilson, forced upon the world a vision of international law as a tool to prevent future warfare. The last of Wilson's 'Fourteen Points', his plan to the US Congress for bringing World War I to an end,[4] provided that 'a general association of nations must be formed under specific covenants for the purpose of affording mutual guarantees of political independence and territorial integrity to great and small states alike'. Wilson insisted that this principle find expression in the Peace Treaty of Versailles over considerable scepticism by his European counterparts;[5] he had such leverage, perhaps, because the entry of the United States into the war had secured the defeat of Germany and the United States was perceived as the guarantor of the Versailles peace. The first 30 articles of the Versailles Treaty became the Covenant of the League of Nations, and Wilson himself presided over the committee at Versailles which drafted the League's Covenant. The League of Nations would presage a new breed of international organisations, and would have an Assembly (in which all member states were represented), a Council (in which a limited set of members would make urgent decisions) and a Secretariat. Disputes between states would be resolved peaceably, by reference to judicial settlement (through a Permanent Court of International Justice), arbitration or resolution by the League's Council. Any act of war against one state would be deemed an act of war against all; all members would be obliged to implement sanctions against the transgressor, and the Council would recommend military action. By that notion, collective security was born, and the League was conceived as a forerunner to NATO.

The League of Nations Covenant said relatively little about the substance of international law; what it did instead was prescribe procedures by which disputes in the field of international law would be resolved, to foreclose war as the default method of dispute resolution. The radical innovation was to create an institutional structure within which questions of international law would be decided, in contrast to what had gone previously when international law had Grotian or Kantian content, but no procedures by which it would be implemented. Equally important was the broad scope of issues the League of Nations regime deemed to fall within the potential scope of international law. The Covenant contained a regime for oversight of League of Nations 'mandates' (that is to say, former colonies of the defeated powers Germany and Turkey, administered after World War I by the victorious nations),[6] and also provided that the League would subsequently expand its competences into the setting of international labour rights, treatment of native inhabitants, people trafficking and drug smuggling, arms control, control of disease and free communications and fair treatment of commerce.[7] Another chapter of the Versailles Treaty created a second intergovernmental organisation, the International Labour Office, with authority to promulgate draft conventions addressing the protection of workforces within member states and, like the League of Nations, with a permanent secretariat. Even by the standards of modern international institutions, the League of Nations was remarkably broad in scope.

Ironically given that the League of Nations structure was so much the work of the US President, the United States was blocked from joining the League by its own legislature. The Senate refused to ratify the League

Covenant out of a concern that it might commit US armed forces to foreign military action without the authority of Congress, contrary to the US Constitution.[8] No such qualms inhibited the United States' later ratification of the UN Treaty and the North Atlantic Treaty, however. Today the League is widely perceived as a failure, through its inability to prevent Axis aggression in the 1930s, and in particular the stepwise territorial advances Hitler's Germany made during that decade that pushed the world towards World War II. This criticism of the League of Nations may be unfair, however, depending on what one compares it with.

The United Nations Organisation was created by the UN Charter, signed in San Francisco in June 1945. This was intended to be a new international organisation, also designed to keep the peace between nations, created in the aftermath of World War II. Its ostensible goals are very much the same as the League Covenant, and the UN Charter is structured in a very similar way to its predecessor. Neither institution had a standing army to enforce the obligation not to go to war. As will be seen in Chapter 3, the jurisdiction of the two institutions' courts (the Permanent Court of International Justice for the League, the International Court of Justice for the UN) were not compulsory for any affected nation and there was no mechanism for enforcing their decisions. Decisions of the Council of the League required unanimity; this was undoubtedly too high a burden to make the Council an effective body in issues of contested and high profile international affairs. But decisions of the UN Security Council can be vetoed by any one of the Council's 'permanent members'. The five permanent members – the United States, France, Great Britain, Russia and China – have often diametrically opposing international agendas, and this seems unlikely to change soon. In the face of major international crises, therefore, the existence of the veto is barely more satisfactory than the League of Nations requirement of unanimity.

The Assembly in both the United Nations and the League, where resolutions can be passed by a simple majority, is denuded of power, having no authority to make decisions of substance. Even if the UN Security Council does pass a resolution against a recalcitrant and warlike state acting in violation of its international obligations, the Council is reliant, just like the Council of the League, upon individual members committing military forces to enforce its strictures. Both the United Nations and the League of Nations might be conceived as attempts at global government: efforts to set compulsory rules about what states may or may not do. But both lack a workable mechanism for independent adjudication or enforcement of those rules. For that reason, the League of Nations was powerless to resist Nazi Germany when it deliberately disregarded the international legal system. In describing the League of Nations as a failure however, we must be careful not to suggest that the United Nations would have done any better. There is no reason why it should have done. One might aver that the United States is a member of the UN but was not a member of the League. However, the United States did not see fit to act against Hitler on its own in the 1930s. It certainly had the means to do so. The reason it did not was because the country was undergoing one of its periodic episodes of international isolationism. If that militated against interfering in a dangerous European military escalation outside the auspices of the League of Nations, it is not clear why the United States would have intervened against Nazi Germany had it been within the League of Nations. Nothing about the League's structure compelled it to do so; and nothing in the UN's structure would have compelled it to do so either.

Both the League of Nations and the United Nations are most interesting for what they do not contain in their charters. While they establish elaborate international institutional mechanisms, and set out procedures for the Assembly and the Council to issue resolutions, neither calls upon national governments to commit troops to a unified international command, neither makes the jurisdiction of the international courts under their auspices compulsory and neither permits small states to outvote powerful ones (or even for powerful states to outvote other powerful states) in any matters of significance. It is not hard to see why provisions of these kinds are absent from both charters. Powerful states have no incentive to agree to create a true world government. The United States, one of the most powerful nations in the world in both 1918 and 1945, would not want to give up real military or legal sovereignty over its affairs. The only possible incentive for any country to do so would be collective security; but the United States no doubt took the view that given the magnitude of its own power, it would be better at protecting its own security alone, than operating within a collective security apparatus.

This logic must have seemed particularly compelling in the aftermath of World War II when there was a real ideological confrontation between liberal democratic capitalism and communism. Significant future threats would come not from rogue states against which allied nations could combine their forces, but from the Soviet Union, a rival empire with few common political values with the United States. Why would the United States agree to an international institutional structure in which the Soviet Union – or any other country – had any say in the circumstances in which the US military could act? The idea was preposterous. It was out of the question – as, indeed, it would have been for the Soviet Union. The most powerful countries would embrace a system of international institutions only to the extent those institutions did not inhibit their sovereign prerogatives to declare war and conduct domestic and foreign policy as they wished. International institutions could not be permitted to take actions contrary to the interests of those nations, or to adjudicate and condemn their actions. The goal of any powerful state in agreeing to a system of international institutions could only be either to use those institutions as tools to control weaker states, or for internal political goals – for a state to associate itself with a set of values that the institution represents.

Imagine 192 families of varying sizes, wealth and strength cohabiting in a village, each of whom carry their own weapons and are used to defending themselves and the territory they claim for their own. For years they fight one another incessantly. Then, one day, after a particularly bloody battle in which a great many people are killed, they sit down and agree to form an institution which will resolve all their differences in a peaceful manner, to prevent future wars. Someone suggests that all families agree to creation of an executive board, consisting of the heads of (say) five families, with their own police force, and with all weapons turned over to that police force. The police and the executive board, it is said, will operate only within the confines of a series of pre-agreed rules. There will be a judicial authority to adjudicate disputes over these rules. This might in principle seem like a good idea to the weakest families in the village, tired of being preyed upon by their more powerful neighbours. But it is hardly attractive to the powerful families, who have far less to fear from the other members of the village. In theory, the powerful families might agree to give up their military autonomy in favour of the executive board to quell the ongoing disputes they have with one another. But such an act of mutual foresight and wisdom would be less likely if each of the powerful families took the view that they had or were about to obtain some comparative advantage that would allow them to be the prevailing power in the future – or if they felt they had some overwhelming military capacity that would never allow them to be dominated, for example a nuclear weapon. The powerful families would be fearful of a truly independent and powerful executive board that might be able to impose decisions upon them – even crush them with violence – and over which they would have only a limited say. Therefore, if the powerful families were prepared to buy into this proposal for collective security, they would insist upon denuding the executive board of real power, or at least ensuring it could act only with the consent of those powerful families. It certainly would not have its own capacity for force, sufficient to threaten them; at most it would have a police force whose members were seconded temporarily to it by the powerful, when those powerful families decided that the executive board's proposed actions were in their interests. In all circumstances, any structure to be created would not impinge upon the powerful families' own freedom of action when they decided that a certain course of conduct, inconsistent with the wishes of other families, was in their interests. Those with power do not, as a rule, freely give it up.

This pessimistic account of the course human beings would pursue in a state of nature diverges from the social contract Rousseau imagined free peoples would voluntarily adopt, because it departs from the implicit assumption in his model that all the parties to the social contract were of equal power and thus all feared the others. In those circumstances of primal equality, it is imaginable that every party would perceive a genuine collective security arrangement as preferable to the status quo. Alas, life is virtually never so. The incentives upon powerful and weak actors to agree collective security arrangements are quite different. The only collective security arrangement a powerful actor will countenance is one in which (s)he provides collective security at his own discretion to weaker actors, with a view to advancing his own strategic interests. This was the model adopted by both NATO and the Warsaw Pact, as the United States and the Soviet Union respectively purchased varying degrees of political domination or loyalty from their allies in exchange for collective security guarantees. Of course every country with an effective functioning government operates some kind of internal collective security arrangement, in which the government, independent of the citizens, adjudicates and enforces rules of law relating to how the citizenry may treat one another. But what is notable is that comparatively rarely in world history has any such arrangement been created by consent. The usual manner by which governments acquire their monopoly over the use of force is not by agreement of those over whom force may be exercised, but through domination of those people by one particularly powerful individual or group of individuals, who subsequently decide to call themselves the government. In time, the distribution of power between different institutions of the government may change, and democratic representation may emerge. But collective security arrangements are, as a rule, initially imposed rather than agreed.

IS VOLUNTARY COMBINATION EVER POSSIBLE?

The two most prominent arguable counterexamples to this proposition, the United States and Switzerland, did indeed involve agreements to create genuine collective security arrangements. In the late eighteenth century, the United States of America voluntarily came together to form a federal government, by way of a set of Articles of Confederation, later to be rewritten in the US Constitution. Interestingly the Articles of Confederation, coming into force on a *de jure* basis in 1781,[9] were insufficiently robust, granting to federal government the power to make war but not to raise taxes or armies. The federal government under the Articles of Confederation was therefore somewhat like the UN, having to go to its member states to ask them for money and troops to sustain its activities. Nor did the federal government have executive or judicial authorities; it was just a legislature, whose edicts the states might or might not observe as they saw fit. However, by 1788 a revised Constitution had been adopted, granting the federal government these extended authorities and also establishing a federal court system and executive branch of government (the President) with the power to raise an army. By the end of the American Civil War in 1865, the US federal government had developed into the undisputed primary military, political and judicial force in the United States.

Switzerland was likewise formed in 1292, as a voluntary confederation of three cantons rebelling against the Habsburg monarchy and who pooled their resources to resist Austrian suppression of the rebellion. To this day the Swiss Confederation has never grown to embrace more than the most elementary federal institutions. There is no nationwide police force. There is only one federal court, being Switzerland's final court of appeal. The list of areas of federal authority is very short, and for most Swiss citizens the only way the federal government intrudes into their lives is in compulsory military service for adult males in the country's militia-based army. The purpose of the militia (which remains one of the largest standing armies in the world proportionate to population) is exclusively defensive, to resist external threats. Switzerland seldom deploys troops abroad, in accordance with its centuries-old policy of neutrality, and rarely in modern times has it deployed troops within its own borders.[10] Collective Swiss pooling of military resources exists not as a tool for adjudication of disputes between the country's cantons but solely as a method for deterring foreign invasion. The decentralised and idiosyncratic features of Swiss government continue today to reflect the unusual circumstances in which the Confederation was formed some 700 years ago.

For both the United States and Switzerland, the dynamic for the agreement to create a central authority was not fear by the sub-federal units of one another, although the inability of the federal government to resolve frequent disputes between the states was one of the motives for abandoning the Articles of Confederation. Instead it was fear of forces outside, and the sense that collective action was necessary to defeat a common enemy. For the United States that enemy was Britain; for Switzerland it was the Austrian Empire. Likewise German unification in 1871, which was for the most part a voluntary combination of individual states formerly within the Holy Roman Empire, was driven by a desire for collective security not between the states themselves but to secure their common borders against hostile enemies (principally France). Moreover, German unification was arguably closer to a larger power in the region (Prussia) absorbing a range of smaller states, as the King of Prussia was proclaimed Emperor of the German Empire. It was less like a voluntary social contract described above, more akin to weaker families asking to join the stronger family and be placed under its protection. Also worth noting is that although the United States entered into a collective security union in 1781, it was only 80 years before 11 states sought to secede from the Union, and were restrained from doing so through violence. As of 1861, when an attempt at secession of the southern states sparked the beginning of the American Civil War, the United States of America could no longer be described as a voluntary relationship between consenting nations.

If voluntary combination to create genuine federal government in a domestic setting is likely only in response to an external threat, then it is little surprise that the League of Nations, and the UN after it, created something less. There is no external threat to the world, in the sense of an extraterrestrial military force. Although such an unworldly danger might be sufficient impetus to create a genuine world government with adjudication and enforcement powers, in its absence an arrangement in which mutually suspicious, even hostile, nations within the global village come together to form a genuinely impartial collective security pact seems quite unlikely. Powerful nations will not be able to trust one another enough, and will not want to give up their comparative advantages. They will certainly not want to share power with less powerful nations. Those less powerful nations may have to be content with aligning themselves behind more powerful nations; that is arguably the common rationale behind NATO and German reunification. The structures created as a result, in any attempt to form Wilsonian global government, will look remarkably like the League of Nations, the United Nations or the Articles of Confederation. Powerful nations will be able to veto decisions; no court will have compulsory jurisdiction over disputes between nations; contribution of troops to common military causes will be voluntary and the individual nations will retain their own military forces.

In the event of a real dispute between powerful nations (such as the Cuban Missile Crisis in 1962), the global governance structures created will only be able to sit impotently on the sidelines, making calculated guesses about which horse to back. Where a powerful nation practises aggression against a weaker nation, and no other powerful nation is prepared to stop it (as in the US-led invasion of Iraq in 2003), the international institution will again be silent, for fear of incurring the powerful aggressor's wrath. Alternatively the international institution may find legalistic or theoretical grounds to support what the powerful country is doing, to engender favour with its paymaster (as happened with the NATO bombing of Serbia in 1999, and its subsequent occupation of the country's southern province of Kosovo). Only where a weak country breaks the international rules, and a powerful country is inclined to punish it for doing so (as in the first Gulf War in 1991), will the international institution be able to speak up in favour of respect for international law. These are the sorts of principles that will likely govern the role of an attenuated international organisation, such as the United Nations, which is the product of an ostensible agreement for collective security that emerges from the agreement of competing nations with different levels of military and economic power.

If this account is accurate, then it strikes at the heart of the liberal thesis. Were liberalism correct about the motivations of states, then powerful states would be willing to give up sovereignty over their own military affairs in favour of robust collective security agreements, rather than the bastardised kinds of collective security exemplified in the League of Nations and the UN. Powerful but beneficent states would agree to create a genuine world government with impartial enforcement institutions, at least between themselves, realising that this is the best way to preserve their mutual internal peace and to cooperate to resist external threats. That they fail to do so in practice is because they are too short-sighted and selfish. However, realism does not perfectly describe the rise of these institutions either. Realism can explain the creation of impotent institutions by the powerful: they are tools for cloaking nakedly self-interested acts of powerful states against weaker ones in the mantle of legitimacy. But it cannot explain why weaker states would go along with the charade. Are they just foolish? That seems unlikely at least as a general theory of international relations, even if it might be true in individual cases. The reason weaker states participate in impotent international institutions is more likely that they calculate they have nothing to lose; powerful states that wish to dominate weaker states will in all likelihood do so, irrespective of the existence or otherwise of an international legal and institutional framework within which to do it. There are domestic benefits of participation in international institutions: for example, where an international organisation promotes human rights, a state's membership and a contribution of funds may become an effective substitute for failure to respective human rights in the domestic sphere.

Weaker states may also calculate that international institutions provide a policy space in which they can exercise a disproportionate influence relative to their size. International organisations may allow states equality of representation of their members irrespective of economic, political or military strength, a status unthinkable for a weak state in the ordinary course of its diplomacy. (Such egalitarianism will rapidly break down in areas of international concern in which powerful nations have strong interests: hence the existence of 'permanent' members of the UN Security Council with vetoes.) In the absence of strong interests advanced by powerful states, international organisations find autonomy within weak competing interests of a multiplicity of ostensibly equal nations. The unholy compromise between powerful and weak states in the creation of dysfunctional international organisations is this: the powerful states can use those institutions as a shroud for legitimacy when they want to push an international policy; weaker states obtain disproportionate influence over issues where more powerful states do not really care. International organisations capture a broad policy space in between the gaps. This is a constructivist explanation of how we have come to create weak solutions to collective security problems.

There are plenty of circumstances in which an international institution will not be buffeted by the forces of its most powerful members in their pursuit of acts of war. The roles of the League of Nations and the United Nations are arguably irrelevant where strong interests of the world's most powerful states are at stake to the extent that they are prepared to spill blood in pursuit of their goals. Nevertheless there are plenty of international episodes of lesser intensity where such an institution may find room for manoeuvre. The League of Nations was not entirely irrelevant; notwithstanding its unsurprising inability to resist German, Japanese and Italian aggression, it achieved some results. Its principal achievement was the resolution of a range of territorial disputes arising out of the decolonisation of the Ottoman and German Empires following World War I, including settlement of German-Polish disputes relating to Upper Silesia, delimiting the borders between Greece and Albania, resolution of the status of Mosul, affirmation of the status of Vilnius within Poland, administration of the Saar territory until its return to Germany in 1935 after a plebiscite and determination of sovereignty over the Åland Islands.

What is striking about these achievements, however, is that in so many cases the decision adopted by the League of Nations represented the military or political status quo. In the dispute over Upper Silesia, a buffer zone between Germany and Poland was recommended by the Treaty of Versailles to be subject to a plebiscite. After a narrow electoral result in that plebiscite, a League Commission recommended partition of the territory in accordance with the linguistic and cultural preferences of its residents. In a dispute over the murder of an Italian General who was engaged by the League to demarcate the Greek-Albanian border, the League's Conference of Ambassadors held the Greek government responsible and ordered payment of compensation demanded by the Italian government; Italian troops had occupied Corfu to enforce their demand. The

Åland Islands had a Swedish population but had been held by Finland since imperial Russian occupation of Finland; again the League resolution involved maintaining the status quo, leaving the territory as part of Finland. Mosul was *de facto* in the British-administered mandate of Iraq; Turkish historical claims to the territory were rejected, supporting the British position.[11] In each case the League's action adopted the course of least resistance, lending international legitimacy to the facts on the ground.

THE GROWTH OF INTERNATIONAL INSTITUTIONS

If the League inevitably had limited room for manoeuvre on issues of international political moment between its member states, it nonetheless found itself busy in a range of collateral, advisory areas. As well as the Permanent Court of International Justice and International Labour Organisation, envisaged by the Treaty of Versailles, a range of other institutions were created under the League's auspices. A health organisation was created, an early precursor of the World Health Organisation. There was a Committee on Intellectual Cooperation, to promote international scientific and cultural work; a Permanent Central Opium Board, to coordinate international policies on narcotics; a Slavery Commission, working to eradicate slavery; a Commission for Refugees (a forerunner of UNHCR) and a Committee for the Study of the Legal Status of Women. All in all, the League became involved in quite a wide range of activities. Its budget expanded from US$3.3 million in 1920 to US$5.2 million in 1929 (equivalent to about US$56 million in 2010). Notwithstanding this growth, it remained a comparatively modest institution; the UN's general budget was in excess of US$2 billion in 2007. Although the League of Nations never had more than 58 members (this zenith was reached at the end of 1934) compared to the UN's 192 current members, the difference remains marked. Moreover, whereas the foregoing figures for the League included all its associated agencies, the US$2 billion figure representing the UN's current budget does not include some 17 UN specialist agencies, which are financed through separate negotiated contributions from those agencies' members. Nor does it include the UN's peacekeeping budget, which was in the region of US$5 billion for the financial year 2005–06.

At the end of World War II, the League of Nations was perceived as a failure for having been unable to prevent conflict, but the United Nations, devised along much the same lines, was nonetheless conceived to replace it. The United Nations would play a far more profligate role in developing a network of international law and international institutions than did its predecessor. It would grow into a very large organisation. The number of staff in the UN 'common system' (a common regime of recruitment procedures, and salary and management grades across the UN and 13 of its specialist agencies) was more than 83 000 in 2008. This did not include staff on short-term contracts, of which no public records are available, but they may add at least 100 per cent to the total. In 1950, the UN had a mere 1500 employees. The operations of the UN and its associated agencies would come to span a remarkable range of activities. The International Labour Organisation (2500 employees in 2009; budget of US$600 million as of 1999) and INTERPOL (500 employees in 2005; budget of €47 million in 2009), an international police cooperation organisation, survived the League of Nations era. In addition, a new range of specialised agencies of the UN emerged in the years after World War II, including the Food and Agriculture Organisation, the United Nations Population Fund, the International Atomic Energy Agency, the International Civilian Aviation Organisation, the International Fund for Agricultural Development, the International Maritime Organisation, the International Telecommunications Union and countless others. Among the larger ones are the United Nations High Commissioner for Refugees (UNHCR), responsible for operations to care for refugees (6500 employees; budget of US$2.5 billion in 2010); the World Health Organisation (2400 employees; budget of $420 million in 2003); the World Intellectual Property Organization (1000 employees; budget of US$310 million in 2010); and the International Organisation for Migration (over 7000 employees and a budget of over US$1 billion in 2008).

At the Bretton Woods Conference in 1944, another slew of international organisations was conceived. Principal among these were the International Bank for Reconstruction and Development (the World Bank) and the International Monetary Fund. The World Bank subsequently multiplied, and now comprises five international organisations employing 10 000 people under the World Bank umbrella; the IMF employs around 2500. A range of regional development banks (at least 11 are in existence at the time of writing) have followed in the wake of the World Bank, and employ several thousand more people worldwide. Still more international organisations grew out of the UN system or in conjunction with it. OSCE, an election-monitoring organisation, had 3500 staff and a budget of over €200 million in 2000. International organisations need not just be the creation of agreements between states. More international organisations can be created by the agreement of international organisations themselves. The International Trade Centre (ITC) is an international organisation created by an agreement between the UN and the World Trade Organisation (WTO). The Global Environment Facility (GEF) is a creation of the World Bank, the UN Environment Programme and the UN Development Programme. Perhaps the GEF and the ITC can enter into an agreement to create a third-order international organisation, although it has not happened yet.

Depending on how one counts, there were 1859 ordinary international organisations in 2001, or 7080 if one adds conferences (such as UNCTAD, the UN Conference on Trade and Development, a sort of autonomous conference-entity which employs some 500 people) and multilateral agreements creating a secretariat (such as the Energy Charter Secretariat, created to oversee the Energy Charter Treaty, which employs some 50 people).[12] No global figures for the annual turnover of international organisations, or the number of people employed by them, exist. But it is clear that taken together they are a significant industry, employing hundreds of thousands of people worldwide and with tens of billions of US dollars in annual revenues. The institutions of global government have undertaken quite an expansion since Wilson's dream and the early years of the League of Nations.

Why did the United Nations and associated international organisations undergo this phenomenal growth? The liberal theorist might argue that in an increasingly interdependent world, there are ever more issues which can be best resolved through international cooperation. The expansion of international organisations represents a realisation of the benefits of international cooperation. Even if the ideals of a global government with impartial and compulsory adjudication and enforcement are too much to expect nations currently to agree to, there are all sorts of other benefits to international cooperation that the creation of international organisations can harness. The World Health Organisation may serve to share medical knowledge and pharmacological innovation across the world. The World Bank fosters expertise in development economics and the skills needed to assist countries to be lifted out of poverty. UNHCR exists as a conduit of specialist expertise through which countries may contribute to refugee relief efforts in distant foreign countries. These are goals which all right-thinking nations would want to pursue; there are tangible benefits to their cooperating to achieve these goals; and international organisations serve as the media of that cooperation. Technology, faster and cheaper transport, ever easier communications and the consequent increased ease for states to take actions which will have an effect beyond their boundaries, have all made the possibility of international cooperation increase exponentially. The growth of international organisations, on the liberal thesis, simply represents the increased opportunities for international cooperation in a globalised world.

There is undoubtedly some truth in this account. One of the reasons ever more policy issues become internationalised is the ease of exchange of information that has become possible due to technological advances. It may now be possible to undertake detailed country comparisons of malaria prophylaxis, because the internet and air travel make such studies easier and the data more readily sharable than was once the case. There may be value in having an impartial organisation monitor and certify elections as fair in emerging democracies; and an international committee of monitors may stake a better claim to be impartial than monitors all of whom hail from a single country. But the challenge for the liberal defence of international organisations is to show why international governmental institutions are better methods of achieving cooperation gains than the nongovernmental alternatives. Cooperation is possible without creating a quasi-governmental international structure. International NGOs can monitor elections, and their judgments may be just as credible. The Carter Center, an NGO in Washington, DC, has a formidable reputation in this area, and works with a fraction of the budget of OSCE. Medical professionals can work with pharmaceutical companies and national health authorities to share medical information. It is not clear what an international organisation can add to international cooperation that would take place anyway through private and public mechanisms.

If an international organisation is a forum for officials from different governments to meet, they can meet anyway; and they always could. Most countries have embassies in most other countries. If international organisations are conceived as centres for expertise, it is not clear why that expertise could not prosper within international private companies and national governments, and without the extravagant expense of international public bureaucracy. If the distinguishing feature of international organisations is conceived as their neutrality, it is far from clear that they are as impartial as they like to present themselves. Many international organisations are perceived as having pronounced political agendas. In Kosovo, UNMIK (the UN territorial administration of the territory between NATO occupation in 1999 and independence in 2008) pushed an independence agenda and thus was perceived as pro-Albanian and anti-Serb.[13] In post-war Bosnia, almost all the international organisations were perceived as pro-Bosniac and hostile to Serb and Croat interests. UN peacekeeping forces in Rwanda prior to and during the 1994 genocide were perceived as attempting to prop up the genocidal Hutu regime.[14] In Darfur, UNAMID (the UN peacekeeping mission in Darfur) is perceived as anti-government.[15] One may infer from this small sample that it may be extremely difficult for international organisations to be perceived as genuinely neutral. Governments (such as the Swiss) or NGOs (such as the Carter Center) may be more able to achieve perceptions of neutrality. In short, it is not clear just what we are paying for in international organisations that cannot be achieved using other, presumably cheaper, means. The only feature unique to international organisations in resolving cooperation problems would be if they possessed an impartial and binding adjudicatory power and an enforcement authority, to bind states to agreements to cooperate. As subsequent chapters will show, this is precisely what international organisations virtually never have, because states consciously agree not to bestow them with that depth of authority.

The danger for the liberal theorist, in promoting international organisations as effective media of international cooperation, is that there is no theoretical account of why they ought to be better at achieving cooperation than other forms of organisation. After all, states cooperated extensively before the era of international organisations, to which the substantial levels of trade and international travel in the nineteenth century are testament. If the only account of international organisations' advantage is to attribute to them a capacity for impartial adjudication and enforcement which in practice states do not bestow them with, then the liberal theorist struggles to explain why these organisations have grown to meet the global expansion in international cooperation. Neither can the realist explain it. For the realist, international organisations are *ex hypothesi* causally irrelevant, being reflections of the international balance of power rather than causative of relations between nations. It is not therefore clear why they would grow at all; why would states pour money into institutions that make no difference? One answer might be false optimism: a misplaced belief on behalf of most of the world's governments that there is a pressing need to expand exponentially the size of international organisations to address all the pressing new problems in international cooperation that emerge year on year. But collective idiocy is barely attractive as a general theory of international relations, even if occasionally in history – as in the Thirty Years War or World War I – it has appeared to approximate to the norm.

The expansion in ostensible levels of international cooperation may instead be considered a coalition of two sets of interests. One is the international organisations themselves, who have every interest in expanding their own spheres of activity, and with them their budgets and staffing levels. As a general rule, bureaucracies are able to expand their budgets beyond the level necessary to fulfil the services required by the citizens to whom they are accountable (in the case of international organisations, those citizens are their member states). This is due to the monopoly the bureaucrat has over assessment of his or her own effectiveness. Typically a bureaucracy's output is not a series of measurable units but a level of activity that is difficult to evaluate. This creates a monitoring problem for oversight agencies, which cannot accurately judge the efficiency of the institutions where there is no point of comparison and no easily measurable output. Only the bureaucracy knows the true costs of providing its services. Because funding comes from outside the bureau, the bureaucracy can overstate its costs to receive a larger budget, and can make 'take it or leave it' budget proposals to the funding agency. In this way, bureaucrats can generate budgets that are perpetually in excess of what the funders' requirements warrant. This type of theory seeks to explain not just the growth in international organisations' budgets, but also the growth of government in western countries.[16] However, the theory is particularly apposite for international organisations, because the lines of accountability to those ultimately paying the bill for bureaucratic growth are so much more diffuse. An international organisation is not directly accountable to a taxpayer; it is only indirectly so through other bureaucracies (the foreign ministries or treasuries of the organisations' member states), who themselves have incentives to perpetrate their own bureaucratic growth.

The incentive for international organisations to enlarge themselves is reinforced by an interest individual states have in the expansion of international organisations' remits. Faced with a foreign policy issue in which there exists domestic demand, referral of the issue to a specialist international organisation is an attractive option. Delegation to a body one does not control alleviates electoral responsibility for failure. Association with an international organisation may permit a state to assert that it upholds or supports a certain value, while committing nothing beyond a marginal sum of money. The international organisation's mandate will be circumscribed in such a way that no real sovereignty (in terms of binding adjudicatory power or enforcement capacity) is attributed to it; and the costs of funding the organisation's expansion will be so thinly distributed across the members as to be barely felt, particularly compared with the costs of any home-grown initiative.

Malaria prophylaxis in the developing world became a hot political issue in the developed world in the 1990s; it was killing many people, particularly in Africa, and immigrants from those countries to the affluent west gave the issue political life. The World Health Organisation (WHO) adopted it, and created a specialist unit to deal with it. Subsequently, staff within the WHO spotted this was not the only epidemic disease capable of creating political pressure in the wealthy west, where the political process might make budgets available for international cooperation. The fight against malaria was combined with battles against AIDS and tuberculosis, and before long a new international organisation, the Global Fund, had spun off from the WHO, with a new staff, a new budget and a new mandate.[17] In 1960 the Food and Agriculture Organisation, which deals with a broad range of issues relating to feeding the hungry (including emergency relief, pest management and policy debates) created a specialist arm, the World Food Programme (WFP), to coordinate emergency food distribution in famines. The WFP subsequently spun off and became an independent organisation. The two institutions now have overlapping mandates. In 1974 a further related organisation was created, the International Fund for Agricultural Development, with another mandate in the same area. It is hard to justify the existence of three international organisations all with such similar functions. Nonetheless, they persist. Domestic pressure groups support each individual institution, and this support is reinforced where international organisations make grants in favour of NGOs. Thus a high political price may be paid by any individual member who withdraws from the institution, once established, as it will be criticised for abandoning the poor or vulnerable. This price is seldom outweighed by the funds saved.

THE GROWTH OF INTERNATIONAL LAW

At the same time as international organisations were expanding, international law was growing, at least in terms of the quantities of treaties. Even in 1967, it was commented that '[o]ne of the most significant developments in international law in the twentieth century is the tremendous growth in the number of treaties'.[18] Under Article 102 of the UN Charter, all treaties are required to be registered with and published by the secretariat of the United Nations. As of the end of 2005, over 46 000 treaties have been registered, organised for publication into some 2200 volumes. Of these, perhaps 50 per cent have been registered since 1990. In 2009, a mean of around 100 treaties a month were being registered. The growth is explosive. There are several reasons why there has been such a glut of treaty-making. With the expansion of economic relationships across the globe, there are ever more reasons for nations to cooperate. A great many international treaties are concerned with economic cooperation, such as removal of barriers to international trade or foreign investment.[19]

Cooperation has also become easier. There may be many reasons why nations want to cooperate, but in the past it was too logistically complex. States may want to agree that they will enforce and respect one another's court decisions. They may wish to agree that citizens of one country living in another will not be taxed twice on the same income or assets, and tax paid to one authority will be offset against taxes due to the other. The modern telecommunications and computer revolutions make complex and detailed agreements far easier to negotiate. Drafts can be exchanged and amendments proposed instantaneously, without the parties even needing to meet. This is also undoubtedly a reason why all modern legal documents have increased exponentially in length, including domestic statutes and commercial contracts. The virtues of brevity are apparently forgone amongst modern legal professionals. Treaties may thus be longer, more detailed and more complex than they were previously. There is a debate about whether this is a good thing, of course: whether the complexity reflects a level of detail desired by the parties to refine the precise scope of their obligations and eliminate ambiguities that frustrate faithful observance of treaties and necessitate recourse to dispute resolution mechanisms, or whether the extra complexity is a mere smokescreen of irrelevant detail designed to keep lawyers busy and well paid. A divergence between the interests of principals and their agents (i.e. lawyers) might explain a growth of length and complexity of legal documentation exogenous to the interests of those the documents are meant to serve.

There is more to explain the exponential growth in international law than just the demands by its users for increased cooperation, or the incentives of lawyers to expand their own workloads. Beyond the interests of both states and lawyers, international organisations have been active campaigners for the creation of ever more international law. International organisations are themselves the creations of treaties; and they are parties to a great many international treaties. Every loan agreement signed by the international development banks and the IMF is a treaty. International organisations often play leading roles in the negotiation and conclusion of treaties. The International Labour Organisation negotiates international conventions relating to workers' rights, of which at the time of writing there are at least 188. The UN High Commissioner for Human Rights negotiates, and gently pushes upon the UN member states, various treaties and conventions relating to human rights of which (depending on how one counts them) there are at least 80.[20] Since international organisations are intentionally created toothless by the states that parent them, one of the activities they can safely undertake even without teeth is the creation of further toothless treaties. They can then monitor and oversee the implementation of those treaties, an activity with which international organisations are perennially preoccupied. A great many modern international treaties create international organisations or vest them with further responsibilities, for which they must be further budgeted, and further staffed. The 1997 Ottawa Convention banning landmines[21] is typical. It gives the UN a variety of roles, including administration of programmes for care and rehabilitation of victims; preparation of national de-mining programmes; receipt of reports of de-mining progress; organisation of 'fact finding missions' by panels of experts where one state accuses another of non-compliance; arranging 'Meetings of State Parties' that make reports and recommendations on compliance; arranging 'review conferences'; and facilitating resolution of disputes. Nowhere in the text, however, does it suggest how to enforce the ban against states that flout it.

The 1980 Convention on the Elimination of All Forms of Discrimination Against Women created a 'Committee on the Elimination of Discrimination Between Women', an institution within the United Nations system, consisting of various experts elected by the signatories. The Committee receives reports and itself reports to the UN's Economic and Social Council. Other UN specialised agencies are also entitled to make representations in connection with those reports. Disputes between states over application of the treaty may be referred to the International Court of Justice, an international organisation considered in the next chapter, although no state signatory to the convention is obliged to consent to the involvement of the Court (and no dispute has ever actually been referred to the Court, for reasons that will be explored in Chapter 3). These treaties are typical. Both were created by international organisations; UN officials managed the multilateral negotiation process. They also create multiple responsibilities for international organisations. Modern international law necessarily involves the creation of international institutions, because international law cannot survive without them. A contract between two parties is worth little without an impartial third party to adjudicate and enforce it. The same logic applies to treaties; yet because states have no interest in creating strong international institutions, the temptation is to lend an air of legal pretence by writing a weak formal institution into the treaty. Thus treaties are replete with monitoring mechanisms, reporting obligations, committees, consultations and representations. The organisations administering these roles are all too aware of their own weaknesses. Permanently under a sense of existential threat, they will be motivated by fear of strong state actors, a desire to appear relevant and to appropriate to themselves further tasks to give the appearance of industry.

The growth in international law is not just a matter of an ever increasing number of treaties. There has also been a considerable growth in what is known as 'customary international law', being the writings of scholars, principles of international law that grow out of the jurisprudence of international courts and tribunals and the writings of international organisations themselves. Ever more has been written about international law in the last 20 years. Well over 100000 scholarly books have been written in the field, with hundreds of academic journals devoted to it. By a consensus adopted by scholars and jurists alike, this material can be drawn upon in deciding the content of international law. Naturally, scholars are supported by international organisations, some of which (including the United Nations and the World Bank) even have their own universities to promote scholarly research. The International Law Commission, a committee within and funded by the UN that exists to promote the development of international law, employs scholars from around the world to write reports. It has spent most of its existence, between its creation in 1948 and 2001, negotiating and drafting its 'draft Articles on the Responsibility of States for Internationally Wrongful Acts', an attempt to codify the principles governing the circumstances in which states may be liable for breaches of international law. The draft Articles do not explain how disputes may be resolved under the rules of any particular judicial forum; nor do they set out any specific rules for how much money a state may be obliged to pay, and to whom, for breaching its international obligations. Such issues would be too contentious. Instead, the draft Articles are confined to a wide ranging series of platitudes, such as prescriptions that 'an internationally wrongful act' must be 'attributable to the state' and 'constitute a breach of an international obligation of the state'. It was anticipated that the draft Articles would be adopted in a treaty.[22] They never were; but that did not stop international courts treating them as definitive statements of international law. Vacuities can be interminably debated; when one's aim is to paper over the cracks of impotence, abstractions of Aquinean dimensions may be of considerable value.

Another way of counting the growth in international law is to chart the creation of international courts and tribunals. There has been an explosion in these institutions since 1990. Some are widely known; others are not. Perhaps the most ubiquitous of these are the international courts established to try war crimes in the former Yugoslavia, Rwanda and elsewhere; the Dispute Resolution Body of the World Trade Organisation, the European Court of Human Rights and other human rights bodies; and a shadowy array of international tribunals convened to hear complaints against states that are alleged to have mistreated foreign investors. We shall consider each of these institutions in due course. However, we shall turn first to a range of international courts established to hear disputes *between states*. These courts have had the potential to adjudicate some of the most profound disputes within the sphere of international relations. If international law could hope to resolve such disputes without the use of force, it would have a major achievement to its name, an armour against which the sceptics and cynics would have few grounds to chip away. Alas, the record of courts established with this aim in mind is more than patchy. To these courts we now turn.

NOTES

1. Samuel von Pufendorf, *De jure naturae et gentium* (1672), developed Grotius's thinking in a natural law direction. (See Carr, C. (ed.) (1994), *The Political Writings of Samuel Pufendorf*, Oxford: OUP.)
2. There is a debate amongst scholars as to whether the Peace of Westphalia genuinely represented such a dramatic development of political philosophy as is traditionally imagined. See e.g. Osiander, Andreas (2001), 'Sovereignty, international relations, and the Westphalian myth', *International Organization*, **55**, 251.
3. See e.g. Kennedy, David (1997), 'International law and the nineteenth century: history of an illusion', *Quinnipiac Law Review*, **17**, 99.
4. The 'Fourteen Points' was a speech delivered by President Wilson to a joint session of Congress on 8 January 1918.
5. See Egerton, George (1974), 'The Lloyd George Government and the creation of the League of Nations', *American Historical Review*, **79**(2), 419.
6. Article 22 of the Covenant of the League of Nations created a Permanent Mandates Commission, ostensibly with responsibility for overseeing management of the former German and Ottoman colonies by the victorious powers. In theory there were three types of mandate, 'A', 'B' and 'C', corresponding to decreasing levels of development and the necessity of increasingly intrusive administration by the mandatory power. In practice the mandatory powers administered the mandates as their own colonies, and the Permanent Mandates Commission was toothless.
7. See Article 23 of the Covenant of the League of Nations.
8. Article I.8.11 of the US Constitution provides for the right of Congress to declare war. The United States has often engaged in foreign military hostilities without Congress's authority. The US courts have refused to intervene in legal debates about the authority to declare war and the consequences of the lack of such a declaration: *Holmes v United States*, 391 US 936 (1968); *United States v O'Brien*, 391 US 367 (1968).
9. Drafting of the Articles of Confederation was completed in November 1777. They thereafter served as the *de facto* system of government used by Congress until their formal ratification in March 1781.
10. The only occasion in the twentieth century when Switzerland deployed its troops internally was the '*fusillade du 9 novembre 1932*', when Swiss soldiers were sent to disperse an anti-fascist demonstration in Geneva. The troops opened fire, killing 13 people and injuring 65. It is important for our purposes that the troops were sent at the request of the Geneva cantonal government. Therefore they were not used by the central government to enforce its writ over a province.
11. For a history of the foregoing and other League of Nations engagements, see Scott, George (1973), *The Rise and Fall of the League of Nations*, London: Hutchinson.
12. These figures are provided courtesy of the Union of International Associations.
13. See Parish, Matthew (2008), 'International officials', *Austrian Review of International and European Law*, **13**, 79.
14. For controversy about Operation Turquoise (the French-led UN peacekeeping mission in Rwanda in 1994), see e.g. *Libération* (2006), 'Validation des plaintes visitant l'armée française au Rwanda', 29 May; BBC News (2006), 'France accused on Rwanda killings', 24 October (citing Rwandan diplomat Jacques Bihozagara as alleging France's partial responsibility for the genocide).
15. See e.g. *Sudan Tribune* (2009), 'Sudan summons top UNAMID official to protest reports of non-cooperation', 4 December.
16. See e.g. Niskansen, William (1971), *Bureaucracy and Representative Government*, Chicago: Aldine-Atherton; Niskansen, William (2001), 'Bureaucracy', in Shughart, William and Laura Razzolini (eds), *The Elgar Companion to Public Choice*, Cheltenham, UK and Northampton, MA: Edward Elgar; Garrett, Thomas A. and Russell M. Rhine (2006), 'On the size and growth of government', *Federal Reserve Bank of St Louis Review*, January/February.

17. The Global Fund to Fight AIDS, Tuberculosis and Malaria, established in 2002, was a spin-off from the WHO but was established as a Swiss foundation in Geneva, albeit one with full diplomatic immunity by way of a Headquarters Agreement with Switzerland, and controlled by a board of trustees representing member states who contribute funds to the Fund. Until 2009 the Global Fund's administration was managed by the WHO; thereafter it managed to wrest itself entirely from the WHO, and for all practical purposes is now an independent international organisation.
18. Jordan, Vincent (1967), 'Creation of customary international law by way of treaty', *United States Air Force Judge Advocate General Law Review*, **9**, 38.
19. Investment treaties and treaties regulating global trade will be considered in Chapters 5 and 6.
20. See the UNHCHR website at www2.ohchr.org/english/law (last accessed 24 June 2010).
21. Convention on the Prohibition of the Use, Stockpiling, Production and Transfer of Anti-Personnel Mines and on their Destruction, opened for signature on 3 December 1997.
22. UN General Assembly Resolution 56/83 of 12 December 2001 'commends [the articles on responsibility of States for internationally wrongful acts] to the attention of Governments without prejudice to the question of their future adoption or appropriate action'. In other words, the General Assembly thought they were a good draft; but they would not become binding until some action of member states to adopt them. This never happened, and hence the articles remain in 'draft'.

3. Irrelevant courts for important disputes

The notion that states could resolve their differences judicially found its origins in the Jay Treaty of 1794, in which the United Kingdom and the United States agreed to refer to arbitration before mixed commissions of British and American jurists various questions outstanding from the American War of Independence. The most important of these was the need to settle the boundaries between the United States and British Imperial Canada. The United States and the United Kingdom again referred disputes to arbitration in the 1871 Treaty of Washington. This treaty resulted in the Alabama claims arbitration, in which the United States complained that the United Kingdom had violated its own policy of neutrality in the American Civil War, in selling vessels to the Confederacy. In the face of domestic support for the Union, the United Kingdom agreed to arbitration to maintain friendly relations with Canada's neighbour; the resulting award of US$15.5 million against the United Kingdom was promptly paid. It is easy now to underestimate the psychological effect this turn of events had upon international lawyers. Although a political fix convenient at the time for the British government, it created the seeds of the idea that an international court could resolve disputes between nations by ordering payment of money, rather than the use of economic sanctions or military force.

THE PERMANENT COURT OF ARBITRATION

In 1899, the Hague Peace Conference met to draw up a convention on the laws of war. Organised by Czar Nicholas II, the driving force behind the conference was Russia's desire to escape the expense of keeping up with the Anglo-German arms race. The Hague Convention that resulted acknowledged disputes should be submitted to arbitration rather than be the causes of war; but it did not make arbitration compulsory. It did, however, create a permanent institution, the Permanent Court of Arbitration (PCA), to administer arbitrations between states. Because recourse to arbitration was not mandatory, states did not agree to it when disputes actually arose. The stronger state would not as a rule agree, because once a dispute arose the stronger nation would take the view that exercise of its superior diplomatic, economic and military muscle would achieve a better result than an arbitral procedure. Despite occupying an extraordinary building in The Hague – the Peace Palace constructed with funds provided by the American industrialist Andrew Carnegie – the PCA has remained something of a white elephant throughout its history as the international tribunal of longest standing. This was the first true international court, and it still exists today. But alas, it has a long history of irrelevance.

Between 1899 and 1914 (the start of World War I) the PCA heard 14 cases, or about one a year. Between World Wars I and II it heard three cases in total. After World War II it heard no cases until 1998. More recently, it decided 18 cases between 1998 and 2009 (an average of slightly more than 1.5 per year), with a number of others pending. The reason why there has been a late 'surge' in the PCA's activity is an interesting one, which will be returned to presently. Nevertheless, it is fair to say that the PCA has never been busy, compared for example to the Queen's Bench Division of the Royal Courts of Justice in London (one of three divisions of that court), before which 4794 cases were commenced in 2007.[1] This is not because states do not have disputes. They have them all the time. It is because they do not consent to submit them to arbitration. It is a cardinal principle of arbitration that no party can be compelled to arbitrate disputes unless he has consented to the process; and states do not usually want to resolve their disputes with other states by a quasi-judicial procedure. It is desperately hard to persuade two recalcitrant disputants to agree to refer a dispute to a legally binding resolution procedure, in arbitration called a *compromis*, once the dispute has arisen. Inevitably, the party with the weaker case will have no interest in an impartial third party deciding the matter, because he will predict that he will lose.

A state may also resist a dispute resolution process because the status quo favours her. She may calculate that without a legal procedure, things will remain as they are, and diplomatic, economic, political or military pressures to make concessions to one's opponents can be resisted. It is only where the final outcome of the dispute is less important than the dispute being resolved, that arbitration is likely to be agreed to between states on an ad hoc basis. Cases of this kind will be relatively rare, and may be limited to disputes where it is important to save face, or where two equally matched opponents are liable to suffer high losses if a minor dispute is not resolved. One such instance was the Taba arbitration, the product of the 1979 Camp David accords settling the war between Israel and Egypt. Under the terms of the Camp David accords, a joint Egyptian-Israeli commission would demarcate the boundary between the two countries.[2] However, the commission failed to reach consensus; thus by a *compromis* signed in 1986, the sides agreed to resolve the issue by binding arbitration. The territory in dispute was small, comprising just a few square miles including a hotel, worth only a few million US dollars. Such a small area of land was not worth a resumption of hostilities; but neither side could be seen to back down. Thus referral of the issue to arbitration, with the attendant delay to allow strong political winds to calm (11 years from Camp David to the arbitration award), made consummate sense. Ultimately the arbitrators found entirely in favour of Egypt;[3] after some political protests, Israel accepted the verdict.

Contrast this with a contemporary hot political dispute, such as sovereignty of the Falkland Islands. It is inconceivable that the United Kingdom would agree to arbitration over the status of those islands. Arbitration would be perceived as an admission that there is some uncertainty over the issue, contrary to the British position that there is no doubt whatsoever as to the islands' legal status. It would also be a substantially more risky proposition than renewed military confrontation, at least in terms of the probability of being the victor. Thus it is not even considered as a possible method of resolving the dispute. For substantially the same reasons, the United States is not about to agree to arbitration of a dispute as to the legality of its 2003 invasion of Iraq. In fact, most disputes between states are so heavily politically contested that they are unsusceptible to arbitral resolution. Where strongly contentious political issues have been subjected to arbitration, the outcome has been somewhat mottled. In 2000, Eritrea and Ethiopia agreed to arbitrate their boundary dispute that had led to a war since 1998, in two separate arbitral procedures. In 2002, one of the two tribunals ruled that the principal disputed town of Badme belongs to Eritrea;[4] in 2005, the other tribunal ruled that Eritrea had been wrong to start a war over the dispute, and was bound to pay reparations to Ethiopia, subject to quantification.[5] The PCA presided over both arbitrations. Taken together, the two decisions were an attempt to fashion a careful compromise between the parties' irreconcilable positions. It would not be plausible to view the process as anything other than highly political.

Nonetheless, these decisions did not have the desired effect. In 2008, a UN peacekeeping mission withdrew from the contested area following Eritrea's decision to cut off fuel supplies to them. In August 2009, the latter tribunal issued two further awards largely cancelling out the award of compensation to Ethiopia. Although Ethiopia was awarded some US$174 million, Eritrea received a counter-award of US$163.5 million.[6] No money has actually changed hands since. At the time of writing Badme remains occupied by Ethiopian troops, despite the Ethiopian parliament having voted to accept the boundary ruling 'in principle'.[7] On 1 January 2010, there was apparently a border skirmish north of the contested town of Zalambessa; Eritrea alleged Ethiopian troops had crossed the border and were repelled.[8] Such peace as exists in the disputed territory is derived not from the authority of the arbitral tribunals' rulings, but from an uneasy ceasefire based upon the parties' joint exhaustion and reluctance, principally for financial reasons, to return to conflict. The arbitration awards were chimeras, having been respected by neither side. The value in the arbitration process, such as it was, lay in allowing the parties to sign a ceasefire that required neither side to make any territorial concessions. It was an exercise in dispute deferral, not dispute resolution. There is too much at stake politically for either side to accept any sort of territorial concession, in the absence of a comprehensive military defeat. Renewed conflict at some future point seems highly likely; in the mean time the two sides have been fighting a proxy war by backing different sides in Somalia's recurrent civil war.[9] The Ethiopia-Eritrea tribunals were not irrelevant; they were part and parcel of a temporary ceasefire agreement that looks likely to break down. They may have been a good thing in preserving the peace, at least for a while. Or they may prove ultimately to be insignificant in a conflict that may rumble on for decades.

Another example of a PCA arbitration over a hot dispute is the Abyei Boundary Commission (ABC). This arbitration is a good example of how political pressure may be brought to bear upon an arbitral process. Abyei is a town in central Sudan, around which there are a number of hitherto unexplored oil fields. The Sudanese Civil War, fought between the Muslim North and the secessionist Christian South, ended in January 2005 with a 'Comprehensive Peace Agreement' (the CPA). That agreement granted the South substantial political autonomy, and permitted it to hold a referendum on independence in 2011. At the same time, the Abyei area is to hold a referendum on whether to join the North or the South. The contested borders of the Abyei area, or 'the area of the nine Ngok Dinka chiefdoms transferred to Kordofan in 1905', were to be determined by an arbitral tribunal called the 'Abyei Boundaries Commission'. The tribunal delivered its report in July 2005,[10] declaring an expansive definition of Abyei, at the expense of northern territory and in particular including territory believed to be rich in oil. Because the Abyei region is expected to vote overwhelmingly to join the South, the North immediately rejected the tribunal's decision. Relations between the two sides quickly deteriorated. Although the North and the South were supposed to participate in joint peacekeeping operations in the area, their respective armed forces face one another off on a new *de facto* front line. In May 2008, clashes between troops of the

North and the South destroyed virtually the entire town of Abyei, leading to scores of dead and displacing tens of thousands of people.[11]

Then, in June 2008, the North and the South agreed to submit the Abyei dispute to arbitration *again*.[12] The new arbitration would be administered by the PCA, and its formal task was to decide whether the ABC had 'exceeded its mandate' in drawing the boundaries of the Abyei area where it did. In July 2009, the new tribunal duly held that the prior tribunal had indeed exceeded its mandate, in failing to give full reasons.[13] The reality was not that the prior tribunal had failed to give reasons, but rather that the new tribunal disagreed with the reasons it had given. The new tribunal then went on to redraw the eastern and western boundaries of the Abyei area, the effect of which was to shrink the size of the region and transfer its principal oilfields to the North. There was little in the way of justifiable legal reasoning in all this. Typically a tribunal exceeds its mandate only where it decides issues the parties have not asked it to decide. There is no evidence the ABC had done that. Rather, its decision had to be the victim of political expediency. The leaders of the North and the South had apparently come to an internationally mediated agreement to refer the matter back to the tribunal, to give the North a larger share of Abyei's oilfields, in advance of a referendum everyone knows will be won by the South. The second PCA tribunal, despite the distinguished jurists sitting upon it, was essentially a tool for rubberstamping a political deal.

Unsurprisingly, both sides immediately accepted the new arbitral award when it was issued. The area remains very unstable and the two sides continue to face one another off. The prospects for peaceful secession of the South from the North in 2011 remain uncertain. If peaceable secession can be achieved, arbitration will have played a part, but not in the way imagined. An arbitral decision did not settle the dispute; if it has really been settled, that settlement was reached by political agreement, to which the tribunal lent its imprimatur. The arbitration process was a smokescreen hiding an underlying political process. The first tribunal reached a decision unacceptable to the North; peace could not be achieved on the basis of that award, therefore the first tribunal's decision had to be rewritten. Arbitration over Abyei was not a neutral and impartial process. It was pure politics.

Apart from the two foregoing recent disputes, there are relatively few other PCA cases in the recent past that have resolved political disputes of great moment. Four other inter-state disputes resolved by the PCA have fallen under the auspices of the UN Convention on the Law of the Sea, designed to resolve maritime delimitation disputes.[14] The most important consequences of these decisions have been delimitation of rights to natural resources. While important to some domestic constituencies, these disputes are seldom issues of such moment that sanctions or war are real risks. Moreover, the international investors needed to exploit these resources will commit only with a judicial ruling but will not commit if countries are at war. A number of other arbitrations before the PCA have been investment treaty arbitrations. These are not disputes between two states at all; they are an entirely different creature, in which a private investor is the claimant and a state is the respondent. We will consider them in Chapter 5. The very few other PCA cases in recent years that do not fall into either of these categories, on the whole, are rather minor affairs. In the 2005 *Iron Rhine Railway* arbitration,[15] Belgium and the Netherlands agreed to arbitrate a dispute over whether to re-open a railway between the two countries. Belgium relied on an 1839 treaty establishing its right to run traffic on the railway; the Netherlands objected on the basis that the railway now ran through a nature reserve. In May 2005, the tribunal held that Belgium could insist upon the railway's being re-opened; but it would have to pay for its modernisation and the two countries would split the costs of construction of a tunnel beneath the nature reserve. This ad hoc settlement may have made good sense in light of the domestic politics of each country. It was another case in which neither side could be seen to lose face within the frame of domestic politics, notwithstanding the comparatively minor issues at stake.

The same was true of the 2004 PCA arbitration award in the case between the Netherlands and France on the Convention for the Protection of the Rhine against Pollution by Chlorides.[16] This was essentially an accounting dispute, over the proportions France owed pursuant to a costs sharing agreement under which Alsace would reduce the level of chloride salts being deposited in the Rhine. The United Kingdom and Ireland have also engaged in arbitration proceedings relating to a dispute about release of nuclear waste from the Sellafield nuclear recycling plant into the Irish Sea. However, no conclusive award has ever been issued.[17] This is more or less the full extent of interstate arbitrations since 1930. The meagre record suggests that very few disputes between states are referred to arbitration; and of those that are, the process can be said to be successful only where the issues are of a comparatively minor order. Where a state is prepared to go to war, arbitration is not likely to succeed. Where war is a danger and the international community has an interest, as in the Abyei arbitrations, the arbitration process may become politicised. Although the PCA was established with the lofty ideal of 'obviating . . . recourse to force in the relations between States [and] ensure the pacific settlement of international differences',[18] it turns out that arbitration only stands any prospect of success where there are no realistic military options. It cannot take the place of war.

Another reason why the PCA may have had so few cases throughout its history is that even when states (or anybody else) agree to arbitrate, the PCA does not have a monopoly on administering arbitral proceedings. Arbitration is by its very nature a private process. Anybody can manage an arbitration, and indeed there is great competition between a range of private arbitral institutions, all vying to provide the best administrative service, the lowest costs, the greatest flexibility and the most prestigious awards. The PCA is a public international organisation, funded in part by the contributions of its members (although it charges fees for its services to litigants) and it does not make a profit. Yet it must sit in competition with the International Chamber of Commerce in Paris, probably the world's busiest arbitral institution by caseload; the London Court of International Arbitration; the Stockholm Chamber of Commerce; and a variety of other highly regarded institutions worldwide. Although the PCA is not prohibitively expensive, it does not have a particularly high reputation for administrative capacity within the world of international arbitration. Its only real comparative advantage is the impressiveness of the building.

A public international organisation cannot effectively compete in the market; indeed, it does not even try to. With a staff of only about 30 people, the PCA is far too small to run anything but the most meagre of case dockets. The 110 states which have acceded to the international conventions establishing the PCA have little interest in its day to day operation. Because the vast majority of them have never been a party to an arbitration before it, and never will be, they care little for whether it works efficiently. The institution could be abandoned tomorrow with little impact. Where states still wish to arbitrate, they can do so, but using a private institution. Thus the PCA's member states have no interest in funding the organisation's expansion to compete with its private counterparts. To be sure, it is unlikely any one of them will pull the plug on its operation, because the institution is so small and therefore so cheap, when its costs are divided between the members, that the political price paid by delivering a message to the effect that 'we withdraw from pacific settlement of disputes' is never worth paying in comparison to the budgetary savings involved. Thus the PCA appears condemned to irrelevant immortality, a hopelessly small secretariat lodged in an enormous building, a folly of monumental proportions to an admirable but unrealistic aspiration that states suspended in a military anarchy will somehow allow their most contentious disputes to be submitted to arbitration rather than contemplate military and economic confrontation.

The PCA was recognised to be a white elephant early in its existence. A small number of claims were submitted to it, but none was of the utmost gravity. When the French consulate in Casablanca gave shelter to deserters of the French Foreign Legion, and French soldiers thereafter beat the Moroccan consular guard, the PCA ruled on the rights and wrongs of the dispute.[19] The PCA likewise ruled upon a dispute between France and the UK as to whether France was entitled to permit dhows in Muscat to fly French flags with the result that they were inviolable from search within the Sultan's waters, thereby hindering British efforts to abolish the slave trade.[20] When the Italian government seized a French vessel and arrested persons suspected to be Ottoman soldiers in the service of the enemy's army, the PCA declared Italian actions wrongful and ordered (limited) compensation.[21] When a joint Dutch-Portuguese survey commission could not agree whether the border between East and West Timor ought to follow a mountain peak or a thalweg, the PCA was good enough to resolve the issue for them.[22] These disputes were more in the nature of diplomatic spats, in which the fact that the dispute was resolved was more important than the direction of its outcome. There was no evidence that the PCA could resolve more fundamental disputes between states, and perhaps the greatest proof that it could not was the onset of World War I.

THE PERMANENT COURT OF INTERNATIONAL JUSTICE

After the Great War, under the influence of Woodrow Wilson, something more ambitious was attempted. The Permanent Court of International Justice (PCIJ) was an organ of the League of Nations, created by the Peace Treaty of Versailles.[23] The rationale for this new institution was said to be the creation of a permanent judicial authority whose judges could interpret and develop international law more consistently than could varied panels of arbitrators under the auspices of the PCA. This was barely a credible rationale; common law systems, in which the law is routinely developed by judicial rulings, benefits from a diversity of courts and judges developing the law. The true innovation of the PCIJ was instead to create a judicial authority to whose jurisdiction states could consent in advance of the dispute, rather than only afterwards. Nonetheless, the PCIJ failed in its creators' aspirations.

The idea of a permanent court, existing to resolve every dispute between countries where negotiated settlements could not be found, was indeed a bold one. But its jurisdiction remained optional. A number of states who were party to the Covenant of the League of Nations agreed to be bound by the decisions of the Court. Some, most notably the USSR, refused to sign the PCIJ statute. Even those who did sign its statute could not be sued before it unless they had expressly consented to the Court's jurisdiction;

and that consent could be limited by reservations, or withdrawn.[24] In practice the vast majority of countries that did accept the PCIJ's jurisdiction as compulsory did so with reservations of one sort or another.[25] This calls for explanation. If states were genuinely motivated to ensure their cooperation problems should be resolved by an impartial adjudicative body, they would surely have agreed to refer all disputes to the PCIJ, without reservation. They would have bound themselves universally to compulsory jurisdiction. In a domestic legal setting, it would never do if individual citizens could declare themselves immune from the jurisdiction of domestic courts in respect of certain crimes and civil matters that they specify in their discretion. The reason this would not work is that some – or maybe even all – people have an interest in breaking the law in certain ways, and are strong enough to resist the compulsions of others to obey it. Some people cannot trust that the courts are truly independent, and thus do not want to accede to their jurisdiction. Still others are nervous that if they accept jurisdiction but others do not, they will be at a disadvantage. The fear of the free rider means that people cannot voluntarily come together to create compulsory jurisdiction. If it is to exist, it has to be forced upon people by a superior outside force.

The mixed record of states in submitting voluntarily to the jurisdiction of the PCIJ shows that this is true for states as much as it is for individuals. Unsurprisingly, it was the Great Powers at the time – Britain, France, Italy and Japan – which refused to accept an international court possessing compulsory jurisdiction. (Not being a party to the League Covenant, the United States was not a party to the Court either.) An initial draft of the Court's statute, granting compulsory jurisdiction over all states, was rejected by British Foreign Secretary Lord Curzon as being 'singularly oblivious to British interests'.[26] Britain's concern was that the judges of the Court would divide on national lines; Britain's expansive interpretation of naval freedom might be ruled unlawful by the Court; continental judges (who would inevitably dominate) have different views of international law from Anglo-American judges; and there was nothing to ensure a losing party might comply with a decision.[27] These reservations were prescient: they gave substance to the argument, presented in Chapter 2, that powerful nations have no interest in impartial international adjudication. The application of principle over force can benefit only the weak, who are more likely to appeal to justice than those who have no recourse to such a notion in pursuit of their self-interest. Britain did not submit itself to the compulsory jurisdiction of the Court until 1929; even then it was subject to a right to refer the matter to the Council of the League, a body on which the United Kingdom had a permanent veto right.

Moreover the fact that states, once they had accepted the jurisdiction of the Court, could withdraw from it, would give the PCIJ a unique political incentive to temper the way it decided cases. The effect upon the PCIJ of having state parties withdraw would, in general, involve a loss of credibility. The credibility loss suffered would depend upon the status of the state withdrawing; if a powerful country withdrew, and signalled that it no longer intended to respect the Court's decisions, the Court would be at risk of looking irrelevant. A weaker country has more to gain from the Court than a strong one, namely an adjudication in its favour where a similar result could not be achieved through the use of military force or economic might. Therefore a weaker nation is less likely to withdraw than a strong one, even if a case goes against it. This is why, in the negotiations over the Statute of the PCIJ, the smaller nations pushed for compulsory jurisdiction of the Court over all nations, whereas stronger nations had reservations over this suggestion, reservations which ultimately prevailed.[28]

Even if a small or weak state does withdraw, the effect upon the Court's reputation will not be as serious as if a large state withdraws. Add to this the iron economic law that stronger states will contribute more to the Court's budget than weaker ones, and thus the functioning of the Court will be more adversely affected by the withdrawal of the former. Thus a court in respect of which jurisdiction is optional to its litigants has a structural incentive to decide cases in favour of strong states and against weak ones, lest it condemn itself to irrelevance and penury through strong states' rejection and criticism of it, and withdrawal of funding from it. Alternatively the Court may be prone to timidity, finding jurisdictional pretexts to decline to hear disputes between powerful countries, or reaching inconclusive rulings designed to cause the least net offence. The Court will prefer complex technical disputes about trivia, which create enormous quantities of work sufficient to justify the Court's budgetary expansion; yet whatever the Court decides, nobody will be too offended. International law can grow, without its organs of adjudication being called upon to decide anything too contentious. Controversy might cause withdrawal, wrecking the entire international law programme. Faced with a heinous dispute between powerful foes, the Court will have to evade the substance of the controversy, lest an aggrieved adversary turns its ire towards the Court, an institution far weaker than the litigants who appear before it.

This is the persistent dynamic of international courts. A domestic court carries the full majesty of the law – meaning that it has enormous, potentially overwhelming, power to see that its judgments are carried out. The ultimate sanction for failure to comply with the orders of a domestic court is forcible seizure of assets, penury, bankruptcy, homelessness, arrest, incarceration, even death, all administered by an impartial bureaucracy determined to uphold the rule of law. By contrast with this ruthless threat of overwhelming force, an international court is weak. Neither the PCA, the PCIJ nor the PCIJ's post-World War I successor, the International Court of Justice, contained within their founding documents any obligation for states to recognise or enforce these courts' judgments. In other words, should the Court issue a decision, whether requiring the payment of money or some non-pecuniary action, no other state is obliged to force them to comply with it. Nor does the Court have bailiffs or a police force. True, the non-compliance with a decision of the Court might be referred to the League Council or the UN Security Council; but the litigants might be represented on that Council, which in any event is hardly politically impartial.

Furthermore the powerful states represented on the Security Council have the same capacity (or lack of it) to force a state recalcitrant in the eyes of the international community to do something it does not want to do, whether or not there is a judgment of an international court asking it to do so. The Court judgment is thus a mere hortatory or legitimising act, persuasive perhaps to countries that do not care, but never liable on its own to override a state's clear interest in some contrary outcome. Without a credible and impartial enforcement mechanism, the Court is reliant upon the good will of the litigants, and international public opinion, for enforcement of its decisions. Should its decisions be ignored, the Court will lack credibility, and interest in its continued work will wane amongst its members. Thus the Court must always be careful not to issue decisions that are not liable to be obeyed. Given it has no means of procuring obedience, this severely hampers the range of orders it is likely to make. In other words, most of the orders it will issue are orders which require no compliance. That way, nobody will notice that the Court's judgments are not being observed.

Operational between 1921 and 1938 (after which the onset of the World War II closed the institution), the PCIJ heard 59 cases in 17 years (or 3.5 a year), although only 53 of these proceeded to judgments. Of those 53, 27 were 'advisory opinions'. An advisory opinion is the product not of a claim brought by one state against another, but a non-binding opinion of the Court issued on a question at the request of the Council or the Assembly of the League.[29] It is not fair to say that all the advisory opinions were strictly non-binding; on occasion the Council would ask the Court to issue an advisory opinion, the conclusion of which would be adopted by the Council in a binding resolution. This occurred in the four Danzig cases,[30] in which an appeal lay from the High Commissioner of the Free City of Danzig[31] to the Council, which might refer the matter to the PCIJ and adopt its opinion. However, it is noteworthy that only extremely rarely were monetary judgments handed down by the PCIJ. In only two cases did the Court order one country to pay another. Germany was ordered to pay France in the *SS Wimbledon* case;[32] Germany had refused a French vessel containing materials destined for military use in the Russo-Polish war access to the Kiel canal on the ground of its neutrality obligations. The Court decided Germany had to pay France 140 000 Francs as reparations for this wrongful denial of access, contrary to the Peace Treaty of Versailles.

In 1923, Germany remained weak, and the Court may have decided this was a good case to establish a precedent for the right to make financial awards. But it would rarely make such awards again. In the 1928 *Chorzów Factory* case,[33] the PCIJ attempted another affirmation of the principle that it could make financial awards. The case famously set the standard of compensation for expropriation in international law, providing that a party whose assets are taken by another state is entitled to a sum equal to the anticipated future profits attributable to the asset.[34] The case was settled before the Court quantified the compensation payable. The defendant was another weak state, Poland. In two other cases, *Serbian Loans* and *Brazilian Loans*,[35] the Court declared sovereign bonds due to private investors. In all other cases brought before the PCIJ, the relief granted, if any, was declaratory, and did not require the defendant state to take any action to implement the judgment. The most daring the Court became was in the *Eastern Greenland* case,[36] where the Court declared Norwegian occupation of Greenland unlawful, but hesitated to order Norwegian authorities or troops to leave it.

It might therefore be tempting to conclude that the PCIJ was wonderfully irrelevant, making not a jot of difference to the activity of states, issuing decisions that could be ignored with impunity. But the PCIJ was not intellectually fallow, even if it was politically impotent. *Chorzów Factory* is now one of the most oft cited precedents in international law setting the standard for quantum of compensation.[37] The *Serbian Loans* and *Brazilian Loans* cases set the standard for the defence of *force majeure* in international law.[38] *Oscar Chinn* was the first case to discuss whether a change of government regulation affecting the economic viability of an investment could amount to 'indirect expropriation'.[39] It would be discussed at length by subsequent investment treaty tribunals.[40] *Société Commerciale de Belgique*[41] set the precedent, likewise subsequently essential in the context of investment treaty arbitration, that where a state entered into an arbitration agreement with a private company, the arbitration awards issued as a result are final and binding and the state is obliged to execute them. *Phosphates in Morocco* developed the concept of exactly when an act is attributable to a state for the purposes of creating responsibility in international law.[42] In the *Treatment of Polish Nationals in Danzig* case, the Court established the principle that national law is not relevant in determining the content of international obligations.[43] Thus at a time when the idea of an international court was new, and its power was exceedingly modest, the PCIJ sought to develop a series of new intellectual disciplines within international law, while at the same time doing so in such a way as not to overstep the realm of what was politically realistic.

The Court exhibited a remarkable mixture of intellectual ingenuity and political cunning. In this it bore something in common with the US Supreme Court in its early years, presided over by its first Chief Justice John Marshall, as that Court tried gradually to establish the doctrine of judicial review of acts of the executive and legislature, a doctrine with very limited precedent at the time in English law. Initially, the propensity of the states to respect the decisions of the Supreme Court was most uncertain, and a brazen rejection of one of its decisions might have sunk the institution. Thus the Court trod carefully. It set out in principle the doctrine of judicial review as early as 1803. In *Marbury v Madison*,[44] the Supreme Court declared the right of the courts to overturn a decision by the executive not to confirm the lawful appointment of a judge; but also declared that the statute giving the courts jurisdiction over the dispute was unconstitutional. Thus the Court managed to create the principle of judicial review of both executive and legislative action, without actually granting the plaintiff the remedy he sought. This would have entailed ordering the appointment of one of the controversial 'Midnight Judges' nominated in the final day of outgoing President John Adams's presidency, an act which might well have brought the other branches of government into open disobedience of the Court. The early days of international courts betray the same sort of caution, and for much the same essentially political reasons.

THE INTERNATIONAL COURT OF JUSTICE

The PCIJ fell into disuse with the onset of World War II. Collocated in the Peace Palace in the Hague with the PCA, it came within occupied Nazi territory in 1940 when Germany invaded the Netherlands. At the end of World War II, the Court was replaced with the International Court of Justice which has existed to the present day. Because the PCIJ was seen as a success, unlike the League as a whole, the new court would, in structure, be virtually a carbon copy of the PCIJ. There would be the same number of judges, appointed in virtually the same way (nomination by states; confirmation by the UN General Assembly) and with the same term of office (nine years). The same system of submitting to the Court's jurisdiction was also required. In other words, submission to the Court is optional for each state,[45] can be subject to reservations and can be withdrawn at any time.

The number of states who have submitted to the Court's compulsory jurisdiction (66) is only a fraction of the 192 member states of the UN who are automatically deemed parties to the Court's statute.[46] Virtually every declaration of consent to jurisdiction under the Court's so-called 'optional clause' is subject to reservations. The United States, Russia, China and France have not submitted to compulsory jurisdiction. The only permanent member of the UN Security Council that currently accepts the Court's compulsory jurisdiction is the United Kingdom. Procedures in the PCIJ and ICJ are extremely similar. The Court is used less frequently than the PCIJ: it has a typical docket of less than two cases per year. This is an average of less than one-seventh of a case per judge per year: not an enormously impressive workload by the standards of modern domestic judges, who may be expected each to deal with tens, or even hundreds of cases a year. Notwithstanding its gentle caseload, the ICJ takes its time in reaching its decisions; each of its cases takes anywhere from one to 14 years to decide. These delays are surely not purely the result of administrative incompetence; as will be seen in later chapters, other international courts, while also very slow, have far higher caseloads. Rather, the reason is that the ICJ uses delay as a political tool.

The case that took 14 years was Bosnia's claim against Serbia for supporting acts of genocide, including the July 1995 Srebrenica massacre. Started in 1993, a decision was not issued until 2007.[47] The reason for the delay was the domestic political consequences within Serbia of making the decision. The decision reached – that Serbia was not responsible for committing genocide but was responsible for failing to prevent it – could, in principle, have provoked a negative political reaction within Serbia, supporting nationalist politicians at the expense of a pro-European emerging political class. Only once pro-European forces were reasonably well entrenched within Belgrade was it safe to release what in earlier, less propitious circumstances, could have been a political bombshell. Hence proceedings were stretched out until 2007. Moreover, this judgment was a masterpiece of political flexibility. Bowing to international public opinion condemning the Serbs for the conduct of the Bosnian war, the Court had to find against Serbia or its judgment would lack credibility in the court of public opinion of the international community and the international law lobby on whose support the court is reliant. Nevertheless, the reparations Bosnia was asking for, which would have properly fallen due had Serbia been found guilty of acts of genocide, would have bankrupted Serbia's fragile economy if paid. Moreover, an enormous financial order made against Serbia could have unpredictable consequences in Serbian politics, potentially derailing its application to join the European Union if such an order were not paid. Indeed Serbian domestic politics would never permit such a payment. Thus the Court's solution was to find that Serbia did not itself commit genocide, but merely that it was culpable in failing to prevent genocide. In such circumstances, the Court ruled, compensation was not appropriate.[48] Thus the ICJ managed to slip between Scylla and Charybdis: it found Serbia culpable, but declined to make an order for damages. Bosnia could claim a moral victory; Serbia could ignore the judgment with impunity; the international community was not distracted in its efforts to draw Serbia into the league of European nations. The ICJ demonstrated itself as the quintessential political court.

On occasion, the ICJ has been somewhat braver than its predecessor in the orders it has made against states. In the *Nuclear Tests* case,[49] New Zealand and Australia asked the ICJ to issue an interim order preventing France from conducting atmospheric nuclear testing in the South Pacific, pending a full hearing of the complaint that these tests were environmentally dangerous and created a danger of nuclear fall-out contaminating their territories. France declared that it considered that the ICJ had no competence to hear the case, and that it did not accept the ICJ's jurisdiction. It refused to participate in the hearings. The ICJ granted the interim measures sought, ordering France not to conduct any further nuclear tests causing deposits of radioactive fall-out on New Zealand territory. Likewise in *Fisheries Jurisdiction*,[50] the United Kingdom brought the 'cod wars' before the ICJ, complaining that Iceland had unilaterally extended its area of exclusive fishing rights from 12 to 50 miles. Again as an interim measure, the Court ordered Iceland not to take any measures to enforce its declaration extending unilateral fishing rights. In its 1971 advisory opinion *Legal Consequences of the Continued Presence of South Africa in Namibia*,[51] the Court declared that South Africa, which occupied Namibia and had applied apartheid policies there since 1948, was 'under obligation to withdraw its administration from Namibia immediately'. In 1975, in its *Western Sahara* advisory opinion,[52] the Court declared the territory of Western Sahara, disputed between Morocco and Mauritania, to be the territory of neither but subject to 'the principle of self-determination through the free and genuine expression of the will of the peoples of the Territory'. In 2004, the ICJ issued its advisory opinion in the *Israel / Palestine Wall* case,[53] declaring the Israeli construction of a wall through West Bank territory to be illegal and requiring it to cease construction immediately and dismantle that already built.

These were all bold orders, instructing states to take actions contrary to their national interests and stated domestic policies. But the tragedy of the Court's irrelevance is that in each case the Court's judgment was totally disregarded. France responded to the Court's injunction not to continue nuclear testing by exploding seven atmospheric nuclear test bombs from June to September 1974. Iceland responded to the ICJ's order in the *Cod Wars* case by attacking British fishing vessels entering its self-declared exclusion zone. After the ICJ's final judgment in the case in July 1974,[54] confirming the British position, Iceland extended its exclusionary zone still further to 200 miles. South Africa ignored the ICJ's *Namibia* judgment in its entirety, the country remaining under South African occupation until 1990. Two weeks after the ICJ judgment in *Western Sahara*, Moroccan troops entered the disputed territory, followed by over 300 000 civilian occupants. By the end of the year, the territory had been partially annexed, and more was annexed in 1979. Aside from a small slither of unoccupied desert behind a defensive wall, Western Sahara is now *de facto* Moroccan territory. The Israeli government flatly rejected the ICJ's *Israel / Palestine Wall* decision, and continued to construct the wall. Even the Israeli Supreme Court upheld the government's decision to construct the wall, issuing a pre-emptive decision nine days before the ICJ's opinion.[55]

In July 2010, the ICJ ruled that Kosovo's unilateral declaration of independence from Serbia in 2008 was lawful.[56] However, it seems absurd to suggest that this decision will make any difference to the facts on the ground. Kosovo is not going to voluntarily merge itself back into Serbia, and Serbia is not going to accept Kosovo's independence. Nor will the Court's decision affect the acts of the international community there, including a substantial EU military and police force, which have been working since NATO occupation of Kosovo in 1999 to establish independent legal and political institutions in Kosovo and have an enormous amount of credibility at stake on the Kosovo project's success. There is also a host of lesser disputes adjudicated by the ICJ in which the parties have ignored its rulings. In 1949 Albania was ordered to pay £850 000 to the United Kingdom for damage to warships and death of personnel arising from illegal mining of its territorial waters.[57] The judgment was never paid; Albanian gold deposited in British banks was seized by the United Kingdom and frozen until 1991 (after the collapse of the communist regime in Tirana), when the case was settled with a modest payment by the Albanian government. In 1991 Guinea-Bissau rejected an ICJ decision favouring Senegal in a maritime dispute.[58] In 1951 Iran ignored an interim order prohibiting nationalisation of the Anglo-Iranian oil company.[59] In 1979 Iran ignored an order to release hostages taken in the US Embassy following the country's Islamic revolution.[60] Malaysia and Romania have ignored ICJ advisory opinions declaring that their citizens who are UN officials are subject to diplomatic immunity and cannot therefore be sued or prosecuted.[61] Nigeria rejected a 2002 decision awarding sovereignty over the contested Bakassi peninsula to Cameroon.[62] Thailand has ignored a 1962 decision awarding sovereignty over the disputed Preah Vihear temple to Cambodia for almost 50 years.[63]

Perhaps the most notorious incidents of countries ignoring the ICJ have been where the United States was involved. The United States withdrew from the compulsory jurisdiction of the ICJ in 1986, following a decision of the Court to uphold jurisdiction in a complaint by Nicaragua that the United States was providing support to rebels and armed movements against its government.[64] Ultimately, the Court ruled that the United States was liable in damages for providing illegal military support to opponents of the Nicaraguan government, a decision which went unsatisfied.[65] In 2005, the United States withdrew from another convention pursuant to which the ICJ could acquire jurisdiction. The Vienna Convention on Consular Relations, which provides for all persons arrested in a foreign country to be provided access to their home state consul,[66] contains an optional protocol in which disputes over whether this right was given proper effect may be brought before the ICJ.[67] The ICJ had decided three cases against the United States in complaints by countries whose nationals were about to be executed, having been convicted of crimes without the relevant consulates being informed.[68] In two of those three cases the individuals were executed notwithstanding the ICJ's interim orders not to execute pending resolution of the case. In the final case in 2003, the United States agreed to conduct a case review for 58 Mexican nationals, but withdrew from the optional protocol shortly thereafter.[69] The incentive to undertake this case review was not the proceedings before the ICJ but the interests of maintaining cordial relations with a neighbour. The United States' response to international legal adjudications against it is to withdraw from the institutions in question. This is not surprising given the country's pre-eminent power in the international sphere. Impartial application and enforcement of international law favours weak countries over powerful ones. Powerful nations will inevitably withdraw, which is precisely why it is bound to remain irrelevant.

Where important national interests are at stake, governments of all hues have shown determination to ignore the ICJ's decisions. This includes both liberal democracies with high rule of law traditions, such as Iceland, the United States and France, and less democratic countries such as South Africa (at the time) and Morocco. What is surprising about the ICJ, given the habit of countries serially to disregard its rulings, is why it ever makes such controversial decisions that are so palpably likely to be ignored. It is as though the ICJ is operating in a parallel universe, in which its decisions are little more than moral decrees about how the world should be. Who benefits from a raft of decisions that nobody takes any notice of? What is the value in their being issued at all? The answer is that there is a range of actors with interests in the law the ICJ develops, and its politically unrealistic decisions. This includes academics who write about international law and international relations; pressure groups, who can use the ICJ's decisions as leverage for justifying their own positions and continued funding; and international organisations, who may justify further fact-finding missions, reports and monitoring. The ICJ's decisions on these controversial issues are tolerated, even if they stand no chance of being implemented.

Angry denunciation of the ICJ by a 'losing' state may be useful to its domestic politicians, giving them a totem against which to rally and providing them with a sense that they will persevere notwithstanding the bias of outsiders against them. Representatives of the 'winning' state will gain moral support for their hopeless position, even though they stand no chance of implementing the ruling. The reactions of Israel and Palestine to the ICJ's verdict in the *Israel / Palestine Wall* case may exemplify these approaches. Academics and pressure groups can agitate. International organisations can note the concern and monitor. It turns out that everybody wins from having an irrelevant court making abstract pronouncements. The ICJ itself also wins, as do the lawyers who work in the field. In the course of writing these monumental judgments, often of great length, the Court develops all sorts of new theories of international law, a complex prism of legal morality through which to view international current affairs, the details of which are available only to international lawyers trained in the arcane arts of construing ICJ jurisprudence. Even if, at this level, international law is irrelevant to and ignored by states, it is deeply relevant to international lawyers. Through promoting an expectation that international law will be used to understand, analyse and judge disputes in international relations, they keep themselves in work. Over the course of nearly 70 years, the ICJ has developed the jurisprudence of international law in manifold directions. Virtually every one of its comprehensive and detailed judgments seeks to expand international law along some new course. Virtually all its judges are legal academics, often of significant distinction. The themes developed by the Court are written about at great length and are enormously influential in legal scholarship.

Behind these exceptional headline cases, where the ICJ adjudicates on issues of fundamental importance in international relations in elaborate intellectual judgments then routinely ignored, lies a second tier of decisions, equally elaborate in content but in which the ICJ declines to make any order of substance. Compliance with ICJ decisions is not at issue in most cases, because the Court rarely orders any party to do anything. In particular, it is noteworthy how few decisions of the Court have ordered payment of reparations; in no such case has the payment ordered actually been made. In *Corfu Channel*[70] Albania was ordered to pay a fixed sum of reparations to the United Kingdom after unlawful mining caused destruction of a British vessel; it failed to do so. In *Nicaragua – Paramilitaries*[71] the United States was declared liable to pay reparations for providing military support to Nicaraguan rebels; it withdrew from the Court's jurisdiction and the case proceeded no further. In *Gabčíkovo-Nagymaros*[72] the Court ordered Hungary to pay compensation for withdrawing from a joint venture project, but did not set the compensation level required, leaving the parties in limbo. The project was never completed and no compensation was ever paid. In the *Hostages in Iran* case,[73] Iran was ordered to pay reparations for unlawful detention of US diplomats; but no amount was ever set or paid.

In none of the Court's other 69 decided contentious cases at the time of writing has any party been ordered to pay any money to another. The relief that Court grants is typically declaratory rather than injunctive, stating the parties' legal positions but not ordering anyone to ensure those legal positions are respected. In the *San Juan River – Navigational Rights* case,[74] the issue was whether Nicaragua was entitled to charge citizens of Costa Rica for visas and tourist cards. The Court held that it was not; but it did not order Nicaragua to stop (and Nicaragua did not stop). The Court commonly declines jurisdiction in contentious cases, in furiously detailed jurisdictional rulings.[75] ICJ cases are procedurally complex, with various parties intervening, numerous procedural orders, high-powered legal teams typically headed by a Foreign Minister or Ambassador on each side; judgments often running into hundreds of pages; separate declarations or concurring opinions and lengthy dissenting opinions given by one or more of the 15 judges, in virtually every case; noisy domestic reactions by the successful and unsuccessful states and detailed analysis and reactions by the various international organisations. However, at least one empirical study has suggested that the judges are biased, making decisions in accordance with the interests of the states of their nationality. The same study suggests that where the Court's decisions actually order a party to do something they are, on the whole, ignored.[76] Notwithstanding the ceremony and complexity of the Court's procedures, proceedings before the ICJ are principally political melodrama, lacking either impartiality or respect by its litigants.

One of the most intriguing illustrations of the political character of the ICJ's judgments, as well as its propensity to issue decisions of no consequence when faced with essentially contested issues, was its 2003 decision in the *Oil Platforms* case.[77] This was another case involving colossal delay on the part of the Court, no doubt on account of the politically contentious nature of the proceedings. In 1992, Iran complained that US warships had attacked and destroyed three Iranian oil rigs. Eleven years later, the ICJ ruled that Iran's complaint failed on the basis that action of this kind was not covered by the Treaty of Amity under which Iran purported to bring its claim. The Treaty, the Court effectively ruled, was suspended in times of armed conflict. This was barely a plausible conclusion in light of prior case law; in *Military and Paramilitary Activities in and against Nicaragua*, the Court had held that breach of an identical term in a Treaty of Amity between the United States and Nicaragua did ground a complaint that the US had taken covert military action against Nicaragua. But in the Nicaraguan case the Court had been stung by subsequent US withdrawal from the Court. It was therefore better that the Court departed from its prior precedent.

Moreover the Court had previously declared, in a jurisdictional phase of the claim,[78] that it did have jurisdiction to hear the complaint of unlawful use of armed force under the Treaty of Amity, leading the United States to lodge a counterclaim under the same Treaty of Amity for Iran's own military activities in 1997–98 in attacking vessels and laying mines in the Persian Gulf. How it now decided that the Treaty of Amity did not apply, at a later stage of the same proceedings, leading it to dismiss both Iran's claim and the United States' counterclaim, was quite a mystery. To add to the confusion, the Court also concluded that a defence available under the Treaty, permitting measures 'necessary to protect its essential security interests', was not available to the United States. Logically, it could only have reached that conclusion had it concluded that the Treaty *did* apply to the dispute at issue; but in fact the Court decided that this treaty-based defence was inapplicable *before* it addressed the question of whether the Treaty was applicable at all. The entire decision was back to front.

As a matter of judicial good practice, it is hard to understand why the Court took 11 years to issue such a confused result, which amounted in effect to abdication of jurisdiction over the two sides' complaints (although without expressly saying so). The reason may be that the Court likes to seize jurisdiction, to keep its docket full; but it does not like to decide cases about armed conflict involving powerful nations. Still less does it like to embroil itself in the midst of disputes between implacable foes, such as Iran and the United States, nor order either party to pay the other any sums of money (a finding which would, logically, have to follow as a result of a finding of wrongful military action causing damage to property). Instead the Court prevaricates, its decisions often exhibiting a confusing web of hazy logic, the final outcome of which must always be that the Court avoids the extremes of political controversy that might threaten its own existence. Its strategy, revealed in *Oil Platforms*, is to give something to both sides while evading the substance of the issue it is presented with.

Given how rare it is that the Court makes orders requiring any party to do anything, the intellectual, diplomatic, public relations and political energy exercised in the course of ICJ proceedings is remarkable. One might be tempted to the conclusion that the process is pure political theatre. The value of the exercise lies in providing a forum in which states may beat their chests in public, without firing weapons at one another. For many disputes, it is simply not worth going to war. A piece of international political melodrama, in which the great minds of international law are brought to bear in a mammoth but inconsequential political process, may be of benefit to all concerned. The outcome will not necessarily be changed by the Court's judgment; but domestic political demands for firm action, and the political urge for expression of moral outrage over entrenched positions, might be satisfied. States may also be able to offload politically charged decisions to an international court where a concession, although necessary to preserve the peace in international relations, would be domestically unpopular.

The ICJ may be irrelevant to outcomes in cases where strong state interests are at stake; but it can be an important political player in the process of defusing political conflicts which are not vital to national interests. Where the most important feature of a dispute is not the outcome but that national pride can be aired, the ICJ can have a useful role. But the sort of tribunal that can effectively play that role has a *modus operandi* very different from that of domestic courts as we usually conceive them. The role for an international court of this kind is to engender delay while a natural settlement may be reached; permit parties respectably and publicly to convey their positions within the mantle of legal reasoning; and ultimately issue a decision that will cause the least damaging future political repercussions. This decision, while politically harmless, must be elucidated in abstract technical terms, to give the impression of impartiality and legitimacy ordinarily associated with legal process. But the procedure is a charade. These ostensible characteristics, of impartial legal reasoning and unemotional application of legal rules to generate an impartial outcome, are borrowed from domestic court proceedings. What is really going on is quite different. The judges are politicians in robes, motivated by the desire to promote the intellectual field of international law, cause the minimum international ridicule of their decisions and provide material to support their sponsors in academia, NGOs and international organisations. This creates an incentive for the Court to issue decisions of maximum intellectual content with minimal practical outcome. On many occasions, for disputes of low value, states are prepared to go along with the charade, to defuse domestic tensions. Where more is at stake, they will simply ignore the Court, or withdraw from it. What never happens however is that an impartial legal institution imposes upon the parties a binding adjudication of their dispute in accordance with objective legal principles. That sort of aspiration is not possible in the anarchy within which states are suspended.

The PCIJ and ICJ had and have the same failings as the PCA. Because submission to the courts' jurisdiction was (and remains) optional and could be withdrawn at any time, the courts have been reluctant to make decisions undermining states. The temptation therefore is to make orders that do nothing or may be easily ignored. Indeed the small proportion of UN member states that have submitted to the compulsory jurisdiction of the ICJ is revealing: for all the advantages of political theatre, on the whole states do not like resolving their disputes in judicial fora. It is too dangerous; while in some cases the theatre may be a welcome distraction from domestic calls to take more radical action, in other cases the theatre may result in some sort of international condemnation or dangerous judgment, as the United States, France, Morocco, Israel and other countries have discovered. Their reactions were simply to ignore the Court's decisions, or to walk away from it altogether. Nevertheless, for all the dangers of an international adjudicatory process, international law has acquired, as with any rules-based system of bureaucracy, a kind of popular legitimacy. The international general public, international NGOs, international organisations, academics and a host of other pressure and interest groups ensure that international law is used as a tool to condemn states who do not act as they may wish. International law, created by states, turns out to be an inconvenient source of adverse publicity for them. One way for states to satisfy domestic pressure to be seen as acting legitimately, and to give the international legal interest groups space for growth without submitting themselves to the dangers of inter-state adjudication, is for states to develop other tribunals purporting to apply international law, but before which states cannot themselves be drawn. The next chapter addresses a series of institutions that do exactly this, namely international criminal courts. These tribunals allow international lawyers ample room to spread their wings; they can (for the most part) be supported by states without fear of being used against them and there is plenty of easy publicity to be gained by domestic politicians from supporting their aims. The origin of these courts is the subject of our next enquiry.

NOTES

1. UK Ministry of Justice, 'Judicial Statistics for 2007', Chapter 3.
2. Article IV(3)(d) of the Appendix to Annex I to the Peace Treaty between Egypt and Israel dated 26 March 1979 provided for a joint commission to demarcate the countries' common boundary.
3. *Taba Arbitration* (Israel v Egypt), Award of 29 September 1988, 27 ILM 1421 (1988).

4. *Eritrea-Ethiopia Boundary Commission*, Decision regarding Delimitation of the Border, 13 April 2002.
5. *Eritrea-Ethiopia Claims Commission*, Partial Award *Jus Ad Bellum* Ethiopia's Claims 1–8, 19 December 2005.
6. *Eritrea Ethiopia Claims Commission*, Final Award Ethiopia's Damages Claims, 17 August 2009; Final Award Eritrea's Damages Claims, 17 August 2009.
7. See BBC News (2004), 'Ethiopia backs down over border', 25 November.
8. Reuters (2010), 'Eritrea says 10 Ethiopian troops killed', 4 January.
9. See Lyons, Terrence (2006), *Avoiding Conflict in the Horn of Africa: US Policy toward Ethiopia and Eritrea*, Washington, DC: Council on Foreign Relations.
10. Abyei Boundary Commission, *Experts' Report*, presented to the Sudanese Presidency on 14 July 2005.
11. See e.g. Amber Henshaw (2008), 'Sudan tinderbox catches fire', BBC News, 24 May.
12. Arbitration Agreement between the Government of Sudan and the Sudan People's Liberation Movement/Army on Delimiting Abyei Area dated 7 July 2008.
13. *Arbitration on Delimiting Abyei Area*, Government of Sudan v Sudan People's Liberation Movement/Army, Final Award, 22 July 2009.
14. These cases are *Guyana v Suriname* (Award 17 September 2007); *Barbados v Trinidad and Tobago* (Award 11 April 2006); *Malaysia v Singapore* (Award on agreed terms 1 September 2005) and *Eritrea v Yemen* (Second Award, Maritime Delimitation 17 December 1999).
15. *Iron Rhine Arbitration* (Belgium v Netherlands), Award of the Tribunal, 24 May 2005.
16. *Netherlands v France*, Award of the Tribunal, 12 March 2004.
17. *MOX Plant Arbitration* (Ireland v United Kingdom), Proceedings commenced 25 October 2001, hearings from 10 to 21 June 2003, proceedings terminated at the request of Ireland on 6 June 2008.
18. Article 1 of the 1899 Hague Convention for the Pacific Settlement of International Disputes.
19. *Deserters of Casblanca* (France v Germany), Permanent Court of Arbitration, Award of the Tribunal, 22 May 1909.
20. *Muscat Dhows* (France v Great Britain), Permanent Court of Arbitration, Award of the Tribunal, 8 August 1905.
21. *French Postal Vessel Manouba* (France v Italy), Permanent Court of Arbitration, Award of the Tribunal, 6 May 1913.
22. *Boundaries in the Island of Timor* (Netherlands v Portugal), Permanent Court of Arbitration, Award of the Tribunal, 25 June 1914.
23. Article 14 of the Peace Treaty of Versailles dated 28 June 1919 made provision for the Permanent Court of International Justice. The first 30 articles of the Treaty of Versailles consisted of the Covenant of the League of Nations.
24. Article 36 of the Statute of the Permanent Court of International Justice.
25. See http://www.worldcourts.com/pcij/eng/documents/1942.12.31_optional.htm (last accessed 13 May 2010) for a full list of the terms and reservations under which states accepted compulsory jurisdiction of the PCIJ.
26. Minute by Lord Curzon, 5 October 1920, PRO W 512/241/98 FO 371/5480.
27. Lloyd, Lorna (1985), '"A Springboard for the future": a historical examination of Britain's role in shaping the optional clause of the permanent clause of international justice', American Journal of International Law, **79**, 28.
28. Lloyd, *ibid.*
29. Article 14 of the Covenant of the League of Nations.
30. The four cases in which decisions of the High Commissioner were appealed were *Polish Postal Service in Danzig*, Advisory Opinion No. 11 (PCIJ, Ser. B, No. 11, 1925); *Jurisdiction of the Courts of Danzig (Pecuniary Claims of Danzig Railway Officials against the Polish Railways Administration)*, Advisory Opinion No. 15 (PCIJ, Ser. B, No. 15, 1928); *Treatment of Polish Nationals in the Danzig Territory*, Advisory Opinion No. 23, (PCIJ, Ser. A/B, No. 44, 1933); and *Access to, or Anchorage in, the Port of*

Danzig, of Polish War Vessels, Advisory Opinion No. 22 (PCIJ, Ser. A/B, No. 43, 1931). There were two other Danzig cases, in which a ruling of the High Commissioner had not first been obtained.

31. The Free City of Danzig, 95 per cent German but with a Polish corridor seperating it from the greater body of post-war Germany, had its own Senate but remained under the authority of the League of Nations. Poland had various rights in relation to it, including the right to represent it in foreign policy, and to operate a railway into Danzig. The High Commissioner of Danzig was an international official created by the Treaty of Versailles, with jurisdiction to resolve disputes between the Free City of Danzig and Poland that arose under the Versailles Treaty or subsequent implementing treaties, or under the Constitution of the Free City. There were many such disputes, and the High Commissioner was perpetually bedevilled by the issues he had to resolve. See Ydit, Meir (1961), *Internationalised territories from the 'Free City of Cracow' to the 'Free City of Berlin'* Leiden: A.W.Sythoff.
32. *Case of the S.S. 'Wimbledon'* (Britain, France and Japan v Germany), Judgment No. 1 (PCIJ, Ser. A, No. 1, 1923).
33. *Case concerning the factory at Chorzów*, Judgment No. 13 (PCIJ, Ser. A, No. 17, 1928).
34. The formula in *Chorzów Factory* for compensation for expropriation is that 'reparation must, as far as possible, wipe out all the consequences of the illegal act and reestablish the situation which would, in all probability, have existed if that act had not been committed'.
35. *Case concerning the Payment in Gold of Brazilian Federal Loans, Contracted in France*, Judgment No. 15 (PCIJ, Ser. A, No. 21, 1929); *Case concerning the Payment of various Serbian Loans Issued in France*, Judgment No. 14 (PCIJ, Ser. A, No. 20, 1929).
36. *Legal status of the Eastern Greenland*, Judgment No. 20 (PCIJ, Ser. A/B, No. 53, 1933).
37. See e.g. Ripinsky, Sergey and Kevin Williams (2008), *Damages in International Investment Law*, London: British Institute of International and Comparative Law, § 4.2.1(a).
38. See e.g. paragraph (7) of the commentary to Article 23 of the International Law Commission's draft Articles on the Responsibility of States for Internationally Wrongful Acts, text adopted by the International Law Commission at its 53rd session in 2001.
39. *Oscar Chinn* (United Kingdom v Belgium), Judgment No. 23 (PCIJ, Ser. A/B, No. 63, 1934).
40. See Weiler, Todd (2004) 'Saving Oscar Chinn: non-discrimination in international investment law', in Horn, Norbert (ed.), *Arbitrating Foreign Investment Disputes*, The Hague: Kluwer.
41. *The 'Société Commerciale de Belgique'*, Judgment No. 31 (PCIJ, Ser. A/B, No. 78, 1939).
42. *Phosphates in Morocco*, Judgment, 1938, PCIJ, Series A/B, No. 74, 10, 28. See also *SS. 'Wimbledon'*, 1923, PCIJ Series A, No. 1, 15, 30.
43. *Treatment of Polish Nationals and other persons of Polish origin or speech in the Danzig territory*, Advisory Opinion, 1932, PCIJ Series A/B, No. 44, 4, 24.
44. *Marbury v Madison*, 5 US (1 Cranch) 137 (1803).
45. As has been confirmed by the ICJ itself. See e.g. *Certain Phosphate Lands in Nauru (Nauru v Australia)*, Preliminary Objections, Judgment, ICJ Reports 1992, p.260, [53].
46. Article 93(1) Charter of the United Nations.
47. *Application of the Convention on the Prevention and Punishment of the Crime of Genocide* (Bosnia and Herzegovina v Serbia and Montenegro), Judgment of 26 February 2007,
48. *Ibid.*, paragraphs 459 to 470 of the Judgment of 26 February 2007.
49. *Nuclear Tests* (New Zealand v France), Order of 22 June 1973, ICJ Reports 1973, 135.
50. *Fisheries Jurisdiction* (UK v Iceland), Order of 17 August 1972, ICJ Reports 1972, 12.
51. *Legal Consequences for States of the Continued Presence of South Africa in Namibia (South West Africa) notwithstanding Security Council Resolution 276(1970)*, Advisory Opinion, ICJ Reports 1971, 16.

52. *Western Sahara*, Advisory Opinion of 16 October 1975, ICJ Reports 1975, 12.
53. *Legal Consequences of the Construction of a Wall in Occupied Palestinian Territory*, Advisory Opinion of 9 July 2004, ICJ Reports 2004, p. 136.
54. *Fisheries Jurisdiction* (United Kingdom v Iceland), Judgment of 25 July 1974, ICJ Reports 1974, p.3.
55. *Beit Sourik Village Council v Government of Israel and the Commander of the IDF Forces in the West Bank*, Decision of 30 June 2004.
56. *Accordance with International Law of the Unilateral Declaration of Independence by the Provisional Institutions of Self-Government of Kosovo*, Advisory Opinion, 22 July 2010, General List Number 141. The Court opined that the declaration of independence was not inconsistent with international law, formally leaving open the question of whether Kosovo had actually succeeded in seceding from Serbia. However, this distinction would in all likelihood be lost on any but the pedantic: Kosovo won, and Serbia lost.
57. *Corfu Channel* (United Kingdom v Albania), Judgment of 15 December 1949, ICJ Reports 1949, p.244.
58. *Arbitral Award of 31 July 1989* (Guinea-Bissau v Senegal), Judgment of 12 November 1991, ICJ Reports 1991, p.53. The case concerned a challenge to an arbitral award effecting a maritime boundary delimitation. The ICJ upheld the arbitral award; Guinea-Bissau nonetheless continued to ignore it.
59. *Anglo-Iranian Oil Company* (United Kingdom v Iran), Order of 5 July 1951, ICJ Reports 1951, p.89.
60. *United States Diplomatic and Consular Staff in Tehran* (USA v Iran), Order of 15 December 1979, ICJ Reports 1979, p.7.
61. *Difference relating to Immunity from Legal Process of a Special Rapporteur of the Commission on Human Rights* (Malaysia), Advisory Opinion of 29 April 2009, ICJ Reports 1999, p.62; *Applicability of Article VI, Section 22, of the Convention on Privileges and Immunities of the United Nations* (Romania), Advisory Opinion of 15 December 1989, ICJ Reports 1989, p.177.
62. *Land and Maritime Boundary between Cameroon and Nigeria* (Cameroon v Nigeria), Judgment of 10 October 2002, ICJ Reports 2002, p.303.
63. *Temple of Preah Vihear* (Cambodia v Thailand), Judgment of 15 June 1962, ICJ Reports 1962, p.6.
64. *Military and Paramilitary Activities in and against Nicaragua* (Nicaragua v USA), Judgment of 26 November 1984, ICJ Reports 1984, p.392.
65. *Military and Paramilitary Activities in and against Nicaragua* (Nicaragua v USA), Judgment of 27 June 1986, ICJ Reports 1986, p.14.
66. Article 36 Vienna Convention on Consular Relations creates the right for consuls to be informed of a national's arrest.
67. Optional Protocol to the Vienna Convention on Consular Relations Concerning the Compulsory Settlement of Disputes. Done at Vienna, on 24 April 1963.
68. *Case Concerning the Vienna Convention on Consular Relations* (Paraguay v USA), 1998 ICJ 248; *LaGrand* (Germany v USA), 1999 ICJ 9; *Case concerning Avena and other Mexican nationals* (Mexico v USA), 2003 ICJ 77.
69. The withdrawal occurred on 7 March 2005. See Quigley, John (2009), 'The United States' withdrawal from the International Court of Justice jurisdiction in consular cases: reasons and consequences', *Duke Journal of Comparative and International Law*, **19**, 263.
70. *Corfu Channel* (United Kingdom v Albania), Judgment of 15 December 1949, ICJ Reports 1949, p.244.
71. *Military and Paramilitary Activities in and against Nicaragua* (Nicaragua v USA), Judgment of 27 June 1986, ICJ Reports 1986, p.14.
72. *Gabčíkovo-Nagymaros Project* (Hungary v Slovakia), Judgment of 25 September 1997, ICJ Reports 1997, p.7.
73. *Case concerning United States Diplomatic and Consular Staff in Tehran* (USA v Iran), Judgment of 24 May 1980, ICJ Reports 1980, p.3.

74. *Dispute regarding Navigational and Related Rights* (Costa Rica v Nicaragua), Judgment of 13 July 2009.
75. See e.g. *Case Concerning Armed Activities on the Territory of the Congo* (Democratic Republic of Congo v Rwanda), Judgment of 3 February 2006; *Case Concerning the Aerial Incident of 10 August 1999* (Pakistan v India), Judgment of 21 June 2000, ICJ Reports 2000, 12.
76. Posner, Eric and Miguel de Figueiredo (2005), 'Is the International Court of Justice biased?', *Journal of Legal Studies*, **34**, 599.
77. *Oil Platforms* (Iran v USA), Judgment on the Merits, 6 November 2003, ICJ Reports 2003, 161. Gratitude is due to Veijo Heiskanen for insights into this case. See in particular Heiskanen, Veijo (2005), 'Oil platforms: lessons of dissensus', *Nordic Journal of International Law*, **74**, 179.
78. *Oil Platforms* (Iran v USA), Judgment of 12 December 1996, ICJ Reports 1996, p.803.

4. International criminal law: victors' justice or an interminable machine?

The idea of trying political and military leaders for 'war crimes' is very old indeed. This should hardly be surprising: after a bloody war in which their young men have been killed, their taxes wasted and civilian life disrupted, the public is baying for vengeance. Thus in 1305 Sir William Wallace, a leading Scottish resistance figure in the Wars of Scottish Independence, was captured in Scotland, transported to London, tried for treason for waging war against the English, executed, and his preserved head, dipped in tar, displayed on a pike on London Bridge. In 1474 Peter von Hagenbach, a feudal lord of the Holy Roman Empire, was tried by an ad hoc tribunal established by the Archduke of Austria for war crimes committed by his forces during the occupation of Breisach. He was found guilty on a command responsibility theory, and beheaded. In 1865 Confederate officer Henry Wirz was tried for abuse of Union prisoners of war at Camp Sumter in Georgia, found guilty and hanged. In 1945 24 Nazi leaders were indicted before the International Military Tribunal, better known as the Nuremberg war crimes tribunal, established by the victorious allies. Of these, 12 were sentenced to death and seven were sentenced to lengthy prison terms. Three were acquitted. In the 1946–48 Tokyo trials, none of the 28 defendants was acquitted by the US-dominated tribunal established by Douglas Macarthur, the US proconsul in charge of post-war Japan. Seven were sentenced to death, 16 to life sentences.

Following the Nuremberg trials, Control Council Law 10 authorised each occupying power in Germany to organise its own further war crimes trials. The United States organised a further 12 such trials in Nuremberg, convicting 142 of 185 defendants (of whom 13 were executed) and tried a further 1672 defendants at mass trials in Dachau. Poland organised trials of over 40 people associated with the death camp at Auschwitz. British authorities arranged seven trials of 38 defendants in Hamburg, for crimes committed at Ravensbrück concentration camp. Many other trials took place, including trials over events in Belsen and Mathausen-Gusen concentration camps (the latter of which resulted in only one acquittal out of 69 and 62 death sentences). A further 5700 Japanese citizens were indicted in US-led war crimes trials. In 1949, the Soviet Union also convicted 12 defendants in relation to biological weapons charges, in the Khabarovsk trials.[1] China also arranged war crimes trials for Japanese citizens in its territory. Adolf Eichmann was captured by Israeli agents in Argentina in 1960 and convicted and executed in Israel in 1962. In 1987 a French court sentenced Klaus Barbie to life imprisonment for war crimes associated with the Nazi occupation of Lyon.

The logic for governments of holding such trials is compelling. Given that judges are selected by states standing in opposition to the political position of the defendant, there is little prospect of too many embarrassing acquittals. Exposure of gruesome details of horrid crimes helps the government prosecuting the trial in pressing its case that costly war was necessary and moral, and satisfies pressure by victims or their families to see justice done. The formal process of trial and judgment legitimises both the wartime actions of the prosecuting government and the political settlement reached after the war is over. It is no wonder, therefore, that war crimes trials are attractive propositions. However, they have for a long time exhibited a concerning lack of theoretical rigour. In each case where a war crimes tribunal has been arranged, the charges have been worryingly ad hoc. It is usually accepted as a rule of criminal law that no person may be prosecuted for an act which was not a crime at the time it was committed;[2] but in war crimes trials, it is typical for the definitions of the crimes with which defendants are charged to be developed only after the event.

The fact that war crimes are, *ex hypothesi*, committed in the midst of war, when all manner of nasty things happen as a matter of course, means that some ingenuity is required in developing offences with which to charge the defendants that do not logically implicate the victorious side's politicians and armed forces. Thus historically, we find indictments raised for all manner of legally colourful offences. Wallace was tried for treason – i.e. betrayal of one's own sovereign – difficult to understand given he was not a citizen of the country (England) placing him on trial. Von Hagenbach was charged with 'trampling the laws of God and men'. Wirz was charged with 'conspiring to impair the lives of Union prisoners of war'. The Nuremberg trials charged the defendants with four crimes: 'common plan or conspiracy'; 'crimes against peace' or 'wars of aggression'; 'war crimes' and 'crimes against humanity'. The defendants in the Tokyo war crimes trials were charged with miscellaneous offences such as 'waging unprovoked war against China', 'waging aggressive war against the United States' and 'deliberately and recklessly disregarding their duty to take adequate steps to prevent atrocities'. None of these criminal offences was adequately defined. In the Nuremberg and Tokyo trials, the offences with which the defendants were charged did not exist, in either domestic or international law, at the time they were charged with committing them. The charters of the military tribunals themselves established the offences.[3]

What is particularly interesting about war crimes trials is that in virtually no case are defendants charged with regular offences under recognised criminal law, such as murder, torture, rape or kidnapping. They are charged instead with specially crafted criminal offences, invented to fit the circumstances in which they are tried. It is worth pausing to ask why this is so. The answer is perhaps obvious: it would be too difficult to convict politicians and military officers with command responsibility of ordinary crimes. There was no evidence that any of the 24 initial defendants at Nuremberg had themselves committed acts of violence. In few cases was there even evidence they had signed orders that others should do so. (Hermann Göring had signed orders for the 'final solution', but there were few other smoking guns.) The elements typical of the crime of murder – for example, sufficient causal proximity between one's act and the defendant's death, and an intention to cause death – would be very difficult to make out against a defendant politician. A politician might have presided over a war in which a group of soldiers had murdered civilians; but if no instructions had ever been issued by that politician condoning such behaviour, then the chain of causation between the politician's conduct and the act of murder seems remote indeed.

It was hard to argue that any direct criminal responsibility in the conventional sense attached to some defendants – for example, Walther Funk, the Director of the Reichsbank, or Albert Speer, Hitler's architect. Nonetheless, they were both found guilty of war crimes and crimes against humanity. The case against the defendants was that they were knowing agents in a government that perpetrated unjustified and terrible war against foreign countries, and atrocities on an unprecedented scale against civilians. Such crimes fitted no easy legal boxes. They were charges of which one could be found guilty by complicity or association. It was far easier to secure convictions on such fuzzy charges than had they been tried under conventional criminal law. This may be one reason why we find exceptionally high conviction rates in the war crimes trials after World War II. In the principal Nuremberg trial, the conviction rate was 88 per cent; in the 12 subsequent Nuremberg trials, 77 per cent; in the Dachau trials, 85 per cent; in the Auschwitz trials, 98 per cent; in the Mauthausen trials, 100 per cent; in the Ravensbrück trials, 92 per cent; in the initial Tokyo trials, 100 per cent; in subsequent Japanese war crimes trials held by the allies, 81 per cent; in the Khabarovsk trials, 100 per cent. By contrast, not guilty pleas in the Crown Court in England typically result in a conviction in approximately 40 per cent of cases.[4] An equivalent figure averaged across the different states in the USA is 68 per cent.[5] Given the levels of atrocities and human suffering necessary to create the political pressure to mount war crimes prosecutions, acquittals in war crimes cases are not politically acceptable to any significant degree, beyond (perhaps) a nominal acquittal level to demonstrate the process is fair. The flexible standard of guilt, developed in *ex post facto* designations of ambiguously defined criminal offences, assist the prosecution and the tribunal in achieving this political result.

The charges levelled against the Germans and Japanese at the end of World War II were not raised entirely in a legal vacuum. An international law of war had been developed since the middle of the nineteenth century, in a series of treaties in which nations agreed to limit their conduct in warfare with one another. In 1856, the Paris Declaration respecting Maritime Law promised neutrality of commercial vessels during war. In 1864 14 states signed the first Geneva Convention, promising that in the course of war on land they would observe the sanctity of medical facilities, impartial treatment of combatants and protection of civilians carrying aid to the wounded. These principles were extended to warfare at sea by the second Geneva Convention in 1906. The Hague Conventions of 1899 and 1907 set out a series of principles for *jus in bello* (conscionable conduct during war), such as humane treatment of prisoners of war, banning the killing of soldiers who have surrendered, proper treatment of civilians in occupied territory, banning the use of poisonous gases, hollow point ammunition, unanchored maritime mines[6] and a range of other wartime activities. The 'Martens clause', a paragraph in the preamble to the Hague Conventions, contained a broad declaration that 'populations and belligerents remain under the protection and empire of the principles of international law, as they result from the usages established between civilised nations, from the laws of humanity and the requirements of the public conscience'.

This formulation was almost entirely vacuous – there was no agreement about what the usages of civilised nations were, nor the requirements of public conscience. The origin of the clause was as a placeholder, pending an inability of the negotiating parties to agree a more comprehensive legal regime.[7] Notwithstanding, it has been referred to on several occasions since then as the origin of the modern international law of war crimes,[8] perhaps precisely because it is so vague that the criminalisation of virtually any conduct can be drawn from it. The undertakings contained in the Hague Conventions would be broadly disregarded in World War I. Although the Peace Treaty of Versailles anticipated the international trial of Kaiser Wilhelm II and lesser German officials,[9] the Kaiser obtained asylum in the Netherlands, and was never prosecuted. Germany refused to extradite other officials considered by the Allies to be responsible for the war, and held just 12 trials in-country, which led to acquittals or lenient sentences. In 1928, the Kellogg-Briand Pact was signed by some 54 nations, including all the Great Powers. By this exceptionally broad treaty the signatory states would 'condemn recourse to war for the solution of international controversies' and 'agree that settlement. . .of disputes. . .shall never be sought except by pacific means'. The third Geneva Convention, signed in 1929, expanded the Hague Convention rules on prisoners of war. The Hague Conventions, Geneva Conventions and the Kellogg-Briand Pact were cited by the Nuremberg tribunal as legal bases for the criminal acts performed by the defendants, as were the provisions of the Peace Treaty of Versailles.[10]

Yet none of these treaties could properly be used as the basis for criminal prosecution. They were obligations undertaken by states towards one another; but treaty commitments do not imply that an individual government servant who participates in breaches of them is criminally liable. The President of the United States should not be put on trial for failing to make good his country's treaty commitments to fund the United Nations. The Nuremberg trials tried to set a precedent that certain sorts of breach of international law were so heinous that criminal liability attached to individuals responsible for their breach; but the legal obligations they cited, namely obligations not to go to war, are so open-ended as to be little more than hortatory. Nations have always gone to war. Even passing over the fact that the tribunal applied *ex post facto* law, the irregularities in the Nuremberg trials (and their German and Japanese successors) were so legion as to bring the process into broad disrepute. These irregularities included brazen partiality of the judiciary; the Soviet judge Nikitchenko, a judge in Stalin's 1930s show trials, had declared the defendants' guilt before the trial even began.[11] The Soviet prosecutor Rudenko later became commandant of Sachsenhausen concentration camp, a Nazi camp in East Germany subsequently used by the NKVD (Stalin's predecessor to the KGB) until 1950.[12] The charge of aggression against Poland was pursued even though it had been authorised by one of the prosecuting allies in the Nazi-Soviet pact and no Soviet officials were being tried for the same crime. There was no right of appeal against conviction and penalty of death. The judges were selected entirely from the victorious powers. The tribunal was not bound by rules of evidence and its decision refers only sparsely to evidence, instead taking 'judicial notice' of whatever facts it saw fit.[13] Exculpatory prosecution evidence was withheld from the defence.[14] Allied troops were mistreating prisoners of war at the same time as trials were underway accusing German defendants of doing the same thing.[15] The Soviet Prosecutors sought to admit evidence of German participation in the Katyn massacre, evidence which must have been false since Russia subsequently admitted the Soviet Union was responsible for the massacre.[16] The Tokyo trials were criticised for exonerating the Japanese Emperor and his family, despite their being the prime movers behind Japanese aggression.[17] The Allies granted immunity to scientists who had conducted germ warfare experiments on civilians and prisoners, in exchange for their data.[18]

What is also intriguing about the Nuremberg and Tokyo judgments is the disproportionately small level of attention given in the rulings to the actions or culpability of the individual defendants. The decisions read like historical narratives, the Nuremberg decision in particular comprising an extended account of the Nazi party's malign motives and aggression, with frequent references to the acts and speeches of Adolf Hitler, who was not on trial. At the end of the Nuremberg judgment's history lesson of some 108 pages (which barely mentions any of the defendants at all), there are then comparatively fleeting discussions of the individual defendants' guilt, comprising an average of fewer than three pages per defendant. There is virtually no discussion of the evidence implicating each individual; they are just declared complicit in the narrative of horrors. There is no reasoning whatsoever about determination of sentences; punishment is dealt with in just one sentence per defendant.[19] It is difficult to escape the conclusion that the verdicts were written with the history books in mind, rather than with a view to providing the defendants with fair trials and carefully scrutinising and adjudicating the evidence against them.

The US prosecutor at Nuremberg, Robert Jackson, defended the trials, saying the defendants were 'the first to be given the chance to plead for their lives in the name of the law'.[20] But the Nazis were some of the first political leaders in history to be executed for losing a war, at least an international one. In prior wars, no matter how bloody, political leaders had never been convicted of crimes and had never been executed by their international opponents. Far from setting a precedent for international justice (or if so, only of the most dubious kind), they set a precedent for international legally sanctioned retribution by the victors. A damning dissent by Indian judge Radhabinod Pal on the Tokyo tribunal argued that the failure of the tribunal to prosecute either the use of the atomic bomb against Japan or western colonialism demonstrated a 'failure of the Tribunal to provide anything other than the opportunity for the victors to retaliate'.[21] The Nuremberg and Tokyo trials were intellectually indefensible within the bounds of international law, and palpably unfair by the standards of natural justice. While it is difficult to sympathise with many of the defendants, these trials were a grubby process, driven by the worst desires for vengeance. The world had seen several years of military horror in World War II. A judicial travesty barely mitigated the evil of what had gone before.

INTERNATIONAL CRIMINAL LAW AFTER NUREMBERG

One might have taken the view that the trials of 1945–48 were ugly aberrations of justice warped by unquenchable political forces in an era where so many people – estimates lie between 48 and 78 million – had died. Yet the Nuremberg trials would lie fallow only for so long, their legacy being resurrected in the late twentieth century. Notwithstanding their well-documented failings, the Nuremberg and Tokyo trials were used as precedents for the re-emergence of international criminal law in 1993. The events which entailed recreation of the international criminal law experiment were of an altogether smaller magnitude. The International Criminal Tribunal for Yugoslavia (ICTY) was established by UN Security Council Resolution 827, passed on 25 May 1993, prompted by reports of atrocities in Croatia and Bosnia, including mass murder and ethnic cleansing. Nonetheless, the numbers of dead in those two wars were of a far lower order than what had taken place earlier in the same century. It is now estimated the Bosnian war left 100 000 people dead, of whom perhaps 75 000 had died by the time the Security Council passed Resolution 827.[22] The Croatian war left about 20 000 dead, of whom perhaps 17 000 had died by May 1993.[23]

There had been far more deadly wars, and atrocities against civilians, in the intervening period since 1945. On historians' estimates, the Chinese Civil War (1945–49) caused the deaths of between 1 and 6 million, with atrocities and famine in Communist China subsequently claiming a further 20 to 72 million in the period to 1961. Between 500 000 and 1 million died in the Chinese occupation of Tibet (1950–51). The Korean war (1950–53) killed perhaps 2 million. Between 1959 and 1988 Hutu and Tutsi atrocities in Rwanda and Burundi caused some 200 000 deaths. Wars in Indochina between 1960 and 1975 killed between three and four million, with Pol Pot's Cambodia regime killing at least 1.5 million between 1975 and 1978. Civil wars and revolution in Ethiopia between 1961 and 1992 killed perhaps 1.4 million, including as many as 1 million in a civil war-induced famine (1984–85). A 1966 coup in Nigeria followed by a civil war that ran until 1970 killed perhaps 1 million. Approximately 1 million died in each of the Bangladeshi Liberation War (1971), war in Mozambique (1975–1992) and the Iran-Iraq war (1980–88). Well over 1 million died in civil war in Sudan between 1983 and 1992. Indeed this list only scratches the surface of international atrocities since the end of World War II. It is therefore worth asking why the wars in Yugoslavia prompted a renewal of the international war crimes movement whereas prior events had not.

One reason may be that the Cold War had ended, and therefore Russian and Chinese cooperation on the project was possible. Another reason is that the crimes were committed in Europe; and the movement for international criminal law had been incubated Europe. Where atrocities were apparently occurring in Europe's own backyard, with the European media and politicians closely engaged, the former Yugoslavia was the perfect opportunity to push for a new international criminal court. Indeed the idea for an international criminal tribunal did not come out of the blue. The 1948 Genocide Convention provided that all states undertake to punish genocide, either in the courts of the state where the crime was committed, or by an international criminal tribunal, where the states had accepted its jurisdiction. This was an empty commitment, since the country where the genocide was committed would probably not have control over the person responsible for the genocide in an international case; and no country was obliged subsequently to assent to an international tribunal.

In 1949 the first three Geneva conventions were updated, and a fourth was added, setting out more detailed rules for protection of civilians during wartime.[24] Yet more extensive rules of war were set out in two 1977 protocols to the Geneva conventions, covering matters as diverse as treatment of journalists, protection of cultural objects and places of worship, perfidy (deceptive surrender) and rights of safe passage for medical aircraft. They even require armies to have legal advisers. Each of the four conventions added a chapter by which states undertook to prosecute 'grave breaches' of them. These provisions created the prerequisites for what would come to be known as 'universal jurisdiction': that is, the notion that any state can prosecute any person for any grave breach of a Geneva Convention, no matter where the breach occurred. The 1949 conventions do not explicitly go that far, but they do provide that each signatory state is obliged to bring contraveners 'regardless of their nationality, before its own courts' or 'if it prefers. . .hand such persons over for trial to another' state.[25] However, none of the Geneva conventions had anything to say on *jus ad bellum*, the circumstances in which states may go to war, rather than what they may do when at war (*jus in bello*). This is important, because many of the charges before the International Criminal Tribunal for the former Yugoslavia (ICTY) would be complaints that war was wrongfully waged (as were several of the charges before the Nuremberg and Tokyo tribunals), not just that the way it was waged was wrongful. The UN Charter sought to set rules for *jus ad bellum*, namely that military force 'against the territorial integrity or political independence of any state' was forbidden, subject to the twin exceptions of self-defence and Security Council approval but it said nothing about criminal liability.[26]

The notion that international treaties would oblige states to prosecute certain types of crime was continued in the Single Convention on Narcotics (1961), the Convention on Suppression of Unlawful Seizure of Aircraft (1970), the Convention on the Punishment of Crimes against Internationally Protected Persons (1973), the Apartheid Convention (1973), the Torture Convention (1975), the Convention against the Taking of Hostages (1979), the Convention on Physical Protection of Nuclear Material (1980) and the Convention on Suppression of Unlawful Acts against the Safety of Maritime Navigation (1988). These international treaties were intriguing. On the one hand they were irrelevant: virtually all nations criminalised the matters they covered anyway. There is no nation where it was legal for a private citizen to possess a nuclear bomb prior to the 1980 Convention. For that reason, all nations were happy to sign up to these conventions. There was also significant political pressure from the human rights lobbies to do so: which nation would want to appear soft on narcotics, hijacking aircraft or hostage-taking? Accordingly, these various conventions had very high rates of signature. These conventions were all drafted or mediated by the United Nations, which could show itself being put to good use when the Security Council was hamstrung during the Cold War and consensus on the use of UN peacekeepers or other solid initiatives was rarely achieved. These treaties also attracted the support of NGOs and pressure groups, keen to highlight whichever global atrocities they were following by reference to some international legal standard.

Although no prosecutions occurred under them at the time, and very few nations changed their domestic laws as a result of these various treaties, they made a profound long-term difference in thinking about international law, due to two intellectual sleights of hand. First, a doctrine was developed by scholars of international law to the effect that if sufficient states signed up to an international treaty, the principles of that treaty would be deemed *erga omnes*[27] – that is to say, such fundamental principles of civilised behaviour that they were binding on all states and owed to all other states, whether or not the states in question had signed them. That way, the outliers could be mopped up, and states could not withdraw. Second, the notion had been created that there were such things as 'international crimes': that is to say, crimes prescribed as such by international (rather than domestic) law. From there, it was only a short logical step to arrive at the notion of an international tribunal to try persons accused of those crimes. If crimes are international, so the reasoning went, it cannot be logical that each state interprets the elements of those crimes in different ways. Moreover states may have political agendas which inhibit prosecutions in certain cases. Due to competing domestic political opinions about his period in power, it would never be realistic to expect the Serbian government to have mounted an impartial domestic prosecution of Slobodan Milošević. To ensure legal uniformity and political impartiality in prosecutions and judgments, an international criminal court is required. This was the direction of thinking amongst international law scholars, practitioners, UN staff and human rights NGOs over the course of 45 years since the end of the World War II.

Preparations to draft a statute for an international criminal court had been underway within the international organisations for some time. In 1937 a League of Nations committee had prepared a draft statute for an international criminal court, but the idea had lain fallow. In 1948 this project was dusted off and a committee of the UN General Assembly again submitted a draft statute in 1951.[28] The UN General Assembly had some doubts about the enthusiasm with which this project was being pursued by international functionaries; it formed a new committee to review the first committee's work, which reported in 1954 with a revised statute.[29] In the same year the International Law Commission, a UN-sponsored committee of jurists, submitted a draft 'Code of Offences against the Peace and Security of Mankind'.[30] These efforts, driven by international organisations rather than states themselves, went nowhere at the time; the General Assembly then suspended this work indefinitely. But in 1981 work on the Code of Offences began again and in 1991 the ILC adopted a draft of the Code. In 1989 the ILC dusted off the statute for an international criminal court yet again, and its draft was coming to maturity just as the Yugoslavian wars were beginning in the early 1990s. The United Nations had kept the legal framework for an international criminal tribunal alive over the long decades of the Cold War, when no member states had any interest in seeing such a tribunal come to fruition. Once the Cold War was over, and as soon as a suitable conflict came along to justify such a tribunal, the UN had an off-the-shelf precedent for presentation to the world.

Thus the intellectual dream of a new international criminal law would be kept on low heat for some 40 years, until global politics were sufficiently propitious to make it a reality. The events that provided this opportunity were the Yugoslavian wars. These wars were suitable because they were highly publicised. The Great Powers had little interest in intervening in bloody civil wars, because there were perceived to be few strong strategic interests in the Western Balkan region at the end of the Cold War. Nonetheless they were very public conflicts, some of the first wars in which daily footage of fighting and civilian suffering were broadcast around the world on the television on a daily basis. Taking place in a corner of Europe, adjacent to Austria and Italy, the western media had easy access to the endless stream of horrors that accompanies any civil war. Yet the west did not want to intervene, because that would have required indefinite military occupation and loss of soldiers' lives, for uncertain national benefit. In the face of calls to do something about the atrocities witnessed from people's living rooms, and without willingness to commit troops, establishment of an international criminal court to try people guilty of atrocities was a convenient way of being seen to act. The UN had a template it could offer immediately; in 1993, it took the Secretary General just three months to present a final statute for the ICTY from the date the Security Council asked him to prepare a draft. The Yugoslavian wars presented a confluence of interests between international law advocates within the UN who would see their project become reality, and the western powers on the Security Council, who could use the new tribunal as a demonstration they were acting decisively on the Yugoslavian conflict without actually risking troops. Thus was the ICTY born.

THE YUGOSLAVIAN AND RWANDAN TRIBUNALS

The statute of the ICTY imbued it with jurisdiction to try four categories of offence, namely 'grave breaches of the Geneva Conventions', 'violating the laws and customs of war', 'committing genocide' and 'crimes against humanity'.[31] Although in each case illustrative lists of culpable conduct were provided (crimes against humanity were defined to include 'murder', 'extermination', 'enslavement', 'deportation' and 'other inhumane acts'), no comprehensive definitions of criminal culpability were provided, of the kind that one finds in domestic criminal codes. To pick just one example, murder is a closely defined term under virtually every western legal system. To establish criminal liability for murder in England, a defendant must be proved to have caused the death of another person, and they must also be proved either to have intended the person's death or intended to cause them serious bodily harm.[32] Complex doctrines exist about liability for murder where the defendant intends an event to occur that makes the death of others possible, or probable, but not inevitable;[33] and where the act of a third party intervenes.[34] Where a defendant encourages another to murder a person and intends that they die, he will be held liable for aiding or abetting a murder;[35] where he does not believe a person under his charge is going to murder someone, he will not be liable for murder.[36] None of these detailed legal rules found expression in the statute or the rules of the ICTY. None of the various international conventions signed since the end of World War II, in which states undertook to criminalise and prosecute various acts, contained any such rules either. Neither did the Geneva

Conventions, nor the Code of Offences against the Peace and Security of Mankind or the International Law Commission (ILC) draft statute. Despite half a century of scholarly theorising about what international criminal law might look like, none of the detailed work necessary to create a robust criminal code had been undertaken.

Instead the ICTY's statute spoke in broad generalities, describing offences in terms more appropriate to a human rights lobbying pamphlet than a comprehensive legal document. No attempt was made to define liability for encouraging or abetting murder,[37] enormously important where one wishes to prosecute military and political leaders rather than the foot soldiers who pull the triggers. No attempt was made to define 'extermination' or distinguish it from 'murder'. 'Genocide' is also a formidably tricky concept for a lawyer to characterise. It was described in the ICTY's statute as entailing 'intent to destroy, in whole or in part, a national, ethnical, racial or religious group', but this standard is difficult to apply with legal accuracy. Any murder involves an intent to destroy at least one person who, as part of some group or other, will amount to a part of it. It turns out that any murder can legally be classified as genocide; if the definition has that consequence, it is obvious that something has gone quite wrong. The desire to wipe out a rival group, driven either by some hatred of the other or by a nationalist plan for ethnic purity of territory, may be more relevant to motive than to the *mens rea*, or mental element of an offence, which will affect the severity of sentence. But a murder remains a murder, irrespective of motive.

Indeed it is hard to understand why, viewed from the perspective of criminal law, genocide should be a separate category of criminal offence at all. Any acts assisting in a genocide would be a very serious crime in any event (such as abetting a murder), carrying the most severe penalties, under any tolerably comprehensive system of domestic criminal law. Genocide is better considered a historical phenomenon, the outcome of a collective attempt by one group of people to eradicate another one in its midst, than a legal category of criminal responsibility attaching to individuals. In making genocide a separate offence, international criminal law has been hijacked by a desire for courts and lawyers to issue definitive historical judgments.[38] There is something final about the pronouncement of a judge, in the way a historian's opinion never can be. International criminal law is co-opted to foreclose historical debate.

The vagaries of the criminal offences created by the ICTY's statute were left for development in the jurisprudence of the court itself. The definition of each crime was subject to judicial elaboration, as indeed were sentencing policies. (The ICTY's statute and rules contain no guidelines on sentencing; any crime may be punished by imprisonment for any period between one day and life.) The tribunal was created to try crimes focused upon historical phenomena, collective events driven by a range of interacting political forces, rather than upon the culpability of individuals who played a role in the events in question. Therefore the tribunal had to find a way of making an individual liable for a collective event. It did this by developing the doctrine of 'joint criminal enterprise', whereby a political or military leader would be made liable for genocide by being a member of a group of people who are jointly responsible for a particular outcome.

This concept goes beyond the common law crime of conspiracy, in which criminal liability attaches to a group of people who expressly agree to act together to achieve some wrongful outcome.[39] The prosecutors at the ICTY could rarely find evidence of any express agreement to commit genocide or mass murder. Pace Göring's written orders for a 'final solution' for Europe's Jews, it is rare for politicians or military leaders to sign documents expressly requiring troops to commit war crimes. War crimes are probably inevitable to a degree in virtually any armed conflict; even with a horde of legal advisers, US troops were accused of serious war crimes in connection with the invasions of Afghanistan (2001–) and Iraq (2003–) and detentions at Guantánamo Bay (2002–). War crimes are typically committed more frequently where leaders are nonchalant or even hostile towards civilians or enemy troops, and there is no sense of accountability or discipline amongst fighting soldiers. Yet such events are exceptionally hard to capture using legal definitions. At the level of command or political responsibility, culpability for war crimes is necessarily a form of guilt by association, in which one person becomes liable for the crimes of another by virtue of being a member of the same group and therefore sharing responsibility for actions undertaken by them. This is the concept behind the term 'joint criminal enterprise' as developed by the ICTY. It is central to modern international criminal law, for without it there would be few successful prosecutions of political and military leaders; yet it is deeply troubling to the criminal lawyer because it is premised upon collective responsibility rather than individual liability.

The concept of a joint criminal enterprise was developed by the ICTY in its very first decision, *Prosecutor v Tadić*.[40] Mr Tadić was a member of a Serb paramilitary group that entered the village of Jakici in northern Bosnia and dispensed random physical violence against its inhabitants. Five Muslims were found dead upon the departure of the paramilitaries. There was no direct evidence that Mr Tadić (or indeed any member of the group) had murdered these five men. Mr Tadić was the only member of the paramilitary group on trial at the time. There were other Serb forces in the area. The trial chamber acquitted Mr Tadić of the murder of these five men. Nonetheless on the prosecutor's appeal, the Appeal Chamber found him guilty of the murders. Whether or not he had personally pulled the trigger, Mr Tadić was a member of a joint criminal enterprise which resulted in the death of these individuals, and therefore he was liable for their murder. In this way, he was found guilty of a crime even though the court, on its own admission, could not be certain who had committed it.

In its decision, the ICTY described 'three distinct categories of collective criminality'.[41] Category One applies where there is a joint intention amongst participants in a group to commit a certain act. Where five people form a plan to assassinate a person, but only one pulls the trigger, all five are guilty of murder. Category Two concerns common 'adherence to a system of repression',[42] and is about joint criminal liability amongst concentration camp guards. If one guard commits an act of murder or rape, all the guards are liable for it. This category is exceptionally controversial. If one prison guard abuses an inmate, why should another guard be liable for that abuse even though he has taken personal efforts himself to avoid any acts of abuse? Category Three is more controversial still. It provides that where a criminal act occurs outside a common design, but is a 'natural and foreseeable consequence of effecting that common purpose', then all the persons who share the common design are liable for the act outside its scope. Forcible removal of civilians from an area may have the consequence – unexpected to all the participants but the primary murderer – that a civilian is killed. Under this doctrine, everyone involved is guilty of the murder, because they should have anticipated that it was the sort of thing that could happen as a result of the activity they were participating in.[43] Whether they actually foresaw this risk is apparently irrelevant. This notion of a 'joint criminal enterprise', in which all participants in a collective act are responsible for all the crimes committed by all other members of the group in question, has been criticised in both judicial opinion and the academic literature,[44] but those criticisms have fallen on deaf ears. The ICTY is a political court, with a political agenda, and the technical niceties of criminal law will not allow it to be deflected from its proper course.

The notion of joint criminal enterprise was extended to a remarkable degree. At the time of writing Radovan Karadžić, wartime political leader of the Bosnian Serbs, is on trial, charged with being a member of a joint criminal enterprise permanently to remove Bosnian Muslims and Bosnian Croats from parts of Bosnian territory; a joint criminal enterprise to snipe at and shell the citizens of Sarajevo during the siege; and a joint criminal enterprise to commit genocide in Srebrenica.[45] Framing his indictment in this way means the prosecution will be able to secure a conviction simply by showing that the event in question occurred: Karadžić was the wartime leader of the Serbs, Serbian armed forces committed atrocities and he should have been able to predict that such events could happen. None of these things is in doubt, and thus his conviction is inevitable. Karadžić will be unable to run the defence that, for example, he knew nothing of events in Srebrenica (being a long distance away from events at the time) or, being a political and not a military leader, he was not responsible for military operations. He was part of a joint criminal enterprise which caused these events. On this legal theory, establishing the defendant's own close association with the events or even his knowledge of them is irrelevant. The tribunal can proceed in its judgment to write a definitive historical account of what happened, and then append a declaration of Karadžić's guilt to the end of the decision. In this regard, the decision convicting him will look much like the decision of the Nuremburg Military Tribunal.

Likewise, the former president of Yugoslavia, Slobodan Milošević, was charged with participation in a joint criminal enterprise which resulted in a campaign of terror and violence against Albanian civilians in Kosovo, forcible removal of non-Serb civilians from parts of Croatia and genocide and persecutions in Bosnia.[46] By charging him with a joint criminal enterprise the Court could focus upon the historical events of the war, rather than the defendant's personal actions relevant to his moral culpability. Ultimately, what Milošević may or may not have done, or known, was irrelevant. Provided the historical events alleged truly occurred, he was to be found guilty no matter what he knew about them. In the ultimate absurdity, Milošević's indictment accuses him of participating in a joint criminal enterprise in Bosnia up to 31 December 1995, after the Dayton Peace Accords ending the war had been signed by him among others. Presumably ending the war was as much an act in furtherance of a criminal enterprise as fighting it. While, like the defendants in the Nuremberg trials, one might find it difficult to have sympathy with Karadžić or Milošević, the process by which these very senior figures' culpability for the admittedly cruel events that took place in the Balkan wars was to be assessed was an historical evaluation more than a legal one. These defendants were not subject to a criminal trial in the conventional sense of the word. Their trials are (or were) not about them but about the events of the war. Those trials are about classifying certain events as 'genocide'. Thus an international tribunal can issue a definitive ascription of an emotionally loaded historical label. The ICTY has little interest in doing individual justice. Its concern is with writing history and in the process, legitimating international law as an arbiter of historical rights and wrongs. If it can secure that role, the future of international criminal law and its practitioners is secured. International law is stealing ground from historians.

A lack of interest in addressing the personal culpability of individual defendants, combined with a lack of incriminating evidence specific to them, rendered the charges of 'joint criminal enterprise' exceptionally common. It has been calculated that 81 per cent of the indictments filed before the ICTY rely upon the notion in one way or another.[47] This is not the only way in which the ICTY has focused upon historical narrative over individual culpability. The prosecutors and judges at the ICTY clearly hold the view that the Serbs bear by far the greatest level of responsibility for the events that occurred during the Yugoslavian war. This view is reflected in prosecutorial and conviction biases revealed in the ethnic background of the defendants. Of the 161 defendants indicted by the tribunal (excluding those indicted for contempt of court, such as the former Court spokesperson Florence Hartmann,[48] 116 (72 per cent) were Serb, 20 per cent were Croat and 4 per cent each were Bosniac and Albanian. Of the 72 cases on which final verdicts have been entered after trial and appeal at the time of writing (March 2010), 61 had resulted in convictions: a conviction rate of 84 per cent.

However, this rate of conviction disguises significant disparities by nationality of defendants. Serb defendants had a 96 per cent conviction rate, Croats 66.6 per cent, and Bosniacs 62.5 per cent. Moreover, there were significant differences in the prison terms to which persons from different national groups were sentenced. Convicted Bosniacs had been sentenced to a total of 47.5 years in prison, or an average of 9.5 years each. Croats had been sentenced to a total of 147 years, or 13.3 years each. Serbs had been sentenced to a total of 770.5 years,[49] or 18 years each. One might react to these figures by replying that the Serbs were disproportionately abusive during the course of the Yugoslavian wars. Moreover they were fighting on three fronts, not just one: they had wars in Croatia, Kosovo and Bosnia, all of which the ICTY has a mandate to address. However, this would not address disparities in conviction rates, which suggest either that the prosecution is bringing cases against non-Serbs that are not as strong or not as well prepared (for example because disproportionate resources are being channelled into prosecutions against Serbs), or the Court is more reluctant to convict non-Serbs on the basis of evidence of a given strength.

Although the Serbs probably were disproportionately abusive compared to the other sides, at least in the Bosnian war, it is not clear that the disparity is as glaring as the ICTY's prosecution figures suggest. Of the approximately 100 000 victims of the Bosnian war, some 65 per cent were Bosnian Muslims, 25 per cent were Serbs and 8 per cent were Croats. These compare to pre-war population ratios of 43.5 per cent Muslims, 31 per cent Serbs and 17 per cent Croats. Certainly Muslims suffered disproportionately during the Bosnian war, but that may in part have been because Serb troops had superior weapons and hardware. Although no equally accurate figures exist for the war in Croatia, the best estimate is that some

20000 people died in the war, of which perhaps 12000 were Croats and 8000 Serbs.[50] Deaths in the 1998–2000 Kosovo war are more contested; one NGO has placed the number of deaths at 13400, of which 69 per cent were Albanians and 18 per cent were Serbs.[51] Figures such as these can never give a true measure of wartime atrocities; some war crimes, such as forced displacement of civilians, can be committed without killing people. Controversy will remain about the extent to which the ICTY exhibited prosecutorial and judicial bias, but the significant skew in favour of prosecuting, convicting and sentencing Serb defendants over others has not been adequately explained, and leaves a lingering anxiety over the partiality of the tribunal. Certainly the popular perception is that Serb aggression was the principal cause of the war; the concern is that the ICTY has been influenced by that perception, in a desire to write a politically acceptable history rather than as an impartial prosecutorial and judicial institution.

If concerns exist about the partiality of the ICTY, that disquiet is multiplied several times for the International Criminal Tribunal for Rwanda (ICTR). Established by UN Security Council Resolution 955 of 8 November 1994, the ICTR was a parallel response to a far more significant loss of life. The ICTR has been the subject of far less critical analysis than the ICTY, a fact which in itself calls for explanation. Despite formally being a very similar structure, with a statute that borrowed heavily from that of the ICTY (including the definitions of the crimes the tribunal has jurisdiction to try, which are virtually identical in each case), it was a far less effective institution. On 6 April 1994, a well-planned genocide of Rwanda's Tutsi minority by militias from its Hutu majority commenced, leaving between 500000 and 1 million dead (including an estimated 75 per cent of Rwanda's Tutsi population) by the time the Rwandan Patriotic Front (RPF), a Tutsi-led military force, overran the country on 18 July 1994. Five thousand people a day were being killed for a hundred days. Less well known than the genocide of Tutsis were the extensive atrocities committed by the RPF itself during the course of the conflict and immediately thereafter. It is estimated that between 25000 and 45000 Hutu civilians died in the course of the RPF's war against the Hutu government; a further unascertained number died after the end of the war in the course of RPF reprisal attacks.[52]

Of the 81 persons indicted by the ICTR, all are Hutus. The tribunal has made no effort to investigate atrocities committed by the RPF (in government continuously since July 1994 to the present day). There can be no doubt that the tribunal displays ethnic partiality. The reason for this is clear enough: the tribunal is wary of crossing the government of Rwanda, in whose territory its prosecutor is operating and whose cooperation is necessary for it to fulfil its mandate. The Rwandan government has been ambivalent enough about the tribunal in any event, dissatisfied that it not located in Rwanda, does not apply the death penalty, wastes money and is exceptionally slow.[53] Given low level hostility by the Rwandan government towards the ICTR, the conventional historical narrative – that all atrocities were committed by Hutus and none by Tutsis – is too convenient for the Tribunal to take the political risk of departing from it.

Indeed the Rwandan government is right that the ICTR suffers from heinous delays. At the time of writing, of the 23 defendants for whom their first instance trials are underway, only three have been in custody at the tribunal's seat, Arusha in Tanzania, for less than five years. Fifteen have been in custody pending trial for more than ten years; of those, two arrived in Arusha in November 1996. The ICTY does not have a formidable reputation for haste either. At the time of writing Ante Gotovina, Croatian military commander responsible for Operation Storm to drive Serb civilians out of Krajina in August 1995, has been in custody without conviction for over four years. The Prlić defendants (charged with persecution of Muslims in Herzegovina) have been waiting five and a half years, Vojislav Šešelj (charged with ethnic cleansing in eastern Bosnia) over six and a half years. However it is not clear why, when the ICTR has had half the case load of the ICTY, its delays should be so much worse. It is also unclear why the ICTR has indicted fewer people when the atrocities it was investigating were so much more widespread than those investigated by the ICTY. Indeed, perhaps the most damning criticism of the ICTR is that it seems superfluous given the willingness of Rwandan courts themselves to prosecute Hutus in connection with the genocide. In 1997, over 92000 genocide suspects were imprisoned in Rwanda. The courts of Rwanda have been exceptionally busy and effective in both prosecuting some of the most prominent organisers of the genocide, and rehabilitating lesser participants under a programme of community reintegration. It is not therefore clear what value was served in taking some 80-odd individuals out of the domestic system and processing them through an international tribunal that lacks credibility or solid support from the Rwandan government.

Notwithstanding, these tribunals have absorbed enormous sums of money in their operation. They have cost well over US$1 billion each over the course of the 14 years in which they have been operating. For 2008–2009, the ICTY's annual budget was US$188 million, the equivalent figure for the ICTR US$133 million. Both institutions are hugely expensive, slow and inefficient. Even the United Nations has become tired of them, forcing both courts to issue completion plans for termination of their activities. Even so in 2010, some 16 years after hostilities ended in Rwanda and 15 years after the end of the Bosnian war, the courts still have significant unfinished caseloads. Even excluding the 11 suspects still at large, the

ICTR has 26 cases yet to reach a first instance judgment and a further 11 awaiting the outcome of appeals. Given that only 39 cases have been finally decided, it is not hard to conclude that after 16 years the tribunal is barely half way through its docket. The ICTY is doing a little better: as of March 2010 it has 25 cases still at first instance trial, plus a further 14 on appeal, compared to 72 cases it has completed following trials. Still, one can expect the ICTY also to continue for some years to come, as the UN Secretary General has himself admitted.[54] The tribunals can keep working notwithstanding their delays because nobody has the courage to say that victims of genocide should not see their tormentors in the dock.

The tribunals are trading on significant groundswells of western European public support for international justice in the face of terrible crimes. They can continue indefinitely, for so long as they have defendants to try. The UN General Assembly will continue funding them, and the ICTY prosecutor continues insisting on the hunt for Ratko Mladić and Goran Hadžić, the tribunal's final outstanding fugitives. Given that apprehension of Mladić, at least, is set as a precondition for Serbia's accession talks with the EU,[55] and given Serbia has shown no inclination or ability to supply them to the tribunal over the last 14 years, we may be waiting a long time. While these men remain at large, and while the extended trials of leading political figures from the Bosnian war such as Karadžić and Gotovina stretch on, the ICTY has a level of political comfort about its future. Nobody can wrap the tribunal up while such important work is outstanding. This is a sentiment the ICTR can trade upon too, even though its outstanding fugitives are names few have heard of in the west. International courts of any kind, even if ad hoc and established to address specific historical events, turn out to be remarkably hard to close down. The only tangible imminent danger to these tribunals is that they may be eclipsed by a new institution, the International Criminal Court (ICC). About that tribunal, albeit still in its infancy, we should now make some remarks, followed by a brief detour into a number of other specialist 'hybrid' tribunals whose developments were motivated by failures in the ICTY, ICTR and ICC.

THE ORIGINS OF THE INTERNATIONAL CRIMINAL COURT

Spurred on by success in persuading the Security Council to pass resolutions creating the ICTY and ICTR, in 1994 the ILC presented a draft statute for a permanent international criminal court, and a series of UN committees thereafter negotiated a statute signed by 120 countries in Rome in 1998. The process was subject to enormous pressure by NGOs, a committee of over 2500 of which established a 'Coalition for the International Criminal Court'.[56] Their influence in the statute of the court established as a result shows. The provisions of the ICC's statute bear many parallels with those of the ICTY and the ICTR, providing for jurisdiction to prosecute 'genocide', 'crimes against humanity' and 'war crimes'.[57] In a throwback to the Nuremberg trials, an extra category of crime was added, entitled 'the crime of aggression', suggesting that the Court would consider complaints of violations of the standard of *jus ad bellum* as well as *jus in bello*. It is no surprise, however, to read in the statute that 'the Court shall exercise jurisdiction over the crime of aggression' only 'once a provision is adopted . . . defining the crime', something which may not happen until at least seven years have passed after the statute has entered into force.[58]

The definition of genocide in the Rome Statute is the same as for the prior tribunals; but the definitions of 'crimes against humanity' and 'war crimes' are elaborated significantly, in evocative and graphic terms. For instance, 'forced pregnancy', a 'crime against humanity', is defined as 'the unlawful confinement of a woman forcibly made pregnant, with the intent of affecting the ethnic composition of any population or carrying out other grave violations of international law'.[59] This type of definition is bizarre. It seems just one very specialist version of the well-established crimes of rape and kidnapping; there seems no good policy reason why so specific an offence should be defined. Similarly, 'enslavement' is defined as 'exercise of any or all of the powers attaching to the right of ownership over a person', including 'in the course of trafficking persons, in particular women and children'.[60] Again, it is not clear why this highly specific definition is necessary beyond a blander definition of kidnapping. Is the intention to exclude adult men from the category of possible victims of enslavement? If not, then why is the final clause of the definition there at all? Perhaps most revealingly, the list of events classified as 'war crimes' is extended beyond the terms of the Geneva Conventions to include an extended NGO-inspired shopping list of ghastly events, including 'physical mutilation or. . .medical or scientific experiments', 'killing or wounding treacherously individuals belonging to the hostile nation or army' (what is a 'treacherous' killing or wounding?), or 'committing outrages on personal dignity' (a matter about which, in the context of war, there could be significant differences of opinion). This is more the language of human rights pressure groups than of legal precision; it bears scant relationship to the language of domestic criminal law.

The crimes defined contain numerous references to generic 'international law', as though that were some established body of doctrine, without taking care to define what is being referred to. Thus 'persecution' is a crime if it is undertaken on 'grounds that are universally recognized as impermissible under international law'.[61] But there is nothing universally recognised in international law; it is the youngest, most fluid and most contested area of law in existence. There is an exception to the crime of 'deportation or forcible transfer of population' where there exist 'grounds permitted under international law',[62] without any attempt to define what those grounds are or to refer to the source of international law setting them out. Then there are crimes so specific and so narrowly defined it is hard to understand the circumstances in which they would be committed. 'The crime of apartheid' is identified as involving 'inhumane acts of a character similar to those referred to in paragraph 1'. Paragraph 1 includes murder, enslavement, torture, extermination, etc.; what acts are similar to extermination or torture but not in fact the same?

The crime of apartheid also contains the proviso that these similar acts must be 'committed in the context of an institutionalized regime of systematic oppression and domination by one racial group over any other racial group' and 'with the intention of maintaining that regime'. What if a person commits acts similar to extermination but with the intention not of maintaining any particular regime but just because (s)he is a sadist? Is a detailed investigation into motive really necessary for the ascription of criminal liability? (Criminal law normally seeks to avoid inspection of motives, at least for the purposes of determining liability if not sentence, on the grounds that they are too subjective to discern and too easy to misrepresent after the fact.) What is an institutional regime of systematic oppression? What about casual or disorganised oppression? When is systematic oppression not undertaken in the context of a regime? Why is the category of 'crimes of apartheid' necessary at all, given the list in paragraph 1, all of which are crimes anyway? Any act falling within the definition of apartheid will inevitably fall *ipso facto* into another category of serious crime. The crimes defined in the Rome Statute also contain a number of remarkably imprecise standards that grant the prosecutor and the court broad discretion. The court has jurisdiction over 'war crimes' which are 'in particular. . .part of a large-scale commission of such crimes'.[63] Does this mean small-scale war crimes are not covered? What is a 'large scale'? Property destruction is a war crime only where 'excessive'. Launching an attack in the knowledge that civilians will be harmed is a war crime if 'clearly excessive'. Who is to determine what is clearly excessive: military men, or international judges?

Good criminal law does not need evocative and alarming descriptions, combined with broad generalisations and subjective discretionary tests. Rather, it is technical and dry. In common law legal systems, ambiguities in definitions of criminal offences can lead to a crime being declared unconstitutional or unenforceable, by reason of its being so vague that a person cannot know in advance, through reading the legislation, just what conduct is and is not being criminalised.[64] The value of such a principle – that people in every walk of life ought to have confidence in the conduct that will land them in jail – was lost upon the drafters of the Rome Statute, who apparently wished maximum flexibility for the court to pursue prosecutions without being tied to narrow, technical or legalistic definitions. By developing international criminal law in its own uniquely florid language, the drafters are encouraging a sort of intellectual ambiguity. Rather than establishing rigorous categories against which a defendant's conduct can be assessed, descriptions at once both vague and highly specialised are subject to casual and imprecise use. Some of the categories of crime listed in the Rome Statute may never be used; others will probably be overused and twisted to fit whatever facts appear before the court. Through its abandonment of definitional rigour, the ICC will be less a court of law, more of a political lobby group appealing to moral outrage to perpetuate its mandate. This is law made by pressure groups rather than by practising lawyers.

Mostly absent from the jurisprudence of the ICTR, the notion of a joint criminal enterprise also crept back into the ICC. A person is liable for a crime if (s)he 'in any. . .way contributes to the commission or attempted commission of such a crime by a group of persons acting with a common purpose'. The contribution may 'be made with the aim of furthering the criminal activity or purpose of the group, where such activity or purpose involves the commission of a crime within the jurisdiction of the Court'.[65] In other words, if a person is part of a group which intends to commit any crime, then (s)he is liable for whatever crime any other member of the group commits, even if (s)he does not know about it and did not intend that it occur. Although none of the current indictments raised by the ICC refers explicitly to the joint criminal enterprise provisions in the Rome Statute, virtually all of them advance similar types of case theory. For instance the indictment against Omar Bashir, President of Sudan, alleges that pursuant to a counter-insurgency campaign, Government of Sudan forces and militias conducted a counter-insurgency campaign which resulted in the commission of 'crimes against humanity'. It is said that Bashir 'played an essential role in coordinating. . .the design and implementation of the. . .counter-insurgency campaign' by virtue of his being '*de facto*. . .Commander in Chief of the Sudanese Armed forces'.[66] Nothing is alleged about his knowledge, intention or even any reason he might have to believe that any crimes against humanity were being committed.

Bashir may or may not have known the Sudanese armed forces were committing atrocities. But the important point is that the prosecution has not apparently seen it necessary to allege that he did. This is surprising; for under ordinary principles of criminal law, if a defendant has no knowledge that a crime is taking place, he cannot be convicted of it. Before the ICC, as before the ICTY, it appears that a defendant's knowledge of what was going on is mostly irrelevant. All one needs to show is that (a) there was a plan to achieve certain war objectives; (b) the defendant was party to that plan; and (c) in pursuance of that plan, wrongful acts were committed. This is well below the standard of criminal responsibility in most domestic legal systems, and in principle it makes convictions of political leaders easy. It remains to be seen what the conviction rate before the ICC will be; after spending several hundred million dollars over the course of seven years, the court has still not completed a single trial. However, if the ICTY's record is anything to go by, conviction rates can be expected to be high. If so, the flexibility incorporated into international criminal law by the concept of a joint criminal enterprise will be one reason why.

There was significant delay in getting the ICC up and running by reason of the refusal of the United States, Russia and China to support it. The ICC would be an independent international organisation and, by signing up to the Court's statute, the member states were agreeing to extradite to the Court any person indicted by it.[67] This feature alarmed the United States in particular, concerned about extradition of members of its own armed forces that operate in theatres all over the world. The United States signed the Rome Statute on 31 December 2000, the last day the treaty was open for signature and in the dying days of Bill Clinton's Presidency. George W. Bush was due to take office on 20 January 2001, and on 6 May 2002 the United States renounced the treaty. It then threatened to shut down the UN peacekeeping mission in Bosnia unless UN peacekeepers were granted immunity from ICC prosecution, a principle which it persuaded the UN Security Council to adopt in Resolution 1422 on 12 July 2002. The United States then started a campaign of negotiating bilateral agreements with other states in which they would undertake not to extradite various categories of one another's citizens to the ICC. At the time of writing the USA has succeeded in negotiating 102 such agreements, with almost as many states as have ratified the Rome Statute. While the ability of one nation to immunise itself almost completely from the jurisdiction of the International Criminal Court was being plainly demonstrated, the Court started grinding into operation, albeit painfully slowly. The Rome Statute came into force on 11 April 2002; this event was critical, since under the terms of the statute the Court has no jurisdiction in respect of crimes that occurred prior to this date.[68] Various appointments of judges, prosecutors and other officials were not completed until November 2003.

It was not until June 2004 that the prosecutor launched his first formal investigation, into events in the Democratic Republic of Congo (DRC). The first arrest warrant was issued only on 17 March 2006, against Thomas Lubanga Dyilo, for use of child soldiers and civilian massacres in northeast DRC. Mr Lubanga was a convenient choice for he was already in custody in DRC, an enemy of the western-backed Kinshasa government and a prisoner of it, and the prosecutor had commenced an investigation at the request of the DRC government. He was transferred to the Hague on the same day as his indictment was issued. The ICC held its first ever court hearing, to confirm the charges against Mr Lubanga, on 9 November 2006. Germain Katanga, a colleague of Mr Lubanga's working in the same area and arrested at the same time, was the next to be transferred to the ICC, on 17 October 2007. Mr Chui, another enemy of the Kinshasa government, followed on 6 February 2008. Further arrest warrants have been issued by the ICC against a Tutsi warlord, Bosco Ntaganda, as part of DRC's ongoing political and military dispute with Rwanda over control and influence in eastern Congo; and against Jean-Pierre Bemba Gambo, the runner up in DRC's 2006 presidential election, a DRC senator, and one of the richest men in the country. The former individual remains at large; the latter was arrested under a sealed (i.e. secret) indictment while in Belgium. From this record, it appears that the ICC exists to support the Kinshasa government's political agenda in eastern DRC; nobody aligned with the Kinshasa government has been investigated or indicted by the ICC. Mr Lubanga's trial began on 26 January 2009 and collapsed on 15 July 2010 amidst judicial complaints that the prosecution was ignoring the court's rulings.[69] The trials of Messrs Katanga and Chui began on 24 November 2009. These are the only trials underway at the time of writing. Mr Bemba is in custody awaiting trial; a fifth defendant, Abu Garda, a rebel leader in Darfur accused of war crimes, is currently released on his own recognisance, having voluntarily attended the ICC in the Hague to face the charges against him in a preliminary hearing. His trial has yet to be scheduled, and it is not known whether he will return to the Netherlands when it begins.

Apart from these individuals, the only indictments issued are against four Lords Resistance Army (LRA) rebel leaders from northern Uganda, the President of Sudan and one of his Ministers, and a Janjaweed militia leader from Darfur. The ICC has been remarkably unhurried in the seven years it has been in existence; and of the individuals it has indicted, there seems little prospect of any of them being extradited to the Court in the near future. The LRA leaders were indicted at the request of the pro-western Ugandan government; no indictments have been levelled against Ugandan government officials arising out of a bloody civil war in the north of the country from 1987 to the present, in which both pro-government and rebel forces have committed atrocities. The Sudanese indictments were raised at the request of the UN Security Council, as part of a programme of pressure to pursue a peace agreement in Darfur. Everybody the ICC has indicted so far has been a black African, either in opposition to an established government supported by the west or a member of the pariah Sudanese government. In its frail political condition, and in the face of rejection of the Court by the USA, Russia, China and Israel, the ICC dares not investigate war crimes committed in the ongoing conflicts in Afghanistan, Israel/Palestine, Russia/Georgia, Iraq or Pakistan, due to the strong interests of the Great Powers involved. War crimes in Iraq were dismissed by the ICC prosecutor as insufficiently serious to investigate.[70] It has no interest in investigating the conflict in Somalia, since there is no government in this lawless land that can extradite anyone. DRC and Uganda are perfect client states for the ICC: the Court can rely upon cooperative governments to arrest indictees. Investigation in Sudan is the product of political expediency, so that the Court may ingratiate itself with the United States and other powers interested in a settlement in the country.

In the face of so modest a case load, it is hard to say whether the trends emerging in the cases the prosecutor chooses to investigate and indict will be replicated in the future. However, it can fairly be said that the Court is in no hurry. The delays in completing trials (at the time of writing Mr Lubanga has been in ICC custody without a verdict for over four years) are hard to understand. They can hardly be put down to docket pressure; Mr Lubanga is the Court's first case. This does not bode well for future cases; should the ICC ever acquire a moderately busy docket (say 10 cases a year, compared with some 400–500 cases a year at London's Old Bailey, each of which typically waits only seven to eight months to come to trial),[71] we may see the ICC develop case delays comparable to the ICTR. The other problem facing the ICC is that now its trickle of DRC-indicted defendants has apparently run dry, it ought not to try its cases too quickly, lest it cannot procure any more defendants and runs the risk of appearing irrelevant through disuse. The ICC has a colossal budget to justify, costing some €80 million in 2007 and €100 million in 2009, with a staff of over 600 people in 2009. These people need something to do; and save for a few cases where unsavoury African leaders hand over their political opponents for trial, and Mr Abu Garda's salutary voluntary submission to the Court aside, it does not seem that the ICC possesses a credible mechanism for compelling defendants to submit to its jurisdiction. Despite the formidable financial resources its swallows, the ICC may be condemned to working at a glacially gentle pace indefinitely.

'HYBRID' TRIBUNALS

While the melodrama of the ICC's indictments was gradually playing out, the ICTY and the ICTR were followed by a series of other hybrid international criminal tribunals, which were ostensibly specialist national courts but with international judges and prosecutors applying versions of international criminal law enacted into domestic legislation. *A priori*, this may not sound like a good idea; but the notion gained ground precisely because the ICTY and ICTR were so phenomenally expensive and slow, yet proved themselves frustratingly durable well beyond the time limits within which their western paymasters wanted to fund them. A number of hybrid courts emerged. The first of these was the Special Panels of the Dili District Court, a series of trial chambers established by the UN Transitional Administration in East Timor after the province voted in favour of independence from Indonesia in a referendum in 1999. The Panels were established to hear allegations of serious crimes committed in East Timor during the course of the Indonesian withdrawal, in which violent clashes were initiated principally by Indonesian security forces and militias loyal to Indonesia. Each sat with one Timorese judge and two international judges. In the period from 2001 to 2006 when they were operational, the Panels tried 88 people, with a 93 per cent conviction rate on a not guilty plea. Although this appears impressively rapid by the leisurely standards of the ICTY and ICTR, particularly given the Panels' relatively modest budget (for example US$6.3 million for 2002), this figure masked some concerning underlying trends. Some 95 per cent of the Panels' budget went to the prosecution. The remaining 5 per cent went to the international judges' salaries. Virtually no funds were made available for the severely inexperienced office of defence counsel, which as a result did not call a single witness in any of the first 14 trials.

Indeed the problems with the Panels were legion. There were no clerks or judicial assistants. For at least the first 18 months no hearing transcripts were taken. Lack of translators frequently delayed proceedings. There were very few appeals (the appeals chamber did not function). None of the Timorese judges had prior judicial experience. None of the high-level leaders were prosecuted. The Panels ceased work with some 514 cases outstanding. Indonesia took advantage of the chaos by setting up its own special court ostensibly to try perpetrators of the Timorese unrest, a system heavily biased in favour of the defendants, and then refused to extradite to the Panels. The Panel system was widely acknowledged as poorly conceived and inadequately executed.[72] If the ICTY and the ICTR were instances of bloated profligacy, the East Timor Panels were examples of what happens where there is no real political interest in an international judicial process. Experienced international lawyers were not recruited; the necessary funds were not made available; the UN refused to criticise Indonesia, because neither the USA nor Australia (the dominant powers in the region) wished to alienate a newly democratic and allied Indonesian government. The court was hamstrung by a lack of international interest in its successful operation. In the absence of that interest, it lacked any kind of accountability, strung out by resident UN officials and with its limited budget unwisely divided.

The next hybrid courts, the Special Court for Sierra Leone, the Extraordinary Chambers in the Courts of Cambodia and the Special Tribunal for Lebanon, can all be dealt with relatively shortly, principally because they all have so few cases. Sierra Leone had suffered from an ongoing civil war since 1991, which pitted the Revolutionary United Front (RUF), renowned for mutilating civilians with machetes, against various military and civilian government regimes. In 1997 the Armed Forces Revolutionary Council (a loose grouping of soldiers) staged a coup against a civilian government, entered into coalition with the RUF, fell out with them and the civil war entered a phase of renewed intensity as the two groups fought one another. ECOMOG (a multilateral armed force established by the Economic Community of West African States) and UN peacekeepers arrived in 1998 to support the civilian government, but failed to stabilise the situation. British troops arrived in 2000, ostensibly to evacuate foreign nationals but stayed on indefinitely, rooting out insurgent groups and encouraging rival military groups to disarm. In 2000 the civilian President agreed with the UN to establish a special court jointly administered by the UN and the domestic government to try the most serious breaches of the laws of war. This tribunal was established in Sierra Leonean law by the Special Court Ratification Act 2002. The court would have mixed panels of domestic and foreign judges and prosecutors, with its seat in Freetown, the capital of Sierra Leone.

The court started work in 2002, but in six years has completed only three trials against eight defendants, of whom three died before conclusion of proceedings. All five remaining defendants were found guilty, with long sentences of up to 52 years' imprisonment. At the time of writing the Sierra Leone Court has no cases. Its sole defendant is Charles Taylor, former President of Liberia, who is in fact on trial in the building of the International Criminal Court in The Hague, due to concerns over security and quality of the judicial process in Freetown, the capital of Sierra Leone. His trial is for all intents and purposes conducted by the ICC, but pursuant to the procedural rules of the Special Court of Sierra Leone. The indictment against Mr Taylor is another example of how case theories in the style of joint criminal enterprise are used to create vicarious liability.

A ten-page document, his indictment contains broad brush accusations of shocking crimes, including mass looting, mass murder and mass rape. However, as is typical with indictments in international criminal courts, it contains no precise dates, does not identify any victims and describes locations in only broad terms (e.g. '[b]etween about 25 May 1997 and 31 March 1998, in various locations, including Kenema town and the Tongo Fields area'). No particulars of Mr Taylor's responsibility for these vaguely described events are provided. It is alleged that he 'planned, instigated, ordered [or] committed' the events referred to; but no details are provided of what his acts of planning or ordering comprised. The language of a 'common plan, design or purpose in which the accused participated' also creeps into the indictment.[73] At the time of writing Mr Taylor has been in custody for four years, but one cannot help feeling that his conviction has an *a priori* inevitability to it. Presumably the Special Court will thereafter simply disappear.

The Extraordinary Chambers in the Courts of Cambodia is another hybrid tribunal with hardly any defendants. Its principal difficulty is that the last of the events it has jurisdiction over took place in 1979; yet the court did not raise its first (and only) indictments until 31 July 2007, ten years after the initial plan for a tribunal was developed within the walls of the UN.[74] Most of the potential defendants are dead. Of the Court's two sole defendants, one is 83 years old; the other, 'Duch', now 68 years old, was 23 when the Khmer Rouge came to power. Although it was thought Duch had pleaded guilty, the trial descended into farce when on the last two days he apparently changed his plea and asked for acquittal and immediate release.[75] On 26 July 2010 Duch was convicted by the Extraordinary Chambers and sentenced to 35 years' imprisonment. Currently no proceedings are ongoing and the court has no hearings scheduled. The court has a full plenum of seven trial judges, nine appeal judges, four investigative judges, four prosecutors and seven pre-trial judges, but no work for any of them to do, and little prospect of finding any more living defendants.

The Special Tribunal for Lebanon, a UN-Lebanese hybrid court 'to prosecute persons responsible for the. . .death of [former] Prime Minister Rafiq Hariri' (who died in a bomb blast in Beirut in February 2005), is another political charade. The Special Tribunal's statute provides that it will apply domestic law; it is not clear what function the tribunal performs that the domestic Lebanese courts could not undertake. Although it has judges, prosecutors, a court building and an Office of Defence Counsel, the tribunal has no defendants, no hearings, no cases and no suspects. The only four people arrested for Hariri's murder were released by order of the tribunal in April 2009, for 'complete absence of reliable proof against them'.[76]

The Court of Bosnia and Herzegovina (or Court of BiH) is also worth considering, as it is sometimes cited as an example of a successful hybrid tribunal.[77] The original rationale for creating this court was a desire, formulated in about 2000, to close the ICTY, which was absorbing far too much money and appeared destined to continue indefinitely. (The Court of BiH did not succeed in this goal; the ICTY remains in full-blooded operation at the time of writing, some ten years later, and as expensive as ever.) Unlike prior hybrid tribunals, the Court of BiH was established not by a formal agreement between the Bosnian government and the UN, but by unilateral dictate of Bosnia's High Representative, its international governor.[78] The institution was driven by a series of international fiats, and therefore it is unsurprising that it has never gained widespread domestic acceptance. Moreover, the Court became hijacked by the international community's agenda in the country, which was to undermine the ethnic partition of Bosnia into a complex array of federal units and subunits at the end of the Bosnian war.

Before the establishment of the Court of BiH, the country's court system was controlled by its federal units, which operated under distinct legal systems and with mutually exclusive geographical jurisdiction. The courts were ethnically homogenous, and had virtually no relationship with one another. The Court of BiH was seen as an opportunity to strengthen Bosnia's central government by creating a multiethnic 'state court' with jurisdiction across the territory of the entire country. As well as having a war crimes chamber, which would take over part of the caseload of the ICTY, the Court would also have a chamber hearing cases of organised crime, and a third chamber, hearing administrative law complaints. In the end, the third chamber was tacitly abandoned: as of 2010, it had never heard a case, meaning that decisions of Bosnia's central government are subject to no effective judicial review. The other two chambers got off to a slow start. Despite the legislation establishing the Court being imposed by international decree in 2000, the first indictment was not issued until late November 2004. The Court would have mixed panels of judges (two international judges and one domestic judge), international prosecutors and domestic defence counsel. The system was adversarial, as opposed to the inquisitorial procedure characteristic of legal practice in former Yugoslavia. Thus domestic defence lawyers were at a disadvantage compared with foreign-trained international prosecutors.

The Court of BiH has faced the same problems of ethnic bias, chronic delay and favour to the prosecution that have cursed the ICTY. Of the 144 defendants indicted by the war crimes chamber so far, 103 have been Serbs, 16 Croats and 25 Bosniacs. At the time of writing, of the sentences handed down by the war crimes chamber, Serbs have been sentenced to a total of 976.25 years' imprisonment, Bosniacs 60 years' and Croats 50.5 years'. Although it is not as prevalent (most of the cases before the Court of BiH do not involve command responsibility theories), the theory of a 'joint criminal enterprise' has crept into the jurisprudence in some cases.[79] Of the cases listed by the Court as completed, the conviction rate on a not guilty plea is 89 per cent. Delay remains the biggest single problem. It is not unusual for defendants to be in custody for two years before a trial even begins; bail is rarely granted; trials typically take 18 months or more to complete; appeals take an extra year, or longer if (as happens relatively frequently) the Appeal Chamber decides to rehear the entire case including all the evidence. If the aim was to speed up trials of war crimes compared to the ICTY, it does not appear to be working. Of the 144 war crimes defendants indicted in five years of the Court's operation, only 43 cases have been finally disposed of at the time of writing. Even if the Court could maintain this pace and issued no further indictments, it would be processing war crimes trials until 2021, some 26 years after the end of the Bosnian war.

In fact the Court's future is in jeopardy. The number of international judges and prosecutors fell from 26 and 15 respectively in 2005, to seven and four by the end of 2009, as the Bosnian Serb Prime Minister took against the Court and frustrated their reappointment,[80] and the Court's political future looks in doubt. For political reasons, the Court of BiH has come to focus on organised crime more than on war crimes, notwithstanding its original *raison d'être*. The organised crime chamber has indicted 313 defendants to date, for a variety of crimes ranging from embezzlement and tax evasion to human trafficking and drug dealing. None of these crimes bears any relationship to international law, and it is difficult to understand why having foreign judges and prosecutors try domestic offences makes much sense. The disproportionate activity in this chamber has been driven by international prosecutors, motivated by international community perception of high levels of corruption and criminality in Bosnian society; fear of institutional weaknesses in the domestic judiciary; relative ease of collecting evidence from more recent events; and a desire to create central state institutions at the expense of Bosnia's federal units. But Bosnia is far from alone in suffering from the twin plagues of organised crime and insufficiently robust domestic judicial institutions. Such frailties do not justify indefinite systems of hybrid international courts which are, in the final analysis, a form of legal colonialism. The longer political goal may be gradually to phase out the international officials on the Court; but there is no evidence that without them the Court of BiH will be able to function.

WHAT NEXT FOR INTERNATIONAL CRIMINAL LAW?

International criminal justice has been nothing if not expansive. The temptation to import international lawyers into post-conflict countries to adjudicate heinous crimes perpetrated in the course of war is perhaps understandable. The lawyers themselves benefit from moral and well-remunerated work and western public opinion, buoyed by effective lobbying by international NGOs, will inevitably be supportive. But the reality of such courts betrays the ideals. International criminal justice is often horrifically expensive, irrelevant, unnecessary, frequently alienates the domestic population and is sometimes grossly unfair. In all cases it exhibits sloppy and politicised jurisprudence. What explanations can be provided for these serial failures?

The explicit political agendas of the founders of these international courts undoubtedly have an important bearing upon the forms they have taken. International criminal lawyers who come to prosecute and adjudicate war crimes want to secure convictions. For the benefit of their own professional records, they want to document that they participated in trials in which abhorrent war criminals were handed heavy sentences for atrocious crimes. In the context of an international court, serious war crimes trials are typically the only (or the principal) cases they will work on. For a domestic court system, the gravest crimes are only a small part of its docket. Conventions regarding the fairness and impartiality of the prosecution and the rights of the accused have developed gradually within the domestic system, often over decades or centuries. Thus those conventions prove durable even in high profile, politically charged cases or prosecutions of the gravest crimes. In courts established outside the context of entrenched domestic legal conventions – indeed, where the judges are drawn from differing national jurisdictions, not all of which may share the same conventions, or may apply them in very different ways – securing impartiality and the rights of the defence may be much harder.

Where the court is established principally or solely to try the gravest crimes, those conventions may be absent or weak, and only lip service may be paid to them. There is political pressure to secure convictions and heavy sentences, to satisfy victims' rights groups and public opinion. Because international criminal courts and their hybrids have no democratic or other accountability, it is rare for external pressure to be brought to bear to ensure impartial or fair procedures. Long delays and extended periods of pre-trial incarceration attract domestic ire in democratic societies, placing pressure upon justice ministries to improve matters. For an international (or hybrid) criminal court, the prime movers are international officials accountable to neither a justice ministry nor any other domestic political authority. Typically they have been appointed by the UN or another international body, itself politically unaccountable. Once they are appointed and the institution is in existence, the international community loses interest in the process. Thus long delays and prosecutorial bias go unchecked; if the quality of defence representation is poor, nobody is too concerned. As with all international organisations budgets spiral, but the expense is tolerated because it is spread thinly between multiple governments. The institutions prove politically impossible to close down once they have reached the expiry of their natural lives, because there is always more work for them to do. In the meantime, international criminal law is developed in ever more abstruse directions by legal scholars, practitioners and judges. The discipline acquires a level of credibility such that it creates its own imperative to be applied in every new post-conflict scenario that arises, notwithstanding arguments that war crimes are better dealt with either by domestic courts or, in the interests of securing the peace, not at all.

This final point is worth dwelling upon briefly in a philosophical context. Those who argue for the advancement of international criminal law typically style themselves as progressive and liberal. As such, the justification of punishment as raw retribution or vengeance is uncomfortable for them. To justify trials and punishments of war crimes, they must appeal either to the notion of deterrence, or to the thought that international criminal law promotes some sort of reconciliation in the aftermath of armed conflict. It is far from clear whether either of these explanations hold water. Certainly neither is true *a priori*, as advocates of international criminal law often seem to assume they are. Indeed there is empirical evidence against both propositions. It is transparent that international criminal law is brought to bear only against defendants who fall out of power. While they remain in office and with political support, their country will never extradite them to an international criminal court. Only once they lose power will they face criminal justice, as Milošević, Taylor and Pinochet discovered. Political leaders fighting wars may be perpetuating conflict precisely to remain in power. Thus they do not factor into their calculations the risk of losing office, and accordingly they work to a presumption that they will never be subject to international criminal prosecution. In the face of international criminal law they may have an incentive to remain in office well beyond a point at which they may otherwise see fit to stand down, for fear of subsequently being made subject to prosecution.

Likewise, it cannot be lost upon political and military leaders engaged in armed conflict worldwide that the risk of prosecution depends upon political factors rather than their conduct during the war. War crimes are prevalent throughout the contemporary world, and in the vast majority of cases go unpunished: consider the actions of the US in Iraq (2003–), the allies in Afghanistan (2001–), the Israelis in Gaza (in particular Operation Cast Lead, an Israeli incursion into Hamas occupied territory in 2009), the Russians and Georgians in their brief war in August 2008, or the prevailing Sri Lankan army in its defeat in 2009 of the Tamil Tigers. None of these wars has been the subject of war crimes prosecutions, nor does it seem likely they ever will be, either because the party committing war crimes was victorious, or because they were the beneficiaries of international political support and thus there is no political will to investigate them. Manifestly, none of the participants in these wars felt deterred by the threat of criminal prosecution. Nor for that matter did the participants in the Serbia-Kosovo hostilities in 1998–99, notwithstanding the existence of significant international public attention and a major ad hoc criminal tribunal already in place and ready to indict and try them should they conduct hostilities in a manner repugnant to international opinion.

The thought that international criminal justice facilitates reconciliation in the aftermath of civil war is superficially attractive, but nebulous in practice. In the former Yugoslavia the activities of the ICTY and, indeed, the Court of BiH have apparently contributed nothing to national reconciliation. Serbs (and to an extent Croats) see these courts as systematically biased against them and incapable of providing a fair trial. In a number of cases they view the defendants as national heroes and martyrs to their cause.[81] Given this attitude, it seems more likely that such tribunals exacerbate ethnic tensions rather than defuse them, reinforcing certain groups' perception of themselves as victims of war crimes (and thus entitled to politically unrealistic reparations, or even the redrawing of constitutional documents and territorial boundaries).[82] Ethnic groups may also see themselves as victims of an unfair and politicised legal process. It is not clear what international criminal justice has added to the unhealthy dynamic of inter-ethnic hostility developed in the Western Balkans over the last 500 years. The ICTR has barely been effective either in this regard; treated by the Rwandan government with scepticism at best, the tribunal has had very little positive impact upon domestic politics. Arguably far more effective at healing the scars of genocide and brutal civil war in that country is the government run programme of rehabilitation and reintegration into Rwandan society of former Interahamwe fighters.[83]

Truth and reconciliation commissions of the kind developed in South Africa[84] may be more effective in promoting social reintegration than are international criminal prosecutions, held at a moral and often geographical distance from the place where war crimes occurred, whose procedures are typically held in low regard and whose phenomenal consumption of financial resources makes local people in poor countries look upon them with a mixture of envy and contempt. Notwithstanding, international criminal law is apparently destined to continue growing. Nobody seems satisfied with it apart from international lawyers, international organisations and the NGOs that have an interest in its continuation. It can continue to expand because any contrary message in the western countries which fund and support it is politically toxic.

What is so intriguing about international criminal law is that it has developed so quickly, from being a purely historical memory of victors' justice at the end of World War II, through to a flourishing, academically respectable and politically unassailable discipline of legal practice in just 15 years since the mid-1990s. Although its tangible benefits to the global polity are negligible, international lawyers were sufficiently astute to observe an autonomous political space within which a brand new discipline of international criminal law could be nurtured. This extraordinary growth was probably due, in the final analysis, to lawyers ruthlessly playing and replaying a political trump card in every post-conflict scenario: the demands of international justice in the face of the horrors of war must be met, and the international community, through its network of international organisations, must pay for it. The international organisations themselves benefited, as they would administer, advise upon, monitor and report upon these new institutions of international justice. Yet international criminal law is not the only field of international law where the political climate was perfectly tuned for explosive growth at the end of the Cold War. To another such area, having developed even more expansively within more or less the same time period, we turn in the next chapter.

NOTES

1. Khabarovsk is a city in the Russian Far East, where the USSR decided to hold war crimes trials in December 1949 that related to Japanese use of biological weapons against Soviet armed forces in World War II.
2. This principle, epitomised in the latin maxim *nullum crimen, nulla poena sine praevia lege poenali* ('No crime, no punishment without prior panel law', first enshrined in the 1813 Criminal Code of Bavaria), is enshrined in Article 7(1) European Convention on Human Rights: 'No one shall be held guilty of any criminal offence on account of any act or omission which did not constitute a criminal offence under national or international law at the time when it was committed. Nor shall a heavier penalty be imposed than the one that was applicable at the time the criminal offence was committed.'
3. See e.g. Article 6 of the Charter of the International Military Tribunal, London, 8 August 1945; Article 5 of the Charter of the International Military Tribunal for the Far East, 19 January 1946.
4. See e.g. Hope, Christopher (2008), 'Number of people escaping jail after a not-guilty plea hits seven-year low', *The Daily Telegraph*, 26 September.

5. See *Felony Defendants in Large Urban Counties, 2004*, Table 19, Adjudication outcome for felony defendants by most serious charge, available at http://bjs.ojp.usdoj.gov (last accessed 23 May 2010). The higher conviction rate in the United States compared with the United Kingdom may be due to the existence of plea bargaining in the former jurisdiction, encouraging defendants in cases where the evidence is border-line to plead guilty to a lesser offence.
6. Articles 4 and 23 and Section III Annex to the Convention with respect to the laws and customs of war on land (Hague II), 29 July 1899; Declaration on the Use of Projectiles the Object of Which is the Diffusion of Asphyxiating or Deleterious Gases, 29 July 1899; Declaration on the use of bullets which expand or flatten easily in the human body, 29 July 1899; Convention relative to the laying of automatic submarine contact mines, 18 October 1907.
7. See von Schaack, Beth and Ron Slye (2007), 'A concise history of international criminal law', Santa Clara University Legal Studies Research Papers Series, Working Paper No. 07-42, September, p.16.
8. See e.g. *USA v Alfried Krupp et al*, Decision of US Military Tribunal III, Nuremberg 10 February 1948; Case IT-95-11 *Prosecutor v Milan Martić*, International Criminal Tribunal for Yugoslavia, Judgment of 12 June 2007; *Trial of Kriminalassistent Karl-Hans Hermann Klinge*, Supreme Court of Norway, Judgment of 27 February 1946.
9. Articles 227 to 229 of the Peace Treaty of Versailles.
10. 'The trials of German major war criminals', Proceedings d the International Military Tribunal sitting at Nuremberg Germany, Vol. 1 (20 November 1945 – 1 December 1945), London: HMSO, 1946, pp.216 *et seq.*
11. Report of Robert Jackson, United States Representative to the International Conference on Military Trials, London, 1945 (Washington, DC: US State Dept., 1949), pp.104–106, 303, quoting Nikitchenko as saying: 'We are dealing here with the chief war criminals who have already been convicted and whose conviction has been already announced by both the Moscow and Crimea [Yalta] declarations by the heads of the [Allied] governments. . .The whole idea is to secure quick and just punishment for the crime.'
12. Utley, Freda (1949), *The High Cost of Vengeance*, Chicago: Henry Rengery.
13. Articles 19 and 21 of the Charter of the International Military Tribunal.
14. Sereny, Gitta (1996), *Albert Speer: His battle with truth*, London: Vintage, p.578.
15. Sereny, ibid.
16. Minutes of the International Military Tribunal, 6 April 1946.
17. See e.g. Dower, John (1999), *Embracing Defeat*, New York: W.W. Norton, pp.323 *et seq*.
18. Gold, Hal (2004), *Unit 731 Testimony*, Tokyo: Tuttle Publishing, p.109.
19. For example, 'Defendant Wilhelm Keitel, on the Counts of the Indictment on which you have been convicted, the Tribunal sentences you to death by hanging.'
20. 'The trials of German major war criminals', 1946, pp.50–51.
21. Quoted in Brook, Timothy (2001), 'The Tokyo Judgment and the Rape of Nanking', *Journal of Asian Studies*, **60** (3) (August).
22. The Research and Documentation Centre in Sarajevo is generally considered to provide the most reliable statistics concerning the Bosnian war. Its 2007 report identified 97 207 Bosnian citizens killed and missing during the war. Some 70 per cent of the deaths occurred in the first six months.
23. Fewer comprehensive studies of deaths in the Croatian war have taken place, but most sources place the number of fatalities at approximately 20 000: see e.g. Grubanović, Saša (2003) 'The first official visit by a Croatian president to Belgrade since 1991 results in surprise apologies from both sides for wartime evils', *Transitions Online*, 15 September. The majority of those casualties took place in 1991; the balance, some 3000, occurred in August 1995, as Croatian forces expelled Serbs from Serb-occupied areas of Croatia in 'Operation Storm'.
24. The first three Geneva conventions, negotiated in 1864, 1906 and 1929, set standards for

treatment of the sick and wounded on land, treatment of the sick and wounded at sea and treatment of prisoners of war respectively. The 1949 Geneva Convention develops the principles set out in the earlier conventions and creates extensive obligations for treatment of civilians.

25. Article 146 Fourth Geneva Convention 1949.
26. The general rule is set in Article 2(4) of the UN Charter. The exceptions are contained in Articles 42 and 51.
27. Perhaps the defining statement of obligations *erga omnes* in international law was made by the ICJ in *Barcelona Traction* (Belgium v Spain) (Second Phase) ICJ Rep 1970, 3, para. 33: 'an essential distinction should be drawn between the obligations of a State towards the international community as a whole, and those arising vis-à-vis another State in the field of diplomatic protection. By their very nature, the former are the concern of all States. In view of the importance of the rights involved, all States can be held to have a legal interest in their protection; they are obligations *erga omnes.* [at 34] Such obligations derive, for example, in contemporary international law, from the outlawing of acts of aggression, and of genocide, as also from the principles and rules concerning the basic rights of the human person, including protection from slavery and racial discrimination. Some of the corresponding rights of protection have entered into the body of general international law. . . others are conferred by international instruments of a universal or quasi-universal character'. The concept is closely related to the notion of *jus cogens* norms in international law, which are regarded as so fundamental by the international community of nations that no derogation is ever permitted. See Article 53 Vienna Convention on the Law of Treaties: 'A treaty is void if, at the time of its conclusion, it conflicts with a peremptory norm of general international law. For the purposes of the present Convention, a peremptory norm of general international law is a norm accepted and recognized by the international community of states as a whole as a norm from which no derogation is permitted and which can be modified only by a subsequent norm of general international law having the same character'.
28. See UN General Assembly Resolution 260B(III) of 9 December 1948; Official Records of the General Assembly, Seventh Session, Supplement No. 11 (A/2136).
29. Official Records of the General Assembly, Ninth Session, Supplement No. 12 (A/2645).
30. Yearbook of the International Law Commission 1954, Volume II.
31. Articles 2 to 5 of the Statute of the ICTY (adopted 25 May 1993 by UNSC Resolution 827, amended 13 May 1998 by UNSC Resolution 1166 and 30 November 2000 by UNSC Resolution 1329).
32. In England and Wales murder is a 'common law offence', whose elements are defined entirely by case law rather than statute. See e.g. *R v Moloney* [1985] AC 905; *Leung Kam Kwok* v *R* (1985) C App Rep 83, PC.
33. See *R v Moloney*, ibid., AC 905 at 925, per Lord Bridge (whether a person who realised there was a probability (but not a virtual certainty or very high probability) that death might result from his conduct but was indifferent to that risk may be convicted of murder); *Thabo Meli v R* (1954) 1 All ER 373 (intent to kill need not be contemporaneous with act of killing for a murder conviction, where both the intent and the act causing death occurred as part of a preconceived plan to murder).
34. For the commission of offences through innocent agents, see e.g. *R v Manley* (1844) 3 LTOS 22, 1 Cox CC 104; *R v Stringer & Banks* [1992] 94 Cr App Rep 13, CA.
35. See e.g. *Smith v Reynolds* [1986] Crim LR 559.
36. See e.g. *R v Allan* [1965] 1 QB 130; *R v Tait* [1993] Crim LR 538. Subjective recklessness may also be sufficient, i.e., the defendant actually foresees the risk of the third person committing the crime, but does not care: *Blakely and Sutton v Chief Constable of West Mercia Constabulary* [1991] RTR 405. See also *DPP for Northern Ireland v Lynch* [1975] AC 653 (a person who knows of another's criminal purpose and voluntarily aids him in it can be criminally liable for assistance).
37. Article 7(1) of the ICTY's statute provides that '[a] person who planned, instigated, ordered, committed or otherwise aided and abetted in the planning, preparation or

execution of a crime. . .shall be individually responsible for the crime'. But none of these terms is elaborated, nor is their *actus reus* or *mens rea* (the necessary physical and mental elements of an offence respectively) defined.

38. Antonio Cassese, formerly President of the ICTY, has confirmed this as his own view. '[V]ictims are prepared to be reconciled with their erstwhile tormentors, because they know that the latter have now paid for their crimes; a fully reliable record is established of atrocities so that future generations can remember and be made fully cognisant of what happened': Cassese, Atonio (1998), 'Reflections on international criminal justice', Modern Law Review, **61**, 1. See also the *Opening Statement of Justice Jackson, Chief Prosecutor for the United States*, in 'The trials of the German major war criminals', Vol. 2, (14 November 1945 – 1 October 1946), London: HMSO, 1947, p.98.
39. A concluded agreement to perform an unlawful act is necessary for the crime of conspiracy to be committed in England; if no agreement is reached then a charge of conspiracy will fail. See e.g. *Mulcahy v R* (1868) LR 3 HL 306; *R v Thomson* (1966) 50 Cr.App.R. 1.
40. *Prosecutor v Tadić*, Case No. IT-94-1, Trial Chamber Judgment 7 May 1997; Appeal Chamber Judgment 15 July 1999.
41. Ibid., para. 195.
42. *Prosecutor v Krnojelac*, Case No. IT-97-25A, Appeals Chamber Judgment 17 September 2003, paragraphs 96 and 203.
43. *Prosecutor v Tadić*, Appeal Chamber Judgment 15 July 1999, paragraph 204.
44. See e.g. *Prosecutor v Simić*, Case IT-95-9-T, Separate Opinion of Per-Johan Lindholm J, Trial Chamber Judgment 17 October 2003; Danner, Allison and Jenny Martinez (2005), 'Guilty associations: joint criminal enterprise, command responsibility, and the development of international criminal law', *California Law Review*, **93**, 75; van der Wilt, Harmen (2007), 'Joint criminal enterprise: possibilities and limitations', *Journal of International Criminal Justice*, (1), 91; Gustafson, K. (2005), 'The requirement of an express agreement for joint criminal enterprise liability', *Journal of International Criminal Justice*, **3**, 11.
45. *Prosecutor v Karadžić*, Case IT-95-5/18, Third Amended Indictment dated 19 October 2009.
46. *Prosecutor v Milošević* (IT-02-54), Second amended indictment (Kosovo) 29 October 2001; Second amended indictment (Croatia) 28 July 2004; Second amended indictment (Bosnia) 22 November 2002. Of particular interest in the *Milošević* case is that the indictments in respect of actions in Croatia and Bosnia were not raised in either case until late 2001, some seven years after the end of the wars in those two countries and indeed after the defendant had been detained and transferred to the ICTY. This suggests the Prosecutor had no plans to indict the defendant in respect of those wars until events in Kosovo in 1999, followed by his fall from power in 2001, yielded his arrest. Only after his arrest was a decision made to indict him for all three wars. The process of indictment was a creature of political convenience rather than legal principle.
47. Danner, Allison Marston and Jenny Martinez (2005), 'Guilty associations', *ibid.*
48. Hartmann was indicted on charges of disclosing a confidential ruling of the ICTY's appellate chamber that suppressed documents revealing Serbia's complicity in the July 1995 Srebrenica massacre. She was convicted on 14 September 2009 and fined €7000.
49. For the purposes of this calculation, for the one ICTY judgment in which the Court handed down a sentence of life imprisonment (Galić, IT-98-29), this has been counted as a sentence of 40 years' imprisonment, the next highest sentence the tribunal handed down.
50. The figure of 12 000 Croat fatalities was provided by Ivan Grujić, Colonel in the Croatian army during the war, during evidence he gave for the Prosecution in the trial of Milan Martić (IT-95-11). Veritas, a Belgrade NGO, lists almost 7000 Serbs killed in those areas of the country in which there were significant Serb minorities, and perhaps another 1500 Yugoslav National army (JNA) (Serb) soldiers were also killed in the war.

51. Data courtesy of the Humanitarian Law Center, an NGO with offices in both Belgrade and Pristina.
52. See the United States Department of State Memorandum dated 19 September 1994 from George E. Moose, reporting UNHCR conclusions of Hutu deaths in reprisal attacks. 'The team estimated that the RPA [Tutsi armed forces] and Tutsi civilian surrogates had killed 10000 or more Hutu civilians per month [in July and August], with the RPA accounting for 95% of the killing'.
53. See e.g. Nieuwoudt, Stephanie (2006), 'Slow progress at Rwandan tribunal', *Africa Crisis Report*, Issue 71, Institute for War and Peace Reporting, 2 August.
54. *Balkan Insight*, 'ICTY will likely need more time to complete work', 17 March 2010.
55. The Dutch government in particular has prevented Serbia's progression towards EU membership while Mladić, which it holds responsible for the July 1995 massacres in Srebrenica in easterm Bosnia, remains a fugitive from the Court. See e.g. 'Netherlands stands firm in opposing deal for Serbia', *EU Business*, 16 January 2008. The Netherlands' position on this issue stems from the fact that Dutch peacekeepers were present in Srebrenica as the massacres took place and did nothing to prevent them, or were even complicit in them.
56. See www.iccnow.org (last accessed 5 July 2010) for information about this coalition, which was formed in New York City in 1995.
57. Articles 5 to 8 of the Rome Statute of the International Criminal Court, 17 July 1998.
58. Articles 5(2) and 121(1) of the Rome Statute. The Statute entered into force on 1 July 2002.
59. Article 7(2)(f) of the Rome Statute.
60. Article 7(2)(c) of the Rome Statute.
61. Article 7(1)(h) of the Rome Statute.
62. Article 7(2)(d) of the Rome Statute.
63. Article 8(1) of the Rome Statute.
64. In US constitutional law this is known as the doctrine of being unconstitutionally vague, derived from the due process clauses of the 5th and 14th Amendments. It is held that these clauses require criminal laws to be drafted in language that is clear enough for the average person to understand. Thus in *Papachristou v City of Jacksonville*, 405 US 156, 92 S. Ct. 839, 31 L. Ed. 2d 110 (1972) an ordinance defining the crime of vagrancy as 'loafing', 'strolling' or 'wandering around from place to place' was held unconstitutional because such activity forms an innocuous part of everyday life. Interestingly this doctrine was also embraced by the PCIJ as a feature of international law: *Consistency of certain Danzig legislative decrees with the constitution of the Free City*, Advisory Opinion No. 27, 4 December 1935, PCIJ, Ser. A/B, No. 65, 1935. In this case the Penal Code of Danzig was amended by Nazi legislators to provide: 'Any person who commits an act which the law declares to be punishable or which is deserving of penalty according to the fundamental conceptions of a penal law and sound popular feeling, shall be punished. If there is no penal law directly covering an act, it shall be punished under the law of which the fundamental conception applies most nearly to the said act.' The PCIJ condemned this provision as too vague to be consistent with the general principles of criminal responsibility.
65. Article 25.3(d) of the Rome Statute.
66. ICC, Indictment ICC-02/05-01/09 of 4 March 2009, pp.6–7.
67. Articles 89 *et seq* of the Rome Statute set out a complex set of provisions for states to arrest and extradite suspects at the request of the ICC.
68. Article 11(1) of the Rome Statute.
69. The prosecutor had failed to comply with an order of the court to release the identity of an individual who had identified several prosecution witnesses. On 15 July 2010 the court ordered an 'unconditional stay of proceedings' and ordered the defendant's release. On 8 October 2010 the appeals panel of the court overturned the ruling and ordered the trial to resume.
70. Moreno-Ocampo, Luis (2006), '*Letter concerning the situation in Iraq*', ICC prosecutor,

9 February available at http://www2.icc-cpiint/NR/rdonlyres/F596D08D-D810-43A2-99BB-B899B9C5BCD2/277422/OTP_letter_to_senders_re_Iraq_9_February_2006.pdf, last accessed, 6 November 2010.

71. Figures averaged from the Central Criminal Crown Court Annual Reports, 2006–2007, 2007–2008, 2008–2009.
72. See e.g. Katzenstein, Suzanne (2003), 'Hybrid tribunals: searching for justice in East Timor', *Harvard Human Rights Journal*, **16**, 245; Cohen, David (2002), 'Seeking justice on the cheap: Is the East Timor Tribunal really a model for the future?', *East West Center Asia Pacific Issues*, **61** (August).
73. The quoted text in this paragraph is from *Prosecutor v Charles Taylor*, Case No. SCSL-03-01-PT, Second Amended Indictment, 29 May 2007.
74. A 'Khmer Rouge Trial Task Force' was formed by the Cambodian government in 1997 to prepare for trials of Khmer Rouge leaders, within UN support, but the institution lacked funding and the first judges were appointed only in 2006 by the UN Secretary General.
75. See Scheffer, David (2009), 'Duch seeks an acquittal and immediate release', *Cambodia Tribunal Monitor*, 27 November.
76. Case No. CH/PTJ/2009/06, *Order regarding the detention of persons detained in Lebanon in connection with the case of the attack against Prime Minister Rafiq Hariri and others*, Order of the Pre-Trial Judge, 29 April 2009.
77. See e.g. *Bosnia Daily* (2008), 'Bosnian War Crimes Chamber's Early Success at Risk', Sarajevo, 15 October.
78. Since 1998 Bosnia's High Representative, an international official created under the Dayton Peace Accords to monitor implementation of those agreements, has taken to issuing unilateral decrees *inter alia* imposing legislation over the wishes of Bosnia's various domestic parliaments. See the Decision establishing the BiH State Court, and the Decision imposing the Law on State Court of BiH, both dated 12 November 2000.
79. See e.g. Case X-KR-06/213 *Kličković and Ostojić*; Case X-KR-08/602 *Pelemiš and Perić*.
80. On 16 September 2009, Serb members of the State Parliament vetoed amendments to state legislation which were needed for international judges and prosecutors to remain working at the State Court beyond the end of 2009. On 14 December 2009, High Representative Inzko enacted decisions imposing the necessary amendments so that these officials could continue in office until 31 December 2012. Inzko's decisions contained a concession to Dodik: foreign prosecutors would continue working on war crimes trials only. On organised crime trials and investigations, it was said they might remain only as 'advisers': see *Balkan Insight* (2009), 'OHR extends international judges' Mandate', 16 December. This did not placate the Republik Srpska (RS) Government, and the RS Government and RS National Assembly issued decrees declaring that they would refuse to abide by those decisions, on 14 December and 28 December 2009 respectively.
81. See e.g. Zimonjić, Vesna (2005), *'Croatians rally behind 'national hero' after general is snatched'*, *The Independent*, London, 12 December; Al Jazeera (2008), 'Karadžić: a national hero?' 'Inside Story', 31 July; Wood, Nicholas (2005), 'Serbia hails surrendered war crimes suspect', *New York Times*, 14 February.
82. This was amongst the demands made by Haris Silajdžić, Bosniac member of Bosnia's Presidency, after the ICJ ruled in 2007 that the massacres in Srebrenica were 'genocide'. See the Statement by H.E. Dr. Haris Silajdžić, 63rd Session of the UN General Assembly, 23 September 2008.
83. The Interahamwe were Hutu militias responsible for the greater part for the massacres in Rwanda in 1994. Many fled into neighbouring Zaïre (later Democratic Republic of Congo) after Tutsi forces took control over the country. For the rehabilitation programme for prisoners who admitted taking part in the Rwandan genocide, see e.g. BBC News (2003), 'Rwanda launches 'rehab' for killers', 31 January; BBC News (2009), 'Rwanda frees genocide prisoners', 19 February.
84. The Truth and Reconciliation Commission for South Africa, established in 1995, was

created to hear evidence of wrongdoing by all sides during South Africa's apartheid era. It encouraged both perpetrators and victims to give testimony, and had the power to grant amnesties to those who confessed of crimes before it. It was developed as a more accessible, and less confrontational, alternative to criminal trials after the end of a period of human rights abuses. The model was subsequently copied in at least 16 other countries.

5. Protecting foreign capital flows: who released the genie?

The International Centre for the Settlement of Investment Disputes (ICSID), part of the World Bank, is a once-obscure institution whose recent exponential growth in workload reveals a fascinating modern history of the development of a new area of international law out of thin air. International investment law, as it is called, is arguably the most important area of international law, because it is far harder for states to ignore it than any other area of international law this book considers. Yet despite its importance, outside the highly specialist and small clique of lawyers who practise its arcane arts it is an area of law the existence of which almost nobody is even aware, and fewer still know anything about. In this chapter we will trace the modest origins and extraordinary growth of this significant, yet mysteriously private, new phenomenon in international relations.

The idea that international law protects cross-border investment has obscure, even violent, origins. Although the nineteenth century saw a number of 'treaties of friendship, commerce and navigation', in which states promised to permit free trade with one another, international law was silent on protection of investments, and instead expropriations of foreign investments were typically dealt with by the diplomacy of the gunboat. In the 1848 *Don Pacifico* affair, a British subject had his home plundered in Athens while the Greek police stood by. Don Pacifico laid a request for compensation before the Greek government; to support his claim, the Royal Navy sent a squadron to the Aegean to seize Greek property equal to the value of his claim, and blockaded the port of Piraeus. After two months, Greece relented and paid the compensation requested. In the words of Lord Palmerston, then British Foreign Secretary, 'a British subject, in whatever land he may be, shall feel confident that the watchful eye and the strong arm of England will protect him from injustice and wrong'.[1] Whatever one makes of this apparent willingness of the British Navy to sail around the world enforcing individuals' private grievances, this was the origin of the notion of diplomatic protection: a state has the right to take up a complaint of expropriation of its citizens' property.[2]

An understanding gradually emerged that expropriating foreign property might yield untoward consequences, but there were no legal principles involved. Gunboat diplomacy by European powers in Latin America became so common towards the end of the nineteenth century[3] that the USA became distinctly nervous, invoking the earlier 'Monroe Doctrine' by which it asserted the right to participate in military actions in Latin America to the exclusion of the European powers. To defuse these tensions, Venezuela agreed to establish arbitral tribunals with several European states to resolve various aggrieved European investors' claims against the country. It was one of these decisions, *Company General of the Orinoco* in 1905,[4] in which a claim for expropriation of contractual rights of an investor was first considered. The French-owned Orinoco company had purchased a concession from the Venezuelan government in the Orinoco basin. Colombia had territorial claims on the land covered by the concession, and was threatening to go to war if it was not returned to them. As a result, Venezuela cancelled the concession. Although the tribunal ultimately denied recovery to the Orinoco company on the basis that cancellation of the concession was justified in the extreme circumstances of impending military confrontation, it recognised in principle that an investor has a right in international law not to be deprived by a government of an investment.

The Permanent Court of International Justice (PCIJ) addressed expropriation of property in the 1925 *German interests in Polish Upper Silesia* case.[5] After the plebiscite and subsequent partition of Upper Silesia following the Peace Treaty of Versailles, the city of Chorzów fell into Polish territory. Chorzów had a well-known nitrate factory, built and owned by a German company, which was promptly nationalised by the Polish authorities. By international treaty the Polish government had promised to respect German property rights in the area for 15 years after the partition; Poland was held liable for expropriation and was subsequently ordered to pay substantial damages. In the *Oscar Chinn* case in 1934,[6] the PCIJ considered a complaint that reduction of the transport tariffs of a Belgian state shipping company on the Congo River breached a private British competitor's 'vested rights' under 'general principles of international law' because it created a '*de facto* monopoly' with which the private company could not realistically compete. The Court rejected the British government's contention, saying the possession of customers and the possibility of profit do not amount to vested rights. Nevertheless the decision left open the door that international law prohibits extinction of vested rights, and the case would later be relied upon as an important authority in international investment law. The next milestone in the field was the 'Hull rule', an assertion by the US Secretary of State in 1942 that nationalisation of US assets by the Mexican government in the interwar period required 'prompt, adequate and effective' compensation.[7] Nonetheless it cannot really be said that there was an international law of investment before World War II. The Hull rule was rejected by socialist governments and former colonies, who considered they had every right to nationalise without compensation, to address capitalist and imperial injustices.[8] Furthermore, international law was mostly irrelevant to investors. Only a state, not an investor, had the standing to raise a legal complaint before the PCIJ; and a state might not – in fact, would almost never – wish to stake its legal credibility in an international lawsuit against another state for the benefit of a private investor.

After World War II, the assertion that there was a branch of international law protecting foreign investment became a tool in the ideological battles between the capitalist west and the communist east. Ostensibly neutral in the Cold War after World War II, the Federal Republic of Germany pledged allegiance to the west in 1955 when it joined NATO. In 1957, a group of German businessmen prepared a draft multilateral convention on foreign investment.[9] The draft was never adopted; but Germany, by then developing as a major capital-exporting state, was keen to show its adherence to free market principles. In 1959 it signed a bilateral treaty with Pakistan, based on the 1957 draft convention, which set out a series of rights for each country's investors when undertaking investments in the other country's territory.[10] The treaty (and the vast majority of the thousands of others which followed it) were one-way streets: although German interests had numerous investments in Pakistan, there were no significant Pakistani investments in Germany.

Under this treaty the Hull rule was formalised. There was a right not to have one's investments expropriated without compensation; a right to transfer funds freely into and out of the country; a right for investors not to suffer discrimination and the like. Pakistan had recently dissolved into two countries, (West) Pakistan and Bangladesh (East Pakistan). Shortly thereafter, there was a military coup in West Pakistan; German investors wanted reassurance that the coup would not jeopardise their investments there, and the new Pakistani military junta wanted to demonstrate their commitment to legal security and differentiate themselves from their rival, socialist-leaning India. The idea caught on. France signed three such treaties (that came to be known as bilateral investment treaties, or 'BIT's) in 1960, with former colonies, Chad, the Central African Republic and Republic of Congo. By these treaties, the new states could indicate their continued security for investors from the former motherland notwithstanding their newly gained independence. BITs also became a badge by which newly independent states emerging from the collapse of colonial empires could indicate their rejection of communism and the forging of new allegiances with non-colonial powers. Germany took the lead, signing a further 31 BITs with developing countries in the 1960s. Switzerland was also enthusiastic, signing 18 BITs in the same period. Neither of these countries had colonies in the aftermath of World War II.

It is important to emphasise the role the Cold War played in developing this area of law. Due to communism's association with revolution and social justice, many newly independent former colonial nations were drawn towards the USSR and communist China and the aid programmes those countries offered, at the expense of close ties with the USA and western Europe. International law became a battleground in this confrontation. In a rejection of the Hull rule, repeated affirmations of the right of states to nationalise private property were passed in the UN's General Assembly between 1962 and 1974,[11] where the USSR and its allies could muster a majority because each newly independent state had one vote and decisions are made by simple majority. These various resolutions were in one sense meaningless: they did not make the slightest difference to how states actually behaved. They were merely an opportunity on the part of the USSR and its allies to needle the United States, by explicitly repudiating the Hull doctrine in an international forum. They were pure political showmanship. BITs were a response to these initiatives in the General Assembly; developing countries who wanted to disassociate themselves from the communist powers, and demonstrate their alignment with the west, could sign BITs to show their commitment to the Hull principle and to the sanctity of private property and foreign investment. BITs grew steadily: by the end of 1969, 72 had been signed; by the end of 1979, 165; by the end of 1989, 385. Throughout this period, the signatories were generally western European and North American countries, on the one hand; and countries in Africa on the other, as they pulled away from communist influence. Thus after the death of its socialist leader Nasser in 1970, Egypt started to enter the western orbit and signed a clutch of BITs. Even socialist Yugoslavia and Romania signed a few in the 1970s and 1980s, demonstrating a level of independence from the USSR. After a late start, the United Kingdom signed its first BIT with Egypt in 1975 and a total of 23 over the next ten years. Ever sceptical of international law, the United States signed its first BIT only in 1982 and remains party to relatively few such treaties.

BITs are remarkable in their brevity. They have only ever been framework documents, sometimes just four or five pages, seldom more than 12, and containing just a handful of articles. The obligations contained in them are rather vague. Each state provides such nebulous undertakings as the promise to provide 'fair and equitable treatment' and 'full protection and security' to investors from the other state. There is almost always a prohibition on 'expropriation' or 'nationalisation' without compensation, although these terms are not generally defined (is *Oscar Chinn* treatment expropriation?), nor is the standard of compensation generally explained. These treaties may also promise treatment 'no less favourable' than that afforded to either national investors (a 'national treatment' obligation), or to treat investors no less favourably than investors from other countries (a 'most favoured nation' or 'MFN' clause). However, no explanation is offered of how to make the comparison. (If British investors may only export from the port of Suez, and French investors may only export from the port of Alexandria, is either treated 'less favourably' than the other? How is this question to be answered?)

BITs almost always contain very broad definitions of what counts as an 'investment', including property, shares and other interests in companies, contractual rights, intellectual property rights and concessions. They are usually expressed to subsist indefinitely far into the future. In light of the myriad potential range of circumstances in which investors may expect that their rights are protected, and over such an extended period of time, it is surprising how short BITs are on detail. The reason is that nobody ever expected them to be enforced. These treaties were political flags, at best indicating receptiveness to foreign investment and commercial friendship with certain nations in the context of the Cold War. Like so many treaties, the language in which they were expressed was so open-ended that it could be interpreted to mean anything.

That these treaties were not really intended to create enforceable commitments was transparent from the fact that, for the first 30 years of their existence, they did not create viable enforcement mechanisms. Most (but not all)[12] BITs up to 1989 contained arbitration clauses where differences or questions of interpretation of the treaty arose. But arbitration claims could be brought only by one state (presumably on behalf of an aggrieved investor, although this is not stated explicitly in most BITs) against another. The arbitration clauses in the BITs are silent as to whether a tribunal could award damages, and if so on what basis. However, the issue remained moot, because no arbitration proceedings between two states have ever been commenced pursuant to a BIT.[13]

In the late 1960s a new innovation emerged. A small number of BIT permitted investors to commence arbitration proceedings, circumventing the requirement to persuade one's government to initiate a claim on one's behalf.[14] British BITs followed this model from the 1970s and the second US BIT did the same from 1983.[15] However, France, Germany and Switzerland, the principal drivers of BITs until the end of the 1980s, did not initially follow the United Kingdom's lead. Even towards the end of the 1980s, their BITs made provision only for arbitration between two states. The thought that an investor could bring proceedings directly remained an Anglo-American innovation. Even then, it was a notion investors themselves did not seem keen to embrace. Before 1995 there was only one claim ever brought under a BIT – at least, only one which has come to light. (In principle, parties to arbitration proceedings may choose to keep the proceedings confidential. However, in practice there has been so much scrutiny of investment treaty arbitration by academics and practitioners that it would be surprising if prior claims had been made but not reported in some fashion.) In 1987 a British company started a claim under the UK-Sri Lanka BIT, complaining the Sri Lankan armed forces had destroyed its fish farm in the course of flushing out Tamil insurgents. Some three years later, the tribunal upheld the complaint, awarding US$460,000. This would prove an auspicious precedent, but nobody realised it at the time.

As the Cold War ended, and political barriers to investment in the former Eastern Bloc came crashing down, bilateral investment treaties suddenly became enormously popular as a way for former communist countries to indicate that they were now open for business. Every country in eastern Europe wanted to sign them. It was apparently a cost-free way of indicating a change of political direction, because the prospect of arbitration claims, based on the record of the last 30 years (only one claim ever brought), seemed remote. Every country in eastern Europe signed at least 20 BITs. The trend caught on. Determined to signal its own new economic openness, China signed a record 94 BITs in the 1990s. Latin American countries, also keen at the time to cast off an impression of being associated with socialist styles of government, started signing BITs. Then developing countries started signing BITs with each other, even though they had no substantial capital flows between them.

The exponential growth of BITs was extraordinary. Between 1989 and 1999, 1,472 BITs were signed – almost four times as many as had been signed in the previous 30 years. Every regime, no matter how autarchic or beyond the pale of international public opinion, could sign BITs in apparent safety, a basic level of permitted engagement in international relations which even the most outcast state could achieve. North Korea signed 11 BITs in the 1990s. Iraq signed a BIT with Morocco three weeks before its invasion of Kuwait in 1990. Communist Cuba signed 47. Bosnia and Herzegovina and Democratic Republic of Congo signed BITs in the midst of civil wars. Soon there was virtually no country in the world which had not signed several BITs. By the end of 2009, there were over 2,600 in force worldwide. They were embraced with abandon, almost a proud badge of the new liberal capitalist consensus and a rejection of the old socialist ideology. Like all international treaties, there was no danger in signing up to such soft law, with its open-ended commitments to provide fair and equitable treatment and full protection and security. Nobody really knew what these phrases meant. They were apparently much akin to the ambiguous verbiage found in so many international treaties, expressions of good will but without bite. As with all soft international law, states reaped the political advantage of public adherence to a formal expression of amity and commercial relations with a partner state, without any subsequent downside involved in obligations of compliance. Or so it was thought.

THE RISE OF INVESTMENT TREATY ARBITRATION

In the clamour to sign up to these apparently empty instruments, capital-importing nations failed to note that a remarkable uniformity was creeping into BITs, the texts of which were controlled by capital exporting nations. Each such western nation had its own model BIT not open to significant negotiation with the poorer capital importing nations, which did not have easy access to international legal advice about the significance of the documents they were signing. Clauses permitting arbitration between investors and the states quickly became the norm. The rights accorded to investors – although vaguely expressed – became more extensive. Nobody thought this mattered; arbitrations had been so few, and thus there was virtually no jurisprudence explaining what arbitral tribunals might take these vaguely worded treaties to mean. But, perhaps inevitably, investors eventually caught on that they could sue states, notwithstanding doctrines of sovereign immunity, using these treaties. Indeed because the categories of investment protection contained in BITs were so wide, investors could sue states for virtually anything. Almost any adverse legislative or executive act may be described as 'unfair', 'inequitable' or contrary to standards of 'full protection and security'. Arbitration proceedings were expensive, extended and damages claims were potentially enormous. In 1928 the PCIJ had ruled, in the *Chorzów Factory* case,[16] that states were liable for losses of future profit where there had been an unlawful expropriation. Investors' lawyers were quick to seize upon these features of the international arbitral process, and the potentially large damages they could claim using the *Chorzów Factory* precedent, to put pressure on governments of developing world countries.

Thus investment treaty arbitrations, in which investors sue states for enormous sums of money in hugely complex proceedings before international arbitral tribunals, emerged as the biggest growth area in international law in the late 1990s. From the single case in 1990, there was no more than a trickle of decisions until 1997, increasing to a record

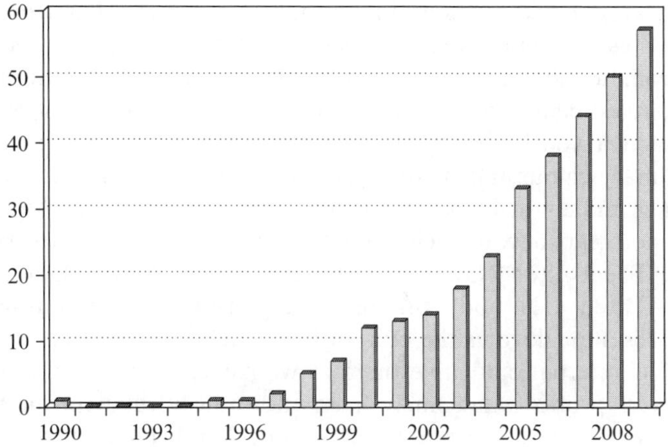

Figure 5.1 Number of investment treaty arbitration decisions, by year of decision, 1990–2009

57 decisions reported in 2009. Although this may not seem like a huge number given the volume of international investment taking place, compared to what had gone before it was a deluge. In 2009 alone investment treaty tribunals heard more cases than the entire contentious docket of the ICJ in its first 40 years. Moreover, in most investment treaty cases huge amounts of money are at stake. Claims before investment tribunals are typically worth tens to hundreds of millions of US dollars. Sometimes (as in the complaint against Russia for improper liquidation of Yukos)[17] they are worth billions. The stakes to small or poor countries are enormous.

For this reason, the costs of litigating investment treaty disputes are also huge, typically amounting to several million US dollars in lawyers' and experts' fees for each party over the course of three to five years of the litigation cycle. Together with an international publicity campaign about the evils of a nation's substandard investment climate, it is a wonderfully effective form of political pressure for an investor to bring to bear upon a government. Unlike any other sort of international court, investment tribunals' awards are enforceable against the defendant countries' assets in almost any country in the world. This is because the 1958 New York Convention on Recognition and Enforcement of Arbitral Awards has been signed by over 150 countries, including every major banking centre worldwide. The Convention provides for virtually automatic enforcement of arbitration awards by the courts of signatory states; the grounds for refusing enforcement are extremely limited[18] and recognition of an investment treaty arbitration award has never been refused. Awards can now be enforced against states' bank accounts in London, New York, Paris or Tokyo. Against a background of blanket doctrines of state immunity that prevent courts from hearing lawsuits against foreign states in most countries' legal systems, investment treaty arbitration is an extraordinary development.

For such a youthful subject, investment treaty law has grown with extraordinary vigour and creativity, driven no doubt by the fact that there is so much money in it that academics, international organisations and practitioners can devote their highest intellectual energies to its development. The United Nations Conference on Trade and Development (UNCTAD), a UN body originally responsible for organising trade conferences, now devotes the bulk of its resources to research and development in international investment law. An elite band of arbitrators and lawyers profits handsomely from enormously time consuming and therefore expensive arbitration procedures. Think tanks and university departments around the world have developed specialisations in the new subject of international investment law. The legal doctrines involved in interpreting the ambiguous and widely drawn categories of legal protection provided by BITs are impressively ambitious. The prohibition on 'expropriation' has been drawn to include 'indirect expropriation' (i.e. depriving an investment of its economic value through regulation – one would query whether the ruling in *Oscar Chinn* would be decided the same way today)[19] and 'creeping expropriation' (i.e. a series of measures that collectively render an investment unprofitable, even if a single such measure would not).[20]

'Fair and equitable treatment' has been interpreted as including an obligation to honour an investors' legitimate expectations (for example imposing restrictions on changing the law after an investment has been made),[21] minimum domestic judicial standards[22] (allowing investment tribunals to act as international courts of appeal) and differential treatment by governments of companies (for example, providing one enterprise with a bail-out or financial support but not another)[23] without what the tribunal sees as a good reason for the discrimination. 'Full protection and security' has been interpreted as an obligation to provide physical protection to an investor's assets in the face of civil unrest or disorder.[24] The fact that domestic law makes no provision for such protections does not matter; international law sits above domestic law, which is no defence to a claim of breach of a treaty.[25] A bizarrely terse and even circular clause found in many BITs, known colloquially as an 'umbrella clause' (which might read, 'Either party shall observe any. . .obligation it may have entered into'),[26] is routinely interpreted to raise breaches by state agencies of their contractual commitments to the level of a treaty violation, to be adjudicated by an investment tribunal rather than a domestic court.[27] 'Most favoured nation' clauses have been interpreted to apply to investment treaties themselves, meaning that if a state has signed another investment treaty with terms more favourable to investors than the treaty under which the claim is brought, the terms of the more favourable treaty are imported into the less favourable treaty.[28] Jurisdictional provisions are also widely interpreted. A company incorporated in a jurisdiction solely to make an investment in another country, without any shareholders or business presence in the jurisdiction of its incorporation, has been held able to bring an investment treaty claim, even though it is nothing more than a 'mailbox' and has no significant connection with the country in which it is incorporated.[29] Even making a loan to an enterprise within a country may count as an 'investment'.[30] BITs have been held to apply retroactively, to investments made before the treaty came into force.[31]

International investment law has also gone multilateral. The North Atlantic Free Trade Agreement (NAFTA), which came into force on 1 January 1994, contained an 'investment chapter' which copied the standards of expropriation, fair and equitable treatment, full protection and security and national treatment from BITs. It also created an investor-state arbitration procedure, the first time a multilateral treaty had incorporated such an innovation. The Energy Charter Treaty was signed in December 1994. This treaty was intended to open up the extractive industry economies of eastern Europe after the fall of communism; 51 states have signed it, and arbitration proceedings can be brought against any of them by investors from any of the others, provided that the investment relates to 'an economic activity in the energy sector'. Again this definition is interpreted broadly; providing technical maintenance services to a nuclear power station suffices.[32] ASEAN (the Association of Southeast Asian Nations) has a 'comprehensive investment agreement' permitting investor-state arbitration, as does the investment chapter of CAFTA (the Central American Free Trade Agreement).

The other significant multilateral institution that has bought into the investment treaty bonanza is the International Centre for Settlement of Investment Disputes (ICSID), the hitherto redundant branch of the World Bank mandated to administer arbitrations. The ICSID Convention was signed in 1966, creating a special secretariat within the World Bank to hear disputes between private investors and foreign states, and appoint arbitrators to resolve them. The World Bank, established by the Bretton Woods conference in 1944, has a development lending mandate. The projects funded by its loans frequently require participation of foreign contractors or investors to accomplish them. Disputes would often arise between the governments managing the projects the Bank was funding, and the contractors retained to implement them. The Bank would commonly be asked to mediate those disputes and had an interest in resolving them to ensure the success of its projects; but as a bank, it had neither the specialist legal skills to resolve disputes nor the political will to get involved in allegations of incompetence, corruption and political infighting that typically characterise the hazards of project finance in the developing world. The innovation was thus to outsource these disputes to external arbitrators, albeit in a process in which the World Bank retained a degree of involvement and control, through establishing the arbitration secretariat within the walls of the Bank. ICSID would be run by Bank staff who would appoint arbitrators; but these arbitrators would be external, and thus the Bank could disclaim responsibility for their decisions. At the same time the arbitrators would maintain close relations with the Bank (such as being appointed to the Bank's advisory boards or to be judges in its administrative tribunals), meaning a level of influence could be exerted over them.

Unfortunately this arrangement did not achieve its objectives, because it overlooked the fact that states must consent to be bound by an arbitral process. Yet they would not consent, because by doing so they would waive their sovereign immunity and thus could be sued by aggrieved investors for potentially enormous amounts of money. Manifold private institutions had always existed to administer arbitrations between states and investors, including the International Chamber of Commerce (in Paris), the London Court of International Arbitration and the Stockholm Chamber of Commerce. But investor-state arbitrations had been rare in practice, because in 'state contracts' (i.e. commercial agreements between states and foreign investors) the state would seldom accept recourse to arbitration, preferring to rely on its own courts which, in the majority of developing world countries, are susceptible to varying levels of influence and direction from the executive branch of government. (Only where the private counterpart has significant bargaining power can it negotiate an agreement where a state waives its sovereign immunity in favour of an international tribunal.) Thus for the first 30 years of its existence, ICSID lay fallow. It was just another venue to administer international arbitration proceedings, in competition with the myriad private organisations worldwide doing the same thing. Yet it had a profound jurisdictional disadvantage compared with those institutions: it could hear only disputes relating to 'investments'[33] (a term which the ICSID Convention did not define); and only where one party is an 'investor' and the other party is a state. Thus the greater number of commercial arbitrations between two private parties, which are the lifeblood of other arbitration secretariats, were denied to it. Until 1996, ICSID had an average caseload typical of the ICJ. Never were more than four cases registered in any one year; in several years there were none.

In the 1990s however, the World Bank was concerned that it was becoming increasingly irrelevant, as international capital markets opened up to sovereign borrowing, supported by a credit rating system for emerging market states. The Bank's share of sovereign lending started decreasing dramatically. Its business model had previously been aimed at lending to sovereigns perceived as being beyond the pale and that the capital markets would not touch. As markets became more sophisticated, the World Bank as a lender lost its sole advantage. As an international public bureaucracy, it was not as competitive as international private banks in the new age. Thus it started looking for things to do beyond just lending money, and ICSID was co-opted for this purpose. In the flurry of BIT signatures in the 1990s, the World Bank presented itself as an expert in matters of foreign investment, and found itself participating in lobbying for and negotiations of investment treaties. The pay-off it received for this activity was that the arbitration clauses in those treaties provided for arbitration before ICSID with remarkable frequency. ICSID portrayed itself as the grand old man of investor-state arbitration, with 30 years' experience and the institutional authority of the World Bank behind it. Capital importing states had reason to embrace a close relationship with the Bank: in the past, at least, it had lent them money when nobody else would. The Bank could therefore be trusted to administer arbitrations, and ICSID arbitration became a default provision in the vast majority of BITs.

The problem with this new role was that ICSID was ill equipped to manage the deluge of investment treaty cases that would come before it. Contrary to the image it had successfully portrayed, it was not an effective and established arbitral institution. Between 1972 and 1996 it had received only 39 cases in total, compared to the many thousands of cases registered before private international arbitral institutions every year. In 1997, the first year when ICSID had the most modest of caseload spikes (ten cases were registered in the course of the year), it was immediately overwhelmed. As a public international organisation, it had terrible trouble managing the recruitment of the necessary staff, appropriations from the Bank's annual budget and even acquiring extra office space. Used to the most leisurely of caseloads, when faced with a real work commitment ICSID ground to a halt. And thus it became renowned for chronic delays, taking weeks to answer letters, arbitrations languishing for years on end before being resolved. Five-year delays became commonplace. The poor quality even of its conference rooms (where hearings were to be held) and administrative support became notorious. By 2003, when the ICSID secretariat was receiving some 30 cases a year (i.e. comparable to the total number of cases received in the first 20 years), matters were reaching crisis point. Several arbitration claims brought before ICSID as a result of Argentina's

1999–2002 financial crisis are still outstanding in 2010. Yet matters did not improve significantly. It was not in the interests of the Bank's members – i.e. states themselves – that it would do so. Faced with huge financial claims arising out of dubious government practices commonplace in emerging market countries, and in respect of which the respondent states cannot assert sovereign immunity, dreadful delay is rather convenient.

DO BITS PROMOTE FOREIGN INVESTMENT?

International investment law is an intriguing field, because it is not clear why it exists at all. It would not exist as a discipline without the rise of the investor-state arbitration provisions, imported into BITs by the British government in the 1970s but not achieving widespread acceptance until the 1990s. By this time there had still been so few investment treaty arbitrations that nobody really knew what effect these clauses would have. There is virtually no historical record of states agreeing that foreign investors can sue them directly; as with the France-Venezuela mixed claims commission in the first decade of the twentieth century, and the two PCIJ cases considered earlier in this chapter, in almost all historical investment claims the investor's home state had served as a filter through which the claim must be brought. One exception is the Iran-US claims tribunal, a body that undertook the bulk of its work between 1981 and 1993, in which private US investors whose assets were expropriated in the 1979 Iranian revolution could bring direct claims against the Iranian government before a mixed tribunal. That the USA had frozen some US$9 billion of Iranian assets abroad, out of which awards (eventually totalling approximately US$2 billion) were to be paid, may give insight into the remarkable circumstances in which Iran was prepared to agree to such a measure.[34]

This exceptional instance aside, that states embrace a novel legal tool so thoroughly, with so bare an empirical record of the consequences, is perplexing. It suggests a sort of collective hysteria, in which states embrace an idea just because other states have done the same. This account is reinforced by the observation that BITs were signed between countries that had no significant foreign investments in either direction. States would agree to submit to arbitration with investors of other states, even though there were very few such investors. There was no constituency of investors to which these BITs were supposed to appeal. Indeed states signed BITs with other states with whom they had no economic relations whatsoever, nor was it likely they would have. Desperately poor developing countries would sign BITs with one another, even though neither state was in a position to export capital to the other. Autarchies would sign BITs. North

Korea has no foreign investment from anywhere (save a small amount from South Korea, with whom it has no BIT.) It may well have been that in the early 1990s, when the convention that BITs should contain investor-state arbitration clauses took off, the risk associated with the presence of such clauses was perceived to be very low. After all, those clauses had been around since 1975, but they had not created any significant litigation. Proceedings instituted by an investor were a theoretical risk only, and the vague language contained in BITs was insufficient to support credible or high-value claims that would curtail a state's sovereignty in any meaningful way.

However, this collective fantasy that there was no practical risk of litigation was dangerous. International investment lawyers spotted the potential to harness an entirely new form of litigation against hitherto immune states. International arbitrators, paid by the case as roving private judges, were happy to oblige. Judicial meaning was imported into the vagaries of phrases such as 'fair and equitable treatment' (by far the most commonly upheld treaty violation). Things states often do, such as taxing, regulating and restricting economic activity, were held to breach treaty provisions, and substantial damages would follow. From out of nowhere, investment treaty law became a force to be reckoned with. The greatest advantage of this new edifice was that it could be driven by private investors, not governments, who had deeper pockets and were more inclined to hire external lawyers than use their own internal legal teams. Thus huge quantities of lawyers' fee income could be generated. These private litigants in public international litigation would be driven by the financial bottom line rather than political considerations, and thus would have far more litigious appetites. When capital-importing countries realised the monster they had unleashed, they must have been horrified.

This account, premised around the notion of collective oversight, does not find expression in the voluminous literature on investment treaty law. The conventional analysis of the rise of BITs is that countries compete to attract foreign capital; and signing BITs with credible investment commitments increases the attractiveness of a country as a locus for investment by foreign capitalists.[35] In other words, clear investment rights, together with a waiver of sovereign immunity, is something which investors want as a precondition for investment and which states want to offer to encourage that foreign investment. In an echo of the economic theory of contract law, BITs are the solution to credibility problems. Investors and states want to enter into arrangements out of which both sides profit. States benefit through foreign investment that creates jobs and economic growth; private investors yield investment returns from successful investments. There are gaps in time between the obligations of each party in these transactions, which require ongoing commitments from each side. An investor needs to know his investment will be fairly treated by the state in which (s)he invests and which has effective sovereignty within the territory of his(or her) investment. (S)he needs to know the state will not pass a law expropriating the investment the week after the final financial payment has been made into the country. States cannot credibly make such commitments due to the existence of the doctrine of sovereign immunity, and thus the cooperation benefits of foreign investment are not realised. Bilateral investment treaties, on this analysis, overcome the cooperation deficit by allowing states credibly to commit themselves. Sovereign immunity is waived and states can be sued if they do not comply. That is the conventional theory of why investment treaties are signed by states.[36] Capital exporting states are lobbied by investors within their territories to create such arrangements. Capital importing states have a direct interest in receiving those investments, and thus agree to the treaty commitments to encourage investments to flow.

In favour of this theory, there appears to be a level of competition between states to sign BITs. It has been shown that states whose principal economic activity consists of secondary industry tend to sign more BITs than states whose focus is primary (extractive) industry.[37] The explanation for this might be that in primary industries, investors have to follow the resources; in secondary industry, they have greater latitude to choose any country where the investment climate is favourable. A factory producing iPhones can be established anywhere land is available, labour is not too heavily regulated, tax burdens are tolerable and sufficient skilled workers are available. Thus countries competing for such investments strain to make themselves more attractive than their competitors, through signature of BITs. However, it is not clear that competition for capital is the only driving motive for signature of BITs. Some states may wish to indicate their openness for business through signing a BIT; other states may have quite different reasons for signing them. North Korea had little interest in encouraging inward investment when it signed its BITs in the 1990s. A more plausible hypothesis is that it wished to use the instruments to assert its standing as a respectable nation in the international community in the face of US efforts to ostracise it. Similarly soft interests – participating in the international community and involvement in international conferences – may have motivated signature of BITs between pairs of states neither of which are capital exporting. Most troublingly for the thesis that signature of BITs is driven by inter-state competition for capital, there is no evidence of any state signing a BIT at the request of a prospective investor, nor any investor or investors' groups having any role in the negotiation of the text of any BIT. If the rationale for the existence of BITs is to facilitate a transaction from which the investor is to benefit, then the existence of the state as a detached intermediary, negotiating on behalf of all the investors from that state but without their participation or consent, is hard to explain.

Of course it is always open to states to provide legally binding commitments to foreign investors, and to waive their sovereign immunity so that those commitments are credible. They can write arbitration provisions into their agreements with investors; these are known as 'state contracts'. States do not need bilateral investment treaties to make credible commitments. As a matter of principle, state contracts are considerably more attractive to both states and to investors than are BITs. For one thing, the obligations they impose upon states are far clearer than those contained in BITs, having been individually negotiated and without the unnecessary medium of the investor's home state. State contracts do not contain ambiguous obligations relating to fair and equitable treatment. Indeed they do not operate in the elusive realm of public international law at all; they operate in the far more certain and clear realm of domestic law. Such contracts generally contain a clause electing upon a specific choice of law, which may or may not be the law of the state where the investment is being made. In state contracts, investors and states will tailor contractual language which sets out exactly the commitments they require of one another. This arrangement will be more attractive to the state: not only will it have a far clearer account of what its obligations are than under an investment treaty, it will also have the opportunity to place obligations on an investor, something which cannot occur under an investment treaty. Unlike investment treaty arbitration, for arbitration under a state contract the investor may be a defendant as well as a claimant. (An investor cannot ordinarily be a defendant to an investment treaty claim because investors are not parties to investment treaties and thus cannot incur obligations under them.)[38]

There are other advantages to state contracts. The relevant state party may be a sub-sovereign federal unit, a local government entity or a public corporation. This may benefit both the state, which will not be liable for the misdeeds of an individual government unit which may in practice have significant autonomy from the central government; and the investor, which has a legal relationship with the unit of government or the public body with which it is actually dealing on a day to day basis. The state can always co-sign and guarantee such a contract if the investor has concerns about enforceability against a sub-sovereign entity which may not hold assets outside the jurisdiction of the investment. In short, if the aim is to elicit a credible contractual commitment from a state, it is hard to understand why either investors or states would choose investment treaties rather than state contracts. Yet state contracts are relatively rare, amounting to just 22 per cent of the ICSID caseload in the period to the end of 2009, compared to a 73 per cent share for cases arising under investment treaties.[39]

One might try to argue that investment treaties are a way of lowering transaction costs associated with state contracts. Rather than negotiate individually with each and every investor, a country negotiates with classes of investor by nationality, using the state of which they are a citizen as their proxy. This theory does not seem very persuasive in light of the definitions of 'investor' frequently appearing in BITs, which often require no closer connection of the investor with the home state to which protection applies than that it is incorporated there. In the *Tokio Tokelės* case,[40] a Lithuanian company had been incorporated by Ukrainian investors to invest in Ukraine. Its shareholding was over 99 per cent Ukrainian and it had no significant connections with Lithuania. Nonetheless the tribunal held the company's investment was covered by the Lithuania-Ukraine BIT. It is a stretch of the imagination to assume that in signing that BIT the Lithuanian government was negotiating on the part of all Ukrainian investors who might wish to incorporate a company in Lithuania to invest back in Ukraine. Furthermore, this argument vastly overstates the transaction costs associated with negotiating state contracts, and vastly understates the transaction costs associated with negotiating BITs. Foreign direct investment is typically worth substantial sums of money, as the large claims that are brought before ICSID attest. The legal expenses involved in negotiating state contracts are trivial compared to the issues at stake.

Consider the commercial analogy. In complex commercial transactions worth far smaller sums of money than the typical value of a foreign investment commitment in an emerging market economy, it remains economically realistic to negotiate detailed commercial agreements, often running to hundreds of pages. The legal fees expressed as a proportion of the transaction value are negligible; and the reason commercial parties negotiate transactions in care and detail is because it obviates the risk of later disputes, the costs of resolving which are a far more significant proportion of the sum at issue. It would be madness for commercial parties to appoint proxies to negotiate general terms of all contracts signed on their behalf, save for the most uniform and specialist transactions. Standard forms for some contracts exist (for example bills of lading and charter parties), but these are highly specialised: quite the opposite of the broad and potentially unlimited array of transactions investment treaties are intended to cover. Even then, such framework agreements often contain extensive and detailed provisions that have previously been carefully negotiated based upon prior experiences. Consider standard form contracts for certain types of derivative instruments, drafted and negotiated by some of the leading marketmakers in these instruments in the world's financial centres. This is a far cry from the casually drafted and perfunctory few pages of a typical BIT. In the commercial context, the standard form terms used for a contractual template are then amended or added to for each individual transaction. This process of tailoring a standard contract to a specific matter seldom happens for investments pursuant to investment treaties.

The most telling problem with an account of investment treaties as resolutions to the problem of states' inability to provide credible contractual commitments is that it misconceives the structure of states' incentives, particularly those governments in the developing world. Many states that sign BITs want foreign direct investment, but some do not care so much for it. Even those that do want it are most reluctant to forego the golden goose of sovereign immunity to receive it, as the comparative paucity of state contracts providing for international arbitration suggests. Countries that are keen to receive foreign investment know what motivates foreign investors to choose their country: political stability, a cheap labour force, advantageous tax regimes, a low level of government regulation and bureaucracy, moderate levels of corruption and a tolerably just domestic court system, all the things Adam Smith thought were important to oil the wheels of commerce when he said '[l]ittle else is requisite to carry a state to the highest degree of opulence from the lowest barbarism but peace, easy taxes, and a tolerable administration of justice'.[41]

In none of these matters does committing to a BIT afford a prospective investor security. It does not change the structure of government, the content of domestic legislation or the quality of local courts. It grants the investor only a prospective and uncertain remedy in a litigation procedure of inordinate expense should things subsequently go wrong. Commercial people are not as a rule motivated by the prospect of looking forward to expensive and uncertain litigation. At best they see it as a necessary evil if their transactions go awry; it is certainly not an alluring prospect. Therefore there is no reason for governments to believe that offering them that opportunity does indeed motivate them to do business within that state. In reality, states have, perhaps until very recently, been signing investment treaties principally for reasons exogenous to national commercial interest. The true reasons are autonomous to the field of international relations, and relate to the value of received wisdom within international organisations, the desire to present an image as a commercially friendly and progressive country and a belief (belied by the very recent rise of investment treaty arbitrations in the last ten years) that they can sign such open-ended treaties at minimal true sovereignty cost.

This feeds into perhaps the most empirically problematic feature of investment treaty law: there is scant evidence that the existence of investment treaty commitments motivates foreign investors at all. Thus even to the extent states do compete with one another for capital by signing BITs, it is not clear that the market within which they are competing is genuine. The evidence suggests that foreign investors do not place much value on the existence of a BIT of which they can take advantage, when they make their investment decisions. There is a wide range of empirical studies that enquire into the correlations between BITs and foreign direct investment (FDI). These studies typically proceed by choosing a data set of developing world (capital importing) countries, counting how many BITs they have signed and measuring the level of FDI the country has received in some relevant time period (for example, comparing FDI flows in the years just before a BIT is signed with FDI flows in the years just after).[42] These studies typically proceed using regression analysis, in which a correlation is drawn between two (or more) variables, for example, number of BITs a country has signed and the quantities of FDI inflow. The inference drawn is that the greater the correlation between the two variables and where other potential determinants of FDI inflow are controlled for, the more likely it is that the cause of a change in FDI inflow is a change in the number of BITs signed. A 2009 UNCTAD paper[43] surveys 15 different such empirical studies, of which ten are broadly sceptical of the existence of any correlation and five are optimistic. It is manifest that using different sample sizes and data sets can produce wildly different results.[44] Even if a correlation can be shown, there are so many different determinants of foreign direct investment that it is not clear studies of this kind can ever be truly conclusive.

Perhaps the most important factors in encouraging foreign investment relate to the internal features of a recipient country, and the number of relevant factors can be exceptionally wide. Consider the potential relevance of the cost of labour, proximity, access and price of relevant primary natural resources (including waterways), skill levels in the labour force, personal and corporate tax rates, language spoken, cultural suitability (there is no sense trying to open a whisky distillery in Saudi Arabia), domestic macroeconomic policy (including inflation and exchange rate fluctuation), incidence of domestic corruption, regulatory burden, historical connections and cultural familiarity, political stability, quality of infrastructure, accessibility of necessary raw materials, openness to imports and exports, legal security (including a tolerably robust judicial system and a public administration that does not extract rents),[45] crime levels, and availability of supporting services and industry. Also potentially relevant determinants of FDI investment are a variety of exogenous factors that may affect capital importing states differently, such as the current stage in the global economic cycle, political and commercial alliances between nation states, market prices of relevant commodities, availability of credit for developing world investments and price elasticity of demand[46] for raw materials and finished commodities which the country produces (or has the potential to produce).

Most studies investigating the correlation between BITs and FDI attempt to control for some such phenomena, using dummy variables in statistical regressions to isolate extraneous factors. But no study attempts to take into account all such exogenous factors. It never could, because the data set is too small. There have been 2,600 BITs, including those for which no significant FDI data is available because the capital importing country in question in fact imports minimal quantities of capital. (Many BITs are paper tigers, being commitments in respect of international capital flows that do not actually take place.) There is a set of perhaps 120 capital importing countries that have signed BITs. Thus there is a mean of perhaps 20 BITs each capital importing country has signed. However, this betrays considerable variation: by the end of 2006, China had signed at least 115 BITs, whereas the numerical majority of capital importing countries had signed just a handful. In all likelihood there are more than 20 variables that have an impact on foreign investment. Therefore in the mean case, there is insufficient data to control for all the variables that a rigorous study would need to take into account. Regression analysis leaves one with a series of simultaneous equations with more variables than data to fit them. Even where a country has signed more BITs than there are variables, the results will hardly be statistically significant for any individual country. Regression analysis assumes large data sets and a small number of relatively straightforward potential determinants. In regressing data correlating BITs and FDI, these studies are attempting to cope with precisely the opposite.

Because virtually every country in the world has signed at least one BIT, it is hard to compare states with a null hypothesis. Nobody can be certain what the current effect of signing BITs is on encouraging foreign investment, because every relevant state has signed at least one. Of course there were times when states had not signed BITs – very few countries in eastern Europe signed investment treaties before the late 1980s. But to infer from this that those states' signature of BITs caused the massive influx of foreign investment eastern Europe experienced in the early 1990s would be quite wrong. The reason was that those markets were suddenly open when they had not been before. BITs were probably mostly causally irrelevant. Investors of all hues and from virtually every capital exporting country went into almost all eastern European countries as quickly as they could. Comparatively sophisticated new markets had just opened and investors eyed opportunities and risks with potentially significant pay-offs. Because there had been virtually no investment treaty arbitrations at the time, the prospect of bringing a claim if one's investment was subsequently expropriated can hardly have weighed upon the mind of any but the most speculative investor receiving the most obscure legal advice. In all likelihood, BITs supervened upon the FDI. They were the results of the markets opening up, not causative of that taking place.

Even in the absence of useful data on the null hypothesis, the temptation exists to say that FDI bears some sort of linear relationship to the *number* of BITs that have been signed. Thus for instance, one might be inclined to suppose that signing ten BITs is ten times more effective than signing one. Such an inference is lent a certainly credibility by the fact that China, a recipient of large amounts of FDI, has signed so many BITs. But that may also be because China is a huge country. The thesis that there is some simple relationship between the number of BITs signed and the levels of FDI received is not particularly plausible. Studies that have examined the relationship between BITs signed and investment coming from the state of the counterpart signatory have concluded there is no significant correlation between signature of a BIT and an increase in FDI from the counterpart.[47] Thus those advancing the existence of a correlation are forced to rely upon the theory that signature of a BIT has a 'signalling effect'.[48] According to this theory, it is not the prospect of being able to bring an investment treaty claim that motivates investors to invest, but a signal that the country is receptive to foreign investments and will treat them properly. This signal will apparently encourage foreign investors to enter the market even when there is no BIT that will protect them. The greater number of BITs are signed, the greater the signal.

This theory seems unpersuasive. Presumably a far better signal is the quality of the country's internal legal system and government transparency, data on which is plentiful and public for nearly every country in the world. Since states virtually never change their domestic legislation or institutions upon signing BITs (they perhaps make the assumption that the obligations imposed by BITs are so generic that their domestic law is already consistent with it), it is not clear that BITs are a particularly good signal of anything. It is not clear why foreign investors would be fooled by so simplistic a signal, without a legal right to enforce the obligations in the BIT (which, on the signal theory, is not a prerequisite for BITs' causal efficacy, because the correlation is not one between signature of a BIT and investment from the territory of the treaty counterpart, but between signature of BITs and foreign investment as a whole). For the signal theorist, BITs need not have investor-state arbitration provisions in them at all. Furthermore, it must follow from the signal account that only states with high traditions of rule of law sign BITs, to demonstrate that they offer secure investment environments. Yet it is known that countries of every rule of law tradition, weak and strong, sign BITs. Perhaps the strong ones have less to worry about – their domestic legal systems are more likely to correct wrongful treatment against foreign investors before a complaint reaches the investment tribunal. But investors will know this already about the country's legal system, through their own due diligence procedures, before committing significant quantities of capital. It is not very plausible to hypothesise that investors use short, ambiguously drafted and obscure international legal documents which may not provide them with any rights at all to evaluate the suitability of an investment environment and make considered investment decisions.

This leads to the point that even to the extent that a correlation can be discerned between foreign investment and signature of BITs, it is not clear that the causal relationship is in the direction from signature of BITs to encouraging foreign investment, but rather the other way round. It may be that markets which are open to foreign investment and which have high standards of rule of law have little to lose by signing BITs. Those countries are independently attractive to foreign investors; the BITs are not necessary to encourage investment. However, such countries have little to risk by signing them, because they already have reasonably strong rule of law traditions and thus their ordinary governmental conduct is unlikely to infringe investment treaty standards. Finally, it does not seem persuasive to suggest that the prospect of being able to bring an enormously expensive and costly claim before an international tribunal should everything go wrong provide significant quantities of comfort to foreign investors. Such events are too remote, and too far out of the minds of commercial people when they negotiate their deals, to significantly impact the investment decision, particularly given that the recovery rate on investment treaty arbitration is so poor (as to which, see below). If the desire to fall back upon a robust and impartial arbitral process is of importance to an investor, it can agree upon an individually negotiated set of detailed contractual obligations, and a tailored arbitration clause, with its host state. Such an arrangement is probably far more satisfactory for the investor than the roulette wheel of the investment arbitration process. About that procedure we should now briefly make a few remarks.

IS INVESTMENT TREATY ARBITRATION ROBUST?

It is sometimes said that there has been an 'explosion' in investment treaty claims,[49] and investment treaty arbitrations have recently been the subject of some publicity. However, perhaps the most remarkable feature of investment arbitration is how few claims are actually brought, compared to the size of FDI flows worldwide and the number of investment treaties in force. Although there are over 2,600 BITs, there are only 100 or so investment treaty claims whose existence is in the public domain. In 20 years, 100 cases is not very many at all, being perhaps the average annual caseload for the litigation department of a medium sized London law firm. The vast majority of investment treaties, therefore, have seen no arbitration. Given the large number of self-appointed experts in international investment law, from academia through practising lawyers, arbitrators and international organisations, there is remarkably little in the way of subject matter for them to be experts about. Without doubt the number of experts outnumbers the number of cases by a significant factor, as do the number of pages of commentary compared to the number of pages of arbitration awards issued. Only a handful of arbitrators, and even fewer law firms, have been involved in more than one investment treaty claim. It is hard for virtually anyone to profess expertise in a subject about which nobody can claim to have had more than passing and limited exposure. On any measure the subject is exceptionally immature. Investors are seldom using the procedure, a fact which calls for explanation.

One of the reasons why there are so few such cases may be that they are fiendishly expensive for claimants and respondents alike to pursue. Anecdotal evidence suggests that a typical claim, including legal costs and a 50 per cent share of each of the arbitrators' fees and the administrative fees of the arbitral institution, costs at least US$1 million to conclude.[50] In some cases the costs of bringing a claim may be as much as several million dollars. Investment treaty arbitration is a serious financial commitment; an investor may prefer to spend that money on a new investment rather than pursuing damages for the failure of an old one. Practising lawyers know that the going market fee rate for litigation services is broadly related to the amount at issue. Therefore claims are typically valued at very high orders. It is not uncommon for claims to be brought with stated values in the region of hundreds of millions of US dollars for loss of expected revenues, following the principle in *Chorzów Factory* that 'reparation must, as far as possible, wipe out all the consequences of the illegal act and re-establish the situation which would, in all probability, have existed if that act had not been committed'.[51] However, it is not clear that investment treaty tribunals are nearly as generous as investors may hope. The common perception, even by experienced commentators, is that investment tribunal awards are enormous, and a few high value awards have captured public attention.[52] However, there are only four known investment treaty awards in excess of US$100 million at the time of writing.[53]

More than 60 per cent of awards where damages are ordered are for

US$5 million or less.[54] Given the considerable costs involved in bringing such claims, even where a claimant is successful the costs of bringing the claim may end up being a significant proportion of the damages award eventually recovered. One study has suggested that for investment arbitrations under the North American Free Trade Agreement (NAFTA)[55] the mean award compared to the size of the claim represents only 2 cents on the dollar.[56] This may be optimistic. Another study suggests that while investors receive a monetary award in 38.5 per cent of cases they bring, the mean size of those awards is only 3 per cent of the amount claimed,[57] leading to a mean recovery rate of only 1.17 cents on the dollar. Add to this significant anecdotal evidence to the effect that respondent states commonly fail to satisfy investment treaty awards against them,[58] and the economics of investment treaty arbitration begin to look distinctly unappealing.

Part of the explanation of this poor rate of recovery may lie in claimants over-exaggerating their damages claims for strategic purposes: they take the view that the higher the level of the claim, the more likely a settlement in their favour. However, the benefits of positional bargaining of this kind are uncertain when all parties are advised by competent legal counsel. Overblown claims which stand no prospect of success will be disregarded. For international arbitration, in which the tribunal has discretion to order that either party pay part or all of the other party's costs, overstating a claim may lead the tribunal to exercise that discretion adversely.[59] The Priest-Klein model predicts that in cases which proceed to a final binding adjudication, plaintiffs will win on average 50 per cent of their expected recovery, irrespective of the legal standard.[60] In short, this is because cases go to trial only where there is a disparity in the parties' perceptions of the relative merits of their positions, perhaps due to the uncertainty of the law. There being no *a priori* reason why the expectations of claimants' lawyers should be further from the actual outcome more often than those of defendants' lawyers, this disparity will be resolved on average 50 per cent in favour of each party. It is a cause for concern that there is such gross deviation from this principle for investment treaty arbitration.

Another explanation may simply be that investment tribunals, being the product of international law, are naturally more disposed towards the interests of the respondent states responsible for creating them through their treaty commitments, than claimants and their lawyers may care to admit. If too many awards of too high a value are issued against states, states may start to withdraw from the treaties that confer their jurisdiction, as has recently occurred for Russia, Ecuador, Venezuela and Bolivia.[61] Part of the problem may arise from inconsistency in investment tribunals' jurisprudence. That investment tribunals have difficulty following the precedents of their predecessors on the most elementary legal issues has been comprehensively documented.[62] Investment tribunals exhibit a mysteriously selective attitude toward the doctrine of *stare decisis*. Where tribunals want to reach a conclusion for which prior authority exists, they are happy to rely upon the decisions of other tribunals as authoritative and binding;[63] where they want to branch out in a new direction, they justify doing so by the assertion that they are not bound by precedent.[64] A number of tribunals have seen fit brazenly to depart from their peers' views of the law.[65] The lack of any central administering authority, hierarchy of arbitral precedents or appellate regime,[66] may be responsible in part for the unpredictable nature of investment treaty jurisprudence. However the perennially changing content of investment treaty law should, in an impartial system, fall as an equal burden on both claimant and defendant, and maintain the Priest-Klein 50 per cent figure. Something else seems to be going on. The principal driver behind the weak figures for claimants' success rates within investment treaty arbitration may be that it is so lucrative for the armies of legal counsel, arbitrators and experts that the poor prospects of recovery are conveniently forgotten. Claims are overstated because legal fees can be increased proportionately.

Claims under investment treaties are jurisdictional thickets, in which many of the most contentious questions between the parties are whether the claimant has a right to bring a claim under a treaty at all. For instance, it is common for investors to fund investments through a company incorporated in a state which has an investment treaty with the country receiving the investment. Is the 'investor' a national of the counterpart state to the BIT simply by virtue of being registered as a company there, irrespective of nationality of the shareholders or the existence of a business presence in the country in question? Precisely this issue arose in *Tokios Tokelés v Ukraine*,[67] discussed above. To recap, the claimant was a company incorporated in Lithuania, of which over 99 per cent of the shares were held by Ukrainian nationals. The company sued under the Lithuania-Ukraine BIT. The tribunal upheld jurisdiction: Ukrainian citizens could acquire protections under international investment law by incorporating a company in a foreign country and then using that vehicle to invest in their own country.[68] This remarkable case is far from alone in a pattern of surpassing jurisdictional findings in favour of claimants. Indeed although almost every investment treaty claim is subject to a jurisdictional challenge, in 88.5 per cent of such challenges the claimant is ruled entitled to continue with his claim under at least some jurisdictional guise.[69] This rate compares most favourably with the International Court of Justice, in which contentious claims have been permitted to proceed over jurisdiction or admissibility objections in some 58 per cent of cases as of March

2010.[70] A cynic might observe that unlike ICJ judges (who are paid a flat annual salary irrespective of caseload), arbitrators have incentives to keep proceedings going; were they to strike out a claim for want of jurisdiction, they would not receive their fees for adjudicating the later stages of the claim.

THE FUTURE OF INVESTMENT TREATY LAW

Because investment treaty arbitration is usually such bad value for claimants, the number of cases brought before investment tribunals will remain modest, in the order fewer than 50 per year. Nonetheless, we will not see states sign significantly larger numbers of investment treaties in the future. States have become wary of the potential risks of large awards from a small number of cases. These cases are concentrated in Latin America, where Argentina was sued for taking emergency measures arising out of its 1999–2002 financial crisis and other left-leaning governments are currently in the process of being sued for implementing nationalisation policies. The original motive for signing such treaties was that they were perceived as cost free, yet experience has shown that they do carry with them significant risks for states. However, the global network of investment treaties is already in place, and withdrawal from the existing regime is politically costly for states seeking to attract capital: far more costly than not signing such treaties in the first place. By the act of withdrawal, one may be labelled as being as attractive to investors as Venezuela's firebrand anti-market President Hugo Chavez, who has declared his intention to withdraw from ICSID.[71] Thus the formal treaty structure for international investment law has reached a natural plateau.

That does not mean the law will remain static, however. Amongst practitioners of international law and the international organisations that have an enduring interest in its propagation, international investment law will remain an appealing mystery, and its elaborate and often inconsistent jurisprudence will continue to evolve at the hands of the group of arbitrators and lawyers who are steeped in its arcane arts. Supported by international organisations with a vested interest in the discipline's continuance, in particular ICSID and UNCTAD, it will be the subject of ever further studies and refinements. All parties involved have an interest in developing the jurisprudence coherently to foster respect for the subject as an autonomous intellectual discipline within the law. However, investment tribunals will remain perpetually hamstrung by competing considerations. Should they rule against states too frequently, states will withdraw. Should they fail to make the economics of bringing a claim sufficiently attractive for investors (i.e. the rate of return is insufficient), commercial claimants will start to notice that the process is a sink hole for legal fees and management time after a failed investment. Those resources may be better used pursuing a new investment rather than raking over the ashes of the old. It is not clear how investment tribunals will react to this tension in their incentives, particularly given that they are decentralised and there is no central body of arbitral or legal authority. It may be that they continue to make comparatively modest awards in favour of investors (i.e. in the order of US$5 million or less) in the majority of cases where they find in claimants' favour. They will reserve for occasional public show very large awards (in the region of more than US$100 million), much as the proprietor of a casino offers a few machines with jackpot payouts to attract customers. States will, on the whole, tolerate the regime, since the burdens it places upon them are for the most part rather modest. Claimants will be deterred from bringing claims due to their continuing high cost and low returns, but not entirely. Thus there will be a continuing modest stream of claims to feed the machine.

The community of international investment lawyers needs to manage this process carefully. In the short history of investment treaty law the subject has come perilously close to killing itself off on at least two occasions, due to strong reactions of respondent states to arbitral proceedings. Argentina has been sued at least 28 times for events arising out of its financial crisis in 2001–2002, when its government converted US dollar denominated debts into freefalling domestic currency by legislative decree. So far, proceedings against Argentina arising out of these events have been successful at least in part in every award issued. Nonetheless, the government has apparently not paid any of the awards against it, and leftist Latin American countries have withdrawn from the ICSID Convention in expressions of sympathy, making the Argentine predicament a *cause célèbre* in their attacks upon principles of a liberal market economy. Investment tribunals could have escaped the trap in which they now find themselves of entering repeated sizeable awards against a single nation, through the development of a doctrine of necessity or *force majeure*; but the early tribunals missed the political significance of the mass claims that were being brought. There is now some evidence that the doctrine of necessity is being broadened by investment tribunals to mitigate the political harm to the discipline of international investment law by the Argentina arbitrations,[72] and this is one advantage of tribunals not being bound by *stare decisis*.

The other serious political risk investment tribunals failed to anticipate was Russia's withdrawal from the Energy Charter Treaty (ECT) in July 2009 after Yukos shareholders sued the government under the Charter for the break-up of the oil giant in 2004. The liquidation of Yukos, at the time one of the largest energy companies in the world (responsible for 2 per cent of global oil production), was a political act by a Russian president determined to rein in Russia's oligarchs and intending to make an example of one oligarch who had undertaken political activities against him. Vladimir Putin would not brook international law being used to interfere so directly in the country's internal political affairs. Russia's withdrawal from the Energy Charter Treaty was a direct consequence of the claim brought against it under the Energy Charter Treaty, a claim which could have been disposed of on jurisdictional grounds.[73] With such formidable natural resources, Russia can pay the political price of withdrawal from investment treaties with ease, and its act of repudiation may conceivably be followed by countries in the Commonwealth of Independent States (CIS), eastern Europe and Central Asia regions that look to Russia for political leadership. At the time of writing, the fall-out from this political mistake on the part of investment tribunals is yet to be quantified.

Investment treaty law is one of the first areas of international law in which there are potentially serious direct financial consequences for states depending upon the direction in which the law develops. In these circumstances, it is surprising this area of law has emerged at all, and the reason it has done so may be down more to a collective misperception by states of the effects of the treaties they were signing than to anything else. Nonetheless, emerge it has, and this area of law now has to operate under a far more burdensome political constraint than some of its more politically irrelevant counterparts that this work considers. The ambiguous legal standards set out in investment treaties are in danger of being developed into too concrete a set of principles by activist arbitrators. Substantial damages claims for loss of expected earnings may turn out to be genuinely entertained by investment tribunals as a matter of course. If these goals are pursued too aggressively, then states will resile from the system and bring it crashing down. Yet if it never hands out rewards, the system will lose favour with the claimants who fund the system so handsomely for its participants. It is not yet clear whether investment tribunals can continue finely to balance these competing financial concerns. But there is a lesson here for international lawyers: international law is at its strongest when developed in politically and intellectually interesting, but financially mostly irrelevant, directions. When international law meets the cruel external world of private financial interests, it is on much more precarious ground.

International trade law, the other area of international law of real financial concern to states, is considered in the next chapter. However, it is an altogether weaker and more pliant creature, due to its deliberately obtuse procedural features, peculiar system of remedies and emasculated regime for enforcement of its decisions. We now investigate this unusual system.

NOTES

1. Hansard CXII (3rd Series) 380–444 (25 June 1850).
2. The first judicial recognition of the principle that a state has a right to complain of a breach of international law by another state injuring one of its citizens was *The Mavrommartis Palestine Concessions* (1924) PCIJ Ser. A, No. 2, 12.
3. Lipson, Charles (1985), *Standing Guard: Protecting Foreign Capital in the Nineteenth and Twentieth Centuries*, Berkeley: University of California Press, p.54 records that Britain alone sent military forces to Latin America at least 40 times between 1820 and 1914 to enforce private individuals' quasi-legal claims against governments in the region.
4. *Company General of the Orinoco* (France-Venezuela Mixed Claims Commission), RIAA X 184, 31 July 1905.
5. *Case concerning certain German interests in Polish Upper Silesia* (Germany v Poland), PCIJ, Ser. A, No. 7, 1926.
6. *Oscar Chinn* (UK v Belgium), PCIJ, Ser. A/B, No. 63, 1934.
7. Secretary of State Cordell Hull: 'The Government of the United States merely adverts to a self-evident fact when it notes that the applicable precedents and recognized authorities on international law support its declaration that, under every rule of law and equity, no government is entitled to expropriate private property, for whatever purpose, without provision for prompt, adequate, and effective payment therefor.' Reproduced in 3 G. Hackworth, Digest of International Law 658-59 (1942).
8. See e.g. Note of 3 August 1938 from the Mexican Minister of Foreign Affairs: 'My Government maintains. . .that there is in international law no rule universally accepted in theory nor carried out in practice, which makes obligatory the payment of immediate compensation nor even of deferred compensation, for expropriations of a general and impersonal character', Hackworth, G. (1942) *Digest of International Law* **3**, § 228, 657.
9. The 'Abs-Shawcroft' draft convention was prepared by the Gesellschaft zur Förderung des Schutzes von Auslandsinvestitionen, a Köln-based society of businessmen, in 1957. For more details see Rood, Leslie (1976–77), 'Compensation for takeovers in Africa', *Journal of International Law and Economics*, **11**, 521.
10. Treaty of 25 November 1959 between the Federal Republic of Germany and Pakistan for the Promotion and Protection of Investments.
11. G.A. Res. 1803 (1962) on Permanent Sovereignty over Natural Resources; G.A. Res. 3171 (1973) on Permanent Sovereignty over Natural Resources; G.A. Res. 3201 (1974) on a New International Economic Order; G.A. Res. 3281 (1974) on the Charter of Economic Rights and Duties of States.
12. See for example the 1963 Switzerland-Liberia BIT, which contains no dispute resolution provisions.
13. At least, none that was made public. As will be explained below, in principle these arbitration proceedings may be kept private. It is therefore at least conceivable that an inter-state BIT arbitration has occurred but whose existence has never entered the public domain.
14. The Indonesia-Netherlands BIT (1968) and the Italy-Chad BIT (1969) are cited as the first such BITs. See e.g. Newcombe, Andrew and Lluis Paradell (2009), *Law and Practice Investment Treaties*, Alphen can den Rijn: Kluwer, pp.44–5.
15. US-Senegal BIT, dated 6 December 1983.
16. *The Factory at Chorzów* (Germany v Poland), Judgment on the Merits, 13 September 1928, PCIJ Ser. A, No. 17, 1928.

17. The Energy Charter Secretariat has described Yukos's claim against the Russian Federation as having a value of US$100 billion, or 6.25 per cent of Russia's 2008 GDP. This is apparently the largest dispute ever litigated in any forum.
18. Those grounds are enumerated in Article V of the New York Convention, and include such technical matters as invalidity of the arbitration agreement; failure to give notice of arbitral proceedings; the arbitral tribunal was not composed in accordance with the parties' agreement or the tribunal acted *ultra petita* (i.e. it decided an issue beyond what it was asked to decide). These grounds are seldom shown. Errors of law or in the factual analysis reached by the tribunal are insufficient to evade enforcement.
19. See e.g. *CME v Czech Republic*, Partial Award 13 September 2001; *Revere Copper v OPIC*, 56 ILM 28.
20. See e.g. *Generation Ukraine v Ukraine*, ICSID Case No. ARB/00/9, Award 16 September 2003, §20.22; *Telenor Mobile Communications v Hungary*, ICSID Case No. ARB/04/15, Award 13 September 2006, §63.
21. See e.g. *Tecmed v Mexico*, ICSID Case No. ARB(AF)/002/2, Award 29 May 2003, §154; *Waste Management Inc v Mexico (No. 2)*, ICSID Case No. ARB(AF)/00/3, Final Award 30 April 2004, §98.
22. See e.g. *Loewen v USA*, Award 26 June 2003, 7 ICSID Reports 451; Paulsson, Jan (2005), *Denial of Justice in International Law*, Cambridge: Cambridge University Press.
23. See e.g. *Saluka Investments v Czech Republic*, Partial Award 17 March 2006.
24. *Wena Hotel v Egypt*, ICSID Case No. ARB/98/4, Award on Merits 8 December 2000, 41 ILM 896 (2002).
25. See e.g. *CME v Czech Republic*, *supra*, §467; *Siemens v Argentina*, Award 6 February 2007, §267; *Kardassopoulos v Georgia*, Decision on Jurisdiction, 6 July 2007, §182.
26. This formulation appeared in the very first BIT, between Germany and Pakistan in November 1959. Equivalent formulations are found in many, even most, BITs.
27. *Fedax v Venezuela*, Award 9 March 1998, 37 ILM 1391 (1998); *SGS v Philippines*, ICSID Case No. ARB/02/6, Decision on Jurisdiction 29 January 2004; *Sempra v Argentina*, ICSID Case No. ARB/02/16, Decision on Objections to Jurisdiction 11 May 2005; *Eureko v Poland*, Partial Award 19 August 2005; *Noble Ventures v Romania*, ICSID Case No. ARB/01/11, Award 12 October 2005; *LG&E v Argentina*, ICSID Case No. ARB/02/1, Decision on Liability 3 October 2006; *Waste Management v Mexico*, ICSID Case No. ARB(AF)/00/3, Award 30 April 2004; *LESI –DIPENTA v Algeria*, ICSID Case No. ARB/03/08, Award 10 January 2005. The earlier case of *SGS v Pakistan*, ICSID Case No. ARB/01/13, Decision on Jurisdiction 6 August 2003, which construed an umbrella clause narrowly, no longer appears to be followed.
28. See e.g. *MTD v Chile*, ICSID Case No. ARB/01/7, Award 21 May 2004; *Bayindir v Pakistan*, ICSID Case No. ARB/03/29, Decision on Jurisdiction 14 November 2005 (in each case importing substantive provisions from another BIT); *Maffezeni v Spain*, ICSID Case No. ARB/97/7, Decision on Objections to Jurisdiction 25 January 2000, 16 ICSID Rev-FILJ 212 (2001) (importing preferable procedural provisions from another BIT).
29. *Tokios Tokelės v Ukraine*, ICSID Case No. ARB/02/18, Decision on Jurisdiction 29 April 2004. This case is discussed later in this chapter.
30. Many BITs explicitly define 'investments' as including loans or the provision of debt facilities. See UNCTAD (2007), 'Bilateral Investment Treaties 1995–2006: trends in investment rulemaking', Geneva: United Nations, p.7.
31. Many investment treaties make explicit provision for this. See e.g. *Generation Ukraine v Ukraine*, *supra*, §11.1.
32. *AMTO v Ukraine*, SCC Arbitration No. 080/2005, Final Award 26 March 2008.
33. Article 25(1) ICSID Convention: 'The jurisdiction of the Centre shall extend to any legal dispute arising directly out of an investment, between a Contracting State. . .and a national of another Contracting State, which the parties to the dispute consent in writing to submit to the Centre'.
34. The Algiers Accords of 19 January 1981, brokered by Algeria between the US and

Iranian governments, provided for release of 52 US hostages in Tehran (after the takeover of the US Embassy in Tehran on 4 November 1979), and established the Iran-US Claims Tribunal to replace litigation between their respective governments and citizens. Iranian debts to US institutions, and other claims of expropriation by US institutions against the Iranian government, would be paid by Iran; otherwise, former property of the Shah would be returned to Iran.

35. See e.g. the discussion by Yackee, Jason (2010), 'Do Bilateral Investment Treaties promote foreign direct investment? Some Hints from Alternative Evidence', University of Wisconsin Legal Studies Research Paper No. 1114, pp.8, 9.
36. See e.g. Guzman, Andrew (1998), 'Why LDCs sign treaties that hurt them: explaining the popularity of bilateral investment treaties', *Virginia Journal of International Law*, **38**, 639.
37. See Elkins, Zachary, Andrew Guzman and Beth Simmons (2006), 'Competing for Capital: the Diffusion of Bilateral Investment Treaties, 1960–2000', Latin American and Caribbean Law and Economics Association Annual Papers, The Berkeley Program in Law and Economics, University of California Berkeley.
38. While this assertion may appear common sense, it has been challenged. See e.g. Veenstra-Kjos, H.E. (2007), 'Counterclaims by Host States in Investment Treaty Arbitration', *Transnational Dispute Management*, **4** (4) (July).
39. Source: the ICSID Caseload – Statistics, Issue 2010-1.
40. See note 28, *supra*.
41. Stewart, Dugald (1980), 'Account of the life and writings of Adam Smith, LLD', in Smith, Adam, Dugald Stewart, Joseph Black and James Mutton (eds), *Essays on Philosophical Subjects*, Oxford: Oxford University Press, section IV.26, p.322.
42. There are many such studies, including e.g. UNCTAD (1998), *Bilateral Investment Treaties in the Mid-1990s*, Geneva: UN; Banga, Rashmi (2003), 'Impact of government policies and investment agreements on FDI inflows', Indian Council for Research on International Economic Relations, Working Paper No. 116; Hallward-Driemaier, Mary (2003), 'Do bilateral investment treaties attract FDI? Only a bit and they could bite', World Bank Policy Research Paper WPS 3121.
43. UNCTAD (2009), *The Role of International Investment Agreements in Attracting Foreign Direct Investment to Developing Countries*, Geneva: UN.
44. Compare Tobin, J. and S. Rose-Ackerman (2003), 'Foreign direct investment and the business environment in developing countries: the impact of bilateral investment treaties', William Davidson Institute Working Paper No. 587; and Tobin, J. and S. Rose-Ackerman (2006), 'Bilateral investment treaties: do they stimulate foreign direct investment?', unpublished. See also Yackee, Jason (2007), 'Do BITs really work? Revisiting the empirical links between investment treaties and foreign direct investment', Legal Studies Research Paper Series, Paper No. 1054.
45. In economics, a rent is a distribution of funds to a resource above the amount required to sustain its use. Thus a system of public administration that charges fees in excess of its operation costs, or extracts bribes from its users, may be described as 'rent seeking'. Rents are inefficient and are characteristic of corrupt public bureaucracies. In properly competitive markets, rent seeking should disappear, since consumers will switch out of a resource in respect of which rents are charged and into another resource where no rent is sought.
46. Price elasticity of demand is a measure of the responsiveness of demand for a commodity to changes in its price. 'Fundamental' commodities, such as oil, have low price elasticity of demand: for an increase in price, relatively speaking demand does not decrease. We keep on driving our cars even when fuel prices are high. Where price elasticity of demand for a country's commodities is low, investors take a risk that a drop in the commodity's price may not be compensated for by increased sales; but also gamble that an increase in the commodity's price will not be offset by decreased sales, thus yielding a bonanza. Where price elasticity of demand is higher, the partial offset in demand caused by price variations may make anticipated profits more stable and less prone to

fluctuations in market prices. Where elasticity is too high, an increase in market price may close down the market in the commodity altogether.

47. See e.g. UNCTAD (1998), *Bilateral investment treaties in the mid-1990s*, Geneva: UN; Hallward-Driemaier, Mary (2003), 'Do bilateral investment treaties attract FDI? Only a bit and they could bite', World Bank Policy Research Paper WPS 3121.
48. See e.g. Neumayer, Eric and Laura Spess (2005), 'Do bilateral investment treaties increase foreign direct investment in developing countries?', *World Development*, **33**(10), 1567, who reject the sceptical conclusions of prior studies that focus upon FDI inflows from bilateral investment treaty partners rather than net FDI inflows from all sources. The authors find a correlation between signature of BITs and FDI in general. If this result is robust notwithstanding the absence of a correlation with FDI inflows from partner signatories, that must be due to some kind of signalling effect.
49. See e.g. UNCTAD (2005), 'Investor-State Disputes Arising from Investment Treaties: A Review', UN Doc. UNCTAD/ITE/IIT/2005/4, p.4; van Harten, Gus and Martin Loughlin (2006), 'Investment treaty arbitration as a species of global administrative law', *European Journal of International Law*, **17**, 121, 124, n.11.
50. Franck, Susan (2007), 'Empirically evaluating claims about investment treaty arbitration', *North Carolina Law Review*, **86** (1), 69 notes that within her data set of arbitral awards about which public information is available, amongst arbitral awards quantifying arbitrators' and institutional fees, the average was US$581,000 (typically divided equally between claimant and respondent); where tribunals ordered one party to pay a proportion of the other's costs, the average so ordered was US$655,000. However, a tribunal may not order a party to pay the entirety of the other side's legal costs, meaning that the average costs actually incurred may be significantly higher. See also UNCTAD, *Investor-State Disputes arising from Investment Treaties: A Review*, ibid. (asserting that the Czech Republic budgeted US$13.8 million in 2005 in the defence of two investment treaty claims).
51. Ibid., Chapter 3, notes 33 and 34.
52. See e.g. Newfarmer, Richard (2005), 'Beyond merchandise trade', in *Global Economic Prospects*, World Bank, pp.97, 118.
53. That is, April 2010. The awards are *CME v Czech Republic*, Final Award 14 March 2003 (US$269,814,000); *France Telecom v Lebanon* (award not public but sum of US$266 million referred to in a France Telecom press release dated 22 February 2005); *CMS v Argentina*, Award 12 May 2005 (US$133,200,000) and Rumeli Telecom *A.S. V Kazakhstan*, Award 29 July 2008 (UD$125 million). There was a fifth, *Enron v Argentina*, Award 22 May 2007, but it was subsequently annulled on 30 July 2007.
54. Franck, Susan (2007) 'Empirically evaluating claims about investment treaty arbitration', *ibid.*
55. The North American Free Trade Agreement, a trilateral treaty between the United States, Mexico and Canada that came into force on 1 January 1994, has an 'investment chapter' that contains treaty protections for investors similar to those found in BITs and also provides for arbitration proceedings between investor claimants and respondent states.
56. Legum, Barton (2004), 'Lessons learned from NAFTA: the new generation of US investment treaty arbitration provisions', ICSID *Review of Foreign Investment Law Journal*, **19**, 344, 346–7.
57. Franck, ibid., pp.48, 58. Franck notes that the mean amount of damages claimed in her sample set was US$343.4 million, whereas the mean amount awarded to successful claimants was US$10.4 million.
58. Argentina, subject to more investment treaty claims than any other sovereign, is believed not to have satisfied the various awards entered against it following the measures it took in 2001–2002 in response to its economic crisis. See Marzoti, Osvaldo (2006), 'Enforcement of treaty awards and national constitutions (the Argentinean cases)', *Business Law International*, **7**, 226.
59. Also worthy of note is that arbitral institutions frequently set their own fees and those

of arbitrators by reference to the value of the dispute, giving claimants another reason not to overstate their claims.

60. Priest, George and Benjamin Klein (1984), 'The selection of disputes for litigation', *Journal of Legal Studies*, **13**(1), 5.
61. Russia withdrew from the Energy Charter Treaty on 30 July 2009. Ecuador's Congress denounced the ICSID Convention on 12 June 2009, and also withdrew from at least nine BITs. Bolivia denounced the ICSID Convention on 2 May 2007. Venezuela denounced the Netherlands-Venezuela BIT on 30 April 2008. On 17 October 2008 the Constitutional Chamber of the Venezuelan Supreme Tribunal issued its Decision 1541, which had the effect of annulling a Venezuelan domestic legislative provision consenting to ICSID arbitration in disputes with foreign investors.
62. Franck, Susan (2005), 'The Legitimacy Crisis in Investment Treaty Arbitration: Privatizing Public International Law through Inconsistent Decisions', *Fordham Law Review*, **73**, 1521.
63. See e.g. *Companía de Aqias del Aconquija & Vivendi Universal v Argentine Republic*, Decision on Jurisdiction 14 November 2005, § 94.
64. See e.g. *SGS v Philippines*, Decision on Jurisdiction 29 January 2004, § 97.
65. Issues of law on which tribunals have entertained divergent analyses include whether non-compliance with mandatory 'cooling off' periods before commencing arbitration affects the tribunal's jurisdiction (contrast *Ethyl Corp v Canada*, Decision on Jurisdiction 24 June 1998, §§ 76–88 with *Enron v Argentina*, Decision on Jurisdiction 14 January 2004, § 88); whether 'most favoured nation' clauses permit a tribunal to import more favourable dispute resolution provisions from another treaty (contrast *Maffezeni v Spain*, Decision on Jurisdiction 25 January 2000, §§ 38–64 with *Plama v Bulgaria*, Decision on Jurisdiction 29 November 2004, §§ 115–119); the criteria for a state of necessity that excuses compliance with treaty obligations (see Parish, Matthew (2010), 'On necessity', *Journal of World Investment and Trade*, **11**(2),1); and whether so-called 'umbrella clauses' elevate breaches of contract to treaty violations (see *supra*).
66. ICSID has a quasi-appellate regime. Article 52 of the ICSID Convention allows a party to an ICSID award to apply for ICSID to convene an 'ad hoc committee' to annul the award. The grounds on which annulment will be granted are very limited, including 'corruption', 'serious departure from a fundamental rule of procedure' and the like. In theory, errors of law are not grounds for annulment. However, in two recent cases, *Enron v Argentina*, ICSID Case No. ARB/01/3, Decision of the annulment committee 30 July 2010, and *Sempra Energy International v Argentina*, ARB/02/16, Decision of the annulment committee 29 June 2010, ICSID annulment committees allowed applications to annul prior awards in each case on the ground that 'the Tribunal ha[d] manifestly exceeded its powers' (Article 52(1)(b) ICSID Convention). Reading the decisions, however, one is drawn to the conclusion that the act of exceeding its powers consisted, in the committee's view, of the tribunal making mistakes of law.
67. ICSID Case No. ARB/02/18, Decision on Jurisdiction 29 April 2004.
68. The chairman of the tribunal, Prosper Weil, so disapproved of the jurisdictional decision that in his dissenting opinion he considered it 'might jeopardize the future of [ICSID]'. He then resigned from the tribunal.
69. Franck, 'Empirically evaluating claims', *ibid.*, p.52.
70. This statistic does not include cases in which either there has been no substantive court decision (save on requests for preliminary measures), or cases where proceedings have been discontinued at the request of the plaintiff. However, it does include two cases (the *Aerial Incident of 27 July 1955* cases) in which the plaintiff states requested discontinuance after a prior jurisdictional ruling in another closely related case that meant the plaintiffs had no prospects of persuading the Court to seize jurisdiction.
71. See e.g. *Latin America Ponders Pullout of ICSID*, Dispute Resolution Journal, 1 May 2007.
72. See *Continental Casualty v Argentina*, ICSID Case No. ARB/03/9, Award 5 September 2008; *Sempra v Argentina*, ICSID Case No. ARB/02/16, Decision on the Argentine

Republic's Request for Annulment of the Award 29 June 2010; and *Enron v Argentina*, ICSID Case No. ARB/01/3, Decision on the Argentine Republic's Request for Annulment of the Award 30 July 2010, all of which suggest that the test of necessity should be interpreted somewhat more favourably in Argentina's favour.

73. Arbitration proceedings were commenced under the ECT by Yukos shareholders on 3 February 2005. Hearings on jurisdiction were held in November 2008. In an award on 30 November 2009, the tribunal upheld its jurisdiction, notwithstanding Russia's withdrawal from the ECT on 30 July 2009. Russia's move may fairly be seen as a pre-emptive strike upon the tribunal, anticipating the jurisdictional ruling going against it. See *Yukos Universal Limited v Russian Federation*, PCA Case No. AA227, Interim Award on Jurisdiction Admissibility 30 November 2009.

6. Self-spite in the regulation of international trade

In Chapter 3, we saw that states are in general reluctant to submit themselves to a system of compulsory dispute resolution between one another. For powerful states, there is little to be gained: a third party adjudicatory regime can never achieve as attractive an outcome as unilateral exercise of that state's military or economic power. For all states, there may be value in the political theatre of such a court: but where strong state interests are involved, states will inevitably ignore rulings that go against them. There is simply too much at stake in one's domestic politics to abide by the rulings of a court that has no effective sanction for non-compliance. Thus international courts are weak, and optional. In this chapter, we address an apparent counterexample to this logic. Apart from being a forum for trade negotiations, the World Trade Organisation is primarily an international court, to which all 153 of its members are required to submit. It exists to resolve disputes between sovereigns relating to government regulation of international trade. Given our analysis so far, why do states agree to such a regime? The answer is that the system is not what it appears. To understand how international trade became the subject of legal regulation, a short detour into the economic history of the subject is appropriate.

THE POLITICAL ECONOMY OF INTERNATIONAL TRADE

Mercantilism, an economic theory that emphasises the importance of exports over imports, and the value of trade surpluses, was prevalent in Europe through to the late eighteenth century. The policy consequences of the theory were import tariffs and export subsidies; it resulted in autarchy within individual colonial empires as each raised tariffs to prevent imports from others, enforced monopolies and imposed bans on foreign competition. The political incentive for mercantilism was the rise of rent-seeking merchants within European political systems, who stood to gain from surpluses derived from their monopoly positions within each nation. The intellectual backlash against mercantilism saw changes in government policy from the early nineteenth century, when Ricardo's theory of comparative advantage explained why free trade would benefit both exporting and importing countries in all circumstances. The benefits of free trade to consumers, combined with the new markets available to domestic producers able now to sell their wares in foreign markets, outweigh the losses suffered by previously monopolistic producers now forced to compete. For all but primary industries, free trade facilitates acquisition of cheaper input commodities for production, which can be sourced in more competitive markets abroad. Ricardo's insight was that the benefits from trade do not require a trading nation to be more efficient in the production of a commodity in order to export it to another. All that is required is that between two nations there is a comparative advantage: one nation produces commodity A relatively more efficiently than another nation produces commodity B. Where Portugal produces both wine and cloth more efficiently than England, there will still be trade in both directions, provided that England is just slightly less efficient at producing cloth, but a lot less efficient at producing wine. In those circumstances, Portugal will export wine to England which will export cotton to Portugal. It is cheaper for Portugal to produce excess wine and trade that for English cloth than it is for Portugal to make its own cloth. Because comparative advantages in two or more commodities exist between virtually every country, trade is beneficial between every set of countries, and trade will occur, save where governments prevent it.[1]

The challenge for those seeking to promote global free trade is that it requires cooperation between governments. Import (customs) duties and import quotas inhibit free trade, as do regulations requiring goods to conform to national standards: the cost of compliance with those standards makes import into the regulating country more expensive than it should be. In EU law, such regulations are known as 'measures equivalent to quantitative restrictions',[2] because the economic effect of such rules is the same as an import quota: a certain level of imports that would otherwise enter the market is frozen out due to compliance costs making the import uneconomical. Export subsidies also distort free trade, decreasing the capacity of domestic producers to compete with otherwise uneconomical imports. Unequal treatment of imports from differing countries decreases the gains from trade, preventing states from exporting commodities in which they have the strongest comparative advantage, because another nation's equivalent commodities are receiving favourable treatment and thus can be sold at a lower price, notwithstanding costing the same or even more to produce. Each of these trade-regressive measures, despite not maximising aggregate welfare, nonetheless benefits some interest groups, principally the domestic producers who drive mercantilist policies. Producers hold a disproportionate influence within a political system when compared with consumers, whose interests are more diffusely spread than those of producers. Although the net benefit to consumers is greater than the net loss to producers, there are more consumers and thus each consumer individually stands to gain less than producers individually stand to lose. Thus the costs of achieving effective cooperation between parties with common interests to lobby for political measures favourable to them are lower for producers than they are for consumers.[3]

Where producers successfully lobby for mercantilist policies within a domestic political system, this damages foreign producers, who will thereby be restricted in their capacity to export to that country. Their only effective remedy, such as it is, is to encourage their government to retaliate with equivalent measures against imports from that state. But retaliation is a bittersweet pill. It may be difficult to frame a measure that will benefit the disadvantaged producer. A retaliatory import tariff against the same commodity will benefit that producer if the two states compete in the commodity. They may not do. If England raises a tariff against Portuguese wine, hurting Portuguese vineyards, there will be little consolation in Portugal introducing a retaliatory tariff against English wine, since England exports no wine to Portugal. Portugal may instead impose import tariffs on English cloth, but that will not benefit Portugal's wine producers: nor will it harm the English wine producers who benefited from the original English import tariff. Rather, a retaliatory cloth tariff will benefit Portuguese cloth producers, and harm English cloth producers, who in turn may lobby the English government again for further retaliation. Within this descending spiral trade wars are born.

Free trade agreements are aimed at addressing the welfare inefficiency of domestic political economy – the disproportionate influence domestic producers may have in a political system to lobby for protectionist measures. The first such agreements emerged in the middle of the nineteenth century, following the decline of mercantilism. Bilateral treaties of 'friendship, commerce and navigation' began developing a rudimentary law of international trade, containing obligations such as the right for vessels of the other nation to dock and import and export, and for traders to go about their business freely. These treaties also typically provided for an obligation not to treat importers and exporters from the other nation any less favourably than traders from any third country (a 'most favoured nation' or MFN obligation), and a duty not to treat them any less favourably than one's own nationals (a 'national treatment' obligation).[4] The first international treaty to cap trade tariffs was the Cobden-Chevalier Treaty of 1860, which reduced French tariffs on British manufactured goods and British tariffs on French alcoholic beverages. In a revealing precedent for modern debates, the treaty was concluded notwithstanding concerns by Emperor Napoleon III that the treaty could jeopardise French jobs. This treaty sparked a series of equivalent bilateral agreements between European states, and by the end of the nineteenth century there had been a global revolution in international trade. Between 1880 and 1913, exports from the UK increased by 135 per cent, from France by 98 per cent and Germany 245 per cent.[5] This was an earlier era of globalisation, based not upon a multilateral trading system in the vein of the World Trade Organisation, but grounded for the most part on bilateral treaties and individual states' forbearance from imposing import barriers.

It might be tempting to consider free trade agreements as solutions to a prisoners' dilemma, but this is not really so. In a conventional prisoners' dilemma, if both parties adopt cooperative strategies, they are both better off than if neither adopts a cooperative strategy. But what makes prisoners' dilemmas acute is that should one party adopt a cooperative strategy and the other not, the uncooperative party gains at the cooperative party's expense. If the USA and Russia agree to eliminate all their nuclear weapons, and the USA honours the agreement but Russia does not, then Russia benefits and the USA loses from the comparative redistribution of political and military global power. The consequence of a prisoners' dilemma is that both sides adopt uncooperative strategies unless they can make a credible commitment to comply with any agreement they may enter into. In the domestic context, this commitment can be made using contracts enforced by impartial courts.

One theme of this book is that in the international context, making credible commitments is very difficult because powerful states will not naturally give away their military and economic power to an impartial third party enforcement system. Unless states accept enforcement of decisions through an impartial procedure, international law commitments are not credible. But the dynamic is quite different for free trade agreements. Where one party pursues an uncooperative strategy, both sides lose, but not as much as where both parties pursue uncooperative strategies. Where Portugal imposes import tariffs for English cloth, but England imposes no import tariffs for Portuguese wine, Portuguese consumers of cloth suffer, as do English producers of cloth. Portuguese producers of cloth benefit; but Portuguese clothing manufacturers will lose out, because they can no longer procure English cloth (available at a cheaper price by exchanging it for Portuguese wine). Economic theory predicts that the net loss to the Portuguese consumers, and to those producers that require cloth as a manufacturing input, will exceed the benefit to Portuguese cloth producers from imposing an import tariff on cloth. Put another way, the welfare-maximising course of action for any state is unilateral reduction of barriers to imports.[6]

Therefore free trade agreements should be self-enforcing. The parties to them have an incentive to comply irrespective of what their counterparts do. In theory, there is no need for either party to make a credible commitment. This is an area of international law in which the problem of inability to enforce ought not to pollute the aspirations of the discipline, and in the nineteenth and first half of the twentieth centuries no thought was given to enforcement or adjudication mechanisms under free trade agreements. To the extent one does not observe perfect compliance with trade agreements, or even unilateral tariff reduction by all states, this is explicable by reference to capture of state power by domestic interest groups – e.g. the Portuguese cloth producers – over the broader social welfare. By capturing public support through playing up fears over job losses, producers may hamper a nation from pursuing the course optimal to its welfare. Nonetheless in a sufficiently healthy democratic system, over time any elite capture of the political process by producers should evaporate; other social interest groups ought to prevail. Free trade agreements make the prospects of collective economic wisdom prevailing greater, since they increase the net utility to a nation compared with unilateral tariff reduction. Once free trade agreements are in place it becomes easier for states to resist producers' capture of the political system, since the government can plead the imperative to comply with its international legal obligations as a defence to the domestic political demand to take protectionist measures. In the long run, the prospects for states voluntarily to comply with their free trade agreement obligations are positive.

SMOOT-HAWLEY AND BEYOND

Free trade took its greatest knock in 1930. The United States had never been quite as committed to free trade in the nineteenth century as had the European colonial powers, for whom trade was an important engine of economic activity, particularly for Britain. The ratio of duties collected to dutiable imports remained in excess of 40 per cent within the United States in the period between 1861 and 1913.[7] After a respite in protectionist measures pushed by President Wilson,[8] the Smoot-Hawley Tariff Act was passed in 1930 to protect US businesses during the Great Depression, increasing the ratio to an unprecedented 53.2 per cent. Retaliation by foreign governments commenced over a year before the act even became law, and heralded a period of retraction in global trade that prolonged the depression and culminated in the Second World War.[9] An appreciation of the contribution of Smoot-Hawley protectionism to economic stagnation and ultimately war was a principal motivation behind the Bretton Woods conference in 1944, which proposed creation of an International Trade Organisation (ITO) to establish common rules for international trade. Although the ITO never came into existence due to US failure to ratify its founding treaty, a multilateral agreement was nonetheless reached on the limitation of tariffs and the establishment of a set of rules to encourage free trade.

The General Agreement on Trade Tariffs (GATT), signed in January 1948, has two principal components. The greater bulk of its text is a series of schedules listing maximum tariff levels for imports into its signatory members. These schedules became ever more voluminous as various 'rounds' of trade talks included ever more commodities subject to tariff maxima and ever more member states were added to the agreement. The treaty itself is a series of detailed trade obligations upon member states, such as an MFN obligation, a national treatment obligation and an obligation for state owned enterprises not to discriminate on grounds of national origin in trade transactions.[10] There is an obligation to allow free transit, and to provide exemptions from customs duties for goods crossing a territory. GATT explicitly allows 'anti-dumping duties' (import tariffs imposed on an import to prevent it from being sold at below cost) and 'countervailing duties' (a duty to offset a foreign government production subsidy), but places limits upon the magnitude of these duties. Import quotas are banned, as are export subsidies; non-export subsidies must be notified to the other parties.

GATT contains very little in the way of dispute resolution provisions. The agreement establishing the ITO contained a dispute resolution mechanism, whereby a committee would hear complaints by GATT parties in the first instance. From the committee there would be an appeal to a plenary session of the ITO's members, and then a further appeal to the ICJ. Because the ITO was still-born, GATT came into force without a clear dispute settlement mechanism. GATT provided that the 'contracting parties' may investigate complaints at the instance of one party and authorise retaliatory suspension of GATT concessions, but it was not clear how this would occur. In the first complaint made, the GATT chairman just made a unilateral and unreasoned ruling that a Cuban consular tax was subject to GATT's MFN rule.[11] Thereafter when a complaint was made, the chairman would establish a working group (subsequently renamed 'panels') to investigate the complaint and negotiate a diplomatic solution. The system developed gradually: from 1952 the panels started issuing 'reports'. Rarely did matters get as far as authorisation to apply retaliatory measures.[12] The Tokyo round of GATT negotiations, between 1973 and 1979, codified these developments. They provided that the GATT conference of contracting parties could form panels to investigate a complaint at the instance of a member. However, the panel regime was relatively weak: the conference of contracting parties could decide to form a panel only by consensus, meaning the party against which a complaint had been initiated could block formation of the panel. The same consensus rule applied to adoption of panel reports.

One might imagine that such a dispute resolution system would never be used, but it was invoked surprisingly frequently. Indeed in three-quarters of cases panel reports were adopted, meaning that the party against whom a finding had been made acquiesced in the decision against her. Key to understanding how such a system could operate is the self-enforcing benefits of free trade agreements: a state will suffer more harm than good from breaching GATT, even if one interest group within the state will benefit. Thus states can embrace a dispute resolution system that finds against them and gives them a pretext for disregarding a harmful domestic lobby. In the majority of cases a formal dispute resolution mechanism was not necessary: given the mutual benefits of compliance, diplomatic negotiation and compromise could prevail.

The spectre of mercantilism was never far beneath the GATT system however, particularly for the United States with its protectionist tradition. Increased legalism within the dispute resolution system, while apparently unnecessary for GATT to achieve its goals, was driven to a degree by the United States. This was ironic given the nation's general opposition to the development of international law that went back as far as its refusal to sign up to the League of Nations. The United States saw a growing trade deficit, and was keen to take measures to prevent its further increase. It therefore wanted to use GATT as a tool to open foreign markets to US exports. A formal legal system, it hoped, would be a technique to pressurise its trading counterparts to achieve this. The United States threatened unilateral retaliations under aggressive domestic trade legislation if the GATT system did not become more robust and allowed the United States to pursue complaints. Section 301 Trade Act 1974, enacted in the midst of the Tokyo round of GATT negotiations, gave the US Trade Representative (USTR) (a government official appointed by the president) the power to take unilateral retaliatory measures on the request of an interested party, if (s)he finds that a foreign government is denying US rights under a trade agreement. An amendment to the statute (known as 'Super 301'), enacted just before the start of the Uruguay round of GATT trade negotiations in 1989, ordered the USTR to draw up a list of priority countries identified as responsible for trade agreement violations. The USTR would then be obliged to initiate investigations under section 301 on its own initiative, threatening unilateral retaliations even without a complaint having been filed. It was under these pressures from the world's largest economy and trading nation that the Uruguay round resulted in an agreement to create the World Trade Organisation (WTO), the first genuinely mandatory inter-sovereign dispute resolution mechanism.

THE WORLD TRADE ORGANISATION

The WTO Agreement, which came into force on 1 January 1995 following the Uruguay round of trade negotiations (1986–1994), contained a raft of new sub-agreements containing rules establishing common standards for domestic regulation in differing areas. These included health measures, rules of origin, pre-shipment inspection, cross-border provision of services, import licensing, intellectual property rights and domestic technical standards. One such sub-agreement, known colloquially as the 'Dispute Settlement Understanding' (DSU), establishes a 'Dispute Settlement Body' (DSB), a permanent international tribunal. The DSU contains three principal innovations. First, it adopted the 'reverse consensus' rule, meaning that requests to create panels, and the adoption of panels' reports, could be blocked only with the consensus of all members. Given the complainant and defendant were both members, that consensus would never be forthcoming, rendering the dispute settlement process mandatory.

Second, a standing 'appellate body' (AB) of full-time jurists was created, to hear appeals from the decisions of panels (whose members, as with the Tokyo panel system, continue to be appointed as arbitrators on an ad hoc basis as and when a request to form a panel is received). Third, the DSU establishes target time scales for proceedings. Disputes are commenced with a 'request for consultations', a mediation process which lasts 60 days. Should no satisfactory resolution be reached, a panel must be established within 45 days. The panel must then issue its report within six months. The AB must thereafter rule within three months. A state found in breach of its WTO obligations must take steps to bring its conduct into conformity within a 'reasonable period of time' (RPT), being a maximum of 15 months. After 15 months, if no conforming action has been taken, the complainant state may apply to a panel for a 'remedy', namely a determination of the appropriate level of retaliatory measures. Those retaliations will take the form of 'suspension of concessions. . .equivalent to the level of nullification or impairment' of the GATT obligation in question.[13] If there is a dispute as to whether measures taken by a defendant state have brought that state into compliance with its WTO obligations, a claimant may request formation of a panel to determine that the remedial measures taken were inadequate.[14]

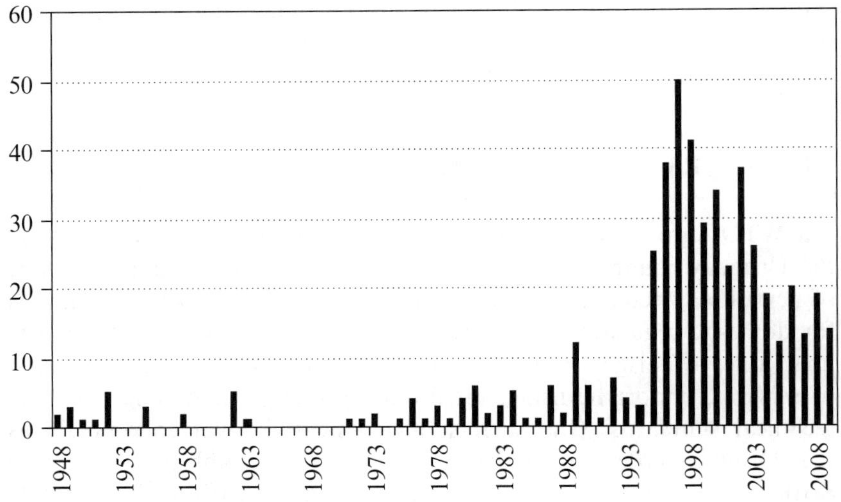

Figure 6.1 Number of GATT/WTO complaints filed 1947–2009

Unlike the ICJ, state parties cannot withdraw from the DSU without withdrawing from the entire WTO system. Although in other respects their procedures are akin to arbitration, decisions of both the panels and the AB are public. The DSB has a significant caseload. While it does miss its deadlines, the DSB does not usually veer too far from the time limits the DSU prescribes. However, cases before the DSB can continue indefinitely, for reasons that will be explored. The new system was certainly more formal, but commentators have tended to overstate the degree to which the new DSU marked a step change from prior procedures. As already noted, prior to the reverse consensus rule, the greater majority of panel reports were adopted nonetheless. Although the number of cases filed per year has been far higher on average since 1995, caseloads rose gradually in the 1970s and 1980s. Part of the post-1995 growth may be attributable to an initial enthusiasm about the new mechanism; after a high of some 50 cases in 1997, since 2005 caseloads have levelled off to a rough average of 15–20 new cases per year. Even if the prior system was ineffective as a matter of legal theory because a defendant could block it, national governments still saw political value in using it. The domestic measures GATT panels ruled against were political distortions from a defendant nation's economic best interests, and thus it was not as hard to swallow a losing judgment as might ordinarily be the case. GATT dispute resolution is litigation of a very unusual kind: the defendant ought to be pleased when (s)he loses.

Perhaps the biggest single change to the GATT dispute resolution system propagated by the WTO was development by the DSB of enormously complex decisions and sophisticated jurisprudence. The essence of GATT law did not change in 1995. However, whereas panels prior to 1995 issued short decisions, at most a few pages, since 1995 both panels and the AB have taken to producing exceptionally long rulings typically running to hundreds of pages. Parties to disputes have submitted vastly complex sectoral economic studies, showing the impact of a given domestic measure upon imports. To bring a claim for breach of GATT's MFN or national treatment obligations, one must show the product which is discriminated against is a 'like product' with some other product that receives more favourable treatment. More favourable regulations for sale of *shochu* (a Japanese spirit) compared with whisky will breach the national treatment obligation only if *shochu* and whisky are 'like products'.[15] One way parties may try to demonstrate products to be 'like' is by econometric analysis, to show strong price cross-elasticity of demand: that is to say, to show that where the price of one increases, the demand for the other commodity increases. (The higher the price cross-elasticity, the nearer the two commodities are to perfect substitutes.)

Parties may thus submit extensive economic studies to support their assertions in WTO litigation. The same is true where authorisation is sought for retaliation: the loss suffered by importers in consequence of a WTO-inconsistent practice must be measured, and tariffs causing equivalent harm must be devised, requiring further detailed economic submissions and analysis. Each case must also analyse in detail domestic legislation with which the panel or AB members may not be familiar, in some cases comparing it with international standards (to which states are obliged to conform their domestic legislation).[16] Detailed jurisprudence has emerged on technical issues such as the burden of proof in relying on GATT exemptions.[17] The decisions of the DSB are the most voluminous area of international law proportionate to caseload. In one case for which a decision had just been issued at the time of writing, concerning US complaints over EU subsidies to Airbus, the report of the panel exceeded 1000 pages, not including six extensive appendices.[18] Although this is one of the DSB's lengthier judgments, decisions of several hundred pages are quite normal.

The reason for these spectacular displays of intellectual energy over the meaning of a single treaty is simple enough: the sums in question warrant it. For developing world plaintiffs, at least, complaints are not managed by government lawyers. Rather, an exporting industry seeking to overcome a rule proscribing their imports asks its government to raise a complaint. The government is content to oblige, provided that the petitioning industry manages the litigation and, most importantly, pays for it. Initiation of a WTO complaint is typically driven by a commercial importer into the defendant state's territory, through a legal mechanism set out in the claimant state's legislation. Defending countries are thus forced also to retain commercial, rather than government, lawyers. Disputes have a commercial rather than political dynamic to them, and lawyers, eyeing the large sums at stake, ensure their fees and output are proportionate, as are the arbitrators' decisions. This also explains why countries in the developed world and large trading blocs bring the bulk of the claims. They have institutional mechanisms such as section 301, and legal expertise, which make it easy for states to bring claims on behalf of their exporters. Smaller countries and countries in the developing world may not have the same sophisticated trade offices within their government or legal expertise,[19] and thus are reliant upon the discretion of the government and the capacity of the government's legal service. For a smaller country, the political ramifications of bringing a WTO claim (especially against a larger country) may be all the greater, and thus the government will consider it imperative that it acts as a gatekeeper. Hence fewer claims may arise.

REMEDIES UNDER WTO LAW

Perhaps the most curious feature of the WTO system, and its single greatest weakness, is in the nature of its regime of remedies and enforcement. There is no compensation ordered for harm suffered as a result of a GATT violation. Panels and the AB just make 'recommendations' that losing defendants bring their conduct into compliance with WTO obligations. For this reason, the violation is almost always ongoing while the panel and the AB deliberate and rule, and for the further 15 months' RPT to comply. The procedure can easily extend for at least three years before the defendant is obliged to do anything or suffers any negative consequences. Because no compensation is due for ongoing harm (and also because neither the panel nor the AB have the power to order a losing party to pay a winning party's costs), defendants have every incentive to drag things out for as long as possible. Therefore appeals are extremely common. If a defendant ultimately fails to comply with the AB's recommendations after the 15 months' RPT has expired, only then can the claimant apply for authorisation to retaliate,[20] a procedure which may then take a further six months. The authority to retaliate, once granted, is not compensatory in character, since retaliation hurts the retaliator. Rather it is a right to inflict private punishment. Whereas in most criminal legal systems punishments are imposed by impartial authorities independent of either the defendant or the victim, in the WTO system the victim is authorised to exact its own revenge. Imagine bringing a complaint to court that your counterpart has breached a contract to buy from you cloth at a certain price. The court agrees that the defendant has breached the contract. However, instead of awarding you compensation for the loss of your sale, it awards to you the authority to breach a contract to buy wine: wine that you want. Breaching this contract will not benefit you; it will harm you, because you will not get the wine you want and will have to buy it from elsewhere at greater expense. The only motivation for using this remedy you have been granted is revenge: cutting off your nose to spite your face. This is the system of remedies within the WTO, and it is palpably perverse.

It is tempting to conclude that the system of so-called remedies under the DSU exists not to benefit the aggrieved claimant who has suffered harm, but instead to protect those who breach the rules.[21] Without a regime for impartial determination of the proper level of retaliatory measures, and a procedural delay aimed at assisting aggrieved complainant states to cool off, those who breach WTO rules place themselves at the risk of potentially unlimited countermeasures. The rationale underlying the WTO remedy system is to reduce the risk of trade wars, by limiting the level of retaliation within a legalistic procedure. Retaliation is an intrinsically irrational mercantilist instinct, because it harms one's own consumers and importers. It may appear superficially attractive because it benefits one's producers who by reason of concentration of interests carry disproportionate political weight within the domestic political system. But their advantages come at the expense of the broader welfare of the nation, which will be enfeebled if trade wars are allowed to spiral out of control. The WTO is a break upon risks of this kind. Of course the WTO, without a genuine enforcement mechanism, cannot prevent unilateral acts of retaliation outside the rules it sets, and trade war escalations, if that is what both parties want. But this is something neither party should really desire (at least not if they are acting rationally), and thus the WTO pulls them into a procedure that permits calmer heads to prevail. Notwithstanding the bold claims of its bureaucrats, there is nothing truly compulsory about the WTO; it is a voluntary system. Where parties volunteer to comply with its rules, this is because they know it is in their mutual interests not to engage in the self-destructive behaviour the system is designed to curtail.

Like all self-help remedies, retaliatory measures create incentives only to the extent that the retaliating party has the power to cause the other side pain. If the United States or the European Union is authorised to apply retaliatory tariffs to imports of cloth, the cloth producer is being frozen out of a very large market. His business may not be able to survive in the face of such tariffs; he will thus lobby his government for repeal of the original offending measures. For smaller and developing world countries, there is little value at all in retaliatory measures, which can inflict little harm. Being frozen out of the Paraguayan or Moroccan market for cloth may make little difference to a cloth exporter's global viability: it is a sanction a country in violation of the WTO, particularly a large one, can live with. The sole remedy available under the WTO is of little deterrent effect where the claimant is a small or economically weaker state. Thus it is not surprising that countries in the developing world make little use of the DSU.[22]

The law of the WTO turns out to have another curious feature. Whereas international law ought to benefit weaker countries, placing principled adjudication over raw exercise of power, WTO law favours powerful countries over weak ones, because its remedies can only be enforced by powerful states. The WTO dispute resolution system has two principal modes of operation: legal reinforcement of powerful countries' bullying tactics against small ones, demanding that they open their markets to the large countries' exports or punishing tariffs will be raised against those countries' exports; and all-out trade wars between the trading superpowers, principally the European Union and the US, that have been locked in mortal combat before the WTO over a variety of different issues since the system's inception in 1995. It is equally unsurprising that there are high rates of non-compliance with WTO rulings. Although the WTO avers that the majority of its rulings are complied with,[23] independent research has established this not in general to be true.[24] The largest of the WTO's members sometimes consider that their domestic exporters' interests and internal markets are strong enough to weather retaliatory tariffs, even if imposed by other large trading blocs. Smaller nations may not have any prospect of having their orders enforced beyond the hope that publicity shames defendants into compliance.

Another serious flaw in the WTO dispute resolution mechanism derives from its status as an exclusively inter-sovereign regime. Private parties do not have standing to pursue disputes, and only states may make claims. However, it is not the state which has an interest (or at least, only a relatively weak interest) in the action to enforce WTO law; it is the exporter. Because claims under the WTO system are driven by commercial exporters rather than by the states themselves, a disparity of interests may arise between the party with an interest in the claim and the party in whose name the claim is brought. Should the claim be successful but the defendant state refuses to comply, the state claimant may not wish to take retaliatory measures which will hurt its own consumers in the process. (As already observed, no rational state would want to do this.) Thus the real driver of the complaint, the exporter, has minimal control over the remedies phase.

None of this is rational. Every time the United States (or any other nation) imposes retaliatory trade sanctions, even with the DSB's imprimatur, its consumers suffer. For instance, for over two years American clothes were subject to retaliatory tariffs within the EC due to the US's failure to comply with WTO rulings in the *US – Byrd Amendment* litigation.[25] This dispute concerned US legislation specifying that anti-dumping duties levied on foreign companies importing goods into the United States would be distributed to (uncompetitive) domestic industries that had made the antidumping complaints. The WTO ruled this practice illegal but the USA refused to repeal the legislation. The US companies that had benefited from the Byrd Amendment were not clothing companies, but they were the ones hurt by the EU retaliatory tariffs. From the EU perspective, although EU clothes manufacturers might relish the suppression of supply and increase in domestic prices this result entails, its consumers would presumably not feel quite the same way. The American clothes those consumers might have wanted to buy – like Levis jeans – were for that period more expensive or frozen out of the market entirely.

The incentive defendants have to drag proceedings out, in the absence of retroactive compensatory remedies, is facilitated by the way the remedies phase is structured. Notwithstanding the timescales contained within the DSU, the deadlines prescribed are often missed. A six-month time scale to a decision in a first instance dispute is exceptionally difficult to achieve even for simple cases within sophisticated and established systems of domestic litigation. WTO disputes are anything but simple, and the practice of the DSB remains relatively immature, the system having been in existence for only 15 years. The culture of the WTO, as an international organisation on occasion hamstrung by its own bureaucracy, scarcely helps to streamline procedure, still less the task of forming panels of multiple arbitrators and legal counsel from around the world that must converge upon the organisation's seat in Geneva for multiple series of fact-intensive hearings. Persuading those same arbitrators, deriving from divergent legal and professional traditions, to agree upon the text of a decision within this time scale, is likewise optimistic.

To expect the AB to undergo the same process within three months is yet more unrealistic, and in practice the first instance and appellate procedures may together take two to three years. Even after the AB has ruled, the procedure can continue virtually indefinitely without a resolution, leading to cases lasting for a decade or more. A state found in violation of its commitments has an opportunity to rectify within an RPT of 15 months. If it takes a remedial measure the adequacy of which is contested by the plaintiff, there must be another arbitration to determine whether the measure is adequate. The DSU contains what is known as the 'sequencing' ambiguity: where a complaining party is dissatisfied with a measure taken by a defendant ostensibly to rectify a WTO violation found by a panel or by the AB, it is not clear what it should do next. One rule within the DSU provides that a claimant may request an arbitration to determine whether the ostensible remedial measures are in fact WTO compliant; another DSU rule provides that where a defendant state does not comply, a claimant state may move straight to an arbitration to determine the level of authorised retaliation.[26]

It is not clear from the text of the DSU whether the latter type of arbitration may be commenced without the former having occurred first. This ambiguity has been seized upon by wily defendants to buy themselves indefinite periods of time to resist compliance. Where a measure is declared non-compliant by the DSB, the defendant state enacts a replacement measure into its domestic legislation that, it alleges, has the effect of remedying the violation. However, the measure remains flawed and unsatisfactory to the plaintiff, which then pursues an arbitration seeking a declaration to that effect. Once the new measure is declared non-compliant, the defendant state invokes another RPT to replace it with yet another remedial measure: and so the cycle of litigation continues. The most notorious dispute that followed this pattern was *US – Foreign Sales Corporations*, in which the DSB found US legislation granting federal income tax rebates to companies that exported products through off-shore subsidies amounted to an unlawful export subsidy. The US response was to enact replacement legislation formally looking different but of materially equivalent effect.[27] However, there have been several other similar cases, and repeated substandard compliance measures subject to renewed arbitration procedures have become a common feature of WTO litigation. While this ritual continues, the complainant has no remedy, and the ongoing measure continues to hurt the aggrieved importers; yet it is never clear when an arbitration to authorise and quantify retaliatory measures can commence. Although in one case the EU and the USA ultimately agreed that the same arbitral panel could simultaneously rule whether a purported compliance measure is WTO-deficient, and if so the level of authorised retaliation,[28] the AB itself has explicitly refused to rule on the issue.[29]

NEGOTIATING IN THE SHADOWS OF TRADING POWER

Another curse of the WTO dispute resolution system is the existence of constant negotiations to update the DSU that have been ongoing virtually since its inception. Before the DSU had even come into force, in April

1994, a Ministerial Decision called for a full review of the new system within four years. Consultations began in November 1997, at just the time when politically loaded cases were creating problems for the credibility of the dispute settlement system. At this time the EU was showing reluctance to implement adverse rulings against it in the *EC – Hormones* and *EC – Bananas* cases,[30] in which the USA had successfully challenged flagship European restrictions on imports of meat from animals fed with artificial hormones, and preferential tariffs for banana imports from former colonies of European powers. As a result the USA was contemplating return to aggressive use of unilateral section 301 trade sanctions rather than resort to the WTO system.[31] Both the EC and the USA submitted papers proposing changes to the DSU in late 1998. Negotiations between the parties on reform to the system were rendered difficult – perhaps impossible – because every change one side proposed was typically made in reaction to a ruling made to which one of the big players objected. Proposals for changes became focused upon correcting the adverse effect of a ruling, changes which the prevailing side would inevitably object to.

Thus the EU and the USA struggled over the issue of sequencing, the United States wanting to move straight to trade sanctions after EC delays in implementing *Hormones* and *Bananas*. The United States was later itself placed on the back foot after its subsequent loss in *Foreign Sales Corporations*. While initially the United States wanted to strengthen enforcement measures, as it found itself the subject of ever increasing numbers of complaints from 1999 onwards, it equivocated. 'Carousel retaliation' also became the object of controversy. This was a threatened United States proposal to revise periodically the list of products subject to retaliation when another country fails to implement a WTO ruling,[32] threatened against the EU to press it into implementing judgments the United States had won. In consequence, in DSU negotiations both sides sought to include provisions explicitly addressing carousel retaliation, the EU draft expressly banning it, the US draft expressly allowing it.[33] Less developed countries have proposed a principle of 'collective retaliation', entitling *all* WTO members to retaliate in the event of non-compliance with a DSB ruling. Unsurprisingly this is unacceptable to developed countries, who would suddenly find they could no longer safely ignore rulings against them at the instance of developing world nations. It is not clear whether, were such a rule to come into force, third party nations would be prepared to retaliate in support of a country's trade complaint. If they were, the reasons might be essentially political rather than having anything to do with trade. The system could become a proverbial jungle of 153 parties picking up any outstanding WTO award as an excuse to impose retaliatory sanctions.

The DSB has been aware that the way it decides its disputes may affect how, or even whether, it operates in the future, and this may affect the way it makes its decisions. This is an inherent problem with any decentralised binding adjudicatory system in which the parties themselves set the rules and are left to implement and enforce them. Panels and the AB are thus inclined to make decisions to preserve their own future. Unilateralism remains a perpetual spectre, whether through threats of carousel retaliation, threats of section 301 actions or trade wars between the large trade blocs. It is in the context of the omnipresent danger of unilateral action that the DSB must make its decisions. Where a powerful country is a plaintiff, should the DSB not take action that satisfies the complaining party, it may go its own way. Where a powerful country is a defendant, should the DSB make a ruling against that defendant which it considers unpalatable and strong enough to resist, non-compliance will follow and the system will fall into disrepute. Retaliatory measures, even if sanctioned by the WTO, are hardly attractive and serve to undermine the structural soundness of the global trade system. Exercise of those retaliatory measures can itself precipitate a trade war, as when the EU started a campaign to fight back against retaliation authorised by the DSB for the USA in *Bananas* and *Hormones*. As a result of retaliation authorised of US$191.4 million and US$116.8 million against the EU in those two cases in 1999,[34] the EU launched a series of complaints against US trade practices, including the attacks on the USA's Byrd Amendment and Foreign Sales Corporation legislation. EU aggression paid off, culminating in a WTO decision in which sanctions of more than US $4 billion were eventually authorised.[35] Even within the confines of the DSU regime, retaliatory tariffs can get quite out of hand.

Trade disputes are ultimately resolved by negotiation in the context of mutual threats. The WTO system, while making the rules each party agrees to abide by clearer, does nothing to change this. One study suggests that overall compliance rates with DSB rulings are poor, and the prospects of compliance with WTO law are significantly reduced if a dispute proceeds to determination.[36] Thus the WTO may be more valuable as a forum for negotiation rather than adjudication. A court system whose judgments the parties see fit to flout routinely is barely worth the bother, even if the quality of its jurisprudence is second to none. This is a brittle system for adjudicating the use of self-help remedies, endlessly fragile and in perpetual danger of breaking down given the constant incentive on the part of the most powerful defendants to ignore rulings, and for the most powerful claimants to impose their own unilateral retaliatory measures if the system does not deliver the results they seek. Because the WTO has no independent enforcement capacity, the system is scarcely better than an anarchy, albeit one veiled in the cloak of legal language and the complexities of jurisprudential logic. The best that can be said for the DSU is that it creates delay while defendants' domestic political problems, that arise from producers' resistance to their free trade commitments, have an opportunity to resolve themselves in favour of the greater good. Such delays can be of great value in facilitating the internal economic readjustments necessitated by the removal of trade barriers.

Nonetheless, we should not see the DSU for more than it really is: a check on precipitous unilateral retaliation. The sophisticated jurisprudence and sectoral studies that have built up around DSB rulings are not contributions to the rule of law; they are contributions towards slowing down what inevitably remains a politicised process. In many cases, the delay is warranted: protectionist trade policies often correct themselves, being the product of a temporary market movement (such as a currency fluctuation or a change in demand). Other times, it is just a matter of giving a domestic producer time to improve the efficiency of its manufacturing procedures. In these circumstances, the delay engendered by a formalistic dispute resolution process can make all the difference, compared with an immediate unilateral retaliation at the instance of one's aggressive exporters, baying for blood. The DSU is an excuse to do nothing for a while, in the anticipation markets will adjust. All this is healthy, but it is a different regime altogether from international law as we might like to conceive it. It is closer to the model of two armies, facing off over a contested piece of land, their generals deferring the dispute until after a peace summit in the hope that in the mean time people back home will come to the realisation that the value of the territory in dispute does not merit the bloody confrontation about to ensue.

THE POWER POLITICS OF RESOLVING TRADING DISPUTES

In these circumstances, it is barely surprising the WTO DSU is less than legally robust. The system must constantly dance on pinheads as huge trading blocs, vastly more powerful than it, use its rules and procedures as an arena in which to do battle. At any point one of them may lose confidence in the system and act unilaterally. The WTO is therefore trying constantly to ensure the world's most powerful nations retain an interest in and sympathy with the system. This inevitably encourages dividing the stakes between litigants so that everyone gets something. There are three ways this occurs.[37]

First, eager to preserve the frail system as nonetheless better than nothing, states may desist from pursuing complaints in which non-compliance is seen as highly likely. The EU followed this course in *US – Helms Burton Act*,[38] which challenged US legislation penalising foreign companies that trade with Cuba. Perhaps realising that the United States would never repeal this legislation under international pressure, the EU commenced the panel process but the panel was subsequently suspended for negotiations, which never achieved a result. The panel's jurisdiction subsequently lapsed and the EU never renewed the complaint; the issue remains outstanding today. Second, the Appellate Body serves as a conciliation mechanism, either reversing high-stakes panel findings against powerful trade blocs, or modifying them so their effect is less significant or to facilitate compliance. Amongst the many cases in which this has occurred just five will be mentioned. In *EC – Computers*,[39] a panel found, upon the request of the United States, that the GATT incorporates a legitimate expectation that the tariff category for a given commodity will not be changed unilaterally by a member. The AB overruled the panel, declaring that this most elementary principle of international law[40] was not part of GATT jurisprudence. In *US – Import Measures*,[41] the 'sequencing' ambiguity was at stake in an EU complaint about retaliatory measures taken by the US after its victory in the *EC – Bananas* case. At first instance, the panel ruled that any GATT panel established to assess the adequacy of remedial measures could also authorise sanctions in the event it found the corrective measures insufficient. If the DSB is supposed to be a credible international court, that would be the only logical view; otherwise the sanctions phase of litigation could be postponed indefinitely, pending repeated deliberately inadequate remedial measures taken following each panel ruling. Nonetheless the AB overruled the panel, leaving the sequencing debate wide open. Any ruling on the issue was bound to create friction; thus natural judicial logic was consciously overturned.

At issue in *US – Shrimp*[42] was US legislation banning imports of shrimp harvested using trawlers not carrying 'turtle excluder devices'. A panel ruled that 'irrespective of their environmental purpose, [the prohibition was] clearly a threat to the multilateral trading system'. Under subsequent pressure from environmental groups outraged at how WTO rules could override environmental regulations, the AB narrowed the scope of the ruling, enabling the USA to make minimal changes to its legislation to ensure compliance, and leaving the environmental regime substantially intact.[43] In a number of other cases, the AB relaxed the criteria set by panels by which environmental measures were to be assessed;[44] environmental lobby groups had made compliance with DSB rulings difficult for member states, and the WTO system needed to relax its rules to make domestic political room for these groups' influence. The AB has learned the hard way that only where the stakes are small should it uphold a finding against a major trade bloc. Thus the WTO is content to find fault in cases concerning safeguard measures,[45] temporary unilateral tariffs to protect a domestic industry in short-term peril which the GATT regime permits in narrow circumstances.[46] With a maximum lifespan of four years,[47] those measures will likely expire within the time period of the WTO litigation process, making them easy targets for WTO rulings: by the time it loses the case, the state raising the safeguards has already achieved what it wanted. Likewise, cases where the impact upon international trade is relatively small are safe targets for the DSB.

Beyond that, adverse decisions may cause major ruptures in the dispute resolution system. The AB is trapped between desire to pursue a coherent body of legal jurisprudence, and the importance of not undermining the system by making rulings which powerful trading blocs will undermine. In *EC – Asbestos*,[48] environmental measures by France banning asbestos were upheld by the AB, even though numerous environmental measures had been struck down in prior cases. The difference was that in the prior cases the complainants had been either the EU or the US. In this case, the complainant was Canada. Ruling against a weaker trading nation was easier in the context of the environmental lobby.

Thus the DSB is one of the clearest examples of international tribunals tailoring their jurisprudence to power politics. Sometimes the system is on the verge of breaking down, as the extended litigation over *US – Foreign Sales Companies* shows. The titanic battles between Airbus and Boeing over EU and US subsidies continues unabated at the time of writing, having been ongoing for over five years with even the first instance stage of the procedure barely completed.[49] The DSB has shown itself stretched to the limit by these cases, as it can do nothing to compel compliance with its rulings in the face of enormous political and commercial domestic interests. It therefore issues rulings that prevaricate and give something to both sides. Moreover, for political reasons states often negotiate to accept less than full compliance. In *EC – Bananas* a settlement was finally reached which brought the EU into compliance only 13 years after the initial complaint was filed.[50] The WTO cannot force states to comply, and yet there is an advantage for all parties in compliance. Therefore it is important that neither powerful claimants nor the DSB place too much pressure on the system such that a powerful defendant will withdraw or disregard rulings such as to undermine it. For smaller countries, by contrast, the system does not look attractive, unless they can append their claims to the complaints of a major trading power, and ride off the back of that party's superior negotiating leverage. Without such leverage, as defendants small states may be picked on by the DSB and found to be in non-compliance, to uphold the 'integrity' of the system. As claimants, the DSB may rule against small states where they bring claims against large countries, to prevent upsetting a major player; even if they obtain an award in their favour, they have no effective means of inducing compliance.

Small countries are thus left on the sidelines in the melée. In Chapter 2, we predicted that a system of international law would benefit weaker states over stronger ones, which is why stronger nations would not fully embrace it. Unusually in international law, the WTO system does not favour small states. Because powerful states can undermine and even destroy the systems in the titanic struggles they unleash upon it, judicial impartiality is severely curtailed to accommodate their interests. The real challenge to the DSU is that there is no certainty the system is any better than the pre-1995 set of trading rules without the institutions that rule upon and enforce disputes. Because the system is, in principle, self-enforcing – and because the dispute resolution mechanism, when invoked, is liable to legitimise retaliations that are harmful – it might just be better if states policed and adjudicated breaches of free trade obligations themselves. It is not clear that the endless disputes over domestic regulatory and environmental measures that WTO litigation has generated are worth the trade retaliations they precipitate. By creating a forum in which disputes can be raised that previously would have lain fallow, it is not immediately clear that the cause of international trade is promoted. Retaliatory sanctions depress international trade; the DSB may give states incentives to retaliate where they may not have done so before. The DSB has spawned national legislation permitting domestic producers to ask or even require governments to bring proceedings.

Notwithstanding these disadvantages in the system, the DSB creates its own interest groups. The WTO itself has grown, from a staff of 400 in 1995 to approximately 1100 in 2010.[51] An array of advisors and experts, NGOs, policy papers and studies have been created, commenting on the WTO's jurisprudence and representing or advising states that appear before it. The notion that sovereigns have agreed uniquely in the WTO to the creation of a genuine world court is deceptive; it is more akin to a referee in a multilateral boxing match who is liable to be ignored, or even be punched himself should his rulings upset one or more of the disputants. These concerns, and the lack of enforcement powers in the hands of the referee, render the referee's decisions perpetually fragile. Nonetheless, that this arrangement resembles a court of law is a myth which an unprecedented array of actors in international relations have an interest in perpetuating. The DSU is legalism for its own sake. It creates a forum in which complaints can be aired, for reasons of political theatre. But it is not clear whether it valuably contributes to the promotion of free trade, the WTO's supposed raison d'être. Even supporters of the institution appear to acknowledge this. In the words of one such scholar:

> [T]he strengthened DSM has not guaranteed compliance of any members with the rules and disciplines of the WTO and has resulted only in inducing more disputes to be brought forward and imposed costs of adjudicating them through the legal process, a cost that is beyond the reach of many of its poorer members. . .[52]

Ultimately the question for advocates of the WTO system to ask is whether creation of the DSB has created greater levels of compliance with GATT than the prior regime. One scholar has suggested that levels of compliance with GATT were high in any event, because signatories to GATT had an incentive to comply with it – all parties benefit from its observance.[53] It is therefore self-enforcing. Moreover, if a party were to deviate from its GATT obligations, it ran the risk of unilateral retaliation. Now the process of retaliation has been rendered more complex. There are delays in the system, and a panel must adjudicate the proper level of retaliation. This process may actually reduce the incentives for compliance with GATT, because the penalties for failing to comply with it are less severe than they might be where unilateral retaliation is ordered. Where a party takes an action it knows violates GATT obligations, it can be confident that the DSB will procrastinate for several years before authorising retaliatory sanctions. At that point, the protectionist conduct may be safely repealed and no international retaliation will have been suffered. Alternatively, a different non-compliant remedial measure may be enacted, subjected to arbitration to determine its adequacy, and the authorisation of retaliatory sanctions may be suspended for yet a further period. The DSB makes GATT obligations tantalisingly easy to breach. Ironically, the DSU may have led to the canons of free trade being undermined rather than supported. The economic argument for the DSU appears increasingly thin.

At the time of writing, the Doha round of trade negotiations, underway since November 2001 to strengthen further the free trade rules under the WTO, has been declared a failure. They broke down amidst mutual recriminations between the major trading blocs, in particular over negotiations to abandon measures to protect domestic agriculture. The reasons for the failures at Doha are not principally related to the DSU, which looks set to stay much the same in structure even if further trade negotiations take place. The original pressure for strengthening the GATT dispute settlement system – a desire by the United States to open foreign markets – has receded, because the United States itself became the subject of punishing DSU complaints that have caused political ruptures in domestic US politics. So aggrieved was Congress at the US$4 billion in authorised retaliatory trade sanctions imposed by the DSU in respect of the *US – Foreign Sales Corporations* dispute that there was even a proposal for a domestic US body unilaterally to review panel decisions[54] – a clear step back from the principle of multilateral legalism. It is not clear what that domestic body could have achieved; it could not 'annul' retaliatory measures, which *ex hypothesi* are imposed by foreign countries and over which Congress has no jurisdiction. It could have served only to authorise unilateral retaliation by the US as complainant notwithstanding the fact that the DSU had not itself provided authorisation.

Nonetheless, it indicates the discomfort the single greatest proponent of the DSU now bears towards the system it pushed to create. Further strengthening of the DSU seems unlikely. With trade talks indefinitely suspended, there will be no agreement to dismantle it, and the DSU will continue to develop its jurisprudence in ever more complex and sophisticated, but increasingly inutile, directions. The DSB seems destined to perpetuate a self-serving judicial activism, in which its arbitrators manoeuvre to avoid being crushed between the rocks of the world's major trading powers, but without the possibility of legislative correction of its decisions.[55] The consensual nature of international relations applies in full measure to the WTO, meaning the parties cannot agree with the requisite unanimity what changes to make to the system. This deeply flawed system appears destined to lumber on indefinitely in its current form.

NOTES

1. The example of trade in wine and cloth between England and Portugal can be found in Ricardo, David (1821), *On the Principles of Political Economy and Taxation*, 3rd edition, London: John Munay.
2. Article 34 Treaty on the Function of the European Union (*ex* Article 28 *ex* Article 30 EC Treaty): 'Quantitative restrictions on imports and all measures having equivalent effect shall be prohibited between Member States'.
3. See e.g. Baldwin, Robert (1982), 'The Political Economy of Protectionism', in Bhagwati, Jagdish (ed.), *Import Competition and Response*, Chicago: University of Chicago Press; Jones, Ronald and Anne Krueger (eds) (1990), *The Political Economy of International Trade*, Oxford: Basil Blackwell.
4. See for example Articles II to IX Argentina-United States Treaty of Friendship, Commerce and Navigation, 27 July1853.
5. Figures derived from data provided courtesy of the Economic History Association. Data is based on price values in domestic currency and thus does not correct for inflation or foreign exchange rate fluctuations.
6. See e.g. Dixit, Avinash and Victor Norman (1980), *Theory of International Trade: A Dual General Equilibrium Approach*, Cambridge: Cambridge University Press.
7. Statistics provided courtesy of the US Department of Commerce.
8. The protectionist Morrill Tariff statute was introduced in 1861, and was one of the

reasons cited by the South for secession. Tariffs under the act were raised again by President Lincoln to fund the Civil War. The Underwood Tariff of 1913 saw a lowering of tariffs to an average of 29.5 per cent.

9. See e.g. Cooper, Richard (1987), 'Trade Policy and Foreign Policy', in Stern, Robert (ed.), *US Trade Policies in a Changing World Economy*, Cambridge, MA: MIT Press.
10. See Articles I.1, III.1, III.2 and XVII General Agreement on Trade Tariffs 1947.
11. *Cuba – Consular Taxes* (BISD II/12), Ruling by the Chairman on 24 August 1948.
12. One earlier case in which a GATT panel did authorise retaliatory sanctions by the USA against the EC was the 'Chicken war'. In 1962 several western European countries placed import duties on chickens from the United States, amid accusations of dumping. In December 1963 the US imposed retaliatory tariffs on starch, dextrin, brandy and light trucks. The so-called 'chicken tax' remains in force against light trucks; the tax is typically circumvented by importing trucks in kit form then assembling them in the United States.
13. Article 22(4) DSU.
14. Article 21(5) DSU.
15. This was the issue in *Japan – Taxes on Alcoholic Beverages*, WT/DS8.10, 10.11/AB/R, Appellate Body decision 1 November 1996.
16. See e.g. Article 2(4) Agreement on Technical Barriers to Trade (the 'TBT Agreement'), requiring that domestic technical regulations conform to international standards; *EC – Trade Descriptions of Sardines*, WT/DS231/AB/R, Appellate Body decision 23 October 2003.
17. Differing rules on burden of proof apparently apply to each of Article XX GATT (general exemptions, for reasons such as protection of health, conservation of natural resources, etc.), an exemption provision in the TBT Agreement, and the 'enabling clause' (a 1979 decision allowing deviation from MFN obligations to promote trade of developing countries): *US – Measures affecting imports of woven wool shirts and blouses from India*, WT/DS33/AB/R, Appellate Body report 23 May 1997; *EC – Sardines, supra.*
18. *European Communities – Measures Affecting Trade in Large Civil Aircraft*, WT/DS316/R, Panel Report 30 June 2010.
19. Busch, Marc Eric Reinhardt and Gregory Schaffer (2008), *Does Legal Capacity Matter? Explaining Dispute Initiation and Antidumping Actions in the WTO*, International Centre for Trade and Sustainable Development, Geneva, December.
20. The authority to retaliate is granted in Article 22 DSU, under the heading 'Suspension of Concessions'.
21. This is the view expressed in Schwartz, Warren and Alan Sykes (2002), 'The economic structure of renegotiation and dispute resolution in the WTO/GATT system', *Journal of Legal Studies*, **31**, 179.
22. For empirical evidence in support of the proposition that economically weaker nations make disproportionately little use of the WTO dispute settlement system, see Busch et al, *Does Legal capacity matter?, ibid.*
23. See e.g. Wilson, Bruce (2007), 'Compliance by WTO Member States with Adverse WTO Dispute Settlement Rulings: The Record to Date', *Journal of International Economic Law*, **10**(2), 397. The author was Director of the Legal Affairs Division of the WTO Secretariat, although he adds a disclaimer that his views are not the official views of the WTO.
24. Busch, Marc and Eric Reinhardt (2002), 'Testing International Trade Law – Empirical Studies of GATT/WTO Dispute Settlement', in Kennedy, Daniel and James Southwick (eds), *The Political Economy of International Trade Law: Essays in Honour of Robert E. Hudec*, Cambridge: Cambridge University Press.
25. *United States – Continued Dumping and Subsidy Offset Act of 2000*, WT/DS217/ARB/BRA, Recourse to Article 22.6 Arbitration Report 31 August 2004.
26. Compare Articles 21.5 and 22.6 DSU. It is the relationship between these two provisions that is the source of the 'sequencing' debate.
27. *United States – Foreign Sales Corporations*, WT/DS108. In March 2000 the AB declared

favourable tax treatment of foreign sales corporations to be an illegal export subsidy, whereupon US Congress replaced the legislation with the Extraterritorial Income Exclusion Act in November 2000, which had substantially the same effect. The EU then challenged this legislation as being an unsatisfactory remedial measure. It was not until 30 August 2002 that a retaliatory tariffs panel authorised the EC to take retaliatory measures worth over US$4 billion. Retaliation lasted almost four years; settlement of the matter was notified on 17 May 2006.

28. *EC – Bananas*, WT/DS27/ARB, Award of the Arbitration Panel 9 April 1999. See Patterson, Eliza (2001), 'The US-EU banana dispute', *ASIL Insights*, American Society of International Law, February.
29. *United States – Import Measures on Certain Products from the European Communities*, WT/DS165/R, Appellate Body Report 11 December 2000.
30. No fewer than five separate DSU complaints were initiated relating to the EU's ban on meat hormones: DS26, DS39, DS48, DS320 and DS321. The EU's preferential banana tariff regime attracted six actions: DS16, DS27, DS105, DS158, DS361 and DS364.
31. See Wolff, Alan and John Magnus (1998), 'America's Lost Leverage', *Legal Times*, 24 August. For a history of the negotiations over reform of the DSU, see Zimmerman, Thomas (2006), *Negotiating the Review of the WTO Dispute Settlement Understanding*, London: Cameron May.
32. See section 407 of the Trade and Development Act of 2000.
33. See Zimmerman, ibid., § 6.4.6.
34. *EC – Bananas* (see note 28); *EC – Hormones*, WT/DS26/ARB, Award of the Arbitration Panel 12 July 1999.
35. The largest single set of retaliatory measures authorised by the WTO was in *US – Foreign Sales Corporations*, WT/DS108/ARB, Arbitration Award 30 August 2002, awarding US$4.043 billion.
36. Busch and Reinhardt, ('Testing International Trade Law') conclude that only two-fifths of DSB rulings result in full compliance; but the concessions the defendant will make are greater prior to a ruling against a defendant than afterwards. See also Reinhardt, Eric (2001), 'Adjudication without enforcement in GATT disputes', *Journal of Conflict Resolution*, **45**(2), 174.
37. It is proper to credit Garrett, Geoffrey and James McCall Smith (2002), 'The Politics of WTO Dispute Settlement', UCLA International Institute Occasional Paper Series 31, July (UCLA International Institute, Los Angeles, CA), as inspiration for this section of the chapter.
38. *United States – Cuban Liberty and Democratic Solidarity Act*, WT/DS38, panel established 20 November 1996, panel suspended at the requested of the EC 21 April 1997, panel's authority lapsed 22 April 1998.
39. *EC – Computer Equipment*, WT/DS62, panel report 5 February 1998, AB report 5 June 1998.
40. For an overview of the concept in the context of international investment law, see the excellent and succinct paper by Yost, Chris (2009), 'A Case Review and Analysis of the Legitimate Expectations Principle as it Applies within the Fair and Equitable Treatment Standard', ANU College of Law Research Paper No. 09–01, Australian National University, Canberra.
41. *United States – Import Measures on Certain Products from the European Communities*, WT/DS/165/AB/R, AB report 11 December 2000.
42. *United States – Import Prohibition of Certain Shrimp and Shrimp Products*, WT/DS58, panel report 15 May 1998, AB report 12 October 1998.
43. See Garrett, Geoffrey and James McCall Smith (2002), 'The Politics of WTO Dispute Settlement', UCLA International Institute Occasional Paper Series 31, July (UCLA International Institute, Los Angeles, CA), 22.
44. See e.g. *US – Gasoline Standards*, WT/DS2/AB/R, AB report 29 April 1996; *EC – Asbestos*, WT/DS135/AB/R, AB report 12 March 2001; *EC – Beef Hormones*, WT/DS26/AB/R, AB report 16 January 1998.

45. See e.g. *Argentina – Safeguard Measures on Imports of Footwear*, WT/DS121/AB/R, AB report 12 January 2000; *United States – Safeguard Measures on Imports of Fresh, Chilled or Frozen Lamb Meat from New Zealand and Australia*, WT/DS177 & 178/AB/R, 16 May 2001, both cases setting onerous standards that states applying safeguard measures will have to meet to avoid those measures being declared invalid by the DSB. See also Sykes, Alan (2003), 'The safeguards mess: a critique of WTO jurisprudence', *World Trade Review*, **2**, 261.
46. Article XIX GATT 1947 permitted the imposition of safeguard measures where increased imports 'cause or threaten serious injury to domestic producers in that territory'. The legal conditions in which safeguard measures could be imposed were refined in the Agreement on Safeguards, negotiated during the Uruguay round.
47. Article 7(1) Agreement on Safeguards. Under Article 7(2), this period can be extended provided 'that the safeguard measure continues to be necessary to prevent or remedy serious injury and that there is evidence that the industry is adjusting'.
48. *EC – Measures Affecting Asbestos and Products Containing Asbestos*, WT/DS135, AB report 12 March 2001.
49. The US and the EU simultaneously filed requests for consultation, on 6 October 2004, each accusing the other of unlawful preferential treatment for their respective aircraft industries. Subsequent complaints were filed on 27 June 2005 (by the EC) and 31 January 2006 (by the USA). See *EC – Measures Affecting Trade in Large Civil Aircraft*; *US – Measures Affecting Trade in Large Civil Aircraft*, WT/DS316/317/347/353. On 30 June 2010 the first instance panel issued its ruling in DS316; at the time of writing Panel decisions in the other three claims are outstanding.
50. The first WTO complaint relating to the EC's banana importing regime, WT/DS27, was filed in February 1996. The Geneva Agreement on Trade in Bananas, WT/L/784, was announced on 15 December 2009.
51. The WTO states that as of 2010 it has 625 permanent staff; but this figure does not include the practice, common to many international organisations, of hiring staff for indefinite periods on back to back short-term contracts, who thereby appear 'off the books'.
52. Srinivasan, T.N. (2007) 'The dispute settlement mechanism of the WTO: a brief history and an escalation from economic, contractarian and legal perspectives', *The World Economy*, **30**(7), 1033.
53. Hudec, Robert (1993), *Enforcing International Trade Law: The Evolution of the Modern GATT Legal System*, Salem, NH: Butterworths.
54. In 2007, both the House of Representatives and the Senate introduced bills that would establish a Congressional oversight committee to review WTO decisions affecting the United States. The bills were entitled the Strengthening America's Trade Laws Act (introduced by the Senate) and the Trade Law Reform Act (introduced by the House). Both bills died in committee.
55. The GATT scholar Robert Hudec advocated a return to the pre-WTO panel system for precisely this reason: he considered that in its autonomy and the impossibility of legislative correction the system had lost touch with the political considerations necessary to make the system workable. 'Almost every commentator who has reviewed the new DSU has expressed some discomfort with the fact that the WTO has no viable legislative arm that can reverse decisions believed to be incorrect. The need for some sort of political review has often been advocated . . . if it is thought necessary to retreat from the present system of unreviewable legal rulings, the only practicable option I can see would be to give every defendant government a veto--a return to the old adoption-by-consensus system.': Hudec, Robert (2002), 'Free trade, sovereignty, democracy: the future of the World Trade Organization', *World Trade Review*, **1**(2), 222.

7. The arid promises of international human rights

What better language can there be for stirring the moral political imagination than discussion of human rights? Since time immemorial, the language of fundamental rights and civil liberties has been invoked by those resisting oppression, fighting for social change and participating in revolutionary politics. Political philosophers, themselves participants in dramatic social change, have also evoked the language of fundamental rights in support of their cause. Cicero, Jesus, Locke, Rousseau, Paine and Nozick[1] have all articulated theories of human rights in support of a social vision. Yet the incorporation of such concepts into international law is a far more recent phenomenon. In one sense, virtually every legal system is concerned with rights: wherever a legal obligation is imposed upon a person, one or more other persons have a right to ensure that obligation is performed, a right which only has meaning if it can be enforced in court. In time, a number of legal systems started to see certain sorts of legal right as more fundamental than others. In the west, in 1188 the Decree of Alfonso IX of the Kingdom of León (in what is now northwest Spain) and the Magna Carta in 1215 in England were early examples of legal documents conferring rights upon citizens. More comprehensive enumerations of individual rights followed in France's Declaration of the Rights of Man (1789) and the United States' Bill of Rights (1791).

However, the notion that all people have supra-national rights, which sit above the domestic legal system of any state, is by historical standards a recent innovation. The Treaties of Westphalia (1648) sought to grant the peoples of the territories in which the Thirty Years War was fought freedom of religious worship; they were promptly undermined upon unilateral renunciation by the Pope.[2] Partition of Europe after the collapse of Napoleon's, and then the Ottoman, Empire in the Congresses of Vienna (1814) and Berlin (1878) developed principles of free religious expression into minority rights, seeking to ensure groups of all religious persuasions would be treated equally in the new multi-ethnic states drawn by these conferences. The same problem of securing fair treatment for religious minorities in the context of shifting European borders was faced in the aftermath of World War I, in which the multi-ethnic Austro-Hungarian

Empire was dissolved and an array of new multi-ethnic states was created. The Treaty of Versailles promulgated a range of minority rights, but its real innovation was to create the first international enforcement mechanism for these rights. A series of so-called 'minority treaties', negotiated at Versailles, provided that an aggrieved individual in territories that had signed such a treaty could petition the Council of the League if they considered their minority rights had been infringed.[3] The Council could thereupon appoint a Minorities Committee to investigate the matter and negotiate a settlement. If negotiations failed, the matter could be referred to the PCIJ. References were made on two occasions, which in both instances involved ethnic criteria in education.[4] These cases were the first examples of human rights being subject to an international mechanism of legal adjudication.

Also important in understanding the rise of an international law of human rights in the early twentieth century is the impact of Marxism, whose long hand extends into human rights law even to the present day. Towards the end of the nineteenth century, trade unions developed into international networks, which pressed for international standards of treatment for workers. There was a perhaps surprising level of acceptance within the international community of the demands of this movement, because in the early twentieth century several countries, including Mexico, Russia, Ireland, Germany, Austria and Italy suffered either revolutions or severe civil disturbances instigated by organised labour movements. The internationalisation of labour rights was seen as a way of defusing this threat. Thus was the International Labour Office (ILO, now the International Labour Organisation) born, charged upon its inception in 1919 with promoting an international labour law. By 1933 the ILO had adopted 40 conventions addressing topics as broad as the maximum working week, maternity leave, working at night, child labour, unemployment, forced labour and freedom to form trade unions. In one sense these conventions, and the organisation that created them, were an irrelevance. None of these treaties created any enforceable rights, and ILO members were free to, and frequently did, ignore the commitments they had signed.[5] The ILO remains legally marginal to the current day, its some 3100 staff performing essentially the same function of producing reports and draft conventions creating unenforceable labour rights in the twenty-first century. However, the workings of the ILO in this early stage are important, because they represent the internationalisation of individual rights. The category of economic and social rights, so important in contemporary human rights discourse, was a creation of the ILO and the early twentieth-century socialists who pushed for the organisation's creation.

The real catalyst for creation of an international law of human rights, however, was the Holocaust. That the Nazis murdered so many people for no better reason than their ethnic identity or political beliefs motivated the thoughts not just that people responsible for such crimes should be subject to criminal prosecution (discussed in Chapter 4), but that individuals should have enforceable legal rights against any such oppression by their own government. These rights would exist in international law to ensure they would be guaranteed even should the most intolerable domestic government come into power, and whatever odious laws it might enact. The original purpose of the various international human rights treaties developed in the aftermath of World War II was protection against the totalitarian barbarism exhibited in Europe's dark historical chapter of inter-war fascism.

It is also important to appreciate the individual influence of both the US President during World War II and of his wife. In his January 1941 State of the Union address, Franklin Roosevelt gave a speech in which he proposed that people everywhere in the world should enjoy 'Four Freedoms': of expression and religion, and from want and fear (of foreign aggression). These ideals found their way into the preamble of the UN Universal Declaration of Human Rights, adopted by the UN General Assembly in December 1948. Eleanor Roosevelt, the late President's widow (Roosevelt died in 1945), chaired the Commission responsible for drafting the Declaration, which set out a detailed array of cultural, economic and political rights of extraordinary breadth. These included the right to periodic holiday with pay, education (which would be compulsory), intellectual property rights, asylum, freedom to travel and protection of the family. Tellingly, there is no mechanism set out in the Declaration for enforcement of these broad and unqualified rights. In the best traditions of the legal systems of the communist Eastern Bloc, the document proclaimed empty rights that any state could safely sign up to because in the absence of any body to adjudicate upon their meaning, hear complaints or ensure their compliance, they were meaningless.

The Universal Declaration was, at best, an aspirational document: its drafters hoped it would acquire moral relevance as a standard towards which domestic governments would be drawn. But it is difficult to see how this effect could be significant. For any country that already has a reasonable records of respecting human rights, the best vanguards of their continued protection are an independent judiciary and a political system responsive to public opinion. An international treaty without domestic legal effect seems causally irrelevant, all the more so where the obligations are so open-ended as to be capable of misinterpretation. In nations where civil rights are not routinely respected, the ambiguous meaning of the treaty, combined with the absence of a body to give authoritative interpretations, likewise renders such international obligations liable to be void of causal content. The most grievous abuser of human rights can claim compliance with a broadly drafted and self-judging standard. Or they may simply ignore the standard because they don't care; there are no consequences of disregarding it. True, international opprobrium may descend upon a nation that treats its citizens despicably; but that effect does not require a treaty. We do not need to legislate for decency; we all instinctively know what it is.

After the Universal Declaration a range of further treaties and institutions emerged over the subsequent years, forged in the heat of human rights idealism. Founded in 1949 by the Treaty of London, the Council of Europe was an embryonic attempt to pursue European union. The treaty created a Committee of Ministers and a Parliamentary Assembly representing European countries. As an early attempt at intergovernmental political union, the Council of Europe was subsequently surpassed by the creation of the European Coal and Steel Community in 1951 (later to become the European Economic Community, now the European Union). However, its lasting achievement was the drafting of the European Convention on Human Rights, whose text was agreed in 1950 and which came into force in 1953. The Convention contained an enforcement mechanism, which we shall return to: it created two part-time bodies, a Commission of Human Rights and the European Court of Human Rights (ECHR). An individual could apply to the Commission, complaining that his rights had been abused by a signatory state. The Commission served as a gatekeeper; if it considered the complaint well grounded, it could refer the matter to the Court.

The western hemisphere soon followed the European example. In 1959, the same year as the ECHR started operating, the Organisation of American States (OAS) formed an Inter-American Commission on Human Rights; in 1965, the commission was given responsibility for investigating human rights issues amongst its members. At the time the Universal Declaration was negotiated, proposals were afoot for a treaty containing an even more extensive list of rights. However, divisions between capitalist and socialist states about what those detailed rights should comprise caused the negotiating committee to split into two, each of which created its own treaty: the International Covenant on Civil and Political Rights (ICCPR) and the International Covenant on Economic, Social and Cultural Rights (ICESCR). Both were adopted by the UN General Assembly in December 1966 and each came into force upon ratification by a sufficient number of states in 1976. Whereas the former treaty provides for individual liberties, procedural fairness before courts and rights of democratic participation, the latter includes rights to employment, social security, food, clothing and housing. Ultimately both treaties were ratified by a majority of states. Each treaty provides for UN committees to monitor state compliance.[6] In addition, both treaties carry 'optional protocols' by which (different) committees may hear complaints by aggrieved individuals.[7] For the ICESCR, that protocol has never come into force.

In 1969 the OAS took another step, creating an American Convention on Human Rights which came into force in 1978. This Convention was most notable for recognising a right to life for the unborn foetus, and also created a raft of economic and social rights in a 1988 protocol. Because it seeks to entrench Roman Catholic proscriptions against abortion, neither the United States nor Canada, the economically and politically most significant nations in the OAS, have ratified it. The Convention creates an Inter-American Court of Human Rights, which works in tandem with the Inter-American Commission on Human Rights in much the same way as their European equivalents did until 1998: the Commission acts as a gatekeeper for complaints, which it will forward to the Court for adjudication if it considers them well-founded. A range of other international human rights instruments were created, including the Convention on Elimination of All Forms of Racial Discrimination (CEARD) (concluded 1965, entered into force 1969); its sister treaty the Convention on Elimination of All Forms of Discrimination against Women (CEDAW) (entered into force 1981); the UN Convention against Torture (1984); the Convention on the Rights of the Child (1989); the Cairo Declaration on Human Rights in Islam (1990); and the Convention on Protection of the Rights of Migrant Workers and their Families (CPRMW, concluded 1990, entered into force 2003).

In 1998 the Council of Europe's Eleventh Protocol abolished the European Commission on Human Rights and established the European Court of Human Rights as a permanent institution with a right of direct petition by aggrieved individual applicants. The work goes on. In 2005 the UN General Assembly created the UN Human Rights Council to monitor and investigate human rights abuses, which replaced the UN Commission on Human Rights. Both these institutions are separate from the committees created under the ICCPR and the ICESCR to hear individual complaints against states that have adopted the relevant optional protocols. A number of other treaties also create new UN committees to monitor compliance and in some cases permit individuals to refer disputes to them. CEARD creates a Committee on the Elimination of Racial Discrimination; CEDAW creates a Committee on the Elimination of Discrimination against Women; the CPRMW creates its own committee. This glut of treaty-making has continued through to the present.

The Convention on the Rights of Persons with Disabilities was adopted in 2006, the Convention for the Protection of all persons from Enforced Disappearance in 2006 and the Declaration on the Rights of Indigenous Peoples in 2007. The African Court on Human and Peoples' Rights was created on paper in 2004, although at the time of writing in 2010 it had still not heard any cases. It will sit in Arusha, Tanzania, taking over the buildings of the International Criminal Tribunal for Rwanda, and in due course will be merged with the African Court of Justice (the African Union's court, another institution at the time of writing existing solely on paper).

THE POLITICAL LOGIC OF HUMAN RIGHTS TREATIES

The proliferation of human rights instruments, particularly since the 1960s, has been remarkable. This is all the more so when one considers the unusual logic which they exhibit. Ordinarily, international treaties create obligations which states owe to one-another. The GATT, considered in Chapter 6, contains obligations upon each state not to raise tariffs or other equivalent measures restricting imports from the territory of its treaty counterparts. These are obligations owed to other states; only states have standing to complain of GATT violations. By contrast, international human rights treaties entail promises by states to one another that they will treat their own citizens in accordance with certain standards (unlike investment treaties, which protect only the other country's citizens). What interest do other states have in these obligations being observed?

The Russian Federation is a party to the European Convention on Human Rights, as is the United Kingdom. Suppose that the Russian Federation tortures and murders its own citizens in Chechnya. The United Kingdom has little interest in this. The people being tortured, and their families, do not vote in British elections, and have no access to the British courts. They are mostly irrelevant to the British political and legal system, and they cannot gain traction within it. Therefore the government of the United Kingdom is not likely to complain about Russian human rights abuses (except where it is seeking ammunition for a broader attack upon Russia on other grounds). Nations are remarkably selective in their criticisms of other countries' human rights abuses, as and when it serves their political interests. The most fundamental principle of treaty law – that it represents a contract between states to cooperate in ways that are mutually beneficial – breaks down for human rights treaties, because there is no substantial benefit to either party from the other complying with its obligations. In one sense, international human rights law represents the most ambitious idealistic aspirations of international law: states sign treaties which none of them has strong interests in other states observing. This is somehow thought to improve the observance of human rights worldwide. The causal mechanism by which this is supposed to happen is entirely obscure. The very idea of international standards of human rights is meant to make observance of those standards more prevalent. How is this supposed to occur?

Imagine a primitive anarchical society in the vein of one of Rousseau's thought experiments, in which the heads of each family enter into a common agreement to treat their family members in certain ways. For example, each agrees to provide education for their children. This is not a credible account of how a domestic education law comes about, because each head of the family has an interest only in the education of his own children, not in the education of the children of any other family. The family head might enter into such an agreement, but his purpose in doing so would be to express his commitment to the principles of education to his family members, not to secure the education of other people's families, an outcome which (at least, comparatively speaking) is not particularly important to him. Thus to the extent the heads of families agreed to create an adjudication and enforcement mechanism for this right of education, it would be weak and only symbolic. Each family head, considered individually, would have no wish that an enforcement tool be brought to bear against him; and would have no interest in the tool being brought to bear against others (unless that individual could hope to control the enforcement mechanism, and use its influence as a proxy for some other interest of greater value to him). Thus at best a weak and ineffectual model would be created; at worst, there would be no enforcement at all. A better political model of how a domestic law compelling parents to educate their children comes into existence might be that domestic interest groups with an interest in universal education (a class of professional teachers, for example) lobby an authority with a monopoly on the legitimate use of force to impose a requirement for universal education upon their citizenry. But that model cannot apply to a right to education created by international treaty, because there is no world government with the monopoly on force.

International human rights treaties share some significant parallels with our thought experiment. There are three reasons a country may sign a human rights treaty. One is as a signal to its own population that it respects human rights and considers them valuable. This may be a particularly significant factor after a period of repressive rule, when an incoming government is seeking to mark a break with the past. Russia joined the Council of Europe (and hence submitted to the jurisdiction of the European Court of Human Rights) in 1996 after the collapse of the USSR;

Spain did the same in 1977 after the end of the Franco regime. Second, some countries with respectable human rights records may want to indicate their support for the principles of human rights to satisfy domestic lobbying groups. The United Kingdom signed the European Convention on Human Rights despite its relatively strong historical record in securing civil rights, because civil liberties are a significant political issue in British domestic politics. The third reason is that states consider such treaties a harmless way of integrating themselves into the community of nations, particularly after a period of international isolation. Thus Taiwan is an enthusiastic signatory of such treaties, as it seeks to give its *de facto* independence from the People's Republic of China an air of *de jure* credibility. European Union nations are enthusiastic signatories, because their political union is based upon international cooperation and nations do not want to be seen as outliers lest they lose influence within the EU's explicitly internationalist bureaucracy.

For none of these reasons, however, is international enforcement of human rights of paramount concern. The most effective method of enforcing human rights is at the domestic level, in the context of a pre-existing court system with direct jurisdiction over the police and other organs of the State that may take actions infringing human rights. An international court makes little intrinsic sense to a country seeking to make a credible commitment to its citizenry, who will be far more impressed with a commitment to improve the quality of domestic police and judiciary. (Commitment to an international tribunal may be a cheap alternative to domestic reform, however; if this is the state's principal incentive, then certainly the signal is more important than the implementation.) If the aim is only to show solidarity with an 'international community', implementation of treaty obligations is mostly irrelevant. The political capital is accumulated from signing the treaty, and far less so from receiving third party adjudications pursuant to it, which as a rule can only harm a country. (Countries rarely accrue political capital from being complemented for their human rights records.) Thus we should not be surprised that in many cases international human rights treaties make no or extremely limited provision for enforcement, because the signatories have no interest in their being enforced.

The optional protocol to the ICCPR permits individuals to raise complaints about breaches of the treaties to the UN Human Rights Committee. Of the ICCPR's 165 signatories, 69 per cent have ratified its First Protocol. The ICESCR has an Optional Protocol allowing individuals to make complaints to a Committee on Economic, Social and Cultural Rights, but as of 2010 insufficiently few states have ratified it for it to come into force. At the time of writing, four other UN committees can hear individual complaints under human rights treaties.[8] However, all five extant committees share a number of weaknesses. They decide complaints only on the basis of written representations. There are no hearings, witnesses do not testify and the committees do not conduct their own investigations. The committees have broad discretion on which complaints to adjudicate; the vast majority of complaints are rejected as inadmissible by the UN secretariat, without any sort of committee adjudication. Where a committee does make a finding of breach of a convention, it has no power to order compensation nor a change of a state's practices; it can only make recommendations. In many cases the state respondents refuse to cooperate with the proceedings or simply ignore them.[9] The committees' reasoning is typically threadbare; even the most serious allegations, such as death in police custody, are typically treated in just a few pages.[10] There is little in the way of jurisprudence. These committees meet only two or three times a year, and their work is perfunctory. It is small wonder that few complaints are adjudicated through the committee system. It is also worth noting that the various UN human rights treaties permit one state to raise a complaint against another; and this mechanism has never been employed. This is unsurprising, and confirms our hypothesis that states have no interest in enforcing human rights treaties against one-another.

Nor are the five UN committees' reports publicised to any great degree. (Their reports are however public documents, unlike much work undertaken by the UN.) That media and politicians take so little interest in the committees' work (few even know these committees exist) means that states violating international treaty commitments do not risk paying even a reputation cost at the hands of the committees. Moreover, to the extent that the policy goal is to secure compliance through reputation costs, it is not clear why UN committees are more effective than private NGOs and lobby groups. There is intense competition between private human rights institutions for the preparation of reports and publicity campaigns concerning global human rights abuses. Their resources are far greater than a handful of UN committees, and in many cases show greater political courage than the United Nations due to their independence from the member states that fund UN operations. There are at least 211 international human rights NGOs at the time of writing,[11] scrutinising the human rights records of governments in virtually every country in the world, often with significant local expertise. These NGOs may have better incentives than UN bodies to uncover civil rights abuses: their continuing funding may depend upon perceptions of their vigilance, productivity and impartiality, whereas the UN's committees continue to receive funding no matter what they do (or fail to do).

Advocates of international human rights treaties might concede that the committee system, even where it exists, is unsatisfactory. However, they persevere with a liberal aspiration that where international treaty commitments exist this mere fact alone induces states to comply with them. The language of moral obligation typically permeates this reasoning: that such treaties represent the highest principles of civilisation gives states a reason in itself to observe them. In the words of the preamble to the UN Declaration of Human Rights, 'the peoples of the United Nations have in the Charter reaffirmed their faith in fundamental human rights, in the dignity and worth of the human person and in the equal rights of men and women'. The thought seems to be that states will enforce their own obligations against themselves, because treaties create a moral atmosphere in which this is acknowledged as the right thing to do. This logic bears the unreal air of Kant's Categorical Imperative: the mere fact that a course of action is morally or rationally required, without more, creates an incentive to act in that way. Perhaps domestic courts will apply international treaty standards in claims that come before them; the regime might be self-regulating as national courts mature and evolve their jurisprudence to meet a credible international standard. Regrettably the empirical record for such optimism is thin, because in countries where human rights violations are severely at issue, the courts are not typically up to the job of protecting them.

There is virtually no state in the world that does not purport to incorporate human rights standards into its most fundamental constitutional documents. The Constitution of Myanmar (Burma) is remarkably progressive, providing for rights of gender equality, freedom of expression, assembly and association, privacy, protection of private property, rights to education and healthcare and rights of due process in criminal procedure. The Constitution of the Russian Federation includes a detailed array of civil rights, with far greater detail than is typical in international human rights conventions. The Constitution of Afghanistan guarantees equality of women before the law. Even the Constitution of North Korea contains provisions guaranteeing human rights.[12] Nevertheless, the courts of these countries do not have formidable reputations for defending their citizens' human rights. If they cannot be expected to defend rights under a domestic constitutional instrument, there seems little reason to believe they will protect rights existing under an international convention. Those trained in law in western Europe and the United States – where civil rights are, on the whole, broadly respected within the context of domestic legal systems – sometimes find it hard to appreciate the dominant attitude towards law that prevails in the rest of the world where, so it is said, there is no 'rule of law' tradition. In the greater part of the world, legal documents preserving rights and obligations are subject to ceaseless interpretation and review, because there are no independent courts impartially or consistently to apply them.

Charters of rights and complex legal rules often exist on paper, because there is political value to a government in conveying the impression both to its citizens and to the broader world of the existence of a sophisticated legal system. But alas, the impression is usually a charade. Without good faith and impartiality on the part of the adjudicatory body, the best law can be construed to achieve the result preferred to the financially or politically powerful. In these circumstances – precisely the political situation in which civil rights are in jeopardy – the aspiration that charters of fundamental rights can make a difference to citizens through determined application by domestic courts is illusory. Although a number of countries purport to incorporate one or more international human rights treaties into domestic law,[13] the rights set out in international treaties are typically far less detailed, and therefore far more open to interpretation, than civil rights contained in domestic law. It is difficult, therefore, to see how courts can adequately enforce international human rights if they cannot enforce domestic human rights.

In conclusion, it is hard to see what international human rights treaties achieve, unless they incorporate their own independent adjudication and enforcement mechanisms. Precious few international treaties do that, and the UN's various committees that hear individual complaints are toothless and perform publicity and reputation functions arguably better undertaken within the private sector. However, there are two international human rights courts in operation at the time of writing. These institutions are remarkable in that they exist at all. Why did states agree to create them? The answer is not immediately obvious.

THE HUMAN RIGHTS COURTS

Two international courts of human rights have been established that hear complaints by aggrieved individuals against states. Yet they are very different creatures. The European Court of Human Rights is considerably older, starting work in 1959; the Inter-American Court of Human Rights began operations in 1987. However, it is logical to consider the latter court first, because the former court underwent a procedural transformation in 1998 leading to a remarkable renaissance, while the Inter-American Court still operates as the European Court used to. Not all members of the Organisation of American States (OAS), of which the Court forms a part, have accepted its jurisdiction, which is optional. The English-speaking members of the OAS are virtually all absent from the Court, including both the United States and Canada, the economically and politically most influential members of the union.[14] Both the Court, sitting in San José, Costa Rica, and the Inter-American Commission on Human Rights, its gatekeeper sitting in Washington, DC, are part-time institutions.

An individual who wishes to complain that his (or her) government has abused his rights under the American Convention must apply first to the Commission, asking that it refer the case to the Court. If it decides to accept the claim, the Commission will correspond with the state in question, seeking the state's assurances that the applicant's human rights will be respected. This process is often private; the Commission has a discretion as to whether to publish applications and its determinations. Only if the Commission is not satisfied by the state's response may the matter be referred to the Court. Sometimes the Commission gives the state a second opportunity to comply with its recommendations. Most frequently, no referral is made to the Court, but no explanation is given as to why not. The criteria the Commission uses in deciding whether to refer a matter to the Court, if any really exist beyond mere political expediency, are opaque at best. No such criteria are published, and the Commission provides no reasoning in its decision to make a reference. Where the Court's jurisdiction is invoked, it is the Commission that makes the application to the Court, not the complainant; the complainant thus has little control over the content of the application the Court receives. Nor does the complainant have any recourse if the Commission, in its discretion, decides for any reason that the complaint should not be referred to the Court. For example, there is no appeal against a decision of the Commission that a complaint is inadmissible; nor can one challenge a decision of the Commission that the state has reacted satisfactorily to the complaint.

Because the procedure before the Commission is often private, it is difficult to assess the precise scale of the Commission's workload. However, it seems to receive a moderate level of use. Of the decisions the Commission elected to publish in 2009, the case numbers went as high as 140; the equivalent number for 2008 was 95. However, these figures hide a colossal backlog. It is not unusual for the Commission to be issuing decisions on admissibility in the late 2000s for complaints received in the mid 1990s.[15] Delays of five to eight years for an admissibility decision are quite normal. Even if the case is declared admissible at this stage, a period of consultations must follow with the state, followed by a ruling on the merits, followed by a failure to comply by the state, followed by a referral to the Court. The system is so slow as to be unusable. The number of cases referred to the Court (proportional to the number of known applications made to the Commission) is small. 2006 was the busiest year on record for the Court, in which the Commission referred 14 cases to it. Approximately ten per year is more typical. The Court may then take a further two years to decide the application, in a process which involves repeating the fact-finding procedures undertaken by the Commission: the process appears unnecessarily duplicative.

From 1987 to 2005 inclusive, the Court decided 125 contentious cases, or slightly fewer than seven per year. The Court has heard cases in which states have acted in abhorrent ways, including flogging a convict with a cat-o-nine-tails;[16] police beating a child to death;[17] abduction, torture and murder by the army of a person suspected of association with a rebel group;[18] military murder, pillage and ethnic cleansing;[19] arrest and incarceration for almost seven years without due process on suspicion of drug trafficking, even though no drugs were ever found;[20] and government-backed paramilitary beheadings of civilians with chainsaws and machetes.[21] The cases that come before the Court are typically so brazen that it is rarely called upon to adjudicate difficult points of interpretation of the Convention. When cases do reach the Court, they usually succeed. The formal plaintiff is the Commission, which gives a recommendation to make a finding against the state, a recommendation with which the Court almost always complies. The Court's remedies are often quite creative, requiring that states place memorials to massacres, or publish retractions of criminal convictions in newspapers.[22]

The Inter-American human rights system is barely judicial in nature. It is hard to escape the conclusion that the Court is not really a forum for resolving a dispute; it is a mode of publicising the most egregious abuses of state power, in countries which in many cases have unfortunate histories of military or police rule. Neither the Commission nor the Court seem particularly interested in complaints unless they are of the utmost gravity. Where atrocious conduct has gone unremedied in the domestic legal system, the Commission tries gently to pressurise the state into taking remedial action. Only if those diplomatic efforts fail to bear fruit is the jurisdiction of the Court invoked, to lend judicial imprimatur to the conclusions the Commission has already reached. Understandably, this regime is not popular with the respondent states. The Court has a problem with observance of its decisions. There is no formal mechanism for enforcement; in many cases, enforcement would be impossible, because many of the creative remedies the Court orders are not financial in nature. There is nothing anyone can do if a state is ordered to erect a memorial to victims of a massacre but fails to do so. It is not clear what rate of compliance exists for decisions of the Court when they are handed down. The other significant problem with the Court, which stems from its lack of popularity, is its meagre budget. At around US$3 400 000 in 2007, it must be the cheapest international tribunal on record. Of this sum, more than half consists of external donations (i.e. sourced other than from state parties to the Convention).[23] Given the delay, the lack of due process, the rubber stamp nature of the Court's judgments, the politicised process which permits only the gravest cases to proceed and the apparently patchy compliance record, it may be better to understand the Inter-American Court's role as a political pressure group in a part of the world historically hostile to human rights, rather than as a genuinely judicial institution.

Until 1998, the European Court of Human Rights employed a similarly two-tiered structure. Aggrieved parties were obliged first to address their complaints to a European Commission of Human Rights, which would assess the complaint for admissibility and, if it found it admissible, would attempt to facilitate an amicable resolution with the state involved. Only if an attempt at mediation failed might the Commission refer the case to the Court. The regime had many of the same failings as the Inter-American Commission. If the Commission decided for any reason not to refer the matter to the Court, that was the end of the matter. It might give no reasons for refusing to do so; there was no right of appeal. The mediatory role was mostly useless: it is a precondition of bringing a claim before the European human rights system that all domestic remedies have been exhausted, meaning in general that court appeals up to the country's highest court must have been pursued.[24] If ever there was an opportunity for a negotiated resolution to a dispute, it would generally have been in the course of these domestic proceedings before the claim reached the international human rights system, where the publicity and extended acrimony might make negotiated settlements all the less likely.

Moreover the Commission was becoming overloaded by cases; a part-time institution, it could not cope with the some 4750 applications filed with it in 1997. There was a sense that, due to its workload, the Commission's decisions were becoming arbitrary. It would reject applications for any reason or none, simply because its budget and staff precluded proper adjudication of all the complaints received by it. Like the Inter-American Commission, the European Commission was also painfully slow, taking several years to do anything with a complaint, even issue a perfunctory dismissal. At this time the European Court, by contrast, was perceived as relatively robust. Although it was also part-time, its caseload was moderate because the Commission served as such a stringent gatekeeper. It was easy enough for the Court to keep a grip on its workload: the Commission ensured that few complaints ever ultimately reached it.

The Commission thus became the sacrificial lamb for the European human rights system's structural failings: delay and arbitrary standards of admissibility. In 1998, the parties to the Council of Europe agreed upon Protocol 11, which abolished the Commission. Thereafter, individuals would have a direct right of complaint to the Court, which would decide upon the admissibility of complaints itself. The theory underlying this radical reform was that all the apparent efficiency advantages of the Court, compared to the Commission, would be adopted for the entire complaint procedure. The arbitrary fashion in which the Commission apparently decided to refer complaints to the Court would become a thing of the past. From now on, admissibility decisions would become matters of public record, adjudicated by the Court itself in accordance with reasoned decisions pursuant to the criteria set out in the European Convention. Delays would be reduced and decision-making streamlined, as the Commission stage in the complaint process was removed.

Alas, the architects of this grand procedural reform neglected to observe that the reason the European Court could operate as an apparent paragon of efficiency was only because the Commission's assiduous refusal to refer more than a trickle of cases to it each year kept its workload manageable. As soon as the floodgates were opened and the Court had to perform the gatekeeping work the Commission had previously undertaken, the Court would become every bit as arbitrary as the Commission had been. Indeed it would be more so; for the abolition of the Commission coincided roughly with a dramatic expansion of membership of the Council of Europe into eastern Europe. With the collapse of Communism in the early 1990s, former socialist states queued up to join western European international institutions, as a mark of their commitment to evolution from socialism to modern standards of liberal democracy. However, these new aspirants to western human rights standards did not have the same traditions of adherence to the rule of law as did their western European counterparts. Corrupt judges, brutal Soviet-era police, obtuse public administration and war in Chechnya all brought a deluge of new cases to the ECHR. Thus Russia, Romania and Ukraine joined the Council between 1993 and 1996, which together with Turkey (a member since 1949, but with a record since the 1980s of human rights abuses in repressing Kurdish rebellions in the country's southeast) account for some 57 per cent of the Court's workload.[25]

Faced with this deluge, the Court ground to a halt. By the middle of 2009 the Court's backlog of cases was around 100 000 and growing. In 2008 the Court received 50 000 new applications and disposed of 32 100 cases. Each year the backlog becomes ever more critical.[26] As a result, applications to the Court take years to resolve, and the delays have become ever longer. At the current time it is quite normal for a case to take six to ten years from application to judgment on the merits.[27] The most scandalous feature of this delay is that in some 95 per cent of cases the Court rejects the application as inadmissible without a hearing and without providing any reasons. Applicants receive a standard form one-page letter explaining that their

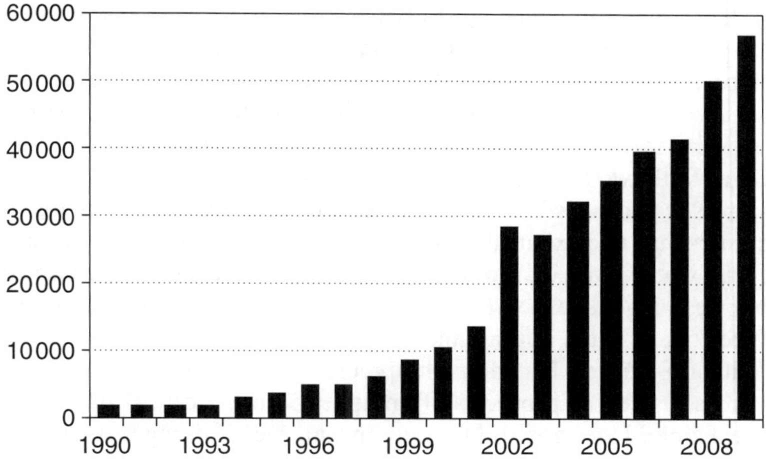

Figure 7.1 *Number of applications to the European Court of Human Rights (or pre-1998, the European Commission of Human Rights) by year, 1990–2009*

application has been declared inadmissible, and that this decision is final and not subject to review. So even for the cases the Court is ruling upon, in 95 per cent of cases the Court is undertaking no publicly available judicial analysis or drafting, nor holding any sort of hearing. A single *fonctionnaire* (judicial clerk) reviews the application, decides it ought to be dismissed and recommends this course to the judge for whom he works. The judge then recommends this same result to a committee of three judges, who issue a decision dismissing the case without reasons. Hundreds of cases at a time are rejected in this manner in the course of brief private meetings to which neither plaintiff nor defendant are invited, which are not open to the public and of which no public record is available. The unfortunate applicant has no idea why his or her application has been dismissed. In these circumstances, it is hard to see how the Court is any better than the Commission. Its decision-making process in the vast majority of cases that come before it is arbitrary, private and unreasoned.

This result is surprising, because the Court's admissibility criteria are not particularly stringent. Applications cannot be anonymous, nor must they be 'manifestly ill founded' or 'an abuse of the right of application'. Nor must they have been already submitted to another system of international adjudication; but this is rarely applicable (usually the only alternative would be the ICCPR committee, which is seldom used for the reasons already described). However, anecdotal experience from the Court suggests that the grounds on which most applications are declared inadmissible is the requirement that applications be made 'only after all domestic remedies have been exhausted,. . .and within a period of six months from the date on which the final decision was taken'.[28] Because there is no clear definition of what it means to exhaust all domestic remedies, this test establishes a dilemma with two horns on which applicants may be impaled. Exhaustion of domestic remedies may typically be taken to mean application to a domestic court and exhaustion of all levels of appeal. However, uncertainties arise where levels of appeal are discretionary or commonly accepted to be hopeless. Does one have to make an appeal where the appeal court is not obliged to accept the appeal, and indeed accepts appeals only very rarely (as with the United Kingdom's Supreme Court)? What if legal counsel has advised that the prospects of an appeal being accepted or successful are negligible? Does one still have to appeal, even if doing so might cause one detriment (for example by incurring a further costs liability)? What if a given tier of court permits parties to make more than one appeal to it? This is typical under procedures of extraordinary review, common in many countries with legal traditions derived from the Austro-Hungarian legal system. Parties may apply multiple times to a Supreme Court for review of a lower court's decision, based upon new facts or arguments. How many times must one apply to the same court, to exhaust domestic remedies? These questions have no clear answer in ECHR case law.

Thus an applicant finds himself (or herself) in perennial danger of falling foul of the Convention's admissibility requirements. Apply to the ECHR before some final theoretical appeal (most unlikely to succeed) has been exhausted, and one risks the claim being struck out for being too early. Apply after the appeal has been made and inevitably rejected, and one risks the claim being struck out for being too late. The exhaustion of domestic remedies may be held to have taken place upon some event earlier than the final action actually taken before domestic courts, and thus more than six months are held to have passed. Both these results are revealed in what little case law is available on the meaning of the 'exhaustion of domestic remedies' test.[29] Because the decision to declare an application inadmissible is usually made by a panel of three judges sitting in private who publicise no record of their reasoning, this legal test is not being developed in such a way as to provide applicants with greater certainty.

This is no great surprise. It would of course be open to the judges of the ECHR to issue decisions on admissibility that elaborate the test of what it means to exhaust domestic remedies. But this would lead to fewer applications being declared inadmissible; and the Court is already so busy that it cannot clear its backlog. The vagaries of the admissibility test, combined with the private and unreasoned manner in which it is applied, are used as a case filter, to reject 95 per cent of applications and leave the Court with a manageable docket. Because the test of admissibility is vague, it is also flexible, allowing the Court to accept such cases as it may find interesting and reject the rest. Such a discretionary approach to accepting applications is not unique. Many countries' supreme courts adopt such an approach; where an application for permission to appeal is declined, no reasons are given. However, those courts are explicit that the judges have discretion to refuse to hear appeals, and will only accept exceptional cases which raise points of law of particular public importance. The ECHR pretends that its portals are open to all applicants, when this is not in fact the case. Because of the fundamental nature of complaints about violations of human rights, it might be thought that a discretionary system before the ECHR – of the kind formerly operated by the European Commission of Human Rights and still operated by the Inter-American Commission – is not appropriate. A victim of a human rights violation should have an absolute right of access to a court. The reality is that the European Court cannot cope with the caseload this absolute right would entail. Thus it engages in legal fictions to introduce a *de facto* discretionary system and cut its docket by 95 per cent. Even then it is severely overworked.

So overstretched is the system that the Court has recently adopted yet further restrictions on admissibility. Under Protocol 14 to the European Convention (which came into force on 1 June 2010), a single judge, rather than three judges, makes decisions on admissibility, again sitting in private and without providing reasons. Cases will be declared inadmissible, amongst other grounds, where the applicant has 'suffered no significant disadvantage'; or 'respect for human rights does not require examination of the merits'. These tests are worryingly opaque, especially where decisions on admissibility will still be taken in private, without a hearing or argument by the parties and without reasons being given. Furthermore, under Protocol 14 a single judge will be able to make decisions rejecting a claim as inadmissible, overcoming even the pretence of convening a panel of three judges to reject claims *en masse*. The judge can sit in his chambers on his own to reject cases. The aim is apparently to increase the figure of 95 per cent to some even higher proportion. The solution to dealing with the Court's backlog is to reject the vast majority of applications out of hand and without any investigation or reasoning. The Court is often cited as a tremendous success,[30] but it is hard to see how this is so if the vast majority of applicants to it are denied access on opaque admissibility grounds without the due process protections of a hearing or a reasoned judgment. The better solutions to the Court's docket problems – increase the Court's efficiency or increase its budget – apparently do not appeal to the member states of the Council of Europe. The reason for this may be that these states are quite content with the system as it currently stands. They never wanted to create an international court of appeal from their domestic legal systems. A court that rejects the vast majority of applications to it and hears only a handful of politically charged cases is far more convenient and tolerable.

In this connection, it is worth noting the sorts of case that do see it through the admissibility procedure and are decided on the merits. They tend to concern issues where there has been significant public attention and where the Court has an opportunity to expand its own jurisprudence in a noteworthy direction on an issue of public interest. This criterion of admissibility is very similar to one of the criteria by which countries' domestic supreme courts accept cases. With a limited caseload capacity, national supreme or constitutional courts see themselves as expanding case law or providing authoritative interpretations of statutes or constitutional provisions only where there is a major policy issue at stake or uncertainty in the law calls for final resolution. Their role is judicial development of the law in controversial or unsettled cases. The European Court of Human Rights may see its role in the same way, as it is eager continually to expand its jurisprudence to find ever more social, legal and political issues within its remit. Thus the Court has opined that rights under the European Convention are relevant to as broad a range of issues as environmental harm,[31] rules of evidence (in particular the hearsay rule and the privilege against self-incrimination),[32] urban planning,[33] the right of prisoners to vote[34] and government regulation of market rates for property rentals.[35]

It is not clear that this role, of perpetual expansion of the boundaries of what count as legally protected human rights, is the proper function of the Court. Its original intended function was as a final backstop against totalitarianism. It was supposed to protect a fundamental core of human rights upon which no democratic government could properly impinge, not develop a supreme federal human rights law that would be imposed uniformly across the Council of Europe's member states. Yet it has sought to adopt this latter role, developing significant and complex jurisprudence that seeks to pre-empt a wide range of contentious moral and cultural issues, including prohibitions on abortion,[36] the right of an unborn child to sue its mother,[37] homosexuality in the armed forces,[38] religious symbols in schools[39] and the status of the Church of Scientology as a legitimate religious institution.[40] In so doing so, the Court pays scant regard to domestic legal traditions that may seek to treat controversial issues in different ways. In the words of one English judge well known for his criticisms of the ECHR, the Court fails to grant states adequate 'margins of appreciation' in their domestic policies.[41] Rather than permit the relatively sophisticated domestic political and legal systems of Europe to resolve contentious issues in which different civil rights are balanced one against the other, or are balanced against broader social goals, the European Court wants to undertake these balancing exercises itself, and impose its resolutions upon all members. This is despite the fact that differing societies balance rights such as freedom of the press and the importance of having a fair trial free from improper media reporting, in different ways. The Court itself clearly considers itself better equipped to make these balancing judgments than are domestic institutions.[42] It considers that the balance should be struck in the same way for all Council of Europe member states, refusing to countenance that different ways of undertaking this exercise may be equally legitimate in countries with different legal cultures.

The reason the Court seeks to undertake this broad role is to provide itself with political relevance. It becomes a participant in contemporary moral and political debates of the day, a role with which it clearly finds itself at ease. This may be why so many run of the mill claims are rejected: they raise issues which there is no political value for the Court in adjudicating. Unfortunately the Court's users are not for the most part driven by the desire of the Court to make pronouncements about social issues: the majority of them are aggrieved by mistreatment by corrupt and oppressive actions of security forces, government administrations and courts in eastern Europe and Turkey. As a general rule, applicants before the Court are less interested in Heathrow night flights (the subject of a much publicised case in which the Court decided to prejudge a decision of the British government to change the hours aeroplanes could land at Heathrow airport, even after the issue had been fully debated in English courts)[43] and more concerned about massacres by Turkish or Russian security forces, claims which (like the vast majority of all complaints) are often rejected as inadmissible. The Court might more valuably focus upon the latter rather than the former.

The reason it does not, and the reason Council of Europe states tolerate the Court's expansionist jurisprudence with so little comment, is intriguing. By focusing upon comparatively minor human rights issues at the tenuous end of the spectrum of issues that are arguably impacted by the European Convention, they keep their antagonism of member states to a minimum. The sorts of contentious moral and political issues on which the Court likes to pronounce are rarely cases in which it is appropriate to award substantial compensation. Indeed the Court's record in granting damages is derisory; its awards are often miniscule, even where the abuses complained of are extremely serious. In *A and others v United Kingdom* the Court awarded €1700 and €3900 as compensation for indefinite detention without trial.[44] For inhumane conditions of imprisonment, including a prisoner having to wash from a squat toilet, the Court awarded 5 million

Greek Drachmas (approximately €14 600).[45] At the upper end of the scale, disappearance, torture and murder by Russian security forces may net the deceased's family in the region of €40 000 to €50 000.[46] In many cases, the Court rules against a state but awards no damages at all, saying merely that the existence of the decision in its favour is satisfaction enough for the applicant.[47]

Furthermore, compliance by states is for all intents and purposes optional. In many cases in which rulings are made against member states, they decline to change their domestic laws to bring them into compliance with the Court's ruling. The regime of modest payments, of a few thousand Euros, is convenient for member states. They can make the payment without significant budgetary harm or domestic political opposition, assert that they have complied with the Court's judgment, and decline to change the underlying legal regime that generated the violation. Where the Court tries to make an order that affects a state's fundamental interests, the state will simply ignore it. In *Al Saadoon and Mufdhi v United Kingdom*,[48] the Court ordered the British armed forces not to hand over two Iraqi detainees to the Iraqi authorities for trial, on the ground that those detainees faced the prospect of execution if convicted. (Protocol 13 to the European Convention bans the death penalty in all circumstances.) The British government simply ignored the decision, transferring the men the next day. In *Sejdić and Finci v Bosnia and Herzegovina*,[49] the Court ruled Bosnia's Constitution, which provides for a tripartite presidency with members from each of the country's three ethnic groups, inconsistent with the Convention. Bosnia and Herzegovina likewise simply ignored the ruling. It was not going to amend its constitution and upset the delicate balance of ethnic interests in a post-war society just to satisfy the Court's abstract theorising about non-discrimination. In the various cases involving murder and disappearances by state security forces, the Court typically orders the domestic government to undertake an investigation. In practice this rarely happens; the respondent state simply pays the compensation ordered and considers that the end of the matter.[50]

When states ignore the Court's judgments, there is no consequence. Its decisions are not enforceable before national courts, unlike international arbitration awards[51] or (within the European Union and the European Free Trade Association (EFTA))[52] domestic court judgments. The only method of enforcement, if it can be called that, is that the Council of Europe is called upon to monitor compliance with the Court's judgments.[53] In principle they can issue reports criticising states for non-compliance or even refer the matter back to the Court for infringement proceedings, but in practice this rarely happens.[54] The ultimate sanction is expulsion from the Council of Europe, but this has never occurred nor has it ever even been considered. Such a measure would harm the Council's budget, the expelled state ceasing to contribute. It is also hard to see how expulsion would promote human rights in the country expelled: thereafter, the Court would cease to have jurisdiction over acts of that state. Because enforcement is toothless, the Court has every interest in ensuring it does not issue judgments that are liable seriously to aggrieve nations and which they are not likely to comply with voluntarily. This is why its damages awards are so modest, and why the Court prefers to steer away from the security forces abuse cases. Individual states agreed to provide the ECHR with jurisdiction over their actions because it would be utterly ineffective and of no danger to states' interests. The Court must live down to that expectation. Until 1998 the Court's jurisdiction was optional (like that of the Inter-American Court). One may speculate that the members of the Council of Europe agreed to make the Court's jurisdiction compulsory only because it already had a track record of not being a serious impediment to their pursuit of important national interests. That record will in all likelihood be preserved.

Russia has recently adopted another intriguing mode of frustrating the Court's activity. When shareholders in the former Russian oil giant Yukos brought an ECHR complaint against Russia for liquidating its assets in an allegedly bogus tax investigation, Russia took to frustrating the claim by appointing and then removing a series of ad hoc judges from the case, who would find themselves unavailable for the Court's hearings. The Russian government agent would also find himself unavailable, leading to the hearings being repeatedly postponed.[55] The case is of exceptional sensitivity for Russia, not just at a political level (it seems difficult to imagine that the break-up of Yukos took place without the direct sanction of the then Russian President Vladimir Putin) but also due to the enormous damages award being sought by Yukos, equal to a significant proportion of Russia's annual GDP.[56] Such an award would be many orders of magnitude beyond any judgment ever previously issued by the ECHR. At the time of writing it is not clear what the Court will do in the face of an enormous claim against arguably the Court's most recalcitrant member, which has taken to vocal attacks upon the impartiality of the Court and the propriety of its procedures in consequence of the ECHR's decision to hear Yukos's complaint.[57]

Other criticisms can be raised against the European Court of Human Rights. One is the composition of its judiciary. Four of its 47 judges are under the age of 40: hardly the experienced jurists one would hope to be sitting upon Europe's court of final recourse. Some 45 per cent (21 out of 47) have never held prior judicial office, perhaps a reason why the Court's deliberations on admissibility are conducted in so injudicious a fashion.

Each member of the Council of Europe gets one judge, irrespective of size. San Marino (population 30 000) and Russia (population 170 000 000) each have one judge. There is a judicial hierarchy: most of the important decisions are written by a handful of experienced judges. Many judges are apparently just treading water, entrusted with *en masse* admissibility rejections but little else. The judicial selection process leaves much to be desired. Each state submits a list of three candidates' names, from which a Council of Europe committee selects one.[58] The only common criterion for candidacy is apparently that the candidate has a law degree.[59] Typically only one applicant out of the three is a serious contender. There is no selection procedure that states are obliged to follow in advancing candidates. Each follows its own procedure (or in most cases, no procedure). The Committee making the choice cannot reject all three candidates; the majority of the members of the Committee are not legally qualified; there is no vetting procedure of substance. It is a lottery as to who ends up sitting on the bench of the European Court. Perhaps this is a reason underlying so many of the institution's failures.

The European human rights system is not what it claims to be: a final recourse, available to all, to redress grievous human rights breaches committed by states. Instead it is a covertly discretionary court that hears applications where it has an opportunity to develop its own jurisprudence in sophisticated new directions. The remedies it offers are mostly of poor value to applicants, and in practice its rulings cannot be enforced if states choose not to comply. It is tolerably easy for the states that have created it to ignore the ECHR, or at least for it rarely to serve as more than a minor irritant. Nonetheless, the European Court has transformed international human rights law into a growth industry. Even though the system borders on the useless for applicants (whose chances of prevailing are always miniscule, and even then they receive little more than moral vindication after years of delay), huge numbers of textbooks have been written, discussing the Court's jurisprudence and advising practitioners on how to take a case to Strasbourg. Because applicants extract so little of value from it and states care little what the Court does (and can cast off or bury its judgments without, for the most part, changing the way their government works), the institution exists for human rights lawyers alone. An entire branch of law has been conjured out of thin air. It is not clear how it advances the original goal of human rights law – preventing recurrence of totalitarian atrocities – to have such a court.

The best that can be said is that the Court's moral authority nudges some countries, which may otherwise have shaky records on human rights, in the right direction. For countries with respectable traditions of observing human rights, the Court looks more like an attempt to seize sovereignty over an ever-expanding set of domestic policy issues and elevate them to an international level. It is not clear why this is desirable, where there is no democratic accountability within the ECHR nor amongst the human rights lawyers that share responsibility for development of this field of law. Were the regime not so ineffectual and easy to ignore, it would be at risk of representing a legalistic tyranny. As things stand, the Court keeps a lot of people busy either writing or discussing its judgments, and creating reams of quasi-intellectual analysis, but without being of enormous benefit to the vast majority its litigants. All the while the case backlog gets larger, the delays get worse, and the greater mass of applicants find their complaints rejected without reasons by private judicial decree. Perhaps more than any other field of international law, the European Court of Human Rights is representative of the constructivist thesis in international relations.

NOTES

1. Robert Nozick is perhaps the least well known of the individuals listed. He was an eminent political philosopher. His 1974 magnum opus *Anarchy, State and Utopia* developed a minimalist theory of the state premised upon the notion that individual rights are absolute and unimpeachable. His work famously opens with the sentence 'Individuals have rights and there are things no person may do to them (without violating those rights).' It is an excellent book (Nozick, R. (1974), *Anarchy, State and Utopia*, New York City: Basic Books).
2. By decree dated 26 November 1648, Pope Innocent X rejected all provisions of the Westphalian peace that gave rights to Protestantism or undermined the rights of the established Catholic church: 'we assert and declare by these presents that all the said articles in one or both of the said treaties which in any way impair or prejudice in the slightest degree, or that can be said, alleged, understood, or imagined to be able in any way to injure or to have injured the Catholic religion, divine worship, the salvation of souls, the said Roman apostolic see, the inferior churches, the ecclesiastical order or estate, their persons, affairs, possessions, jurisdictions, authorities, immunities, liberties, privileges, prerogatives, and rights whatsoever, – all such provisions have been, and are of right, and shall perpetually be, null and void, invalid, iniquitous, unjust, condemned, rejected, frivolous, without force or effect, and no one is to observe them.'
3. Among the countries that signed treaties with such provisions were Poland (in the 'Little Treaty of Versailles'); the Kingdom of Serbs Croats and Slovenes; Czechoslovakia and Austria (in the Treaty of St Germain-en-Laye); Bulgaria (in the Treaty of Neuilly-sur-Seine); Greece (in the Treaty of Sèvres); Romania; Hungary (in the Treaty of Trianon); Bulgaria; Turkey (in the Treaty of Lausanne); Albania; and the Baltic States.
4. *Rights of Minorities in Upper Silesia*, Judgment of 26 April 1928, PCIJ, Ser. A, No. 15, ruled ethnic criteria for admission to school unacceptable. *Minority Schools in Albania*, Advisory Opinion of 6 April 1935, PCIJ, Ser. A, No. 64, ruled against closure of minority schools.
5. At the time of writing an intriguing alternative method for enforcing international labour standards may be emerging. The Dominican Republic-Central America-United States Free Trade Agreement (CAFTA-DR) contains an obligation upon each party to enforce effectively its labour laws. Treaty signatories may insist that a complainant of breach of this obligation be referred to arbitration, with fines of up to US$15 million per annum being imposed if default is found. On 30 July 2010 the US Government

announced that it had filed a formal request for consultations against Guatemala, a precursory step to arbitration proceedings, for breach of this obligation. However, the United States was explicit that its motive was not the welfare of Guatemalan labourers but protection of its own workforce. Lax labour standards would allow Guatemalan enterprises to compete unfairly with US ones. In other words, the motive in bringing the complaint is trade protectionism. See Office of the US Trade Representative (2010), *USTR Kirk Announces Labor Rights Trade Enforcement Case Against Guatemala*, press release 30 July.

6. Articles 28 *et seq* ICCPR; Articles 16 to 22 ICESCR.
7. For the ICCPR, the Optional Protocol was opened for signature by General Assembly Resolution 2200A(XXI) of 16 December 1966, and came into force on 23 March 1976. For the ICESCR, the Optional Protocol to the ICESCR was adopted by the UN General Assembly only on 10 December 2008 and was opened for signature only on 24 September 2009. It has not yet been ratified by enough countries to come into force (ten ratifications are necessary).
8. These are the Committee on the Elimination of Racial Discrimination, the Committee on the Elimination of Discrimination against Women, the Committee against Torture and the Committee on the Rights of Persons with Disabilities. In each case a complaint against a state is admissible only if a declaration or optional protocol has been adopted. For details see http://www2.ohchr.org/english/bodies/petitions/index.htm (last accessed 13 July 2010).
9. See e.g. (just recent examples of a common trend) Communication No. 1209/2003, *Rakhmatov v Tajikistan*; Communication No. 1231/2003, *Safarovs v Tajikistan*; Communication No. 1241/2004, *Mukhammadiev v Tajikistan*, Views adopted 1 April 2008, 92nd session of the Human Rights Committee. In these cases the applicants alleged severe torture by the police while in custody, leading to forced confessions and wrongful convictions. The Tajik government simply ignored the proceedings. The Committee recommended the victims be compensated and released from prison early. It is not clear what action if any the Tajik government took on these recommendations.
10. See e.g. Communication No. 1186/2003, *Titiahonjo v Cameroon*, Views adopted 26 October 2007, 91st session of the Human Rights Committee. The deceased's wife launched a complaint that her husband had been medically neglected in police custody and this had led to his death. More than five years after she filed the complaint, the Committee concluded that her claim was well founded and that Cameroon ought to grant an effective remedy. Its decision was five and a half pages long. This was another case in which the state respondent simply ignored the proceedings and took no part in them.
11. Figures courtesy of Duke University library, Durham, NC.
12. Or so it is reported. (The document is not apparently public.) See *Associated Press* (2009), 'North Korea's new constitution mentions human rights', 28 September.
13. This is particularly so for the European Convention on Human Rights, which in Germany has the status of a federal statute, under Article 59(2) Grundgesetz and the *Bundesverfassungsgericht* decision of October 14, 2004, 2 BvR 1481/04 – *Görgülü*. In the United Kingdom, section 3(1) Human Rights Act 1998 places an obligation on public authorities to give effect to legislation 'so far as it is possible to do so. . .in a way that is compatible with the Convention rights'.
14. The only English-speaking member of the OAS that has accepted the Court's jurisdiction is Barbados.
15. See e.g. Report No. 56/08 dated 24 July 2008 (complaint received on 19 February 1996); Report No. 59/08 dated 24 July 2008 (complaint received on 17 December 1993); Report No. 35/09 dated 27 March 2009 (complaint received on 8 October 1999); Report No. 88/09 (complaint received on 23 December 1998).
16. *Caesar v Trinidad and Tobago*, Judgment of 11 March 2005, Inter-Am Ct H.R. (Ser. C) No. 123 (2005).
17. *Bulacio v Argentina*, Judgment of 18 September 2003, Inter-Am Ct H.R. (Ser. C) No. 100 (2003).

18. *Sánchez v Honduras*, Judgment of 7 June 2003, Inter-Am Ct H.R. (Ser. C) No. 99 (2003).
19. *Moiwana Village v Suriname*, Judgment of 15 June 2005, Inter-Am Ct H.R. (Ser. C) No. 124 (2005).
20. *Calderon v Ecuador*, Judgment of 24 June 2005, Inter-Am Ct. H.R. (Ser. C) No. 129 (2005).
21. *Case of the 'Mapiripán Massacre' v Colombia*, Judgment of 15 September 2005.
22. *Mapiripán Massacre* and *Calderon* respectively, *ibid.*
23. Filippini, Leonardo (2008), 'The strengthening of the inter-American Court of Human Rights', ADC (Asociación por los Derechoes Civiles), Buenos Aires.
24. Article 35(1) European Convention on Human Rights: 'The Court may only deal with the matter after all domestic remedies have been exhausted, according to the generally recognised rules of international law, and within a period of six months from the date on which the final decision was taken.'
25. This figure is courtesy of Chatham House (2009), 'European Court of Human Rights: A Court in Crisis?', International Law Discussion Group Meeting Summary, June.
26. These delays are periodically reported by the media. See e.g. BBC News, 'Mammoth backlog prompts European rights court reforms', 19 February 2010.
27. Chatham House, 'European Court of Human Rights', *ibid.*
28. Article 35(1) European Convention on Human Rights.
29. Thus in Application 21287/02 *Prystavavska v Ukraine*, Decision of 17 November 2002, it was held that there is no obligation to pursue discretionary remedies such as requesting a court to revise its decision, before applying to the ECHR. The applicant had asked the domestic court to revise its decision before applying. In the intervening period more than six months had passed since the exhaustion of domestic remedies, and thus her application was declared inadmissible. Contrast this with Application 26323/95 *Kiiskinen v Finland*, Decision of 1 June 1999, in which the Court held that applying to the domestic court for revision of its decision should have been attempted, and thus the application to the ECHR was declared inadmissible for failure first to exhaust domestic remedies. Alternatively the Court may simply decide that a domestic step the applicant took was inappropriate, and thus the six month time limit had started running in the mean time (and expired): Application 49859/99 *Rezgui v France*, Decision of 7 November 2000.
30. See e.g. Helfer, Laurence (2008), 'Redesigning the European Court of Human Rights: Embededdness as a Deep Structural Principle of the European Human Rights Regime', *European Journal of International Law* **19**(1): 125 (describing the ECHR as the 'crown jewel of the world's most advanced system for protecting civil and political liberties'); Helfer Laurence and Anne-Marie Slaughter (1997), 'Toward a Theory of Effective Supranational Adjudication', *Yale Law Journal*, **107**, 273; Janis, Mark, Richard Kay and Anthony Bradley (2000), *European Human Rights Law: Text and Materials*, 2nd ed., Oxford: Oxford University Press; Ryssdall, Rolv (1996), 'Opinion: The Coming of Age of the European Convention on Human Rights', *European Human Rights Law Review*, **18**; Tomkins, Adam (1997), *Civil Liberties in the Council of Europe*, in Conor Gearty, ed., *European Civil Liberties and the European Convention on Human Rights: A Comparative Study*, Leiden: Martinus Nijhoff; Reding, Andrew (2000), 'Europe Overtakes US on Frontiers of Human Rights Law', *Pacific News Service*, 17 January.
31. Application 36022/97 *Hatton v United Kingdom* (2003) 37 EHRR 611, dissenting opinion of Judge Costa (the President of the Court); *López Ostra v Spain*, Judgment of 9 December 1994, Series A, No. 303-C; (1995) 20 EHRR 277.
32. For the ECHR's commentary upon the hearsay rule, see Application 26766/05 *Al Khawaja and Tahery v United Kingdom* 20 January 2009. On the privilege against self-incrimination, see Application 43/1994/490/572 *Saunders v United Kingdom*, Judgment of 17 December 1996; Applications 15809/02 & 25624/02 *O'Halloran and Francis v United Kingdom*, Judgment of 29 June 2007. Hoffman discusses these cases critically and in further detail (see note 41).
33. Application 20348/92 *Buckley v United Kingdom*, Judgment of 25 September 1996; (1997) 23 EHRR 101.

34. Application 74025/01 *Hirst v United Kingdom (No. 2)*, Judgment of 6 October 2005, (2006) 42 EHRR 41.
35. *Mellacher v Austria*, Judgment of 19 December 1989, Series A, No. 169, (1990) 12 EHRR 391.
36. Application 25579/05 *A, B and C v Ireland*, hearing on the merits 9 December 2009; Decision pending at the time of writing (assessing the permissibility of Ireland's blanket prohibition of abortion with the European Convention).
37. *Paton v United Kingdom* (1981) 3 EHRR 408.
38. Applications 33985 & 6/96 *Smith and Grady v United Kingdom*, Decision of 27 September 1999 (prohibiting discharge of homosexuals from the armed forces).
39. Application 30814/06 *Lautsi v Italy*, Decision of 3 November 2009 (banning crucifixes in school classrooms); the matter was subsequently referred to the Grand Chamber, which held a hearing on 30 June 2010. The Grand Chamber's ruling is pending at the time of writing.
40. Application 18147/02 *Church of Scientology Moscow v Russia*, Judgment of 5 April 2007.
41. Lord Hoffman, *The Universality of Human Rights*, Judicial Studies Board Annual Lecture, 19 March 2009.
42. Hoffman, *ibid*, discussing Application 59320/00 *von Hannover v Germany*, Judgment 24 June 2004. In this case the ECHR overruled the German Bundesgerichtshof (Federal Court of Justice, Germany's highest court) in its decision balancing the privacy rights of the applicant (who was a public figure) against the freedom of the press to publish family photographs.
43. Application 36022/97 *Hatton v United Kingdom*, *supra*. The issue in the case was whether noise and sleep disturbances engendered by a limited night flight regime for Heathrow airport violated the right to respect for private and family life under Article 8 of the European Convention on Human Rights. A significant minority of the Court, including the President, dissented that the applicants' right to family life were violated. A majority of the Court, while declining the Article 8 claim, held that English judicial review proceedings were an inadequate forum for the applicants to air their complaints about breach of their Article 8 rights.
44. Application 3455/05 *A and others v United Kingdom*, Judgment of 19 February 2009. The case related to UK anti-terrorism legislation permitting indefinite detention without charge of foreign nationals suspected as involved in terrorist activities.
45. Application 28524/95 *Peers v Greece*, Judgment of 19 April 2001.
46. See e.g. 74237/01 *Baysayeva v Russia*, Judgment of 5 April 2007 (video emerged of applicant's husband being beaten by Russian troops before being taken away; applicant awarded €50 000); 68007/01 *Alikhadzhiyeva v Russia*, Judgment of 5 July 2007 (Russian military vehicles seized and abducted opposition Chechen politician; presumed murdered; award of €40 000); 69481/01 *Bazorkina v Russia*, Judgment of 27 July 2006 (victim beaten and executed by Russian army on video; award of €35 000).
47. This is more common where there is no case of physical harm or mistreatment. See e.g. Application 11002/05 *ASLEF v United Kingdom*, Judgment of 27 February 2007 (right of trade union to choose its own members). Alternatively nominal awards are made. This is common in discrimination cases: see e.g. Application 45330/99 *SL v Austria*, Judgment of 9 January 2003 (discriminatory age of consent for homosexual and heterosexual sexual intercourse). In some cases findings are made of human rights violations with extremely serious consequences, but nevertheless no award of compensation is made. See e.g. Application 36009/08 *MB & others v Turkey*, Judgment of 15 June 2010 (applicants deported to Iran in violation of Court's interim measure, where they faced religious persecution).
48. Application 61498/08 *Al Saadoon and Mufdhi v United Kingdom*, Indication on Interim Measures of 30 December 2008; Judgment on the Merits of 2 March 2010. Nevertheless the applicants were granted no compensation.
49. Applications 27996/06 and 34836/06 *Sejdić and Finci v Bosnia and Herzegovina*, Judgment of 22 December 2009.

50. For instances in the Russian context see footnote 42, *supra*.
51. International arbitration awards are enforceable under the 1958 New York Convention on Recognition and Enforcement of Arbitration Awards by the courts of all state signatories. By far the majority of the world's trading nations have signed the New York Convention.
52. EC Regulation 44/2001 provides for near-automatic enforcement of the judgments of the courts of any EU member state by the courts of any other EU member states. The 1988 Lugano Convention extends almost exactly the same regime to members of the European Free Trade Association.
53. Article 46 European Convention provides that 'The High Contracting Parties undertake to abide by the final judgment of the Court in any case to which they are parties. The final judgment of the Court shall be transmitted to the Committee of Ministers, which shall supervise its execution'. However, the Convention does *not* provide that states are obliged to enforce judgments against one-another (as they may be required to do so with arbitration awards under the New York Convention). The Committee of Ministers has a series of Rules for the Supervision of the Execution of Judgments (adopted 10 May 2006, at the 964th meeting of Ministers' Deputies), but the Committee relies upon updates from the state concerned as to the measures it has taken. In principle the Committee may refer the matter back to the Court for infringement proceedings, but in practice this virtually never happens. Even if it did, it is not clear what such a reference could achieve beyond adverse publicity.
54. An example of a case in which the United Kingdom has resisted enforcement is *Hirst v United Kingdom* (note 34 *supra*), where the United Kingdom has declined to implement the ECHR's ruling that prisoners should have the right to vote. There is no political will to give effect to this ruling, which seems destined to be ignored indefinitely far into the future. The judgment has now been outstanding for over five years with no effective enforcement measures taken. However, the worst offender for refusal to comply with ECHR judgments is Turkey. According to statistics prepared by the Council of Ministers, as of 30 June 2007 Turkey was responsible for 17 per cent of cases in which compliance with the ECHR's judgment was outstanding. The next offender on the list was Italy, responsible for 9 per cent of the cases in which compliance was outstanding. The number of cases in which compliance was outstanding had risen from 1607 in 1999 to 6017 as of 30 June 2007.
55. Application 14902/04 *OAO Neftanaya kompanija YUKOS v Russia*. See Khordokovsky & Lebedev Communications Center (2010), 'Hearing in Yukos v. Russia Case Postponed', press release, London, 12 January.
56. The damages sought in the Yukos claim before the ECHR are some US$42 billion (or approximately 3 per cent of Russia's GDP in 2008), making it the largest ECHR claim in the Court's history. The claim was declared admissible in a ruling dated 29 January 2009 and a hearing on the merits was held on 4 March 2010. At the time of writing the Court's judgment is pending.
57. See Charter, David (2009), 'Yukos shareholders take case to Strasbourg', *The Times*, 30 January.
58. Article 22 European Convention.
59. Article 21(1) European Convention sets the sole qualifications for appointment: 'The judges shall be of high moral character and must either possess the qualifications required for appointment to high judicial office or be juriconsults of recognised competence.' This test is so flexible as to be virtually worthless.

8. The allure of judicial trusteeship in the European Union experience

Discussions of international law typically proceed in parallel with those addressing the law of the European Union, as though they are two parallel lines that never meet. On its face this is bizarre, since EU law is the creation of a series of international treaties. Europe's transnational institutional regime commenced with the Treaty of Paris (1951) that established the European Coal and Steel Community (ECSC). The next step was the Treaty of Rome (1957), creating the European Economic Community (EEC), and the structure was further developed by subsequent pan-European treaties from the Single European Act (1986) to Maastricht (1992) to Nice (2001) to Lisbon (2007). These treaties successively led the ECSC to evolve into the EEC, then the European Community (EC), and finally the European Union (EU).[1] These treaties create a two-tier system of international courts, the General Court of the European Union (formerly known as the Court of First Instance) and the European Court of Justice. These courts have the task of ruling upon the interpretation of the law created by these treaties and, in some cases, of adjudicating disputes.

Whereas there are many critics of international law, there are fewer critics of EU law. (Although there are plenty of critics of the European Union, their criticisms tend to be aimed at the EU's Byzantine political system rather than specifically at its legal system. However this may be a false dichotomy: the interdependence of the two will be explored in the course of this chapter.) Indeed those who are well known for their criticisms of international law sometimes seem stumped by the apparent success of EU law. Typically, they retreat to contrasting the European experience with that of the rest of the world, and suggesting that it is inappropriate to apply lessons from the EU to the system of international law more generally.[2] Yet to adopt such an approach is to beg the question: is EU law genuinely in a category of its own amongst systems of international law? If so, what differentiates it, and what explains its relative success? This chapter aims to cast some light on these issues.

The origins of the European Union lie in many of the same aspirations for international cooperation and foreclosure of conflict that drove the expansion of other areas of international law in the aftermath of

World War II. The Treaty of Paris created the European Coal and Steel Community and was signed in 1951 between France, Germany, Italy and the Benelux countries, when wartime destruction was a recent memory. The principal idea behind the ECSC was to create a common market for French and German coal and steel, and to integrate the signatory countries' coal and steel industries to such an extent that political cooperation would become obligatory to achieve economic growth. Thereby it was hoped another war would be made impossible, for coal and steel production had been central to Germany's war effort. Of course another European war never did occur; whether the ECSC was responsible for that achievement, it is hard to speculate, but the basic principles and institutional structure of the Community laid the groundwork for the European Union that would develop over the subsequent decades.

Under the Treaty of Paris, import tariffs within the Community were banned. A 'High Authority' (an embryonic predecessor to the European Commission, with a cabinet of international officials appointed by the member states) could also impose maximum and minimum tariffs on coal and steel trade with third countries. Members were obliged to remove restrictions on cross-border migration of workers in the covered industries. The Treaty contained the world's first international competition laws, banning anti-competitive agreements and abuse of dominant market positions and regulating mergers. Discriminatory pricing of coal and steel products was prohibited. The High Authority could impose production quotas in the event of declines in demand or shortages. The High Authority could also provide loan guarantees. A Court of Justice was established to adjudicate disputes under the Treaty; this institution developed into the European Court of Justice that exists today. There was also a Council representing national governments and an Assembly that represented national parliaments. The regime was funded through a uniform levy on coal and steel production.

Although limited both in economic scope and the countries involved (only six countries were initially signatories to the Treaty of Paris), the ideas underlying the treaty were revolutionary. The innovation consisted in creating international organisations with a mandate to intervene directly in the domestic affairs of member states. The High Authority could issue directions on matters such as wage rates for labour, the annulment of anti-competitive agreements, prohibitions of mergers and market pricing decisions, and it created an international tax regime. In fact the High Authority's formal powers were sparingly used; the regime's principal interventions were the issuing of modernisation loans to ailing industries seeking to recover after the war, and on social issues, providing funding for improving workers' accommodation and redeploying workers who lost their jobs as the European coal and steel industries contracted in the second half of the twentieth century.[3] The ability of the Court of Justice to enforce the law of the ECSC was never tested. Nevertheless, the basic structure of the ECSC evolved into the EEC with the Treaty of Rome in 1957. This Treaty, while retaining essentially the same institutional structure, created more elaborate economic obligations upon its member states. The free movement of all workers was guaranteed, not just those in the coal and steel industries. There was also to be free movement of goods, meaning an abolition of all tariffs and quotas, and 'measures having equivalent effect'.[4] There was to be 'freedom of establishment' of business in other member states, and freedom of movement of capital. Competition rules prohibiting cartel agreements and abuse of a dominant market position, and regulating mergers, were to be applied across all industries; to procure equality of competition between companies from different countries, 'state aid' (meaning government subsidies to an industry or equivalent measures) was to be restricted. These principally economic standards were the most important founding principles of the EEC.

Initially it was somewhat unclear what the practical consequences would be for states that embraced these obligations set out in an international treaty. What did 'free movement of workers' involve? Did it require any citizen of any member state automatically to be granted a work permit for any other state? What about his family? Was he entitled to social security benefits? Did the Treaty create direct rights for such workers, who could enforce them personally against domestic immigration authorities? Did free movement of goods entail abolition of administrative fees on customs imports, or customs checks? How, if at all, did it affect national regulatory rules affecting sale of goods? If goods are obliged to satisfy different safety or consumer information standards in differing states, do those amount to restrictions upon the freedom of goods? The obligations set out in the Treaty of Rome were broad and lacked detail. No definitions were provided of 'workers', 'goods', 'establishment', 'freedom' or 'restrictions'. The Treaty of Rome's most important obligations appeared to be sweeping statements of principle typical of the international treaties this book has considered. Beyond broad aspirations towards pan-European principles of economic unity, it was not clear what these obligations really entailed.

However, the unique feature of EC law was the way in which these general treaty commitments were transformed into a concrete set of legal obligations upon states, and binding rights enforceable by workers, exporters and businesses. In the groundbreaking 1963 case *van Gend en Loos*,[5] the European Court of Justice (ECJ), the EEC's international court, ruled that the Treaty of Rome's prohibition on customs duties[6] had 'direct effect'. By this it meant that obligations created by the Treaty could be enforced by private individuals who suffered as a result of its breach. Such an obligation would ordinarily be enforced not by the ECJ itself, but by domestic courts. Many, but not all, obligations under the Treaty of Rome would be 'directly effective' in this way. Free movement of workers and of goods, in practice two of the most important rights under the EC Treaty, would be directly effective.[7] The ECJ also ruled that EEC law would be 'supreme' over national law, meaning that national courts must disapply inconsistent domestic legislation to give effect to EEC law[8] and must interpret domestic legislation consistently with EEC legal obligations.[9] Even where EC law cannot be enforced directly against member states (for example because states have a measure of latitude as to how to implement it), private individuals who have suffered loss as a result of inadequate implementation can sue states for damages, even where such a right does not exist under national law.[10]

In time, the various vague commitments contained in the Treaty were fleshed out in considerable detail. The prohibition on restrictions upon free movement of goods was interpreted as forbidding import licences, certificates of origin, foodstuff purity rules, advertising restrictions and rules encouraging exploitation of intellectual property.[11] All such measures could potentially discriminate against importers who had to comply with national standards not applicable in their countries of origin. This is so even if the domestic regulatory rule does not expressly discriminate against foreign sourced products, but just sets a standard distinct from that in another member state.[12] The right of free movement of workers was ruled to include the right for both a worker and his family to enter a state for the purposes of looking for work, the benefit of social and employment law protections of the state in which the worker is a guest and a prohibition of domestic restrictions upon the use or recognition of foreign educational qualifications.[13]

The ECJ has taken every opportunity to construe the rights in the Treaty of Rome (and indeed in the other forms of EU law, in particular Regulations and Directives enacted by EU institutions pursuant to the Treaty of Rome) as expansively as possible, consistent with creating a free market within the EU's borders. It is no exaggeration to say that the ECJ has developed EU law so broadly that it now intrudes upon large swathes of national policy that were previously considered the province of states; it overrides national laws on the same issues; and it places a significant compliance burden upon states to ensure that all their EU legal obligations are satisfied. It is commonly said, even by the ECJ itself, that the EU treaty regime involves significant abrogation of domestic sovereignty in favour of a European legal order.[14] None of this was obvious from the text of the Treaty of Rome.

These bold strides in ECJ jurisprudence are difficult to understand in the context of the themes of this book. On the realist thesis, the ECJ ought never to have issued any of these decisions: they were far too daring. Constantly nervous of the risks of states withdrawing from the treaty regime or from the jurisdiction of the Court, or even simply ignoring the Court's decisions, the Court should have enacted far weaker rulings that might elaborate EU law in interesting intellectual directions but would not risk alienating the states that created it. The ECJ clearly felt it had sufficient political authority to push EU law in expansive directions. One commentator has described this as the 'judicialisation of EU governance',[15] by which he means that the ECJ has played perhaps the most important role in developing the scope of EU law, a role more pronounced than that the individual member states have in mind when they agree to treaties and other legislative acts. In other words, the ECJ has expanded the scope of EU law beyond that which states apparently intended to create. What member states intended to be at best a vague and open-ended set of treaty commitments, the ECJ has developed into a robust regime of international law. Under a realist analysis of international law, it seems astonishing that states should allow an international court to do such a thing. In any other context, surely, the states would ensure so audacious an institution is closed down or politically weakened. What is it about the ECJ that has enabled it to achieve so much of substance, where other branches of international law have achieved little but expenditure of money, employment of international civil servants and authorship of elaborate textbooks?

THE INSTITUTION OF THE EUROPEAN COURTS

To answer this question, we might begin by considering some of the statistical similarities between the European courts and the other international courts we have been considering. Taken together, the European Court of Justice (ECJ) and the General Court (the two institutions sit in the same building and to a great extent share the same staff) are a monumental institution in Luxembourg. There are 27 judges on each court (one from each EU member state), nine additional quasi-judicial figures called 'advocates general' in the ECJ, a docket of some 1221 cases received by the two courts in 2008, a backlog in the same year of 1945 cases, a budget for 2009 of some €315 million and a staff of about 2000. Delays of between 18 months and three years from receipt of a case to its final disposal are quite normal; case disposal times have improved significantly since 2000. The EU courts might therefore be argued to bear some similarities with the European Court of Human Rights in Strasbourg. While somewhat faster than the

ECHR, their consumption of budget and deployment of staff are even more extraordinary than most international tribunals.

One might seek to cite the EU courts as paragons of inefficiency characteristic of international tribunals. However, it is worth considering carefully these courts' roles. Unlike the ECHR, the ECJ does not have a general jurisdiction to hear private applicants' complaints. Its 'original jurisdiction' is very limited, to actions brought by member states or EU institutions for annulment of an illegal act by an EU institution; and acts by the European Commission (or other member states) against member states for failure to failure to fulfil their EU legal obligations. It also hears 'references' from domestic courts within the EU. These references are not appeals; the domestic court, not the parties, decides to refer a matter of EU law to the ECJ for a ruling, where the principle of law is unclear. Thus in virtually all cases a right of access to the ECJ for litigants is limited either to the public authorities of member states or to EU institutions. The court exists essentially to resolve disputes between member states and EU organs, or to issue rulings on uncertain points of law (again at the request of EU states). The ECJ is thus closer to the ICJ or the WTO DSU as a form of international dispute resolution than it is to the ECHR or investment tribunals. In the former, claims are brought only between states (or between states and the EU's international institutions); in the latter, private individuals may bring direct claims before international tribunals.

The General Court does permit direct claims by private individuals. However, those claims may be brought not against member states but only against EU institutions, for violation of their legal duties. The threshold for bringing such a claim is that the measure complained of is of 'direct and individual concern'[16] to the private applicant: broadly, that it must have an effect upon the applicant distinct from effects upon any other private individual. A general measure that affects a class of individuals of which the applicant is just one member will not suffice. In practice, by far the majority of acts challenged under this provision are decisions of the European Commission's Competition Directorate, imposing fines or other penalties for breaches of EU competition law. Thus when Microsoft was fined €497 million by the Commission for abuse of a dominant position in software bundling, and ordered to release an unbundled version of its Windows operating system and to divulge source code sufficient for competitors to produce rival software, it appealed (unsuccessfully) to the General Court (at the time called the Court of First Instance).[17] Thereafter, appeals from the General Court to the ECJ lie on points of law only, which rarely succeed.

The majority of EU competition law decisions are now dealt with by domestic competition authorities, not by the European Commission, which has restricted the cases which it will investigate to 'the most serious infringements' with a significant international element.[18] Where (as in the majority of cases) a complaint is investigated by a domestic authority within a member state, any right of recourse against such an investigation will lie only to the domestic courts, not to the EU courts, even though the domestic authority will be applying EU competition law. Indeed this is a general feature of EU law: although it is propagated by a series of international institutions, including the Commission, the European Parliament and the European Council, for the most part it is enforced and adjudicated by domestic courts. Although EU law states that it reigns 'supreme' over contrary domestic law,[19] in much the same way as does federal law over state law in the United States, for the most part it is domestic courts that are left to interpret, apply and enforce it.

In theory, domestic courts are obliged to refer points of EU law to the ECJ where there is no appeal from the domestic court in question. (Lower courts have a discretion whether to refer.)[20] However, this obligation applies only where determination of the point of EU law is 'necessary' to resolve the dispute. In practice the domestic court will make a decision as to whether resolution of the point of EU law is necessary, since the ECJ cannot compel a court to refer a point of law to it. The ECJ itself has confirmed the existence of a discretion by national courts to determine whether a point of law is 'necessary' for resolution of a case.[21] Furthermore, references are only necessary where the principle of EU law in question is unclear, itself a matter of judgment for the referring court.[22]

The *de facto* discretionary nature of the referral regime is confirmed by the wide discrepancies in the numbers of referrals made by each state's courts. Thus in the period 2000–2008, German courts made 510 referrals to the ECJ, Italian courts 354 and Dutch courts 203; in the same period, British courts made 157 referrals and the Spanish courts 144.[23] Proportionate to population size, German courts referred cases to the ECJ almost two and a half times as frequently as British courts; Dutch courts almost five times as frequently. Since accession in 2004, Slovenia and Malta have never referred a case to the ECJ; Romania, Bulgaria and Cyprus have referred a case each just once. Different members have enormously different propensities to use the ECJ's referral system. To a great extent, use of the Court is optional. Domestic courts in member states may defer to the ECJ for a ruling on a point of EU law; or they may just decide the point themselves, or indeed circumvent the issue by deciding EU law is not pertinent to the case before them. Although there is no obvious robust method of testing the hypothesis, a great deal may turn upon domestic judicial attitudes to EU law and to the quality of their judicial peers in the EU. Traditionally, the English courts have shown something of an aversion to the style of reasoning prevalent in the ECJ, and have expressed concern over the delays involved in the referral process, which may explain the lower reference rates from the United Kingdom.[24]

The jurisdiction of the ECJ is not entirely optional for states: slightly less than half its caseload consists of infringement actions against member states for failures to implement their EU legal obligations. These actions are usually initiated by the Commission, or more rarely by other member states. The statistics comparing the number of cases commenced against individual countries are revealing. Italy, Greece and tiny Luxembourg are by some way the predominant defendants to such actions, having 128, 115 and 96 infringement actions commenced against them in the period 2004–2008, respectively.[25] The United Kingdom suffers comparatively little from the Commission's wrath, being the defendant to only 38 such actions in the same period: the lowest of any large EU nation in the EU 'old 15' member states that joined the EU prior to 2004. Where these actions are brought, they succeed in 91 per cent of cases.[26] The relief granted is principally declaratory, the Court concluding that the state's laws or actions are inconsistent with its obligations under EU law.

Although in theory the Court has jurisdiction to impose fines if it issues a ruling that is subsequently ignored,[27] only exceptionally rarely is such a fine ever issued. The first ever such fine was imposed only in 2000, some 48 years after the Court's creation.[28] Anecdotal evidence suggests that states do on the whole comply with adverse infringement decisions issued by the ECJ, although no reliable data is available. The infringement system seems moderately robust; certainly the ECJ is not afraid to issue rulings against states, and the reason proceedings for the imposition of fines are so rare may be because, on the whole, states are inclined to comply with rulings of the ECJ against them. In many cases states may be fully aware that they are not in compliance with EU law; often infringement actions relate to failures to implement EU directives by enacting corresponding domestic legislation within the two year grace period typically provided.[29] Action before the Court by the Commission, typically taking two years or more, may give the domestic government breathing space to implement its EU obligations. Sometimes EU law goes unimplemented for extended periods of time, without action before the ECJ; but the Commission's own statistics suggest that the level of voluntary compliance by member states with EU directives is overwhelmingly high (over 97 per cent for the old 15).[30]

Many of the traditional problems of compliance with and enforcement of international law do not seem to apply within the EU system. In particular, the ECJ does not appear to be concerned about making rulings of non-compliance against the member states that created it, for fear that they withdraw from or disregard the system. Nor is there a problem of member states lacking incentives to enforce EU treaties, discussed for human rights treaties in Chapter 7, which may cause obligations to lie fallow without anybody caring to ensure their compliance. The treaties create the European Commission, with its own independent right to bring court action, as the principal institution charged with enforcement. Furthermore, EU law requires individual states' domestic courts to receive claims for damages brought by private plaintiffs against non-compliant states, where the plaintiff has suffered a loss as a result of the state's failure to implement EU law.[31] Thus states are obliged to enforce EU law against themselves, a consequence of the doctrine of supremacy of EU law. In theory, there are no exogenous sanctions for failure to comply with this regime. The EU has no army of debt collectors or bailiffs, and the European Court cannot freeze bank accounts of recalcitrant states or take over their affairs. By analogy with the other systems of international law considered by this book, the system may appear precarious. But it has built itself into a remarkably strong autonomous system. This is an apparent anomaly, and it deserves some explanation.

THE LEGAL SYSTEM WITHIN THE EUROPEAN POLITICAL STRUCTURE

Perhaps the principal difference between the EU legal system and other systems of international law is the existence of a major institutional infrastructure with legislative and executive powers. The EU treaties themselves are only a small part of EU law, a feature which distinguishes EU law from other forms of international law. Most EU law consists of 'regulations' and 'directives', adopted by one of the various legislative procedures set out in the two principal EU treaties. These are the Treaty on European Union (TEU), signed in Maastricht in 1992, and the Treaty of Rome, signed in 1957, subsequently renamed the EU Treaty (in 1993) and then renamed again as the Treaty on the Functioning of the European Union (TFEU) in 2009. Depending on the policy area and the authorising provision of the TEU or the TFEU, these legislative acts may have been proposed and adopted by any or all of the Commission, the European Council, the Council of the European Union or the European Parliament, institutions each created by the TFEU or its predecessors. The interaction between this array of international institutions within the European Union is enormously complex. This is the result of historical accident, irreversible bureaucratic growth and political compromise over countries' wish to exercise more or less close powers of veto of an EU initiative in different policy areas.

In most areas, legislation can be proposed only by the Commission. The Commission is a quasi-executive institution, consisting of a cabinet of 27 commissioners, each of which is nominated by one member state and who as a whole are subject to approval by the European Parliament. (The Parliament must vote to approve the entire slate of Commissioners; it cannot veto individual members of the Commission.) Commissioners are meant to be independent of national government and national interests, although in practice this principle sometimes frays: a number of commissioners have simultaneously participated in national elections while holding office,[32] and sometimes operate within the Commission with their sending states' interests very much in mind.[33] The European Council (entirely distinct from the Council of Europe, introduced in Chapter 7 as the oversight body for the ECHR) has no formal legislative powers at all. Nonetheless it is enormously important in the legislative process due to its composition: it consists of the heads of government of all the member states, plus the President of the European Commission. Since the Lisbon Treaty came into force in 2009, the president of this body is considered the European president (the first such president is Herman van Rompuy, the former Belgian prime minister). In practice the European Council sets EU-wide policy at its four or more meetings per year, and no legislative initiative stands a chance of success if it is inconsistent with the direction set by it.

The Council of the European Union (likewise distinct from the Council of Europe), also known as the Council of Ministers or 'Consilium', is a meeting of 27 national ministers from each member state; exactly which minister attends depends upon the topic at issue. The Consilium also has a 'Presidency', being a member state, that changes every six months. Virtually all draft EU legislation must be approved by the Consilium; depending on the area, the threshold for approval is generally qualified majority voting (QMV) or, for a small number of policy areas, unanimity. The threshold for QMV depends on the issue, but typically involves a measure being supported by an absolute majority of member states (i.e. 14 out of 27) representing 74 per cent of the members' voting rights. (Each member has a given number of votes very loosely correlated to population. From 2014, the rules on both what can be enacted by QMV, and the number of votes required, will be liberalised by the Lisbon Treaty.) Where a state is outvoted under the QMV procedure, it may refer the matter to the European Council for a decision, the only circumstance in which the latter body has formal legislative power.

Since 1979 the European Parliament has been a directly elected body. The EU's citizens elect members of the European Parliament (MEPs) every four years. Where an initiative is adopted by QMV, the Parliament can propose amendments to draft legislation on both first and second readings. Weaker than national parliaments, the European Parliament's formal approval is not required for a law to take effect, but on the second reading an initiative can be rejected by an affirmative decisions of an absolute majority of MEPs. Where the Parliament's proposed amendments to draft legislation are not accepted, the legislation must ultimately be abandoned. (Where unanimity is required within the Consilium, the role of the Parliament is generally only consultative and it can be overriden.)

This convoluted system is the product of a series of muddy historical compromises enmeshed in a confusing succession of treaties negotiated to address specific concerns of the member states at different periods of the Union's development. In particular, the existence of three presidents (of the European Council, of the Consilium and of the Commission) is particularly confusing, and points to a remarkable diffusion of power amongst different nodes within the network that seems to ensure no decision can be made without the utmost consultation and consensus. There can be little doubt that were the system created from a *tabula rasa* today, it would not be so contrived. It can readily be concluded that the system is irrational: it is not the most efficient method of achieving the goal of distributing federal power amongst a set of sovereign states of differing sizes.

The US Constitution, which sought to achieve substantially the same result, was (more or less) a *tabula rasa* system and procured the balance between sovereignty and population through a bicameral legislature, in which one house (the Senate) would have each state send the same number of members and the other (the House of Representatives) would receive delegates proportionate to states' populations. By contrast, the European system is trapped within the folds of a dense 60 year history since the creation of the ECSC. Nevertheless, this complexity has yielded some significant benefits: the ceaseless participation of national representatives in so many different institutions has sustained a greater level of acceptance of the EU's decision-making process. Each nation participates with representatives in the Commission, the European Council, the Consilium, the parliament and the European courts. Due to the participation in the legislative process of so many institutions in which each member state is represented, an unhappy member can create, at the very least, delay and friction at multiple turns. Thus a culture of consensus has prevailed historically, providing reluctant member states with opt-outs from the most controversial EU initiatives, such as the common currency, the 'social chapter' (creating minimum EU-wide employment law rights) and the 'Charter of Fundamental Rights' (an EU-wide international human rights treaty).

At the same time the expansion eastwards of the European Union in 2004 and again in 2007 has diluted the voting power of the bloc's integrationist Franco-German axis, rendering sceptics of European federalisation such as the United Kingdom more amenable to the prospect of QMV and less concerned that it will be outvoted by its Franco-German rivals. In the modern politics of the European Union can be found traces of the balance of power that characterised nineteenth-century European diplomacy. The eastward movement of the European Union has rendered pan-European decision-making vastly more complex, embracing as it has a number of nations such as Poland and the Czech Republic in which Euro-scepticism has significant political currency. Institutional reform and legislative processes have therefore been retarded. The European Union's principal challenge at the time of writing is shoring up a shaky single currency in the face of high debt burdens and threats by Euro members to default on their sovereign debt. Faced with these impediments, further progress towards federalisation of the European political system may prove burdensome in the near future.

THE POLITICS OF THE JUDICIARY IN THE EUROPEAN UNION

Within this culture of consensus the European Court of Justice has taken a dominant role, precisely because it is not hidebound by the sclerotic machinations of the EU's manifold political institutions. Populated by judges with a remarkably unitary agenda of advancing the common market goals of the EU system, the EU's courts have managed to achieve a great deal. No judge would accept an appointment in Luxembourg without significant sympathy for the EU system; many of the judges are academics involved in development of EU law, and thus they share a common vision of EU law to a far greater degree than national politicians from member states share a common vision for the EU as a whole. There is a coherence of purpose within the ECJ that is lacking elsewhere in the EU's institutions, save perhaps within the Commission (which has only executive, not legislative, power and must always ultimately answer for its policy proposals to the European Council).

Thus the judges of the EU's courts are able to agree upon expansive interpretations of the EU's treaty provisions that a consensus of national politicians in the Council or Consilium would never be able to muster. Because revision of the EU's treaties requires unanimity of its 27 members (unanimity which very nearly evaded the Union for the Lisbon Treaty and its predecessor, the European Constitution), any interpretation of the EU treaties that is promulgated by the Court of Justice is essentially irreversible. To a great extent like the Supreme Court of the United States,[34] the

EU's judicial function is not subject to effective legislative check, giving the Court enormous power.

The ECJ is reliant for the most part upon domestic courts to enforce and further interpret EU law as the ECJ has developed it. Indeed this is the essence of the referral system: references from domestic courts to the ECJ on points of law are voluntary. If a national court system were to become too unimpressed with the ECJ's jurisprudence, it could simply stop referring cases to it and decide points of EU law as it saw fit (or evade the entire discipline by deciding that no such points were ever determinative of claims before it). Moreover, the ECJ is in a weaker position than the US Supreme Court, because there is no system of lower federal courts within the European Union for whom loyalty to EU legal principles can be taken as given. However, for the most part the ECJ has not found national courts uncooperative in this sense, because it has co-opted them to its cause. First, the European courts undertake a continual charm offensive towards both domestic judges and legal academics, engaging with them wherever possible, inviting them to conferences at the Court in Luxembourg and appealing to them as the most politically independent branch of national governments to endorse the EU's new legal order. Second, EU law has achieved an intellectual robustness lacking in much international law. It has a complex regime of treaties and EU legislation with which to work; and it has done a tolerable job of knitting these diverse sources into a coherent whole, while embracing legal principles and traditions from diverse member states, such that domestic lawyers have gradually become comfortable considering the system a natural extension of their own.

EU law also gives judges powers they may wish they had under their national systems. Domestic legislation perceived as unfair or giving the state too much power may be disregarded or interpreted to mean something different, because EU law is supreme. States and by extension public authorities may be found liable in damages, whereas normally remedies against public institutions would be circumscribed by domestic legislatures. EU law grants autonomy and power to judges, and for that reason they are liable to like it. Even where the methods of its reasoning are radically out of kilter with those of domestic legal systems, in time the domestic judiciary of a nation can reach an accommodation with EU law. This is a particular issue in common law countries, where the close historical and analogical readings of statutes and case law fit ill with the 'teleological' prescriptions of EU law that looks to the results of interpreting a law in a certain way rather than textual intent.[35]

Nonetheless, the traditions of judicial independence in common law countries means that common law judges are likely to implement EU law, once they have become accommodated to it, even against a prevailing domestic political tide. Where national courts are uncooperative or have a habit of disregarding EU law (as is particularly the case in some recent eastern European accession states), that does not necessarily matter. Provided there are sufficient states in the old 15 whose courts are prepared faithfully to interpret and implement EU law, the system remains tolerably robust. In time the courts of the new eastern European members, in many cases lacking the judicial independence necessary to implement legislation over the political will of national politicians, as an historical hangover from Communist periods of government, will improve. At that point, the benefits to the domestic judiciary of following the ECJ's direction will prevail.

Even if the domestic judiciary can be captured by the EU courts through a combination of charm, intellectual appeal and promises of power, it is always open in principle for domestic legislatures to tear away the newly found authorities, founded in EU law, from the domestic judiciary. They might legislate to the effect that notwithstanding their country's membership of the European Union, their courts are not to apply EU law. Such a move would lurch the EU into crisis. Whereas passive judicial resistance to EU law often goes unnoticed (in such cases the matter never gets to the Luxembourg courts, because the domestic courts do not refer it there), overt legislative resistance, far more politically loaded than the abstract musings of a jurist, would be front page news. The Commission would be obliged to refer the matter to the ECJ as an infringement proceeding against the state; given the ECJ's pronouncements upon the supremacy of EU law, such a measure would have to be denounced by the Court; threats of fines (or worse) might follow. The member state would have to back down – or the system would collapse. This dramatic escalation has never in fact happened, because the economic benefits of continued EU membership are so significant that no one state wants to bring the system down. The safety release valve where the ECJ does overstep the mark of what is politically palatable is that domestic courts quietly ignore its edicts or desist from referring cases to it. Provided that domestic legislation is superficially compliant with EU law, the Commission also ignores domestic non-compliance in so far as it is judicially sanctioned. Only in the most extreme cases, it is hoped, will domestic courts ignore EU law; given a tolerably independent judiciary, that will require a significant well of domestic political pressure. Where it does happen, the fact that EU law is being disregarded will be wrapped inside a riddle of judicial reasoning, such that everyone can comfortably pretend it is not happening.

Such is the role of domestic courts in enforcing and applying EU law. Most of the judicial heavy lifting is not done by the European courts at all. Indeed on a reference to the ECJ from a domestic court, the Court of

Justice is not permitted to pronounce upon any facts, nor upon any issue of domestic law. It is obliged to consider points of EU law in isolation, on the basis of presumed hypothetical facts. Because it is left to national courts to implement the EU law as divined in the abstract by the ECJ, the exercise of domestic judicial discretion may release political pressures created by ambitious ECJ jurisprudence. Although it cannot force them to be so, the ECJ hopes that domestic courts will remain faithful to the task, because it gives domestic courts several reasons to want to implement EC law.

Thus it is no surprise that some of the ECJ's most controversial recent judgments have involved attempts to take powers away from national courts. English courts have traditionally granted themselves jurisdiction to issue 'anti-suit injunctions', that is, orders restraining participation in foreign legal proceedings that have been commenced contrary to an exclusive jurisdiction agreement in a contract, providing for disputes to be resolved in a given judicial forum or in arbitration. The ECJ's attempts to restrict the capacity of English courts to do this[36] have met with ferocious resistance and, given the foregoing narrative, this course is potentially politically dangerous. The ECJ relies upon its investing domestic courts with new authorities to secure their loyalty; taking pre-existing authorities away may undermine the edifice of fidelity it has been patiently building with the English judiciary since the UK's accession to the EEC in 1973.

Ultimately, domestic courts have a liberty to interpret or ignore EU law as they see fit. The fact that EU law grants individuals rights against their own governments that did not previously exist in domestic law does not matter so much; the member states of the European Union can live with that. While there are no European federal courts by analogy with lower federal courts in the United States, and while there is no system of European federal bailiffs to enforce judgments based upon European law, the system will remain susceptible to the frailties of periodic domestic judicial resistance to its edicts. But the ECJ has an intellectual and political latitude to go on pronouncing new milestones in European jurisprudence because, being almost invisible for political purposes, it is embedded so deeply within the European political system that political attacks upon it are rare and are unlikely to succeed. The Commission, with its expansive executive powers and unaccountable unelected presidential officials, is a far easier political target for Euro-sceptics than the intangible yet respected Court of Justice.

In this way, the European court system manages to preserve a level of intellectual integrity that escapes its counterparts elsewhere in the network of international law. It has latitude to develop EU law in directions contrary to member states' wishes, because it is just one part of an institutional network which every member state has a strong vested interest in preserving. Other elements of the network prove far more susceptible to attack. The courts can rely upon being defended by the Commission and other actors within the EU institutional system. Everybody involved knows that development of EU law means propagation of the EU system in ways the more overtly political institutions of the EU cannot hope to achieve. As EU law becomes more expansive, the Commission will have more work to do in monitoring and enforcing it. Because the Commission realises the European Court of Justice to be a valuable co-conspirator in advancing its integrationist European aims (and because it needs to cultivate the Court's good will if it is to win the various cases which come before the European courts and before which the Commission is a party), the European courts can rely upon the Commission to protect its prerogatives. Thus the European courts are rarely subject to criticism by those who are familiar with their operation. The Commission will guarantee the Court always has an adequate budget: hence its large new premises, built during the first decade of the twenty-first century at a cost of over €500 million, to house the expanded 27-judge courts, and the availability of new personnel and resources to manage the Court's backlog.

Due to the subtlety and novelty of its jurisprudence, which permits lawyers and academics alike to write at great length on its methods and workings and creates a discipline of experts, the ECJ is popular with lawyers. Because domestic judges (for the most part) have an incentive to support its work, it can rely upon domestic courts for enforcement and implementation. It does not need to infringe upon domestic judicial sovereignty through acquiring its own enforcement regime or by creating lower federal courts – a measure that might well produce extraordinary resistance amongst domestic legal and judicial classes. It cannot be certain of its decisions being implemented in all cases by domestic courts over which it has no effective control. But that may not be a bad thing; where disobedience occurs, it is a discreet political pressure release valve. The important feature of this disobedience is that it does not raise the political stakes such as to engage domestic politics and jeopardise the entire European system. Thus quiet judicial disobedience, where it does occur, can be tolerated and need not distract the European courts from the integrity of their jurisprudence. The system that has been constructed, in part through a series of historical treaty accidents, proves remarkably stable.

THEORISING ABOUT THE EU LEGAL SYSTEM

One might view EU law as the pre-eminent example of the constructivist thesis. EU member states have created an international legal system over which they have genuinely lost significant control. Led by the Court of Justice and the Commission, EU law is now set upon an autonomous trajectory quite out of kilter with the original aspirations of the states who agreed to it. Rather that trajectory is set by an autonomous class of European lawyers and administrators, who have managed to capture a political agenda without being entirely bound to the interests and demands of the member states that founded the system. It is inconceivable that such a system would have been created by rational and well-informed heads of government representing member states in primordial negotiations about creating a European Union. Yet through gradualist development from the origins of the ECSC, this is the system we have ended up with, and it appears highly durable. The ideological freedom of European officials to develop EU law as a discipline relatively unhindered by the politics of the Council or the Consilium rests upon its being a quiet cog within a network of European institutions, the collective survival of which is more important than any individual inconveniences European law might impose upon its members. The dramatic changes required of national laws in the fields of consumer protection or immigration, driven by expansive interpretations of Treaty provisions relating to free movement of workers and goods, has had an impact upon national sovereignty at least as significant as the various pieces of legislation drafted by the Commission and approved by the Consilium. The Consilium works by national consensus, or at least only after the political concerns of reluctant members have been fully aired. The Court of Justice, a highly intelligent yet mostly untamed beast, feels fewer such constraints. In the language of one scholar, whereas the Consilium acts as an 'agent' of its principals' perceived interests, the Court acts more like a 'trustee' of their 'real' interests:

> A Trustee court, by definition, possesses the capacity to expand or contract its own zone of discretion, through interpreting the law, and the scope of its own powers. Consider the constitutionalization of the treaty system. The Treaty of Rome originally contained no supremacy clause, and the Member States did not provide for the direct effect of Treaty provisions or directives. The Court, in collaboration with national judges under Article 267,[37] secured direct effect and supremacy; in effect, it rewrote the Treaty. As a result, Article 267 developed into a decentralized mechanism for enforcing EC law; it connected individuals and firms with a stake in European law to the legal system, through national judges; and it generated a steady stream of cases alleging Member States non-compliance which the ECJ used to construct a sophisticated jurisprudence.[38]

One has to be careful with the use of the term 'trustee', an expression that lends an air of legal legitimacy to an institution doing something other than what its members want it to do. To describe a thief as a trustee over stolen goods does not change the fact that the goods have been stolen and cannot be retrieved, even if the thief purports to be using those goods for the victim's real interests. Nevertheless there is something of a consensus that this thief is handling the stolen jewellery for the most part wisely. An early theory of the European Union's propensity for integration, developed by the American political scientist Ernst B. Haas, captured the insights of the EU's potential for success as an international organisation well before even the groundbreaking 1963 *van Gend en Loos* judgment, in which the principle that EEC treaty obligations create private rights in domestic law was first articulated.[39]

Haas's 'neofunctionalist' theory hypothesised that the European Economic Community could achieve a level of integration greater than that initially intended by the states who signed the treaties. According to Haas, this could happen by three means. First, there would be a transfer in domestic allegiances: over time, citizens, interest groups and enterprises within states would come to see more value in the international institutions within the European Economic Community than in domestic political institutions. Second, there would be 'positive spillover effects': the benefits of integration would create incentives for further integration. Hence the ECSC became the broader EEC, and the EU was expanded eastwards to create a still larger internal market from which its members have benefited. Third, the international institutions created would acquire 'technocratic automaticity', meaning an ability to take executive decisions and develop policy goals independently of the states on whose behalf they supposedly act.[40] Haas came to despair of his own theory, as he observed the intrusion of national politics into the functioning of the EEC during the course of the 1960s. In 1965 France boycotted the Consilium over the Commission's proposal for agricultural reforms.[41] Haas's hopes for the transfer of citizens' allegiances from domestic to international institutions have not survived modern nationalist European political movements and a sense of alienation amongst Europe's population in their attitudes towards the EU. There remains a sense that EU institutions are unaccountable, remote and irrelevant to peoples' everyday lives. However, his theory turned out to be more prescient for the expansion of powers of the European judiciary. While it was the ECJ that first embraced Haas's technocratic automaticity, more recently a professionalised European Commission has acquired both power and ideological independence from the states which send Commissioners. It is legally accountable only to the Court of Justice, with which it shares much the same set of political values.

Haas's neofunctionalism was derived from an interwar scholarly movement, 'functionalism'. This saw the principal dynamic in international relations not as relationships between states, but common interests and needs shared by non-state actors.[42] On this theory inspired by Wilsonian liberalism, the selfish realist behaviour of the nation state would wither away, in favour of a supranational legal order that would greater satisfy people's real needs. Almost Marxist in sweep, functionalism was an optimistic movement, as were Haas's aspirations for what European integration could achieve. The thesis of this book so far has been that as a rule, international law has developed on its own mostly dysfunctional autonomous trajectory independent of the goals of nation states. That returns us to the opening question of this chapter: how can it be that the likewise autonomous trajectory of European law has developed relatively satisfactorily, and with sufficient substance to give weight to the functionalist thesis?

For all the frustrations that exist with the European Union system, and for all the weight of contested legislation emerging from Brussels and domestic dissatisfaction with the bulging and multifarious European Union institutions, the EU appears to have yielded tangible economic benefits. These include promoting trade in goods and services through a free market, ease of travel and migration to alleviate labour shortages, coordination of Europe-wide economic and policy problems from environmental pollution to peacekeeping, reducing barriers to trade raised by differing domestic standards of product and service regulation, promoting robust competition law to the benefit of consumers and (arguably – although the jury remains out on its success) creating a single currency to reduce transaction costs of interstate commerce, eliminating exchange rate uncertainty, reducing inflation and economising on foreign currency reserves. The EU has also emerged as a major global economic power, able to use its collective bargaining strength as the world's largest economic bloc to negotiate preferential international trade arrangements with third parties. If it is difficult to count the achievements of growth in other areas of international law, the EU is apparently the exception, the glittering jewel in a sea of otherwise effete international legal relations.

The reason why this is so is that even if the activism of the Court of Justice was not anticipated, the original founders of the ECSC did indeed intend to create a system of international government, whereas the creators of other international organisations did not. Although the benefits to states in most instances of international institution-building are principally identification with some abstract goal such as world peace or human rights, that was not the dominant motivation of the founders of the modern European legal order. Scarred by two world wars, the creators of the ECSC including Robert Schuman, Jean Monnet and Konrad Adenauer[43] were quite deliberate in their intention to abandon part of their respective nations' sovereignty to an international order. Their goal was not mere political advantage in the name of cooperation; it was to entangle their nations' economies to such an extent that war would become unthinkable. The system became successful and other nations, historically more defensive of their sovereignty, signed up to the model to reap its economic benefits. Without the horrors of war so deeply ingrained in the psyche of the system's architects, this genuine abandonment of sovereignty could probably never happen again.

Likewise, had the model not yielded significant economic dividends, other nations on the edge of the system would have had no interest in paying the sovereignty price of joining, and it would have remained a truncated version of its current expansive form. Some of the features of the current system are to be deprecated, including its unaccountable and lumbering bureaucracy, its excessively complicated decision-making procedures, a voluminous budget of some €120 billion per year (of which almost 50 per cent is devoted to agricultural subsidies and a further 30 per cent to regional subsidies) and the blizzard of legislative initiatives its bureaucracy has incentives to propagate. Nonetheless, it is not clear such a system could ever evolve other than in the piecemeal fashion in which the EU emerged. Its members would simply never agree to such an abrogation of their sovereignty on their own initiative. It had to be taken away from them by judicial and bureaucratic stealth, which is why the complaints of a democratic deficit within the European Union are simultaneously both so penetrating and so misplaced. A genuinely democratic system would never have achieved such results; the undemocratic bureaucratic waste of the system is a price that must inevitably be paid for its success.

In principle, the system might still go awry. Should the culture of enlightened bureaucracy corrode, the system might become insufficiently responsive to members' sovereignty concerns and members might withdraw or insist on renegotiating their treaty commitments. The legal edifice on which EU integration stands is perpetually at risk of being undermined by the demons of member states' realist politics. Nonetheless, the system is apparently flexible enough to accommodate such gremlins. Even the collapse of the Euro (seriously countenanced in 2010 as a possible result of the Greek and Irish debt crises) might not undermine all the other achievements the Union has accomplished. The occasional irritations of ECJ jurisprudence are currently a small price for member states to pay for the economic and political benefits the system yields as a whole. Given the political exposure and public criticism levelled against other EU institutions, it seems difficult to believe it would be overstretching by the EU's legal system that brought the structure down. For now, it seems that the ECJ is safe to continue developing its jurisprudence in whatever direction it chooses, insulated by a begrudging respect developed over decades of cultivating careful relationships with national judiciaries. EU law is insulated deep within a system with far more vulnerable weak points than the Luxembourg courts.

By the same token, the hope that other systems of international law might transform themselves into an EU model seems destined to be dashed. The extraordinary circumstances in which states expressly agreed to pool sovereignty to prevent further conflict, in a continent scarred by a century of devastating wars, seem unlikely to be reproduced elsewhere any time soon. Thus the complex institutional network anticipated by the ECSC, in which international institutions are granted genuine powers to intrude into countries' domestic affairs, will not exist. Without those institutions, there will be no protected political space within which an autonomous international judicial system can be fostered and can develop a genuinely robust jurisprudence. In short, without real efforts to create an international government, the idea of international law cannot work. The ECJ has proved a success because it was a Court appended to a real, if initially embryonic, system of international government. Its ostensible analogues in Strasbourg, Geneva and The Hague are politically exposed, because they exist without the protection of international governing institutions. Thus they are far more susceptible to sway perilously in the international political winds.

INTERNATIONAL LAW IN DOMESTIC COURTS

Finally, it falls to be asked whether other areas of international law might be enforced in the domestic context. EU law is enforced not truly by an international court but by domestic courts taking their leads from an international court and given proper incentives by it. Might other international courts play an equivalent role? This certainly is the hope of some advocates for the European Court of Human Rights, who see the problem of that court's backlog as being resolved ultimately by persuading domestic courts to grant redress for Convention violations so that the European Court in Strasbourg need not step in.[44] However, this seems an over-optimistic aspiration. Within Europe, national courts do not feel beholden to the jurisprudence of the European Court of Human Rights, even if national legislation prescribes that they should be. Courts from countries with strong rule of law traditions take the view that fundamental rights are enshrined within their own legal systems, and thus the European Court has little to add.

The English courts have been conducting trials for centuries, over which they have evolved sophisticated standards for what counts as 'fair'. They may take the view that the Court in Strasbourg, composed in significant part of judges from countries with no rule of law tradition or one significantly less venerable, has nothing to teach English judges about such matters.[45] As to countries with lower rule of law traditions, the jurisprudence of the Court may be routinely ignored precisely because domestic judges do not feel politically empowered to issue decisions against the interests of their governments. It is not clear how the risk of a judgment from the European Court of Human Rights some three to five years after all domestic appeals have been exhausted is supposed to cause an improvement in the human rights jurisprudence of courts which fear to defend human rights in the first place because of the political pressure to which judges are subject. The notion that the jurisprudence of the European Court of Human Rights will mysteriously filter down to domestic courts and start being implemented by national judges seems unrealistic as a general rule. The national judiciary has no incentive to do so.

Of course it is always possible that national judges selectively embrace parts of international treaties, to reinforce a result they wish to reach but which might be regarded a stretch of domestic law. The recent evolution of a common law of privacy in England and Wales is replete with references to the European Convention rights to privacy and respect for private and family life.[46] Even the United States Supreme Court has referred to the European Convention on Human Rights to justify a constitutional ruling.[47] However, where a domestic court does not wish to follow an international court's lead, it will not do so. Unlike a domestic appeal court, an international court has no effective form of sanctioning or embarrassing a domestic judge. International law is easily disregarded; indeed some judges make a point of criticising it and expressly refusing to consider it.[48] Given the absence of a consistent system of incentives for domestic judges to apply international law, its observance in domestic courts will be patchy, as even some advocates of international law concede.[49] By contrast, the EU's legal system is so institutionally rich, and the economic incentives for domestic government compliance so compelling, that a higher level of observance can be expected. Even then, there is significant empirical evidence of non-compliance by domestic courts with EU law in cases where references to the ECJ are not made.[50] The process of pushing member states' courts faithfully to implement EU law is an ongoing one, and there are no judicial guarantees of compliance, whatever the ECJ may decree about the supremacy of EU law.

The distinctive features of the European legal regime are twofold: a genuine international government, with an independent executive with enforcement powers, and a system of incentives for domestic courts to embrace EU law. This permits them to strengthen their powers against their own governments in the field of administrative law. Still the regime of compliance is imperfect, because the ECJ frequently issues rulings to which member states are adverse. It has been observed in particular that states are opposed to ECJ rulings increasing the power of the courts to annul domestic legislation.[51] Thus one may expect political pressure to be exerted upon domestic courts not to implement its rulings. That pressure may be presumed more likely to succeed in member states lacking sufficient judicial independence. Even in the realm of the European Union, the influence of international law is sometimes uncertain and patchy.

Nevertheless, because the European Union courts are so embedded within other EU institutions, they remain invulnerable to many of the political winds that blow over other international courts. By fortuity or design, the European Court of Justice has found itself in a position where it can develop a field of international law without being held hostage to state interests.[52] Subject to far less scrutiny than its sister institutions, the Commission, Parliament and Consilium, the Court has found remarkable freedom of action. Even though implementation of its rulings is variable, the Court has found itself in a 'trustee' role. One may properly have mixed feelings about this. Some of the Court's judicially imposed structural reforms to the European internal market have been admirable in their commitment to free market principles and in their efforts at undermining domestic protectionism. The court has stepped forth where domestic politicians feared to tread.

The ECJ has embraced a role in some ways parallel to that of the US Supreme Court, which through its flexible and evolving interpretation of the brief and open-ended US Constitution embraces difficult political decisions too divisive to be resolved by the legislature. Sometimes the other branches of the US government protest when the Supreme Court decides such issues; defenders of the institution may suggest that it is precisely due to the polarised and sensitive nature of political debate about issues such as abortion, freedom of religious expression and wiretapping that it is politically acceptable for nine judges, appointed for life, to decide these issues rather than elected politicians. Yet the dissimilarities between the US Supreme Court and the ECJ are pronounced. The process for appointment of Supreme Court judges is extremely public and subject to the most penetrating levels of scrutiny. Moreover it is explicitly political: the US president nominates, the US Senate approves and the perceived political record of the candidate is important at all stages of the process. The average US citizen can name many or all of the US Supreme Court judges. The average lawyer practising within the EU is tested to name even one judge at the ECJ, whose appointment process is shrouded in secrecy (and is different in each member state). Decisions of the ECJ are rarely publicised; decisions of the US Supreme Court are routinely front-page news.

The voting preferences of Supreme Court judges are subject to searching analysis to discern their political preferences. In the ECJ there are no dissenting judgments, making analysis of the work of individual judges impossible. In several important respects the justices of the US Supreme Court are directly accountable to public opinion, both before and after appointment. The Supreme Court has a legitimacy amongst the US voting public which the ECJ cannot pretend to have amongst the European public, many of whom are not aware even of the institution's existence.

Autonomy in international law helps evade the constraints and competing nationalisms of domestic politics. Yet the danger of an unaccountable court is obvious. The influence of the ECJ has been considerable in affecting the domestic political and economic life of the EU's citizens, from groundbreaking judgments on immigration and deregulation of national markets to strengthening anti-discrimination law. But what if the Court went off the rails? Or what if the Commission went off the rails, and the Court refused to rein it in? Being unaccountable to any political body, the danger remains that the ECJ's jurisprudence takes an unacceptable turn and there would be little anyone can do. Of course member states could start ignoring the Court; and there is evidence that in some cases they already do so. But given the propensity of some national courts to observe the ECJ's rulings on many occasions, and the absolute nature of the doctrine of the supremacy of EU law, the hope that domestic courts might deliberately disregard their legal obligations in cases where the ECJ steps incautiously hardly seems attractive as the only escape valve available. Although its record to date might be regarded as largely benign, the ECJ represents a danger. The jurisprudence of the Court risks spinning off in untoward directions. Were that to happen, the EU project might be fatally damaged. Implementing international political change through explicitly expansionist judicial decree has the potential to be profoundly dangerous. There is no *a priori* reason why the decisions of an international court must be enlightened, and there is a legitimate debate about the proper speed of EU integration, which a court ought not to pre-empt. To conclude that any international court has a monopoly on wisdom is a reckless illusion.

NOTES

1. These changes in nomenclature have led to confusion about the proper name of the European Union's legal system. Until 1992 (the Maastricht Treaty on European Union) the phrase 'European Union' was not used. Although the Maastricht Treaty first referred to a 'European Union', this moniker had no legal personality. The 'European Community' was a set of common institutions for administering the treaties establishing the EEC, the ECSC and EURATOM, the European Atomic Energy Agency. These

institutions were responsible for the legal obligations relating to all three 'pillars' of the EU, so the phrase 'EC law' was adopted. With the 2007 Lisbon Treaty the 'pillars' were abolished and the European Community was renamed the European Union. At the time of writing both the phrases 'EC law' and 'EU law' are used interchangeably.

2. See e.g. Posner, Eric (2009), *The Perils of Global Legalism*, Chicago: University of Chicago Press, p.159 *et seq*; Rabkin, Jeremy (2007), *Law without Nations? Why Constitutional Government Requires Sovereign States*, Princeton, NJ: Princeton University Press, Chapter 6.
3. See Gilbert, Mathieu (1970), 'Dans l'histoire de la CECA, du rose et du gris', *Le Monde*, 9 May.
4. Article 30 EEC Treaty: 'Quantitative restrictions on importation and all measures with equivalent effect shall. . .hereby be prohibited between member states'. This provision became Article 28 of the Nice consolidated version of the EC Treaty. It is now Article 34 Treaty on the Functioning of the European Union (as the Treaty of Rome was renamed by the 2007 Treaty of Lisbon).
5. C-26/62, *NV Algemene Transport-en Expeditie Onderneming van Gend en Loos v Nederlandse Administratie der Belastingen*, 1963 ECR 1.
6. Article 12 of the Treaty of Rome provided that 'Member States shall refrain from introducing between themselves any new customs duties on imports and exports or any charges having equivalent effect, and from increasing those which they already apply in their trade with each other'.
7. See e.g. C-41/74 *Van Duyn v Home Office* [1974] ECR 1337 (free movement of workers); C-2/73 *Geddo v Ente Nazionale Risi* [1973] ECR 865 (free movement of goods).
8. C-6/64 *Costa v ENEL* [1964] ECR 585; C-106/77 *Simmenthal* [1978] ECR 629, 643, [17]; C-10-22/97 *IN.Co.GE.'90 Srl* [1998] ECR I-6307. EC law distinguishes two closely related concepts, 'direct applicability' and 'direct effect'. The former means that a provision of EC law becomes a provision of national law without further action by the state; the latter means that a private individual has a right of action in respect of breach of the principle of EC law. Direct applicability implies supremacy; a principle of EC law must be directly applicable if it is to be directly effective, but the reverse does not necessarily hold.
9. This is called the doctrine of 'indirect effect': see e.g. C-157/86 *Murphy v An Bord Telecom Eireann* [1988] ECR 673; C-14/83 *von Colson v Land Nordrhein-Westfalen* [1984] ECR 1891; C-106/89 *Marleasing SA v La Comercial Internacional de Alimentacion SA* [1990] ECR 4135.
10. C-6&9/90 *Francovich v Italian Republic* [1991] ECR I-5357; C-46&48/93 *Brasserie du Pêcheur SA v Bundesrepublik Deutschland* and *R v Secretary of State for Transport for Transport, ex parte Factortame Ltd* [1996] ECR I-1029.
11. C-51-54/74 *International Fruit* [1971] ECR 1107; C-8/74 *Procureur du Roi v Dassonville* [1974] 2 CMLR 436; C-120/78 *Rewe Zentral AG v Bundesmonopolverwaltung für Branntwein ('Cassis de Dijon')* [1979] ECR 469; C-286/81 *Oosthoek's Uitgeversmaatschappij BV* [1981] ECR 4575; C-60-61/84 *Cinétheque* [1985] ECR 2605.
12. In C-267-268/91 *Keck et Mithouard* [1993] ECR I-6097, the Court of Justice withdrew slightly from its prior expansionist view of the scope of the prohibition of restrictions upon free movement of goods, holding that 'selling arrangements' (as opposed to 'requirements to be met by the goods themselves') would fall outside the scope of the prohibition on domestic regulatory rules if they were not discriminatory on their face. There was a sense that the jurisprudence had become *so* expansionist that it involved excessive interference by European law in domestic regulatory and consumer regimes. *Keck et Mithouard* therefore involved a step back from the Court's prior position.
13. C-48/75 *Procureur du Roi v Royer* [1976] ECR 497; C-44/72 *Marsman v Rosskamp* [1972] ECR 1243; C-19/92 *Kraus v Land Baden-Württemberg* [1993] ECR I-1663.
14. See e.g. C-6/64 *Costa v ENEL* [1964] ECR 585: 'By creating a community of unlimited duration, having its own institutions, its own personality, its own legal capacity and capacity of representation on the international plane and, more particularly, real

powers stemming from a limitation of sovereignty or a transfer of powers from the states to the Community, the member states have limited their sovereign rights, albeit within limited fields, and have thus created a body of law which binds both their nationals and themselves'.

15. See Stone Sweet, Alec (2010), 'The European Court of Justice and the judicialization of EU Governance', *Living Reviews in EU Governance*, **5**.
16. Article 263(4) TFEU (ex Article 230(4) ex 170(4) EC Treaty) : 'Any natural or legal person may. . .institute proceedings against an act addressed to that person or which is of direct and individual concern to them. . .'.
17. T-201/04, *Microsoft Corporation v Commission of the European Communities*, ECR 2007 II-03601.
18. See Article 11 Commission Notice 2004/C 101/5 of 27 April 2004.
19. See Declaration 17 of the Consolidated EU Treaties (the Lisbon Treaty): 'The Conference recalls that, in accordance with well settled case law of the Court of Justice of the European Union, the Treaties and the law adopted by the Union on the basis of the Treaties have primacy over the law of Member States, under the conditions laid down by the said case law. The Conference has also decided to attach as an Annex to this Final Act the Opinion of the Council Legal Service on the primacy of EC law as set out in 11197/07 (JUR 260): Opinion of the Council Legal Service of 22 June 2007. It results from the case-law of the Court of Justice that primacy of EC law is a cornerstone principle of Community law. According to the Court, this principle is inherent to the specific nature of the European Community. At the time of the first judgment of this established case law (Costa/ENEL,15 July 1964, Case 6/641) there was no mention of primacy in the treaty. It is still the case today. The fact that the principle of primacy will not be included in the future treaty shall not in any way change the existence of the principle and the existing case-law of the Court of Justice.'
20. Article 267 (ex 234 ex 177) Treaty on the Functioning of the European Union.
21. C-283/81 *CILFIT*: 'courts or tribunals. . .have. . .discretion. . .to ascertain whether a decision on a point of law is necessary to enable them to give judgment'. Of course a judgment as to whether a point of law is *acte clair* is likewise a matter of judgment and thus discretion.
22. This is the '*acte clair*' doctrine (there is no need to refer a point of law if it is reasonably free and clear from doubt). In *CILFIT*, ibid., para. 16, the Court held that this test would be satisfied where 'the matter is equally obvious to the courts of the other Member States and to the Court of Justice'. It is not clear that this imposing standard is observed by domestic courts in practice, who do not as a matter of course analyse the jurisprudence of all 27 member states' domestic courts in determining whether to make an Article 267 reference.
23. These figures are provided courtesy of section C, Court of Justice (2009), Annual Report, Luxembourg.
24. See e.g. *Bulmer v Bollinger* [1974] 2 All ER 1226 (concern at not overloading the ECJ through making an excessive number of references); *Henn & Darby v DPP* [1981] AC 850 (Lord Diplock contrasting 'teleological rather than historical methods to interpretation of Treaties and other Community legislation' with the English judicial approach to legislative construction).
25. That Luxembourg is the subject of so many infringement actions proportionate to its size (with a population of less than 500 000, the second smallest EU member state after Malta and the smallest of the old 15 EU pre-2004 member states), is intriguing. It may be because the EU courts and the European Commission offices responsible for preparing infringement actions are based in Luxembourg. The institutions' civil servants live there and thus have great familiarity with the country's legal systems and its weakness. Luxembourg's small size and corresponding political weakness, combined with its strongly pro-European sentiments (much of its wealth derives from the presence of EU institutions on its territory), may also make it an appealing victim for test cases.
26. These statistics are drawn from the Court of Justice's 2009 annual report, see note 23.

27. Article 228 (ex 171) Treaty on European Union (TEU).
28. C-387/97 *Commission v Greece* ECR 2000 I-05047 (failure to comply with prior judgment requiring clean-up of environmental waste; fine of €20 000 per day imposed until compliance). It is not clear from the judgment who was to determine when compliance had been undertaken, nor how much (if any) of the daily fine was collected.
29. Each Directive sets its own timescale within which member states must enact domestic legislation giving effect to it, typically within an 'implementation' clause. See e.g. Article 33 Directive 2006/54/EC of 5 July 2006 (on equal opportunities and equal treatment in employment): 'Member States shall bring into force the laws, regulations and administrative provisions necessary to comply with this Directive by 15 August 2008 at the latest or shall ensure, by that date, that management and labour introduce the requisite provisions by way of agreement. Member States may, if necessary to take account of particular difficulties, have up to one additional year to comply with this Directive. . . .'
30. See 21st Commission annual report on monitoring the application of Community law, Brussels 30 December 2004, COM(2004) 839.
31. C-6&9/90 *Francovich v Italian Republic*, see note 10.
32. Examples include Louis Michel (Commissioner for Development and Humanitarian Aid, who participated in Belgium's 2007 elections); Romano Prodi (President of the Commission; participated in the 2001 Italian elections while still president; subsequently became prime minister of Italy); Anna Diamantopoulu (Commissioner for Employment and Social Affairs; resigned after winning a seat in the 2004 Greek elections).
33. See Eppink, Derk-Jan (2007), 'Former Top Official: Dutch Naïve in EU', NIS News Bulletin, 20 March .
34. An amendment to the US Constitution requires approval of three-quarters of the states: see Article V. However, the legislative (and executive) check upon the Supreme Court comes principally through the appointment process. Unlike the ECJ, the Supreme Court contains some dramatic ideological fissures between its judges, who must be nominated by the president and approved by the Senate to take office. In both the nomination and approval processes the ideological hue of the candidate Justice is important to his or her approval and subject to close scrutiny.
35. See *Henn & Darby v DPP* [1981] AC 850, 905, per Lord Diplock: 'The European Court, in contrast to English courts, applies teleological rather than historical methods to the interpretation of Treaties and other Community legislation. It seeks to give effect to what it conceives to be the spirit rather than the letter of the Treaties: sometimes, indeed, to an English judge, it may seem to the exclusion of the letter. It views the Communities as living and expanding organisms and the interpretation of the provisions of the Treaties as changing to match their growth'.
36. See C-116/02 *Gasser v MISAT* [2003] ECR I-14693; C-159/02 *Turner v Grovit* [2004] ECR I-3565; C-185/07 *Allianz SpA v West Tankers Inc.* [2009] All ER (D) 82 (Judgment 10 February 2009). For one instance of (much) negative English commentary on the *West Tankers* ruling see e.g. Spence, Alex (2009), 'Lawyers fear West Tankers ruling could harm London', *The Times*, 10 February.
37. Article 267 TFEU, ex Article 234 (ex Article 177) EC Treaty, provides for national courts to refer points of law to the ECJ. This footnote is explanatory of the reference contained in the quotation and does not form part of the original quotation.
38. Stone Sweet, 'The European Court of Justice', *ibid.*
39. See note 5, *Van Gend en Loos* established the principle of direct effect, discussed above.
40. Haas, Ernst B. (1958), *The Uniting of Europe*, Stanford, CA: Stanford University Press.
41. See Ludlow, Piers (2006), *Decommissioning the Empty Chair Crisis: The Community Institutions and the Crisis of 1965–6*, London: LSE.
42. For an overview of the history of functionalism see Rosamond, Ben (2000), *Theories of European Integration*, New York: Macmillan.
43. Schuman was a post-war prime minister of France who went on to become the first president of the European parliament. The 1950 Schuman Declaration was a proposal

on which the ECSC would be founded. Monnet, a French diplomat, was behind the Schuman Declaration and became the first president of the ECSC's High Authority. His Action Committee for the United States of Europe, founded in 1955, was responsible for much of the thinking behind establishment of the EEC. Konrad Adenauer, Chancellor of Germany from 1949 to 1963, was responsible for German support for the European project.

44. Chatham House (2009), 'European Court of Human Rights: a court in crisis?', International Law Discussion Group Meeting Summary, June.
45. This was apparently the view of Lord Hoffman, formerly Senior Law Lord. See Hoffman, Chapter 7 note 23.
46. Article 8(1) European Convention, discussed *inter alia* in *A v B plc* [2003] QB 195, 202; *Reynolds v Times Newspapers Ltd* [2001] 2 AC 127; *Campbell v MGN Newspapers* [2004] UKHL 22.
47. *Lawrence v Texas* 539 US 558 (2003) (overturning a law banning homosexual sodomy). Justice Kennedy, writing for the majority, cited the ECHR case C-7525/76 *Dudgeon v United Kingdom*, Judgment 22 October 1981.
48. Justice Scalia on the US Supreme Court is perhaps the best example of this trend. See e.g. Scalia, Antonin (2004), 'Foreign legal authority in the federal courts', *Proceedings of the American Society of Intenational Laws*, **98**, 305; for a discussion see Waters, Melissa (2004) 'Justice Scalia on the use of foreign law in constitutional interpretation', T*ulsa Journal of Comparative and International Law*, **14**, 140.
49. See e.g. Kirby, Michael (2001), 'The Common Law and International Law – a dynamic contemporary dialogue', *Legal Studies*, **30**(1), 29.
50. See e.g. Stone Sweet, Alec (2004), *The Judicial Construction of Europe*, Oxford: OUP, Chapter 3, undertaking a study of the implementation of C-8/74 *Dassonville* (1974) ECR 837 (which struck down domestic consumer protection regulations as inconsistent with the EEC treaty obligation to facilitate free movement of goods) in France, the Netherlands and the UK, found that the majority of domestic judges were not applying *Dassonville*. See also Vegter, Marlies and Sacha Prechal (1992), 'On indirect discrimination and discrimination on grounds of pregnancy/maternity', Report of the Network of Experts on the Implementation of the Equality Directives, European Communities, finding that implementation by domestic courts of the ECJ's ruling in C-96/80 *Jenkins* [1981] ECR 911 (creating a notion of indirect sexual discrimination, a concept hitherto unknown in most domestic EU legal systems) was extremely patchy and slow to take effect.
51. See Stein, Eric (1981), 'Lawyers, Judges, and the Making of a Transnational Constitution', *American Journal of International Law*, **75**, 1.
52. Stone Sweet, *The Judicial Construction of Europe*, p.129 *et seq*, observes that free movement of goods cases were litigated in the ECJ against larger states more than against smaller states, and those states lost these cases more frequently, suggesting a real independence of the ECJ from its members. Were the Court beholden to powerful states, one would expect the opposite result.

9. The future of an illusion

Some illusions evaporate when their contradictions are exposed. Freud predicted religion would gradually whither as society realised the vacuous intellectual basis on which the phenomenon was premised, and the primitive psychological needs it fulfilled. Human society would become sufficiently rational that a collective appreciation of the false role of religion would gradually emerge, and people would stop practising it. Freud made this prediction in 1927.[1] With the benefit of 85 years of hindsight, it is far from clear he was right; considered on a worldwide scale, religious belief is as strong as ever. So it is with international law. While its stated benefits and rationale are revealed as illusory, it stands little prospect of declining as citizens come to perceive its manifest fallacies. The global polity has too much invested in this illusion for it to recede. If this book aims to expose error leading to the correction of wrongs, it cannot hope to succeed, for historical forces are against that course. The only thing this work can hope to do instead is glumly to chart the inevitable. This prediction distinguishes the constructivist thesis from the realist. Were the realist's account correct, one might imagine international law would disappear, since it is a costly and periodically inconvenient irrelevance to those who have created it. The point can be pushed further: the realist has trouble explaining why international law was developed in the first place. The constructivist, by contrast, can harness the power of ideas to explain why international law was both created, persists and even grows. The account the constructivist offers of the causal efficacy of ideas is a disquieting one, because it suggests that in politics bad ideas may trump real interests. The prevalence in the twentieth century of corrosive ideologies of Marxism and fascism attests to this thesis. The purpose of this concluding chapter is to sketch a theory of what the constructivist's account involves.

The international law this book has discussed was born of ideas rather than interests. The three principal historical events that served as fulcra for the growth of the discipline were the end of World Wars I and II and the conclusion of the Cold War. Out of wasteful and destructive global confrontations were born new aspirations for international cooperation. These events are not the first occasions in human history when governments have used the end of a conflict as an opportunity to impose some new rational blueprint on the international order. The past is littered with such attempts. After the Thirty Years' War wreaked havoc on Europe, the Westphalian Peace in 1648 saw the emergence of new principles of sovereignty, meaning non-interference by the government of one territory in the affairs of another. Tolerance of religious minorities was another new international principle that emerged from the same era. After Napoleon's defeat, the Congress of Vienna in 1815 carefully redrew the borders of continental Europe to achieve a delicate balance of power between its principal protagonists. That balance of power persisted until World War I, unravelling gradually only after Bismarck's unification of Germany in 1871. Although these historical shifts were engineered by international treaties, they did not entail the creation of a vast autonomous discipline of international law, adjudicated upon by international courts, monitored and supervised by a range of international organisations.

That idea is a curiously unique feature of the twentieth century. It can probably be traced to one man, Woodrow Wilson, and to one country, the United States. Although there were a few embryonic predecessors in the Permanent Court of Arbitration (1899) and the International Telecommunications Union (1865), the ideas of a League of Nations and a Permanent Court of International Justice, to adjudicate disputes between states without recourse to war, were intellectually revolutionary. Roosevelt drew on Wilson's work in seeking to create institutions that would preclude a recurrence of the horrors of World War II. In time, the idea flourished. International organisations grew to cover every conceivable field of international cooperation. Detailed systems of law arose governing states' obligations to their own citizens (human rights law), other states' investors (investment treaty law), other states' exporters (WTO law), obligations of leaders in time of war (international criminal law) and regional unions (EU law). There was a delay in realising the maximum extent of these aspirations, engendered by the Cold War which hampered effective international cooperation across the capitalist-communist divide. Unshackled by the end of the Cold War, international institutions flourished, and with that international law exploded. The expansion cannot apparently be restrained, and international law now forms a tight web that embraces virtually every aspect of human activity. Not even the sky is the limit: the United Nations has its own UN Office for Outer Space Affairs.

We might conclude from the discussion pursued in this book that the ideas Wilson and Roosevelt nurtured were bad ones. International law cannot achieve its aspiration of orderly and moral regulation of states' behaviour, because it has no mechanism for enforcement. Thus impartial international adjudication is in perpetual danger of being undermined by political pressures. If a judicial decision cannot be rendered and enforced impartially, that will colour the sorts of decision the tribunal issues. The content of those decisions will then be driven by an overriding aim that they are not undermined through being ignored or openly flouted. In time, parties to cases before those tribunals will lose confidence in the impartiality of the system, which appears in structure no better than the melée of international power politics. The same reasoning applies to international organisations, with mandates to monitor and observe international law. Because they are funded by and thus dependent upon the states supposed to be responsible for implementation of international law, they have vested interests not to undertake their functions in a fashion contrary to the interests of their most powerful members. It is not clear what the international organisations that administer international law add to the balance of power. Indeed they seem the epitome of it: each state's influence within an international organisation tends to be proportionate to its power in the world. If things were otherwise, powerful states would depart from the organisation. The publicity international organisations give to international issues may impose reputation costs on states; but those costs are not obviously higher than the reputation costs states have always suffered for acting oppressively or unfairly, and which they may incur in any event under the glare of the international media and NGOs.

Nonetheless, states continue to bind themselves to international treaties, and continue to fund international organisations and international courts. Even if theory and experience prescribe that international law is not the panacea for the propagation of a new ethical world order, nonetheless states continue to create more of it. Have they not learned their lessons from the litany of failed experiences of international cooperation that have populated international relations since 1918? Why do they not withdraw funding and denounce treaties? In the answer to this question lies the key to understanding the enduring popularity of international law. Therein lies the heart of the constructivist thesis that this book has been seeking to illustrate.

POLITICAL YIELDS OF INTERNATIONAL LAW

The value for states in signing the greater bulk of contemporary treaties lies principally not in their observance, but in their signature. The act of agreeing to a series of treaty commitments may be the most effective way of satisfying domestic political demand. A section of the British public wants the British government to take action on human rights abuses in some distant corner of the world: for example, Burma or Tibet. There is nothing the British government can realistically do to influence human rights in such places. Commercial and geopolitical interests may preclude overt opposition to the acts of a foreign sovereign. International human rights treaties, combined with ineffective monitoring activities by the UN, thus serve a valuable purpose in satisfying the domestic human rights constituency. They enable the British government to maintain that it is doing something about international human rights abuses, in combination with its partners in the United Nations. It is contributing to the maintenance of human rights abroad in the most effective means possible: through international cooperation. The British government may thus demonstrate its commitment to international law.

Nonetheless, the efficacy of these institutions is illusory. Human rights abuses continue in Tibet and Burma, and are affected not one jot by the global network of human rights treaties and the various branches of the UN responsible for monitoring and implementing them. The British government has no interest in exposing the charade; as long as there is an approximate consensus that international cooperation can make a difference, domestic pressure to take self-damaging unilateral action is relieved. For a country such as the United Kingdom, signature of human rights treaties may be a signal not to one's treaty partners of one's commitment to human rights, but to one's domestic constituents. Like so much in politics, the signal of intent is frequently more important than the implementation. Thus the ineffectiveness of international law is not necessarily of great concern. It is a way for governments to take a position on an issue without making a significant commitment. International organisations give effect to the lie: notwithstanding their ineffectiveness, their functionaries, together with the academics and NGOs that support them and profit from their existence, will give the impression of cooperative industry to resolve the world's problems.

This symbiotic relationship is convenient for all. States have an opportunity to delegate to a hallowed sphere of international cooperation some of the most taxing issues on which they feel domestic political pressure. Many of the world's problems are insoluble; but for the politician seeking election such a gloomy message may not be attractive. Wilsonian optimism is far more appealing as a response to domestic interest groups applying public pressure over human rights, climate change or foreign civil wars. Even in more ruthlessly commercial spheres such as foreign investment flows or international trade, the same logic applies. The obligation to subject a trade dispute to the protracted procedures of WTO dispute resolution may be an effective excuse for not immediately buckling to domestic producers' demands for retaliatory tariffs in response to a perceived foreign measure damaging domestic industries. Although there is less direct evidence for the theory, investment treaties may relieve the governments of capital exporting states from the obligation to insert themselves into debates over the treatment of investors' foreign assets. There are tangible benefits to democratic states of promoting a comprehensive system of international law, in removing a host of issues from the sphere of domestic politics.

By contrast, the incentives for an undemocratic human rights abuser to sign an international treaty are somewhat different. Such nations are typically less concerned with appeasing a domestic constituency by signing up to a treaty; rather, they are concerned with appeasing international public opinion. A poorer, undemocratic country may be reliant upon the good will of fellow nations for aid, expertise, investment and trade. Democratic fellow nations may place pressure upon such countries to accede to international treaties, as signals of their commitments to given values. It may be easier for a donor nation to commit international development funding to a country which has publicly committed to international human rights treaties, irrespective of their actual domestic human rights records. Similarly, investment treaties and WTO membership demonstrate an ideological commitment to principles of liberal economic development that may facilitate political support from nations where that ideology holds sway.

On this theory, international legal commitments are signals; but they are not (as was considered in Chapter 6) commitments to foreign investors or importers. Rather they are signals by states either to their own citizens, or to other states, that they care about certain values. Wilsonian liberalism achieved one concrete result: it made adherence to certain ideologies, including respect for human rights and commitment to free trade and open markets, important components in the dialogue of international relations. These are now values about which significant parts of domestic electorates apparently care. Interest groups and NGOs push for such values to be reflected in states' foreign policies. Thus governments have to purport to care about them too; but the real interest of democratic domestic governments in the human rights records of foreign countries is low. Even their interest in the economic records of foreign countries is not intrinsically that high. A small subset of US foreign investors may be upset if Ecuador's politics takes a lurch to the left and foreign businesses start to be nationalised by the Ecuadorean government. Those businesspeople may form an interest group that places pressure upon the US Government to take action. Nevertheless there is little the US Government can really do, short of invasion. Attempts to support opposition groups in plotting a coup d'état (as happened in Venezuela in 2002) or decades of unilateral sanctions (such as those in place against Cuba since 1960) have failed to dislodge ideologically hostile regimes. Such actions may do more harm than good, causing further suffering to US investors. Nevertheless, protection of investments has acquired an almost moral force in the vocabulary of US foreign policy. Thus a recent proliferation in the network of investment treaties to which the USA is a party allows the US government to demonstrate its commitment to the Wilsonian ideal.

International organisations are the voice giving international expression to these goals. These institutions naturally benefit from the abundance of ideals in the sphere of international relations. They hold a natural sway over states, because they offer immediate gratification for money being spent. As soon as a new global or regional problem emerges, the UN or one of its sister organisations can easily argue for the creation of a new agency to coordinate and monitor the situation. Such a solution is virtually irresistible for governments feeling political pressure to do something, because there is nothing more substantial that they may be able or want to do. Take the example of civil wars and regional wars. International moral principle mandates what one international organisation calls a "responsibility to protect",[2] and thus to intervene, in the wars of others when (as is inevitably the case) the humanitarian costs of those wars grow. The depth of penetration of modern journalism means that virtually no such war, or its humanitarian catastrophes, can be kept secret from international public opinion.

Thus virtually every global trouble spot, no matter how obscure, has a UN mission tailor-made to respond to it. These missions give expression to the thought that there should be intervention and international action over the problem, but without any individual nation committing more than notional levels of troops, funds or political responsibility to dealing with it. These international missions often persist indefinitely. Indeed the lower the profile of an international dispute, the greater incentive states may have to send an international organisation: lacking a will to do anything more substantial, an ineffective UN mission is just about the optimal level of commitment for them, consistent with being able to say they are doing something. MINURSO, the UN Mission for a Referendum in Western Sahara, has been in existence since 1991. (Unsurprisingly, no referendum has occurred; Morocco occupies the greater bulk of the contested territory and has no interest in permitting a referendum to proceed.) Likewise, the UN has had a mission in Cambodia since 1991. MINUSTAH, the UN mission to Haïti, has been in place since 1993. UNFICYP, the UN mission in Cyprus, has existed since 1964. Wherever there is a low profile frozen conflict, one will find a long-lasting UN mission.

In many cases these missions appear mere stopgap measures in the face of irreconcilable disputes. The international community creates them because it does not know how, or is not prepared to commit the resources, to achieve a more sustainable solution. Yet once such missions are created, nobody wants to take responsibility for closing them. Problems always remain, and international organisations are persuasive advocates for the viewpoint that they encourage stability and remain the international community's eyes and ears in a troubled region. The same logic applies to virtually every international organisation: once established, they carve for themselves a niche in the theatre of global cooperation that nobody wants to take responsibility for foreclosing. The political cost to closing an agency associated with international development, promotion of global health, stabilisation of a fragile society, promotion of human rights or environmental protection, for most countries is just not worth paying. Domestic interest groups will attack the country's ethical record. Other countries may likewise come under internal pressure to shun that state. The only advantage to a state of departing from membership of an international organisation is to save a modest proportion of the institution's global budgetary contribution. Only where an international organisation singles out a state for treatment contrary to a very strongly held interest can the political price of departure be justified, as when the United States withdrew from compulsory jurisdiction of the ICJ in the wake of the *Military and Paramilitary Activities against Nicaragua* (Nicaragua v USA) case.[3]

Most of the time, international institutions are not foolish enough to act so precipitously. Thus once created they endure. The greater bulk of their efforts must be directed towards institutional public relations, to ensure that they continue to represent some widely acknowledged global ideal. Provided they exert themselves effectively in that direction, at least, they will survive. Such institutions also seem to benefit to a degree from the positive feedback identified by Haas's neofunctionalist theory: once a core set of issues is internationalised, an incentive arises for further issues to be internationalised in similar ways. Because internationalisation becomes associated with positive norms such as cooperation, morality and law, domestic political pressure will suggest international law and organisations as solutions to new foreign policy problems. Because international organisations channel funds towards academics and NGOs, those institutions will become lobbyists for the internationalisation process. Provided internationalisation continues to create political dividends for countries under political pressure to address foreign policy issues in which they might have little genuine interest, it will appear to be good value for money. International law will continue to grow.

In this context, we should observe how ironic it is that the country responsible for the creation of the new international legal order is also the quickest to repudiate it. The optimism of two US presidents, Woodrow

Wilson and Franklin D. Roosevelt, was responsible in large part for laying the foundations of the international order which we observe in all its institutional glory today. Yet in the contemporary era their ideas appear embraced more fervently by Europeans than by their own countrymen. The United States is commonly perceived as the most reluctant amongst liberal democratic nations to comply with its international obligations or to resolve issues by international cooperation. In the past decade, recent history abounds with instances of the United States turning its back on international institutional cooperation, from debates over the treatment of prisoners in accordance with international standards in Guantánamo Bay, Cuba, to US intransigence at the Doha round of WTO negotiations, to US reluctance to ratify the Kyoto Protocol on reduction of greenhouse gases, to refusal to ratify the Rome Statute of the International Criminal Court, to persistent refusal to pay the UN its share of the organisation's annual dues.

We observed previously that there is something particularly American about the aspirations for international cooperation: a belief that a rules-based legal system, and application of principles over interests, is the most effective mode of resolving disputes. American legalism has influenced international law through its presidents and the drafting of the UN Universal Declaration of Human Rights by Roosevelt's widow. It is therefore perhaps the most damning indictment of this attempt to transpose Kantian ethics into international relations, that the United States, the early architect of this project, has come to denounce it so comprehensively. The reason why this happened is clear: as the most powerful nation in the world, the United States has little to gain from international cooperation. It can act unilaterally, and by its very nature international law cannot restrain unilateral actions. To facilitate self-interested unilateralism in the face of moral norms, the United States has developed its own domestic narrative of hostility to international law. On this account, international institutions have been captured by interest groups hostile to US interests, which justifies the US government's periodic disregard of international law. The International Criminal Court might be used to bring politically motivated prosecutions against US soldiers; the UN is a forum for grandstanding foreign tyrants from Iran and Venezuela; international trade agreements entail undermining US producers and damaging jobs by flooding American markets with low-grade Chinese imports.

Yet even though it disregards international law with some frequency, the United States remains enormously influential upon its content, involved in drafting the latest class of investment treaties, playing a large part in drafting the WTO Agreement, North America Free Trade Agreement (NAFTA), the Dayton Peace Accords, the Rome Statute of the International Criminal Court and a host of other international treaties. International organisations cannot afford to ignore the United States; they remain suspended within the balance of power, and cannot remain immune from the greatest power's influence. It is testament to the political skills of those institutions' managers that they continue to thrive in the face of indifference or, at times, hostility of the world's most powerful nation. One reason may be that there remains a sufficient number of occasions, even for the United States, when international law can achieve its domestic political value of deflating the pressure felt from interest groups to take a certain course on issues of foreign policy. UN peacekeeping missions are a godsend when the USA does not want to send its own troops into a particular trouble spot.

COMPARING CONVENTIONAL THEORIES OF INTERNATIONAL COOPERATION

The notion that international cooperation carries political value in name (signing treaties) rather than in effects (seeing them observed) sits in flat contradiction to some prevalent theories of international relations, which see the value of treaties as procuring effective international cooperation of some kind. For realists, treaties are akin to private contracts, albeit ones for which there is no impartial third party enforcement mechanism. Nonetheless, they can still result in partial compliance, to the extent that it is in principle in the interests of each party that the other side perform its obligations under the treaty in question, and provided that tit-for-tat retaliation may follow non-compliance. Performance will be imperfect: in some cases the benefit to one state of breaching a treaty will be greater than the disadvantage to that state of its counterpart engaging in tit-for-tat retaliation. (We saw examples of this logic in Chapter 6, when we noted the incentive for large states to breach their international trade obligations to small states, confident that the small state could impose no sanction or comparable harm.)

The liberal idealist also sees states as having interests in cooperation, but to achieve non-self-interested goals. For the idealist, sovereigns enter into human rights treaties to promote moral values that they share in common, and with whose terms they will naturally comply because democratic states have domestic incentives to act altruistically. Such treaties provide positive reinforcement for a state's natural inclinations, and a checking mechanism for the occasional times when a liberal democratic state goes off course. The value in the system lies in procuring a global polity in which principles of cooperation and ethical conduct are routinely observed; if all international law was complied with, that goal would be achieved. The distinctive feature of the constructivist theory this book has presented is that it asserts the existence of political forces mandating the creation of international law but which are uninterested in achieving any particular end. One important factor in the dynamic of contemporary international relations is deontological: unconcerned with consequences, it represents the battle of ideas. Where strong state interests are at stake, the desire for a nation to be associated with ideas or ideology will never override that state's genuine interests. Where the interests are weaker, states may be prepared to give association with ideas some weight in their trade-offs against results. This is because states are not simple actors with linear sets of interests such as the pursuit of GDP or the pursuit of territory.

Particularly in democracies, states are enormously complex amalgams of different interests, between which prudent politicians have to strike delicate compromises. Many of those interests will demand, as a precondition of their support for an elected government, that it pursue the state's interests in a narrow sense of the word: the economy must remain strong, and the territory must remain intact and subject to central government control. But many other interests, albeit weaker, will demand that the government intervene in a variety of other intangible matters. Diaspora populations may demand intervention in foreign civil wars. Environmentalists may demand allegiance to global green policies as a condition of their votes. A society's intelligentsia, which often wield political influence by shaping public debate, may demand action on human rights and global tragedies. Lawyers – a particularly powerful interest group in many western societies – may press for development of international law out of which they can extract rents.

To achieve sufficient political consensus to govern, states may need to satisfy a variety of these interest groups, and with only limited resources. Often, it will be sufficient that support for a group's interests is denoted in some symbolic way. In many cases, symbolic support is all that can be offered. There is nothing the United Kingdom can do unilaterally to prevent global warming, for all the power of the environmental lobby, because by any absolute measurement it is not one of the world's principal emitters of greenhouse gases. Nevertheless the environmental lobby may need to be offered something. International law and organisations are tools in the portfolio of democracies to satisfy the demands of domestic interest groups. Because responsibility for international organisations is diffused so thinly amongst their members, once the issue has been internationalised the state can abdicate responsibility for the outcome. In elevating an issue to the international sphere in this way, a state takes a limited risk: it is losing control over an issue to a substantially autonomous international policy-making authority, which may make all sorts of pronouncements and exhortations as it sees fit. But there is an element of the prisoners' dilemma in this risk; provided other states are prepared to make such a delegation, the international organisation will adopt its autonomous course irrespective of whether the state in question also makes such a delegation. With enough members behind it, the International Criminal Court has started work notwithstanding the United States' refusal to participate. Therefore a state might as well make the delegation in any event, and reap the benefit of disposing of the issue from its domestic agenda. The more rational consequentialist course would be for all states to agree not to internationalise issues; but given the other prisoners will internationalise, all prisoners might as well do so.

If this is the true incentive for states' accession to the instruments of international law, then it is not surprising the institutions created as a result are so ineffective. States want them to be so. If they must create autonomous institutions as a method of alleviating domestic political pressure, then they may not be keen for those institutions actually to achieve things. That would be a dangerous encroachment upon states' sovereignty. Far better for the United Nations to be a perennial talking shop than that it makes decisions potentially adverse to the Great Powers' real interests: hence the convenience of veto votes in the UN Security Council. In ejecting impossible political issues from their domestic orbits, states have every interest in creating impotent colossi, appearing to bear inordinate responsibilities but in fact bearing none. The world of international relations bears more than a faint analogy to an orbit of space debris far above the world. While junk satellites are forever circulating above us, periodically crashing into one another and creating further detritus, we peoples of the world carry on far below, ignoring and even oblivious to the political refuse we have ejected into space.

THE RE-EMERGENCE OF A MULTI-POLAR WORLD

Writing in 2010, it appears that in the future international relations will be ever less dominated by a single military and economic power. In the nineteenth century, the world was multi-polar. While the British Empire was perhaps marginally the pre-eminent superpower, it by no means exerted global hegemony. The nineteenth-century unification of Germany created a dominant military and economic force in continental Europe. In the aftermath of its civil war the United States developed as a credible economic power in the western hemisphere; with the turn of the twentieth century, it also emerged as an impressive military force under its expansionist President Theodore Roosevelt. The French Empire remained an economic force through its African and Indochinese possessions. The Dutch held real influence in Southeast Asia, the Belgians in Central Africa. In the aftermath of World War I, the power of the European empires waned, while the economic might of the United States became increasingly apparent. The rise of Stalin saw the Soviet Union develop into a superpower that was able to rival American military dominance in the aftermath of World War II. The Communist economic model proved unsustainable without the iron hand of Stalinist oppression, and in the aftermath of the collapse of the Warsaw Pact, the United States emerged as the sole superpower.

These changes in the balance of international relations – from multipolar to bipolar to unipolar centres of power – broadly coincided with changes in attitudes towards international law. As the predominant themes in geopolitics became influenced by an ever-smaller group of dominant nations, the prospects for international cooperation through international organisations and international law increased. In the nineteenth century, international organisations counted for little. As the balance of power between the United States and the European empires became more finely balanced in the interwar period, international organisations emerged, spearheaded by the League of Nations. In the standoff between the United States and the USSR, international law flourished through the United Nations. After the demise of the Soviet Union the world entered a period of US hegemony, and the discipline exploded into the plethora of international organisations and international legal systems we see today. Is this a coincidence?

A number of new economic powers are now emerging, and with their rise we find a change in the relative balance of political and military influence. China is faced with formidable domestic problems, including rural poverty, weak infrastructure, nationalist secession movements in the west of the country and pressure for greater popular political representation. Nevertheless its status as a principal trading partner with both the United States and the European Union has meant its foreign policy preferences cannot easily be ignored. China has also started building a significant military force using the tax revenues from its new-found trade surpluses, giving it increased leverage over the disputed island of Taiwan, protected since 1949 by the US military. It has developed an overseas aid and development programme, and Chinese companies have appeared increasingly frequently as foreign investors in Africa and Latin America. To a lesser extent, both India and Brazil have developed as regional economic and political powers in consequence of rates of economic growth throughout the first decade of the twenty-first century that outstrip those found in Europe or the United States. Parts, at least, of the developing world are catching up. A number of nations, including Russia and states in the Middle East, are prospering from elevated world market prices for oil and other natural resources; as those resources are consumed and commodity prices increase as a result, their wealth will increase at the expense of the developed nations that consume these resources. Increasing numbers of nations are apparently destined to acquire nuclear weapons, with corresponding changes in regional balances of power.

It might seem naïve to assume that with these rising powers, the dialogue of international relations will remain dominated by a European-American discourse in which Wilsonian or European internationalist themes will predominate. In the future, distribution of global geopolitical power may be spread more diffusely amongst a plurality of nodes, many of which do not share the liberal traditions which international law purports to embody. Moreover, a return to the balance of power between competing nations, with no one state dominating the international order, may render international cooperation more troublesome. No one nation will be able to impose its values upon the rest of the world, as arguably the United States (and to a lesser degree, western Europe) have done in the course of the twentieth century. Will this herald a return to a nineteenth-century model of international law? One inference might be that in the absence of an intellectual consensus about the ideals international organisations ought to embody, those institutions will wither. There will no longer be an incentive for states across the world to be seen to embrace the liberal goals these institutions embody, because in the new global marketplace between nations far less will turn upon finding favour with the United States or the European Union. International law and international organisations as we currently think of them will become the preserve of only a select few nations, such as those in the European Union, which share a set of values pertaining to the moral value of international law. Other nations will abandon the charade, more comfortable doing business with one another in an unrestrained anarchy in which the reality of states' power relations is uncushioned by the mirages of legalistic international cooperation.

This analysis may look superficially attractive, and ultimately it can be tested only by experience. However, it may underestimate the tenacity of the international organisations created so far, and the inventiveness of the interest groups the contemporary international legal framework has empowered. International organisations have proven themselves adept at catering to the requirements of developing powers, mid-size countries and nations outside the western orbit. The UN General Assembly provides a forum in which the economically weak and small developing world nations each have the same voting power (one country one vote) as powerful nations. This is particularly evident in the voting procedure for the Human Rights Council, which includes amongst its members countries with such dubious human rights records as Libya, Mauritania, Malaysia and Russia.[4] In accordance with the principle of political neutrality espoused in its Articles of Agreement,[5] the World Bank breezily lends money to international pariahs such as Iran, Syria, Iraq and Zimbabwe. (It refuses loans to Burma solely on the ground that Burma is in default on repayments under other loans.) INTERPOL is content to share information on its database with Iran and Cuba, despite their mottled records of impartial policing. Even reclusive North Korea can boast membership of the UN and 13 other international organisations.[6]

International organisations, and the international legal regimes they represent, allow countries of all hues a level of international respectability. No matter how discordant with international standards their conduct is, those states find a place at the international table. The autonomy of international organisations permits them to create relationships with every state, and propose the public relations services they offer to all nations, including the next generation of presumptive heirs to international economic and political power. It is difficult to predict with certainty what an economically powerful China will want from a network of international organisations. At the current time she receives development funding, cheap loans, association with moral norms despite a poor human rights record and a level of protection of her trading surpluses despite an artificially devalued currency. In the future she may look for more. In all likelihood the international organisations, desirous of China's support for them and indeed for her continued funding, will find ways of giving her the things she wants.

International organisations have proved themselves flexible in adapting to the changing political environment. Provided they can continue to do so, they may well preserve themselves through any dramatic shift in the balance of global power. The world will remain a realist anarchy; indeed with the draining of the comparative advantage of military and economic dominance away from the United States over time, it may become more of one than it is today. Already the United States is no longer the world's policeman; it has found itself with a propensity to become bogged down in muddy local conflicts in Afghanistan and Iraq that serve neither its interests nor the interests of global stability. In the future it may retreat into isolationism; or it may make further ill-judged military forays into global affairs, which will further confirm its relative decline. Either way, America's Wilsonian propensities to think in terms of moral values rather than state self-interest will become ever less of an influence within the world as other ruthlessly self-interested nations acquire greater relative prominence. But one long-standing influence the twentieth-century period of US hegemony may have had upon the world is the institution of an illusory global legalism in which international institutions are created in ambitious, but ultimately futile, attempts to resolve global cooperation problems.

THE GRIP OF DELUSION

Why is the idea of global cooperation, although misconceived, so perennially alluring? The answer may be the attraction of the modernist premise: that as members of a society develop more sophisticated relationships with one another, society can improve itself and move towards some ideal of political organisation. As with national society, so the same advances can be achieved for the global society. It was arguably Hegel who first captured this vision at its most acute. Out of international wars and perennial conflicts, thought Hegel, emerge higher forms of living. From the errors of mankind's endless cycles of self-destruction emerges hope. We humans learn from our prior mistakes, and thus the wanton loss of life experienced in the world's most destructive conflicts was not wasted. Wilson anticipated creating a world order in which the horrors of World War I trench warfare need never be repeated. The *realpolitik* consensus of nineteenth-century European politics need not, thought Wilson, be extended to the New World. A new international order would be forged based upon reason, peaceful negotiation and judicial resolution. The vehicle for this optimistic rational future would be the League of Nations, and a host of international legal instruments that represent the triumph of law over force. No matter that in the domestic context at least, law is not respected without the ever-lingering threat of overwhelming force.

Nonetheless, this thought represented a new beginning after the unreason of World War I resulted in the death of 16 million people, the majority of whom were young men. Their lives would not be wasted. Likewise after World War II, the horrors of fascism would forever be precluded by a new international order based upon human rights that would render the atrocities committed by the Nazis and their allies unthinkable. The autarchy that characterised the Great Depression and the Smoot-Hawley tariff regime would be foreclosed permanently by a general agreement on trade tariffs. The destruction of World War II would be overcome by an International Bank for Reconstruction and Development, which would rebuild Europe from its ashes. Macro-economic shocks in the vein of the Wall Street Crash could be prevented, through an International Monetary Fund to provide emergency funding in response to economic crisis.

Communism had created conflict that had brought the two poles of the world to the brink of mutually assured destruction, and had condemned large swathes of the global population to penury through a wasteful economic system and had deprived nations of the most fundamental civil liberties. Thus a new cluster of grand ideas was assembled to prevent the world again falling under such a tyranny. International investment law would provide guarantees of liberal market treatment of foreign investments, precluding the return of socialism. The international investment flows fostered in consequence would be buttressed by a reinforced global trading regime, and the WTO was born. The European Union and human rights principles were diffused eastwards, ensuring eastern Europe could never again fall under the yoke of Stalinist tyranny. The world could never slip back into a communist malaise.

The aim of international law was to stamp out the various structural problems, crises and horrors with which rulers were faced in the twentieth century. The most destructive century on record would be preparatory to ushering in an altogether more liberal, humane and perfectly balanced global polity. To paraphrase one popular thinker in the late twentieth century, history itself would be brought to a conclusion.[7] The errors of the past would be eliminated through a new global consensus based upon principles of liberal democracy, free markets and respect for human rights. International cooperation would be the touchstone of this new world order. The power of ideas in politics is profound: these notions created an influential new international institutional architecture, a new discipline of international law, and employed hundreds of thousands of new international civil servants worldwide. The cities of Washington, DC, Geneva, Brussels, New York, Vienna and others would never be quite the same again. The very dialogue of foreign policy would become irreversibly infected with such arcane abstractions as obligations under international law and the legal personality of the United Nations.

Alas, the aspiration that the tortured course of history can be brought to an abrupt conclusion through the emergence of saintly new ideas for international cooperation is illusory. There is something deeply attractive about it for the human psyche. Taken objectively, the empirical record of international relations is so depressingly bleak that we would despair were we not able to fantasise about a world order in which the perennial cycles of murder, warfare and abuse that litter foreign relations could be fractured. International law feeds off this compelling desire to find a solution to the anarchy of inter-nation egotism. Whatever the best intentions of those who press such ideas into effect within the global polity, they do not fit within the sharp edges of the jigsaw. Nobody wants to appear to reject them explicitly, such is the extent to which these notions are loaded with moral force. Nevertheless at the appropriate time they will be tacitly ejected from the global jigsaw, because the relationships between states simply do not work in this way.

What is left is an array of international institutions that, although confined within the power relationships of states' mutual rivalries, can feed off the desire for allusions to a higher world order. The success and influence of international organisations lies in their representing the supremacy of ideas over interests. Although ideas have no such causal supremacy no practitioner of the dark arts of international relations can admit as much, lest (s)he be condemned by domestic pressure groups. International organisations are thus relegated to a causal limbo between the world as it is and as we would pretend it to be. Through the desire of statesmen to pay lip service to principle and pay homage to the compulsion of hypocrisy, international organisations can find scope to influence the world. But their influence is of a muted form. They can appeal to the better natures of their sovereign interlocutors. They can project themselves as the expositors of principle, compromise and ethics. Like the popular member of the club, everyone will want to be associated with them. In this way they can attract funds, staff and mandates; they can grow. But like demagogues whipping up the vengeful mob, when the pack surges off to battle, international organisations stay well behind the lines, because they carry no arms. They remain elusive magicians in the dark arts of ideas, operating in the background; but they are never at the front line of international relations, which in the final analysis are driven by the superior might of one nation over the forces of another.

Although their founding impetus has waned, the institutions created as a result of political commitment to faux ideals persist. Indeed they remain formidable global actors. International law is a remarkably durable institution despite being for the most part quite useless, representing unachievable aspirations. International justice is a seductive mirage, one human society seems compelled to pursue by reason of its own innate casuistry. Perhaps it represents a profound weakness in human nature: the desire to believe that human selfishness can be overcome by moral standards in principles of social organisation. If such illusions could be conquered, the world would appear a far starker place, but a more honest one. Alas, it appears that they cannot be. Lies keep individuals sane; perhaps they keep societies and nations sane too.

NOTES

1. Freud, Sigmund (1927) *Die Zukunft Einer Illusion*, Leipzig, when and zürich: Internationaler psychoanalytischer Verlag; an English translation followed in 1928.

2. The Report of the International Commission on Intervention and State Sovereignty (ICISS) entitled its 2001 report 'The Responsibility to Protect'. ICISS was established by the Canadian government in response to UN Secretary General Kofi Annan's 2000 annual report to the UN General Assembly, in which he called upon the international community to establish consensus upon the principles in which humanitarian intervention by one country in another would be permissible.
3. This case is discussed in Chapter 3.
4. For criticism of the political compromises involved in membership of the UN Human Rights Council, see *New York Times* (2006), 'The Shame of the United Nations', 26 February.
5. See Article IV(10) Articles of Agreement of the International Bank for Reconstruction and Development: 'The Bank and its officers shall not interfere in the political affairs of any member; nor shall they be influenced in their decisions by the political character of the member or members concerned. Only economic considerations shall be relevant to their decisions, and these considerations shall be weighed impartially in order to achieve the purposes stated in Article I.'
6. These are the food and Agriculture Organisation, the International Civil Aviation Organisation; the Inter-Parliamentary Union; UNCTAD; the International Telecommunications Union; the UN Development Programme; the UN Education, Scientific and Cultural Organisation; World Health Organisation; the World Intellectual Property Organisation; World Metrological Organisation; the International Maritime Organisation; the International Committer of the Red Cross; and the Non-Aligned Movement.
7. Fukuyama, Francis (1992), *The End of History and the Last Man*, New York: Free Press.

Index